Studies in Church History

57

(2021)

INSPIRATION AND INSTITUTION IN CHRISTIAN HISTORY

INSPIRATION AND INSTITUTION IN CHRISTIAN HISTORY

EDITED BY

CHARLOTTE METHUEN

ALEC RYRIE

ANDREW SPICER

PUBLISHED FOR
THE ECCLESIASTICAL HISTORY SOCIETY
BY
CAMBRIDGE UNIVERSITY PRESS
2021

Published by Cambridge University Press
on behalf of the Ecclesiastical History Society
University Printing House, Cambridge CB2 8BS, United Kingdom

First published 2021

ISBN 9781316514801

ISSN 0424–2084

SUBSCRIPTIONS: *Studies in Church History* is an annual subscription journal
(ISSN 0424–2084). The 2021 subscription price (excluding VAT), which
includes print and electronic access, is £106 (US $193 in the USA, Canada and
Mexico) for institutions and £66 (US $106 in the USA, Canada and Mexico) for
individuals ordering direct from the Press and certifying that the volume is for
their personal use. An electronic-only subscription is also available to institutions
at £93 (US $148 in the USA, Canada and Mexico). Special arrangements exist
for members of the Ecclesiastical History Society.

Previous volumes are available online at www.cambridge.org/StudCH

Printed in the United Kingdom by Bell & Bain Ltd
A catalogue record for this publication is available from the British Library

Contents

Contents

Preface

The theme of Studies in Church History 57 is *Inspiration and Institution in Christian History*. This fruitful theme was proposed by Professor Alec Ryrie, President of the Ecclesiastical History Society during 2019–20. The volume comprises seventeen peer reviewed articles drawn from the range of communications and keynote lectures given at the Ecclesiastical History Society's Summer Conference at the University of Durham in July 2019 and at its Winter Meeting at Carrs Lane Conference Centre, Birmingham, in January 2020.

This topic has resulted in a rich and wide-ranging collection of articles which reveal the complexity of the interplay between institution and inspiration in the Church at all periods of its existence. We are grateful to Professor Ryrie for proposing this theme and for his able presidency. We thank also all who offered contributions and submitted papers for consideration for the volume, and those who peer reviewed the contributions, thereby helping the society to ensure that the volume is of the highest quality. Dr Tim Grass continued his meticulous work as assistant editor.

The careful planning and engagement of the society's conference secretaries, Dr David Hart, succeeded by Professor Elizabeth Tingle, ensured that the Summer Conference and Winter Meeting went without a hitch. They were supported by the society's secretary and treasurer, Dr Gareth Atkins and Simon Jennings, and by the conference teams at St Chad's College Durham, and Carrs Lane Conference Centre.

The Ecclesiastical History Society offers two annual prizes for articles accepted for publication in Studies in Church History. In this volume, the Kennedy Prize, for the best contribution by a postgraduate student, was awarded to Elise Watson, for her article 'The Jesuitesses in the Bookshop: Catholic Lay Sisters' Participation in the Amsterdam Book Trade, 1650–1750'. The President's Prize, for the best contribution by an early career scholar, goes to Dr Clive Murray Norris for '"A blessed and glorious work of God, …

attended with some irregularity": Managing Methodist Revivals, *c*.1740–1800'. Both articles demonstrate excellent scholarship as well as an innovative exploration of the theme.

Charlotte Methuen
University of Glasgow

Andrew Spicer
Oxford Brookes University

Contributors

Hazel J. Hunter Blair
    Postgraduate Student, University of Lausanne

Sam Brewitt-Taylor
    Witney

Dominic Erdozain
    Visiting Scholar, Emory University

Claudia Jetter
    Postgraduate Student, Ruprecht-Karls Universität, Heidelberg

Josef Lössl
    Professor of Historical Theology and Intellectual History,
    Cardiff University

Grant Masom
    Department of Continuing Education, University of Oxford

Teresa Morgan
    Professor of Graeco-Roman History, University of Oxford;
    Nancy Bissell Turpin Fellow and Tutor in Ancient History,
    Oriel College

Clive Murray Norris
    Research Fellow, Oxford Centre for Methodism and Church
    History, Oxford Brookes University

Roger Ottewill
    Southampton

Helen Parish
    Professor in History, University of Reading

Andrew Poxon
    Postgraduate Student, Durham University

Contributors

Alec Ryrie
> Professor of the History of Christianity, Durham University

Neslihan Şenocak
> Associate Professor of History, Columbia University

Matleena Sopanen
> Postgraduate Student, Tampere University

Rhiannon Teather
> Postgraduate Student, University of Bristol

Elise Watson
> Postgraduate Student, University of St Andrews

Tim Yung
> Postgraduate Student, University of Hong Kong

Abbreviations

ANF	A. Roberts and J. Donaldson, eds, Ante-Nicene Fathers, 10 vols (Buffalo, NY, 1885–96 and subsequent edns)
ARG	*Archiv für Reformationsgeschichte* (1903–)
BL	British Library
CChr.SL	Corpus Christianorum, series Latina (Turnhout, 1953–)
CERC	Church of England Record Centre
ChH	*Church History* (1932–)
CPReg	*Calendar of Entries in the Papal Registers relating to Great Britain and Ireland* (London / Dublin, 1893–)
CRL	Cadbury Research Library
CSEL	Corpus Scriptorum Ecclesiasticorum Latinorum (Vienna, 1866–)
CWTM	Yale Edition of the Complete Works of St Thomas More (New Haven, CT, 1963–)
DRChH	*Nederlands archief voor kerkgeschiedenis / Dutch Review of Church History* (1900–2005)
EETS	Early English Text Society
ET	English translation
GCS	Die Griechischen Christlichen Schriftsteller
HistJ	*Historical Journal* (1958–)
JBS	*Journal of British Studies* (1961–)
JECS	*Journal of Early Christian Studies* (1993–)
JEH	*Journal of Ecclesiastical History* (1950–)
JMedH	*Journal of Medieval History* (1975–)
LMA	London Metropolitan Archive
LPL	Lambeth Palace Library
n.d.	no date
NF	Neue Folge ('new series')
n.pl.	no place
n.s.	new series
ODNB	H. C. G. Matthew and Brian Harrison, eds, *Oxford Dictionary of National Biography*, 63 vols (Oxford, 2004), and subsequent online versions
PG	J.-P. Migne, ed., Patrologia Graeca, 161 vols (Paris, 1857–66)
P&P	*Past and Present* (1952–)
PWHS	Proceedings of the Wesley Historical Society (1897–)
RO	Record Office

RSTC	A. W. Pollard and G. R. Redgrave, eds, *A Short-Title Catalogue of Books printed in England, Scotland, & Ireland and of English Books printed abroad 1475–1640*, revised edn, 3 vols (London, 1976–91)
s.a.	*sub anno* ('under the year')
SC	Sources Chrétiennes (Paris, 1941–)
SCH	Studies in Church History
SCJ	*Sixteenth Century Journal* (1970–2006)
SHCM	Studies in the History of Christian Missions
s.n.	*sub nomine* ('under the name')
SP	*Studia Patristica* (1957–)
TNA	The National Archives
TRHS	*Transactions of the Royal Historical Society* (1871–)
UL	University Library
Wing	Donald Wing, *Short-Title Catalogue of Books printed in England, Scotland, Ireland, Wales and British America and of English Books printed in other Countries, 1641–1700*, 2nd edn, 4 vols (New York, 1998)

Introduction

A Christian church is a paradoxical entity. All churches trace their origins back to Christianity's archetypal moment of inspiration, the day of Pentecost, when tongues of fire rested on the apostles and the Spirit stirred them into unexpected and turbulent life; and beyond that moment to Christ himself, who had much more to say by way of criticizing religious institutions than he did about establishing new ones in their stead. The Holy Spirit has remained at the heart of most Christian doctrines of the church ever since, and one of the Spirit's defining qualities is that the wind blows where it wills. And yet a church is and must of necessity be a human institution, with structures, traditions, laws, offices and finances. The story of Christianity's history is in large part the story of how these two threads – the inspirational and the institutional – have been woven together: sometimes one in the ascendant, sometimes the other, sometimes unravelling, but never parting company completely. A church which no longer seeks inspiration is merely a fossil. And a Christian community without institution is not merely doomed: it is an impossibility, since no human community can endure without *some* structure, however fluid or implicit.

One recurrent dynamic at work here is what Weber called the routinization of charisma, in which a community dominated by the personality of a founder or early leader is compelled, after that person's death or departure, to replace them with institutional forms that serve as a kind of effigy, filling their seat but doing so lifelessly. That process is matched by one of sheer scale, as communities are compelled to regularize their structures through numerical growth or geographical spread. And it is true that we can see these processes at work again and again in Christianity's history, as indeed in many other spheres of life. Contrast the freewheeling fluidity of the early Pauline letters, urging that the Spirit not be quenched, with the prudent legalism of the later Pastoral Epistles, a sign of what was to come.

Yet it is not enough to see this as a matter of relentless withering and ossification, for two reasons. First, most obviously, attempts to quench the Spirit or to routinize charisma generally fail. Sometimes fresh upsurges of inspirational religion take place within existing

Studies in Church History 57 (2021), 1–5 © The Author(s), 2021. Published by Cambridge University Press on behalf of Ecclesiastical History Society.
doi: 10.1017/stc.2021.1

church structures, sometimes outside, and sometimes they cross from one to the other; some cultures and ages experience them more frequently than others; but they will come, sooner or later, as unpredictable as the weather and as inevitable as the climate. The instinct that institutional religion is a hindrance to true Christianity – perhaps even its opposite – is evergreen, whether it be the Desert Fathers shaking the dust of a supposedly corrupt urban church from their feet, or the medieval beguines who chose to bypass monastic establishments they no longer trusted, or the nineteenth-century Americans who wanted to rediscover or create a pristine, republican Christianity. Alexander Campbell, one of the founders of the Restoration movement, claimed that he hoped 'to read the scriptures as though no one had read them before me ... I am as much on my guard against reading them to-day, through the medium of my own views yesterday, or a week ago, as I am against being influenced by any foreign name, authority, or system whatever'.[1]

But this rarefied anti-institutional purity eventually, and inevitably, ended the way countless other anti-institutional revolts had before: in the foundation of new institutions, in this case the denominations such as the Churches of Christ, into which the Stone-Campbell movement eventually splintered. The only alternative, as some of the radical anti-institutionalists of the 1960s discovered, is an institutional self-immolation so complete that a movement simply ceases to exist.

So Christianity's history is a recurrent spiral of inspirational outbreak, institutional containment and renewed inspiration. Martin Luther proclaims a gospel of Christian freedom; establishment Lutheranism settles into a static orthodoxy; Pietism challenges it with a religion of the heart; Pietism itself swiftly adopts surprisingly rigid norms; the Moravians challenge it in turn. 'A Pietist', the Moravians' founder Count von Zinzendorf observed wryly, 'cannot be converted in so cavalier a way as we can. ... We ride, and the Pietists go on foot.'[2]

But secondly, and more interestingly, there is more to the institutionalization process than this. Sometimes – normally, indeed – it

---

[1] Quoted in Nathan O. Hatch, *The Democratization of American Christianity* (New Haven, CT, and London, 1989), 179.

[2] Quoted in W. R. Ward, *The Protestant Evangelical Awakening* (Cambridge, 1992), 136–7.

fails entirely. Sectarian movements collapse, wither or spin out of control as quickly as they had flared up: routinizing charisma is easier said than done. There was a moment when the Moravians seemed poised to inherit the whole evangelical movement, but, under-institutionalized as they were, they then blew themselves apart with financial scandals and a swerve into idiosyncratic devotional practices that most of their contemporaries found bizarre. Christianity's history is dotted with eras of inspirational creativity and sectarian formation, from the earliest church onwards: most of these new movements quickly gutter out, usually with a whimper, occasionally – especially in the case of certain apocalyptic movements, which use predictions of the imminent end of days to avoid institutional constraints – with a bang.

Yet some flourish. They tend not to be the movements that fossilize, or those that clamp down most effectively on the disruption of inspirational religion. They are the ones which learn to manage it. They build institutions which work with the grain of inspiration: to discipline, house-train and direct it, not to suppress it. They may even intensify it. They develop structures which are flexible enough to accommodate and benefit from inspiration but supple enough to contain it. The early church's development of episcopacy – a collective-security system in which authoritative local leaders could generally manage their own affairs but could also call on, or restrain, one another when necessary – is the archetype of such a system, an institution whose ability to manage the wildly fissiparous tendencies of early Christianity without squeezing the life from it gave it a totemic status that endures to the present. Or again, the Benedictine rule could hardly be described as *routinizing* charisma; we might rather say that, in the manner of monastic winemakers, it bottled charisma, to be laid down to mature and uncorked when needed. In the Reformation era, the primary reason why the diverse and quarrelsome family of the Reformed tradition has come to be known as 'Calvinism' is that Calvin found an institutional expression – the fourfold ministry, synodical government, cell-churches, endogenous discipline – which enabled the movement to spread like bindweed in the most inhospitable of environments. Mid-seventeenth-century England saw a surge of sectarian creativity: the Muggletonians, Diggers and Fifth Monarchists came to nothing; the Baptists and the Quakers found structures that endured, structures that governed them loosely enough for them to flourish, tightly enough for them to hold together. John Wesley came late to the revivalist party in the eighteenth century, but by using the established Church of England as a matrix on which Methodist movement's connexional system could be grown, he created an institution which outspread and outlasted most of its rivals.

This is not to suggest, like a low-rent management consultant, that there is an organizational secret sauce for ecclesiastical success: much less that this volume will reveal it. Plainly, institutional structures that have nurtured inspiration in some eras have choked it or been overwhelmed by it in others. The relationship between institution and inspiration in Christian history is not a formula, but a complex and unpredictable dance, in which neither dancer is particularly surefooted but in which, for all the mis-steps, the show has – so far – kept going. This volume of essays consists of reports from the sidelines. Some articles consider cases where the dance has found its rhythm and flowed smoothly, even gracefully; some look at moments when the dancers have not been in time, or have indeed reached the stage of kicking each other in the shins or walking away entirely – only to discover, of course, that neither one can manage on their own. These are stories about how formal structures of authority have negotiated with the fluid reality of charismatic leadership; about how even institutions that have managed to absorb inspirational movements with delicacy and grace have nevertheless changed them profoundly in the process; about how institutional memory has meshed with inspirational revival, since both of our dancers are deeply aware of the depth of the traditions they follow. We read about how institutions have picked their paths between suppressing, ignoring, condoning, manipulating and celebrating inspirational movements; how inspirational movements have rejected, negotiated with, exploited, succumbed to or taken over institutions, or simply flourished safe within their walls; or, often, how they have whipped up new institutional structures of their own, which, in the way of things, mostly crumble or subside in a generation or two. Inspiration may feel more ephemeral than institutions, but in long historical perspective it may be that the opposite is true.

The two conferences from which these articles were taken were held – although we did not know it at the time – on the cusp of the COVID-19 pandemic which began in early 2020. Producing a volume under those circumstances has been a trial for the contributors, whose access to libraries and archives has been sharply curtailed, and for the Ecclesiastical History Society as a whole. The society has done what institutions do best when facing unexpected crises, that is, to adapt and press on: and we all owe a considerable debt to the society's officers and committee, who have ensured that, a year on, the institution is stable, financially sound and shaping itself to the emerging circumstances. As to whether its inspiration has deserted it, that is for readers of this volume to decide.

Alec Ryrie

Two Aspects of Early Christian Faith

Teresa Morgan*

Oriel College, Oxford

'Faith' is one of Christianity's most significant, distinctive and complex concepts and practices, but Christian understandings of faith in the patristic period have received surprisingly little attention. This article explores two aspects of what Augustine terms fides qua, *'the faith by which believers believe'. From the early second century, belief in the truth of doctrine becomes increasingly significant to Christians; by the fourth, affirming that certain doctrines are true has become central to becoming Christian and to remaining within the church. During the same period, we find a steady growth in poetic and imagistic descriptions of interior faith. This article explores how and why these developments occurred, arguing that they are mutually implicated and that this period sees the beginning of their long co-existence.*

The idea and practice of 'faith' have been central to Christianity for longer than its recorded history.[1] No concept or praxis is invoked more often by followers of Jesus Christ, from the earliest letters of Paul onwards. Within a few years of the crucifixion, what we now call Christians were referring to themselves as 'the faithful'. By around the turn of the first century they were calling their organization 'the faith'. Throughout their history, Christians have appealed to faith more often, in more varied contexts, than adherents of any other ancient or modern cult or religion.[2]

* Oriel College, Oxford, OX1 4EW. E-mail: teresa.morgan@classics.ox.ac.uk.
I am grateful to Alec Ryrie and the committee of the Ecclesiastical History Society for the invitation to speak at its 2019 Summer Conference, and to participants for their stimulating responses to the paper.

[1] 'Faith' is a placeholder for the complexity of Greek *pistis*, Latin *fides* and comparable terms in other languages of early churches, whose meanings include 'trust', 'trustworthiness', 'faithfulness', 'good faith', 'a pledge', 'a guarantee', a legal trust, a rhetorical proof, 'belief' and (among Christians) the 'new covenant', the content of doctrine and 'the faith'.

[2] Teresa Morgan, *Roman Faith and Christian Faith:* pistis *and* fides *in the Early Roman Empire and Early Churches* (Oxford, 2015), 103. Why *pistis* language became so important to Christians so early remains uncertain. Calling people to trust in God may go back to Jesus himself: ibid. 350–2. Other Jewish groups in this period self-designate as

Studies in Church History 57 (2021), 6–31 © The Author(s), 2021. Published by Cambridge University Press on behalf of Ecclesiastical History Society.
doi: 10.1017/stc.2021.2

It is therefore surprising how little detailed investigation there has been of how early Christians understood faith. In New Testament studies, certain aspects of *pistis* and its relatives – the lexicon we most often translate with the language of 'faith' or 'belief' – have been discussed extensively, including the meaning of the phrase *pistis Christou* in the Pauline corpus, and the use of *pisteuein* in the Gospel of John.[3] With a few exceptions, such as the relationship between *pistis* and *gnosis* in the thought of Christian Platonists, and some aspects of Augustine's thinking about *fides*, understandings of faith in patristic writings have received very little attention.[4] Until recently, there has been no historical study of faith in all its complexity at any period.

This article draws on a two-volume study, currently in progress, of Christian faith from the earliest Christian records to the fifth century. The first volume, *Roman Faith and Christian Faith*, investigates the treatment of *pistis* in the earliest Christian writings. The second traces the development of ideas and practices of faith from the second to the fifth century. What follows offers an overview of two strands in the evolution of faith which reflect the themes of institutionalization and inspiration, outlining how these strands develop over three centuries and how they are both distinct and interdependent.

The definition of faith most familiar to church historians and theologians is that of Augustine in *On the Trinity* (13.2.5). Augustine divides *fides* into *fides quae* ('the faith which is believed', the content of doctrine) and *fides qua* ('the faith by which it is believed', what

---

(for example) wise, pure or faithful, so 'the [truly / properly] faithful' may have begun as a self-designation among Jewish Christians: ibid. 238–9. The absolute trustworthiness of God and Christ was part of early preaching at a time when trust, especially in people, was widely perceived as difficult and precarious: ibid. 36–122. *Pistis* language is unlikely, however, to have arisen to refer to believing in the resurrection (although it also came to mean that), because *hoi pisteuontes* and *hoi pistoi* are used interchangeably for 'the faithful', and the latter cannot mean 'believers': ibid. 239–41.

[3] Ibid., especially 262–306, 347–93.

[4] Notable exceptions include Oscar Cullmann's essay collection, *La Foi et le culte de l'église primitive* (Paris, 1963); Ignacio Escribano-Alberca, *Handbuch der Dogmengeschichte*, 1/2a: *Glaube und Gotteserkenntnis in der Schrift und Patristik* (Freiburg im Breisgau, 1974); Mark Elliott, '*Pistis Christou*', in Michael F. Bird and Preston M. Sprinkle, eds, *The Faith of Jesus Christ* (Milton Keynes, 2010), 277–90; Oliver O'Donovan, 'Faith before Hope and Love', *New Blackfriars* 95 (2014), 177–89. These make significant contributions on specific questions, such as the evolution of creeds, the relationship between *pistis* and *gnosis*, and whether Christians sought to imitate the faithfulness of Christ.

takes place in the mind and heart of believers). This is not an ideal definition. It overlooks the meaning of *pistis* / *fides* (central in texts of the first and second centuries and still widely attested in the third and fourth) as the relationship of trust and faithfulness between God, Christ and the faithful. It elides the meaning 'the faith', in the sense of the new covenant or the cult as a whole, and glosses over the complexity of what both Christian and non-Christian writers describe as taking place in the mind or heart. In Augustinian terms, however, this article investigates two aspects of *fides qua*: the attitude of belief that certain doctrines are true (what philosophers sometimes call 'propositional belief'), and the varied and colourful imagery through which Christians explore what it means to have faith in one's mind or heart.

Between the second and fourth centuries, both propositional belief and the imagery of interior faith become increasingly important to Christians. Propositional belief gradually becomes institutionalized, in the sense that affirming publicly that one believes certain propositions to be true becomes central to becoming and remaining Christian. The imagery of faith, meanwhile, becomes increasingly inspired, in the sense that it becomes an ever more creative, varied, colourful and dynamic means to describe how people experience their interior life of faith. This parallel evolution, I suggest, is no accident, but constitutes part of the development and internal self-regulation of an increasingly complex and highly successful cult.

THE INSTITUTIONALIZATION OF PROPOSITIONAL BELIEF

Belief that certain things are true has been part of Christian thinking from as far back as we can trace. In 1 Corinthians 15: 3–11, for example, written in the early 50s, Paul tells the Corinthians, 'I handed on to you as of first importance what I also received: that Christ died for our sins in accordance with the scriptures; that he was buried; that he was raised on the third day in accordance with the scriptures ... so we preach and so you believed (οὕτως κηρύσσομεν καὶ οὕτως ἐπιστεύσατε).'[5] For very early Christians, however, it was not believing itself that admitted one to the community or kept one there. That took a further step: putting one's trust in God and Christ.

---

[5] Biblical quotations are taken from the New American Bible, Revised Edition.

This distinction should come as no surprise. Under the Roman empire, almost everybody believed in the existence of a vast number of gods, heroes, divine men, spirits and demons. Nobody worshipped them all, not only because there were so many, but because many were specific to a particular locality or family or had a limited sphere of action.[6] In Christian contexts, the distinction between belief and religious commitment is less obvious in Greek than in English, because the verb Christians most often use for committing to God and Christ, *pisteuein*, can mean both 'to believe' and 'to trust'. In context, however, it is normally clear which meaning is in play. Paul and other early writers undoubtedly expect members of their communities to believe certain things about God, Jesus Christ and God's action in the world, but when they call them to commit to Christ, they use *pistis* language in its sense of 'trust'.[7]

Early Christian writing, in general, has limited interest in belief. Gospels, sayings collections, acts, apocalypses, letters, hymns, prayers, spells, oracles and sermons all use *pistis* language, but nearly always in a relational sense. From around the turn of the first century, however, some writers become increasingly interested in belief, in two contexts: internal wrangles among the faithful about what to believe and debates between Christians and outsiders.

Even in these contexts, before the fourth century Christian writers do not typically discuss what they or others believe using *pisteuein* or *credere*. They prefer the language of thinking or knowing: *nomizein, dokein, doxa, gnōsis, phronēsis, putare, noscere, opinio*.[8] It is only in the fourth century that Christians begin regularly to use *pistis / fides* language to refer to right belief. There are two likely reasons for the shift. The first is what we might call 'concept creep': Christians are so invested in *pistis / fides* language that, over time, they apply it to more and more aspects of the cult, and since 'belief' is a possible meaning of *pistis* and *fides*, it is there to be used. The second is the influence of Platonism.

---

[6] Whether all Jews were strictly monotheistic in this period is debated, but believing (for instance) that multiple supernatural powers existed or that Elijah or Enoch was taken into heaven by God did not necessarily entail worship: Carey C. Newman, ed., *The Jewish Roots of Christological Monotheism* (Leiden, 1999); Larry W. Hurtado, *One God, One Lord: Early Christian Devotion and Ancient Jewish Monotheism*, 3rd edn (London, 2015).

[7] Morgan, *Roman Faith*, especially 212–443.

[8] This is why historians speak of 'orthodoxy' (right opinion) rather than 'orthopisty' (right faith or belief).

Among Greek speakers, Plato and his followers use *pistis* atypically, to refer to beliefs which are based on the evidence of this world, which in their view are unreliable compared with knowledge of the world of ideas.[9] In the late Roman republic and early principate, however, we encounter a number of intellectuals (including Cicero, Plutarch and Origen's Celsus) influenced by Platonism who are also deeply and explicitly interested in the nature and validity of mainstream cult. Plato's specialized usage of *pistis* creates a difficulty for them, because mainstream cult involves beliefs about the gods which are based on this-worldly evidence, such as the fulfilment of prophecy and the recorded successes of the gods in healing people or ending wars. Many middle Platonists are concerned to defend this-worldly reasons for believing certain things about the gods. Probably because of their debt to Plato, they often use *pistis* / *fides* language to do so.[10] Early Christians, some of whom are also much interested in Platonism, are also keen to defend their cult against accusations that it is irrational. Some of these discuss Christian *pistis* in terms which are increasingly influenced by Platonism.

A few examples must suffice. Justin Martyr was born about 100 CE. In his *Dialogue with Trypho* he describes how, as a young man, he investigated several schools of philosophy, including Platonism, before discovering and converting to Christianity. During the 150s Justin composed an apology, addressed to the imperial household, defending Christianity against contemporary accusations that it was immoral, irrational and seditious. Most of his defence of Christianity's rationality is couched in the language of thought and knowledge, but occasionally he uses *pistis* language, in very much the way that religious middle Platonists use it, to suggest that there are this-worldly bases on which it is rational to believe:

> We have received, by tradition, that God does not need the material offerings that human beings can give, seeing that he himself provides

---

[9] I am indebted to Mark Edwards for sharing his unpublished essay, '*Pistis* and Platonism'.

[10] For example, Plutarch, *Moralia* 165b, 359f–360b, 417a; idem, *Life of Numa* 4.3–4, Lucian, *Icaromenippus* 10; idem, *Alexander* 38, cf. Teresa Morgan, '*Doxa, praxis* and Graeco-Roman Religious Thinking', in James Carleton Paget, Simon Gathercole and Judith Lieu, eds, *Christianity in the Second Century: Themes and Developments* (Cambridge, 2017), 200–13; John Wynne, *Cicero on the Philosophy of Religion: On the Nature of the Gods and On Divination* (Cambridge, 2019), 50–82.

[us with] everything. We have been taught, and persuaded, and believe (δεδιδάγμεθα καὶ πεπείσμεθα καὶ πιστεύομεν) that he accepts solely those who imitate the good things which pertain to him: temperance, justice, and philanthropy ...

The coming into being at first was not in our power; and in order that we may follow those things that please him, choosing them by the powers of reason which he has given us, he persuades us and leads us to *pistis* (πείθει τε καὶ εἰς πίστιν ἄγει ἡμᾶς).[11]

The idea that we please God by deploying the reason God has given us and imitating the divine virtues, and that we can do this because of the teaching we have received, parallels contemporary middle Platonism (and, indeed, Stoicism).[12] Justin does not define what he means by Christian *pistis*, but by linking it twice with persuasion he implies that it is the outcome of teaching applied to reason, and therefore that it is a cognitive function: something like belief.

A generation later, another apologist goes a little further. Athenagoras of Athens (born *c.*133) was also a philosopher, probably a Platonist, and a Christian convert. His *Apology*, also addressed to the reigning emperor and his son and dated to 176–7, is a plea for equal rights. Like Justin, Athenagoras claims that Christians are moral people and loyal subjects of the emperor. Like Justin's, his *Apology* uses mainly the language of thought and knowledge rather than that of *pistis*. In one passage, however, he claims that Christians share many of their views with poets and philosophers, including that, ultimately, there is only one God.[13] This being the case, it is outrageous that Christians, uniquely, are accused of atheism and challenged 'to prove what we think and have rightly believed (ὅ τι καὶ νοοῦμεν καὶ ὀρθῶς πεπιστεύκαμεν), that there is one God' (7.27).

'What we think and rightly believe' is a telling phrase. From the second century onwards, Christians were accused by critics of urging converts, 'Do not think, just believe'.[14] Athenagoras insists that Christians both think and believe, echoing a phrase, *pistis orthē*,

---

[11] Justin Martyr, *Dialogue with Trypho* 10.60–1, 63. Translations are mine unless otherwise noted.

[12] For example, Epictetus, *Discourses* 2.14.11–14; cf. Maximus of Tyre, *Oration* 27.7b–9d; Alcinous, *Introduction to Plato* 28.3–4.

[13] For this view Christians adduce the this-worldly evidence of prophecy: Athenagoras, *Apology* 7.28–9.

[14] Origen, *Against Celsus* 1.9.

'right belief', which goes back to Plato's *Republic* (10.601e). For Plato, 'right belief' has useful qualities but is inferior to knowledge. Later Platonists and writers who invoke Plato, however, use *pistis orthē* and *doxa orthē* approvingly, of right beliefs or opinions which are part of piety and which are appropriately held by those who are in a process of gaining knowledge of the divine.[15] Athenagoras therefore implies that Christian *pistis* is part of a thought process about the divine which philosophers share and which leads to knowledge. To claim this, however, he has to present Christian *pistis* as belief rather than (for instance) as trust.

Almost a generation later again, Clement of Alexandria takes a more sustained interest in *pistis*, especially in the *Protrepticus*, addressed to non-Christians, and the *Stromateis*, addressed to Christians. This article cannot do justice to the complexity of Clement's thinking, but his contribution to the evolution of Christian understanding of *pistis* is decisive: partly because he is a serious philosopher with a particular interest in Platonism, who is deeply interested in the relationship between *pistis* and knowledge, and partly because he profoundly respects the letters of Paul, and wants to do justice to Paul's conviction that *pistis* brings human beings into their right relationship with God and stands at the heart of that relationship.

Clement develops a multi-stage theory of *pistis*.[16] At its simplest, it can be the kind of pre-rational trust or belief in things we take for granted which all human beings practise every day.[17] At a more sophisticated level, it is a belief-response to things that are self-evident to reason.[18] When, for example, in the gospels, we encounter the Word of God in Jesus Christ, Clement claims that we are encountering something self-evident to reason, to which we respond with *pistis*.[19]

---

[15] Plutarch, *Moralia* 404b; Josephus, *Against Apion* 2.256.4; *Anonymous Commentary on Plato's Theaetetus*, 2.52, 3.14, 3.16, 15.9; cf. Plutarch, *Moralia* 333b, 379b–c; John M. Dillon, '"Orthodoxy" and "Eclecticism": Middle Platonists and Neo-Pythagoreans', in idem and A. A. Long, eds, *The Question of Eclecticism: Studies in Later Greek Philosophy* (Berkeley, CA, 1988), 103–25.

[16] See especially Eric Osborn, 'Arguments for Faith in Clement of Alexandria', *Vigiliae Christianae* 48 (1994), 1–24; Salvatore R. C. Lilla, *Clement of Alexandria: A Study in Christian Platonism and Gnosticism* (Oxford, 1971), Section 3.

[17] Clement, *Stromateis* 1.6.27, 2.9.45, 2.12.55. For Clement faith is always a free choice: e.g. ibid. 2.2.9, 2.4.12.

[18] Ibid. 2.3.13.

[19] Ibid. 2.11.48–9, 5.1.5–6.

For Clement, reason and *pistis* are both, ultimately, gifts from God, although both must be exercised by the faithful.[20] The early stages of *pistis* make further rational thought and enquiry possible. By building on faith with investigation, we can begin to understand and to know God, and to judge the truth of claims about God.[21] This leads to a further level of *pistis*: that which we have in the truth of something which has been demonstrated by reason. This highest level of *pistis* is very close to, if it is not identified with, *gnosis*, knowledge of God and even (in Platonic fashion) assimilation to God.[22]

In this summary, two points are of particular interest. Clement makes the most sustained early attempt to syncretize Christianity and Platonic philosophy, and in the process makes belief central to *pistis*. And he applies his understanding of *pistis* to his reading of an authoritative early writer, shifting the centre of gravity of Paul's *pistis*, in his interpretation, from trust in God and Christ to belief. Clement's approach is summed up at the beginning of the *Protrepticus*, in an image of what Christ, the Word of God, does for the faithful: 'I am the door [Christ says], which we who seek to understand (*noēsai*) Christ must discover so that he may throw heaven's gates wide open to us. For the gates of the Word being intellectual (*logikai*), are opened by *pistis* (*logikē*).'[23]

Clement marks a new high-water mark in the *philosophopoiesis* of Christianity. He is not the last writer, however, to push the meaning of *pistis* towards belief. He is followed, among others, by his fellow Alexandrian and perhaps fellow school-member Origen, in his invective *Against Celsus*.[24] *Against Celsus* was written in the late 240s, in belated response to a late second-century work by Celsus, who, on the basis of internal evidence, was a Platonist and polytheist. From Origen's extensive quotations and citations of Celsus's *Logos Alēthēs* (*True Doctrine*), Celsus seems to have been extensively interested in *pistis*. His account is apparently that of a mainstream polytheist of his day. *Pistis* is both trust in the gods and belief,

---

[20] Ibid. 1.7.38, 2.4.48.
[21] Ibid. 2.2, 2.9–12, 2.4.14–15, 5.1.
[22] Ibid. 7.10.55, 57, 2.22.126.
[23] Ibid. 1.10.2–3.
[24] Elsewhere, Origen does not match Clement's interest in *pistis*, but focuses more on the importance of knowledge (in which he is followed, notably, by the Cappadocians).

based on this-worldly experience, that certain things are true about the gods.[25]

Celsus detests Christians, who, he thinks, are cowards and charlatans who tell the vulnerable and ignorant, 'Do not ask questions, just believe' (1.9). In attacking Celsus, Origen tackles Celsus's concept of *pistis* explicitly. Unexpectedly, he largely agrees with it. Both writers hold that *pistis* can mean trust in the divine (1.19–21, 2.3–4), although Origen thinks that such trust is particularly suitable for the uneducated who cannot aspire to knowledge (6.13).[26] Both hold that the pious should be able to prove that what they believe is reasonable, and Origen thinks Christians can. Their scriptures (by which he means the Jewish scriptures) are very ancient, and writings that have stood the test of time always bear credence (5.3). Many Christian doctrines (such as that God is one and good) are shared by contemporary philosophers (1.4–5). And Christianity is proved right by its consequences (1.6, 1.55): we can believe in the incarnation, for example, because it has a beautiful effect on the character, implanting 'a wonderful meekness and tranquillity, and love of humanity, and kindness and gentleness' (1.67).

Origen, however, is also conscious of the limitations of what can be proven. If Christian preaching, he observes (1.62), had been based entirely on reason, then Christian *pistis*, like that of the philosophers, would have been belief in the wisdom of human beings rather than the power of God. Human reason is limited. We deal with its limitations by exercising *pistis* in another sense: that of rational risk. Every day – when we go to sea, get married or plant our fields – we trust that the things we do will turn out well. We do so in part on the basis of experience, but in part by taking a risk (1.11, cf. 1.31, 3.39). We trust in God in the same way, and this is acceptable (1.11), because risk-based trust is rational. There is always a gap between what we can infer from evidence and the uncertain future, and trust leaps into that gap.[27] In a sense, here, Origen is talking of trust as a 'leap of

---

[25] Teresa Morgan, 'Origen's Celsus and Imperial Greek Religiosity', in James Carleton Paget and Simon Gathercole, eds, *Celsus in his World* (Cambridge, forthcoming).

[26] He assumes that even the uneducated hold trust-based beliefs: Gunnar af Hällström, *Fides Simpliciorum according to Origen of Alexandria* (Helsinki, 1984), 20–42.

[27] The idea that trust is a rational risk is now a commonplace of trust theory in the social sciences, but this passage is highly unusual among ancient writings (cf. Arnobius, *Adversus nationes* 2.8), although his point, that we plant in the belief that we will reap, etc., casts trust as justified (experience-based) belief, not rational risk.

faith', but not in the modern sense of the phrase. He advocates not deliberately non-rational trust or belief, but rational risk. By making this argument, however, Origen highlights the cognitive element even in trust, and shifts the centre of gravity of Christian *pistis* further towards believing.

All these writers are encouraged by interactions with non-Christians to present propositional belief as central to Christian *pistis*. At the same time, a different set of conflicts pushes some Christians in the same direction: disputes among the faithful about their understanding of God and Christ.

It is worth noting that, as far as we can tell, in very early Christian communities, thinking something different from what one's neighbours think (about the nature of Christ, say, or the resurrection) may provoke argument, but there is no sign that it leads to formal expulsion from the community.[28] The first people who are said, in so many words, to be expelled from a church for departing from a community's teaching and believing the wrong thing, are Valentinus and Marcion of Sinope in the mid-second century, according to Tertullian.[29] Tertullian normally uses *fides* language in the mainstream Latin sense of 'trust' or 'loyalty'. Occasionally, however, usually when he is discussing Marcion, he invokes a more propositional meaning.

In *Against Marcion*, Tertullian introduces Marcion as 'a monster more philosophical than Christian. Because Diogenes the Cynic used to go about, with a lantern, at midday, looking for a real man, but Marcion has lost the God whom he had found by dousing the light of his faith (*extincto lumine fidei suae*)' (1.1.5). Marcion, in Tertullian's view, holds wrong views about God (he thinks that the God of Christians is not the God of the Hebrew Scriptures) and the nature of Christ (he is a Docetist). The 'light of [Marcion's] faith', the thing that ought to guide him to God, is therefore what he thinks is true about God and Christ.

This makes right belief foundational to *fides*, but not necessarily identical with it. In *On the Flesh of Christ*, however, Tertullian goes

---

[28] As opposed to idol-worship or incest, for example, which Paul already thinks are grounds for expulsion in 1 Cor. 10: 21 and 5: 4–5 respectively.

[29] Writing several decades later: Tertullian, *On the Prescription of Heretics* 30.2. Judith Lieu observes that even in the mid-second century, claims of excommunications are anachronistic: *Marcion and the Making of a Heretic* (Cambridge, 2015), 396.

further. Marcion holds that it is irrational to think of God as taking on human flesh. Tertullian objects that it is only irrational in human reason. He appeals to 1 Corinthians 1: 25: 'the foolishness of God is wiser than human wisdom'. He concludes: 'You [Marcion] are not a Christian, because you do not believe what, being believed, makes people Christians (*non es Christianus, non credendo quod creditum Christianos facit*)' (2.4). In this move, Tertullian identifies being a Christian with believing that certain things are true.[30]

These examples show something of how pressures on Christians from inside and outside the cult, together with their own interests and those of their interlocutors, edge some writers increasingly towards thinking of *pistis* less as a relationship of trust or faithfulness between God, Christ and humanity, and more as belief. This in itself, however, does not constitute the institutionalization of belief. That requires a separate step: the development of creeds.

INSTITUTIONALIZATION AND THE CREEDS

The history of the creeds is a topic of much current debate to which this essay does not seek to contribute. It assumes only what is least controversial: that creeds develop out of baptismal interrogations, and that there are credible indications of their existence from at least the second century, though direct evidence comes, at the earliest, from the third.[31] If creeds begin life as baptismal interrogations, then they are always institutional: they define community membership. It does not follow, however, that they are always understood as

---

[30] Eric Osborn, *Tertullian, First Theologian of the West* (Cambridge, 1997), 48–64; cf., probably a little later, Novatian, *On the Trinity* 1, 11, emphasizing the importance of *fides* and *credere* in the truth (as opposed to heresy). Irenaeus, *Against Heresies*, occasionally clearly uses the 'belief' register of *pistis / pisteuein* (e.g. 5.20.1, fragment 36), but often refers to (for example) the '*kērygma* and *pistis*' (e.g. 1.3.1) received, distinguishing the content of preaching (or 'preaching of the truth', e.g. 1.3.2, cf. 1.9.4) from *pistis* in it. The slightly later *Refutation of All Heresies* still prefers *homologein, alētheia* or *alēthēs logos*, for example, when speaking of what the faithful believe.

[31] *Apostolic Tradition* 21.11–18; on reconstructions of the text, see Wolfram Kinzig, Christoph Markschies and Markus Vinzent, *Tauffragen und Bekenntnis. Studien zur sogenannten 'Traditio Apostolica', zu den 'Interrogationes de fide' und zum 'Römischen Glaubensbekenntnis'* (Berlin, 1999); Wolfram Kinzig, ed., *Faith in Formulae: A Collection of Early Christian Creeds and Creed-Related Texts*, 4 vols (Oxford, 2017), 1: 153–61. All surviving versions of the earliest baptismal formulae use *pisteuein / credere* language.

propositional. The terms used of them suggest that, before the fourth century, they are not.

Early creeds are called *ektheseis* (expositions), *mathemata* (lessons) or, most often, *symbola*. A *symbolon* is a token, a guarantee, or any kind of official document, such as the token carried by imperial messengers.[32] These terms suggest that early creeds are thought of as summaries of teaching which act as an identity marker. This is far from a new observation, but it has not been connected with the question about what kind of faith is at stake when Christians use or invoke a creed. If creeds are identity markers, however, there are many aspects of Christian identity to be marked other than propositional beliefs, including trust in God, worship of Christ, obedience to teaching, acknowledgement of episcopal authority and presence at communal rituals. If creeds are summaries of teaching, that teaching may include much beside propositions, such as the narratives of the Scriptures and authoritative early Christian writings, stories about the saints or the history of the church. We cannot assume that early Christians understood the identity they assumed and affirmed by saying early creeds as based on propositional beliefs, much less as defined by them.

Evidence of how creeds are put together and used, and the way their formally closest relations are used, also suggest that encoding propositional beliefs is not their earliest function. Liuwe Westra has argued that the hypothetical proto-Roman creed is constructed in part out of Christological acclamations, which at some point after about 150 CE were fused with a trinitarian baptismal formula.[33] Comparative evidence suggests that this is a plausible picture. Acclamations are ubiquitous in classical antiquity, and many of them sound very like Christological formulae, and some not unlike Christian creeds:

Hail to Zeus the victor![34]

Hear, O Israel, the Lord your God, the Lord is One![35]

---

[32] This is also a meaning of *pistis / fides*. *Symbola* are used as tokens of membership in some mystery cults: Kinzig, *Formulae*, 1: 6, 61–144; Plutarch, *Moralia* 611d; Apuleius, *Apology* 56; Origen, *Against Celsus* 6.22.

[33] Liuwe H. Westra, *The Apostles' Creed: Origin, History, and some Early Commentaries* (Turnhout, 2002), 71–2.

[34] Aeschylus, *Agamemnon* 174–5.

[35] Deut. 6: 4.

Great is Artemis of the Ephesians![36]

Holy is God, the father of all, who is before the first beginning, whose purpose is accomplished by his own powers; who wills to be known, and is known by those who are his own; holy are you, who by your word have constructed all that is ...[37]

Throughout the ancient Mediterranean and Near East, acclamations act as identity markers and forms of worship. They imply beliefs, but their purpose is less to define or police beliefs than to affirm worshippers' commitment to a divinity.[38]

Acclamations also have a close relationship with the affirmations which are made when one person or group pledges allegiance to another. The baptismal question-and-answer in the *Apostolic Tradition* begins: 'Do you *pisteueis* [believe in, trust in, make your commitment to] one God, the Father Almighty, and his only-begotten son Jesus Christ, our Lord and our Saviour, and his Holy Spirit, Giver of life to all creatures'. The candidate responds: '*Pisteuo.*' This formula is strikingly similar to the tripartite affirmation which new subjects make when they become part of the Roman empire:

'Are you the ambassadors and spokesmen sent by [for example] the Collatine people, to surrender yourselves and your people?'

'We are.'

'Is your people sovereign over itself?'

'It is.'

'Do you give yourselves and your people, your city, land, water, boundaries, shrines, utensils, and all things, divine and human, into the power of the Roman people?'

'We do.'[39]

---

[36] Acts 19: 28.

[37] *Poimandres of Hermes Trismegistus*, libellus 1.31.

[38] T. Klauser, 'Akklamation', *Reallexikon für Antike und Christentum* 1 (Stuttgart, 1950), 213–33; Charlotte Roueché, 'Acclamations in the Later Roman Empire: New Evidence from Aphrodisias', *Journal of Roman Studies* 74 (1984), 181–99.

[39] Livy, 1.38.1–2, cf. Polybius, 36.4.2, Plautus, *Amphitruo* 258–9; see Morgan, *Roman Faith*, 98–9. On the role of question and answer in admission to Roman Jewish communities, see Michel Dujarier, *Le Parrainage des adultes aux trois premiers siècles de l'église* (Paris, 1962), 82–9.

This is the Roman formula for *deditio in fidem*, the ritual by which new allies give themselves into a relationship of trust and loyalty with Rome. If Christians did not derive their idea of pledging *pistis* / *fides* to God, through a set of questions and answers, from the Roman empire, they surely accomplish something very similar by it, and it makes good sense that the resulting formula becomes known as a *symbolon*.

Creeds operate as identity markers, acclamations and affirmations or pledges of faith. Acclamations are also closely related to, and often embedded in, prayers and hymns, from the Homeric hymns through the Hebrew psalms to the offering prayer: 'My father was a wandering Aramean'.[40] Hymns and prayers commonly include, or allude to, stories about the god who is being worshipped or the past relationship between the god and his or her worshippers. It has occasionally been noted, though it has not been much explored, that creeds also make good sense as summaries of stories. Frances Young observes:

> There is a sense in which creeds are not themselves a system of doctrine ... It's as though the essential content is ... a *story* ... [Creeds] are summaries of the gospel, digests of the scriptures. As Cyril of Jerusalem put it in his Catechetical Lectures (V.12), 'Since all cannot read the scriptures ... we comprise the whole doctrine of the faith in a few lines.'[41]

Cyril is one of many sources attesting that much of the content of pre-baptismal instruction consisted of the contents of the Scriptures, full as they are of stories, acclamations, prayers and hymns, and that creeds were taught shortly before baptism as a summary of that teaching.[42]

If creeds emerge as summaries of teaching, summaries of stories, pledges, tokens of allegiance and acclamations, while Christian 'faith' language begins life focused primarily on trust and faithfulness rather than on belief as defining the divine-human relationship, gradually, Christians' disputes with each other and with non-Christians encourage them to make more and harder claims to knowledge and truth, and increasingly to use *pistis* / *fides* language

---

[40] Deut. 26: 1–11. Kinzig suggests that Deut. 6: 4 and this passage are the nearest ancestors in the Hebrew Bible to Christian creeds: *Formulae*, 33–4.

[41] Frances Young, *The Making of the Creeds* (London, 1991), 4.

[42] Thomas M. Finn, *Early Christian Baptism and the Catechumenate: West and East Syria* (Collegeville, MN, 1992), 3–5; William Harmless, *Augustine and the Catechumenate*, rev. edn (Collegeville, MN, 2014), 35–130.

of those claims.[43] This process reaches a crux in 325, at the Council of Nicaea, where the creed negotiated in response to Arianism includes, for the first time, material explicitly formulated to express what are claimed to be doctrinal truths. This creed is validated by the institutional authorities of the emperor and assembled bishops; it is used to baptize, and to assess the orthodoxy of existing community members. This is the moment when (at least in that form of Christianity endorsed by the emperor) Christians achieve 'orthopisty': propositional belief becomes institutionalized as definitive of being Christian. Significantly, it is after Nicaea that the phrase 'the true faith' (*pistis alēthēs*, *vera fides*) becomes widespread in our sources.

AN EXPLOSION OF INSPIRATION: IMAGES OF *FIDES QUA*

From the development of orthopisty, we turn to a very different aspect of early Christian faith. From the beginnings of Christian tradition, *pistis* had been imagined as active and dynamic. For Paul, it enables people to be forgiven and made right with God.[44] In a saying of Jesus, it has the power to move mountains.[45] With that exception, the early language of faith is not strongly imagistic, nor do early writings explore explicitly what faith is.[46] From the second century, however, especially in pastoral and devotional writing, we find a steady increase in imagery which explores what faith is and does.[47]

Given that faith has always been understood as leading to healing or release from sin, it is not surprising that some images are of healing or purification.[48] John Chrysostom and Augustine, for example, both

---

[43] Accounts of the evolution of orthodoxy and of creeds still typically assume that belief and specific beliefs were crucial to Christians from the earliest formation of churches, but this overlooks the dominance of trust / faithfulness meanings of *pistis* / *fides* language in early writings, such as recently Wolfram Kinzig, 'From the Letter to the Spirit to the Letter: The Faith as Written Creed', in idem, *Neue Texte und Studien zu den antiken und frühmittelalterlichen Glaubensbekenntnissen* (Berlin, 2017), 293–310.

[44] For example, Gal. 2: 16, Rom. 3: 21–6.

[45] Matt. 21: 21 = Mark 11: 23, cf. 1 Cor. 13: 2.

[46] The apparent exception is Heb. 11: 1, but this is a description of how *pistis* works rather than a formal definition.

[47] What follows focuses on images which appear multiple times in multiple (at least three and often a dozen or more) authors; these have the best claim to represent not just one author's idea but ideas that were widely shared and formed part of Christian *mentalité*.

[48] Peter Chrysologus, *Sermons* 57.1 (faith is like a flaming coal taken from the altar to purify our lips).

make much use of the idea of faith as medicine: 'the medicine of all the wounds of the soul', as Augustine calls it.[49]

One might think that the faith which is medicinal would be the content of doctrine. Occasionally it is, but more often it is the faith by which the faithful believe. Almost all images of faith are used to describe both how and what Christians believe. This convergence may seem surprising and potentially confusing, but there are good reasons for it. Images draw heavily on a relatively small group of authoritative early texts, especially the emerging canonical gospels. Christians are also keen to hold the different meanings of their faith language together. They imply that it is no accident that the act of trusting or believing in God and Christ, the new covenant and the content of doctrine are all called *pistis / fides*, and using the same imagery of them all is one way to express – if hardly to explain – their integrity.

The fact that faith can act as medicine for the soul does not necessarily imply that it is wholly under the believer's control. Between the second and fourth centuries, it becomes increasingly common to affirm that faith is a gift from God. This idea has roots in 1 Corinthians 12: 9, where *pistis* is a gift of the Spirit, and Galatians 5: 22, where it is a fruit of the Spirit, and it becomes a significant theme, not least in fourth-century debates about grace and free will. The imagery of faith, however, does not polarize grace and free will as some argumentative writing does. More often, it seems to reflect a sense that faith is complex. It is given to Christians, but they have to accept it; it does something they cannot do for themselves, but they also have to exercise it. For John Chrysostom, for instance, faith is an oak tree planted in the soul which the faithful person must tend.[50] For Ambrose, it is the drachma which the woman who has acquired it loses, and has to find again in order to save her soul.[51]

Another cluster of images focuses on the salvific function of faith, specifically its ability to elevate the soul from earth to God or heaven. 'Faith lifts the soul up from earth to God', says a second-century collection of gnomic sayings, *The Sentences of Sextus* (402). For Clement,

---

[49] Augustine, *Letters* 143.1, cf. John Chrysostom, *Homilies on John* 33.1; Paulinus of Nola, *Poems* 19.200–5.
[50] John Chrysostom, *Homilies on John* 54.1.
[51] Ambrose, *Letters* 7, *to Iustus* 2.

in the *Paidagogos* (1.4.1), faith is a ship's rope by which we haul ourselves up to God, while for Ephrem the Syrian in one of his hymns on faith (84.1), the faith of the thief on the cross possesses him and raises him to paradise.

Most images of faith, however, focus less on heaven or the afterlife, and more on the role of faith in this life. This is a striking development. The earliest Christian writings say very little about what faith does, or what the faithful do with it, after their conversion, except that one must continue to be faithful.[52] From the second century, however, Christians become increasingly interested in the role of faith after conversion: no doubt, at least in part, because they expect to have more life after conversion. As one late antique dice oracle says, 'Do not abandon the faith that is in your heart: it is helpful to you.'[53]

Sometimes faith is described as foundational for the church or for Christian life. In the second-century apocalypse *The Shepherd of Hermas*, Hermas is given a vision of the church as a tower which is in the process of being built.[54] All the parts of the tower stand for God, virtues or various groups of Christians, and the whole structure is supported by seven women (3.8.2) who form an eclectic group of virtues. The first and most foundational of these virtues is Pistis, because, as the church herself says, 'through *pistis* the chosen of God are saved.'[55]

The most widely used image of faith in this life, however, is that of a ship, which carries the faithful across the turbulent seas of life, bearing them up, weathering storms and bringing them safely into the harbour of heaven.[56] One might think that the faith we sail in would be 'the faith': the cult or the church. Sometimes it is, but more often it is the faith of the faithful. Tertullian describes its action in *On Idolatry* 24:

> [A]mid the reefs and inlets [of vice], the shallows and straits of idolatry, faith navigates, her sails filled by the Spirit of God; safe if cautious,

---

[52] Morgan, *Roman Faith*, 220–2, 314–15, 336–8.

[53] Vatican Coptic Papyrus 1.53, ET in Marvin W. Meyer and Richard Smith, *Ancient Christian Magic: Coptic Texts of Ritual Power* (Princeton, NJ, 1999), 253.

[54] Vision 1, 2.1; 3, 2.4–5.

[55] Cf. John Chrysostom, *Catechetical Oration* 1.19 (faith is the foundation on which everything else is built).

[56] For example, Ephrem, *Hymn on Faith* 2.6, 49.6, 69.6; Cyril of Jerusalem, *Catecheses* 5.7; Ambrose, *On Faith* 1.45–6.

secure if intently watchful. But for those who are washed overboard, there is a deep there is no swimming out of; those who run aground suffer inescapable shipwreck; for those who are engulfed ... every wave suffocates; every eddy sucks one down into hell.[57]

Without faith, says John Chrysostom, we are like people trying to cross the sea without a ship. They can swim for a while with their hands and feet but, as they get further out, they are swamped by the waves.[58] For those who think of their spiritual journey as terrestrial rather than maritime, faith, according to Prudentius's *Psychomachia* (362–6), weaves new clothes for those setting out on their journey; it shines a light on the way;[59] and, according to Paulinus of Nola, it strengthens the hearts of the faithful when they are afraid.[60]

As the faithful travel, faith plays several further roles in their lives. In two popular images, faith is guide and teacher. 'May *pistis* guide you in all good actions', say the Sentences of Sextus (166).[61] A famous early example of *pistis* as both leader and teacher appears on the late second-century tombstone of Abercius of Hierapolis, in Asia Minor:

My name is Abercius, disciple of the holy shepherd [Christ] ... It was he who taught me trustworthy knowledge, and it was he who sent me to Rome, to see the queen of cities, and to see a Queen with golden robes and golden shoes ... Everywhere Pistis led the way; everywhere she fed me with fish from the spring, great and pure, caught by a holy maiden ...[62]

The queen with golden robes is probably the Roman church, while the fish which Pistis feeds to Abercius may well be *fides quae*, the content of doctrine. Pistis's feeding of Abercius with fish may also echo

---

[57] We are used to the image of heaven as a palace, city or kingdom, but in these images it is always the harbour, surely reflecting that the most potent everyday Mediterranean experience of safety was of reaching harbour after a sea journey.

[58] John Chrysostom, *Homilies on John* 33.1, cf. Augustine, *Sermons on Matthew* 75.2.

[59] For example, *Oxyrhynchus Papyri* 18.430; Ambrose, *Hymns* 4.25–8.

[60] Paulinus of Nola, *Poems* 26.99–103.

[61] Cf. Prudentius, *Against Symmachus* 2.91–3; Cyril of Jerusalem, *Catecheses* 4.6; Ephrem, *Hymns on Faith* 80.9.

[62] W. Wischmeyer, 'Die Aberkiosinschrift als Grabepigramm', *Jahrbuch für Antike und Christentum* 23 (1980), 22–47, at 24–6; ET in Peter Thonemann, 'Abercius of Hierapolis', in Beate Dignas and R. R. R. Smith, eds, *Historical and Religious Memory in the Ancient World* (Oxford, 2012), 257–79, at 259.

the feeding of the five thousand; if so, then Pistis here acts like Christ, a theme to which we will return.

On Christians' journeys, whether literal or metaphorical, faith is often a nurturing or a comforting presence. Two tombstones from late antique Gaul refer to her (in a very Roman expression) as *alma fides*: '*Alma Fides* procured (*conferre*) for [someone whose name is lost] the height [or 'support'] of apostolicity, and when he died he went up to heaven.'[63] For Ambrose, in an evening hymn, 'watchful faith with cooling care' soothes the fevered brows of the faithful as they fall asleep.[64]

In more extreme situations, faith does more. Peter Chrysologus, in a sermon, describes the martyrdom of St Laurence on the gridiron. This horrible death, as Peter describes it, is made bearable with the help of faith:

> Next, someone brought out the well-known gridiron for martyring Laurence ... by roasting him. He was bound fast by iron, but he regarded that gridiron of torture as a bed of rest ...

> We admire his patience. Let us admire this as a gift from God. In this case his faith was not burning painfully in him: it was even consoling the man who was being roasted. Why was faith consoling him? Because it was keeping [him] faithful [to] the One making promises ...[65]

The divine gift of faith seems to take Laurence's pain away.

For Prudentius, in the *Harmatogenia*, when the soul of the faithful person finally reaches heaven, Faith is there, like Abraham or Godself, to clasp it to her bosom and let it unload all its troubles: 'Then, as the exiled soul returns to be reinstated in her heavenly country, white-haired Fides receives her to her bosom and comforts her nursling with tender affection, while [the soul] plaintively describes the many toils she has endured since she took up lodging in the flesh.'[66]

---

[63] Françoise Descombes, *Recueil des inscriptions chrétiennes de la Gaule antérieures à la Renaissance carolingienne*, 15: *Viennoise du Nord* (Paris, 1985), 95, cf. 39.

[64] Ambrose, *Hymns* 2.21–4.

[65] Peter Chrysologus, *Sermons* 135; ET in *St Peter Chrysologus, Selected Sermons; and St Valerian: Homilies*, transl. George E. Ganss, Fathers of the Church 17 (Washington DC, 1953), 224. In the last sentence, *quia fidelem tenebat promittentem*, 'because it was keeping faithful the one making promises', is surely wrong, since God does not need to be kept faithful, while it would be odd to describe Laurence as making promises at the point of death.

[66] Prudentius, *Harmatogenia* 852–5. *Cana fides* is another phrase with Roman origins.

In several of these passages, faith is more or less strongly personified. Before exploring personification a little further, however, it is worth summarizing the cumulative shape and effect of these images so far. Images of faith, among many authors and across many genres, describe faith as saving and changing the faithful. It acts as the foundation of their lives and carries them through life to a safe harbour. On the way, it supports them, comforts them and relieves their suffering. It teaches them and guides them, and, one way or another, ensures that eventually they reach heaven. These images convey vividly not only how important faith is, but how people imagine it as a dynamic force at the centre of their lives, and life itself as a project to which faith is essential. This makes faith extraordinarily precious, a theme which no-one captures better than Ephrem. In his hymns on faith, faith is a priceless pearl (16.6) which a merchant offers to his king as the most valuable thing he owns. It is a peeled grape (16.8), the most luxurious thing a vinedresser can offer his master. It is a beautiful bride (20.7), who should be carried in triumph through the marketplace.

The drama of these images should not mask the fact that for most Christians, most of the time, especially by the fourth century, life was probably not especially dramatic or dangerous. This, in itself, may be one reason why faith imagery develops as it does. It is often observed that by the fourth century Christians no longer expect the final cosmic battle or the return of Christ imminently, and persecution and martyrdom are no longer a regular risk. It is sometimes suggested that monasticism and asceticism develop in part as a response to this lessening of risk: as an alternative framework of life in which those with a particularly dramatic and dynamic sense of their life of faith can live it out. The imagery of faith, I suggest, does something similar for all the faithful. It creates a 'mental set', in which everyday life is a cosmic drama in which all the faithful can take part.

Most dramatically of all, faith helps the faithful to fight for their faith, and even fights for them: defending them against attack, bearing the brunt of their suffering in martyrdom, and seeing off the devil. It is in these roles that faith is most strongly personified. The idea that faith fights for the faithful has Christian roots in Ephesians 6.16, where *pistis* is a shield.[67] In later writers, the shield often becomes a

---

[67] Cf. Tertullian, *On the Games* 29; Gregory of Nyssa, *Letter to Ablabius*, lines 1–12, in Ekkehardus Mühlenberg and Giulio Maspero, eds, *Gregorii Nysseni Opera*, 5: *Ad*

weapon. Armed with the word of faith, says Cyril of Alexandria in his *Commentary on John*, we destroy arguments and every obstacle to the knowledge of God, while Ambrose tells us that every martyr's faith is his sword.[68] By the fourth century, Faith is sometimes the one wielding the weapon: Paulinus of Nola, Gregory of Nyssa and Augustine are among the writers of this period who talk about Faith going into battle on behalf of the faithful. No description of faith as a warrior, however, is more famous or influential than that of Prudentius in his poem, the *Psychomachia*.

The *Psychomachia* is an epic account of the war for the Christian soul between the virtues, led by Fides under the generalship of Christ, and a host of vices:

> Fides first takes the field to face the doubtful chances of battle, her rough dress disordered, her shoulders bare, her hair untrimmed, her arms exposed ...

> See, first Worship-of-the-Old-Gods (*Vetera cultura deorum*) ventures to match her strength against Fides' challenge, and strike at her.

> But she, rising higher, smites her foe's head down, with its fillet-decked brows; lays in the dust that mouth that was sated with the blood of beasts, and tramples the eyes under foot, squeezing them out in death ...[69]

Prudentius's personifications have received abundant attention from both literary critics and theologians.[70] The poem can be seen as the

---

Ablabium, Quod non sint tres dei (Leiden, 2010), 37; John Chrysostom, *Homilies on Genesis* 46.2; Paulinus of Nola, *Poems* 15.145–52. The idea also has abundant parallels in Fides, the divine hypostasis of Jupiter, and other personified qualities which help, and sometimes fight for, human beings in Greek and Roman cult, myth and literature. Christian personification also owes something to the biblical personification of wisdom, although Jewish personification of wisdom seems to fall away in this period: Peter Schäfer, *Mirror of His Beauty: Feminine Images of God from the Bible to the Early Kabbalah* (Princeton, NJ, 2002), 79–117.

[68] Cyril, *Commentary on John* 2.182 (on John 1.32–3); Ambrose, *Hymns* 10.25 (on the martyrs of Milan); cf. Jennifer R. Strawbridge, *The Pauline Effect: The Use of the Pauline Epistles by Early Christian Writers* (Berlin, 2015), 57–73.

[69] Prudentius, *Psychomachia* 21–33.

[70] See especially Macklin Smith, *Prudentius'* Psychomachia (Princeton, NJ, 1976); Brenda Machosky, 'The Face that is not a Face: The Phenomenology of the Soul in the Allegory of the *Psychomachia*', *Exemplaria* 15 (2003), 1–38; Marc Mastrangelo, *The Roman Self in Late Antiquity* (Baltimore, MD, 2008); Ad Putter, 'Prudentius and

culmination of the classical theme of the gods at war which goes back to Homer, and the beginning of a long medieval tradition of large-scale allegory. Personification also offers a powerful mechanism for capturing all the meanings of faith (or hope, love or other key Christian qualities) under one helmet: Fides, for example, at different points in the poem, is a gift from God, the trust of the faithful, 'the faith' in the sense of the cult, and true doctrine.[71] The personification of faith heightens that sense which has just been discussed, of faith as a force at the centre of Christian life, and life as a drama to which faith is crucial.[72] Few life experiences can be more dramatic than hosting a bare-armed heroine inside you while she battles for your soul.

This article cannot do justice to Prudentius's personification of faith, much less to his practice of personification as a whole. It is, though, worth mentioning briefly two aspects of the former which add something to our understanding of the role of imagery in general to early Christian understandings of faith.

The *Psychomachia* begins with a prologue which traces God's command to the faithful to make war on the vices back to Abraham. Most of the poem consists of a series of duels between Fides, Pudicitia, Patientia, Mens Humilis and others, and their opposites, interspersed with lengthy speeches urging the reader to repentance and Christian life. Prudentius presents the battle as taking place within a human soul, and most commentators assume that the soul is doing battle with itself. A few have argued that the virtues and vices represent opposing forces in the battle between God and the powers of the world, or even that they are echoes of the deified abstractions of Greek and Roman cult.[73] All these theories have something to commend them, but all leave questions unanswered.

---

the Late Classical Biblical Epics of Juvencus, Proba, Sedulius, Arator, and Avitus', in Rita Copeland, ed., *The Oxford History of Classical Reception in English Literature*, 1: *800–1558* (Oxford, 2016), 351–70.

[71] Cf. Prudentius, *Psychomachia* 5–6 (gift from God), 868–74 (faith of the faithful), 29–39 ('the faith'), 726–827 (the true faith).

[72] In the *Psychomachia* an unusually large number of qualities are personified and portrayed as crucial to Christian life. Elsewhere, after faith, wisdom, truth, hope and love are the qualities most often personified. *Logos* is invariably identified with Christ and as such operates differently from other personifications.

[73] For example, Smith, *Psychomachia*, 126–31; Kenneth R. Haworth, *Deified Virtues, Demonic Vices, and Descriptive Allegory in Prudentius'* Psychomachia (Amsterdam, 1980); James J. Paxson, *The Poetics of Personification* (Cambridge, 1994), 66–7.

The idea that there is tension between virtues and vices within the soul goes back to Plato, although philosophers do not normally talk about progress in virtue as a war. Prudentius's terminology of virtue and vice is undoubtedly philosophical, but his picture of what is happening in the soul owes more to the Pauline epistles, in particular the idea that the faithful are given various qualities as gifts by the Holy Spirit, and the idea that the faithful are fighting a war in themselves against the devil.

In the prologue (13–14), Prudentius says that the example of Abraham reveals that a *bellicosus spiritus* must do battle and overcome the monsters in our enslaved heart (*cor*).[74] When all the vices have been expelled, Christ himself 'will enter the humble abode of the pure heart and give it the privilege of entertaining the Trinity' (prologue 59–63). Prudentius appeals to Christ to tell him 'with what fighting force the mind (*mens*) is armed' (5–6). He already knows the answer: the troops are the virtues, under Christ's leadership (11–20).

Prudentius's list of virtues does not exactly match any other such list (of which there are many in Greek philosophy, Hellenistic Judaism and early Christianity), but nearly all of them are qualities familiar to Christians as either gifts or fruits of the Spirit in 1 Corinthians 12: 4–11 or Galatians 5: 22. *Pistis*, as has already been noted, appears in both lists. As has also been noted, the idea that qualities, which have been given to us, help us to fight the devil, appears several times in early epistles, most famously in Ephesians 6: 10–17. In those passages, the qualities the faithful put on are not their own virtues, but gifts from God which enable them to defend themselves in the cosmic war with the devil. The psychology of this poem therefore owes something to philosophy but rather more to the Pauline epistles. It is never fully articulated, no doubt because developing a theory of the soul was not Prudentius's prime concern, but the poem conveys a strong sense that the most important thing a Christian soul can do is to be receptive to Christ: to let Christ and his troops into itself to do their work.[75] This implies a rather different psychology from the philosophically informed theories which

---

[74] Smith argues that *mens*, *anima* and *spiritus* are not exact equivalents but are often hard to differentiate: *Psychomachia*, 141–59. Many Latin writers use them in ways which are difficult, if not impossible, to distinguish: Morgan, *Roman Faith*, 447–50.

[75] This idea may be another with a Pauline origin, if Prudentius had in mind Gal. 2: 20.

patrologists attribute (often rightly) to other writers.[76] Prudentius has little or no sense that what matters in faith is knowledge, reason or the control of the best part of the soul over the rest of the soul or the rest of the self. He focuses on openness, receptivity and acquiescence to Christ.

As we have seen, Prudentius is by no means the only writer who personifies faith, especially when the life of faith is being imagined as a battle. In scenes of combat, the imagery of faith reveals not only something of these writers' psychology, but also some notable theology.

Poem 15 is one of several in which Paulinus celebrates the birthday of St Felix of Nola, who was believed to have been martyred during the Decian persecution or soon after. Here, he is describing how a martyr's faith holds out under persecution: 'Faith defeats [men armed with steel] through [its] awareness of heavenly truth; it measures the future life against immediate death, and it joyfully restores to God the mind which is victorious over the conquered body, and transports it to the delighted stars' (15.147–52). This is figurative but not perhaps a very developed personification; but Paulinus continues:

> So [Felix] eagerly stood his ground like a wall against the savage foe. His blooming faith lent him fresh strength in his old age. Concentrating his mind on heaven, mindful of Christ, forgetful of the world, he bore God in his heart and his person was filled with Christ. His body now no longer contained him; he seemed a sanctified, greater being, and his eyes and countenance shone with heavenly glory. (15.171–6).

It is a recurring theme in martyrologies that the martyr either puts on, or feels, the presence of God or Christ, and that the presence of God with a human being causes shining.[77] Here, however, we find Fides supporting Felix, alongside God and Christ.[78]

This is not an isolated passage. We have already encountered Faith behaving very like Christ on Abercius's tombstone and in a sermon of Peter Chrysologus, where she consoles St Laurence on the gridiron and takes away his pain. In his *Hymn in Honour of St Laurence*, Prudentius goes even further. He describes how, in Christianity's battle

---

[76] The study of patristic psychology in general would benefit from more attention to its scriptural and early Christian roots.

[77] Eusebius, *Ecclesiastical History* 5.123, 42; 8.7.2; *The Martyrdom of Perpetua* 18.2; *The Martyrdom of Pionius* 22.4.

[78] In the event, Felix is not not martyred on this occasion, as Paulinus goes on to tell.

with mainstream cult, 'Fides fought in arms, not sparing her own blood, for by death she destroyed death and spent herself to save herself'.[79] This is a remarkable image. The language of salvation and the destruction of death unmistakably references the saving death of Christ. The phrase 'by death she destroyed death' virtually quotes 2 Timothy 1: 10. Here, therefore, Fides – Laurence's faith or perhaps 'the faith' – acts like Christ himself. She re-enacts Christ's saving death, and is imagined as continuing Christ's saving work on earth in the ongoing battle with idolatry.

In these passages, Faith constitutes a form of God's ongoing presence with the faithful, very much as do the risen Christ and the Holy Spirit. Either she enters people and inhabits them, like Christ or the Spirit, or she is with them, supporting them, as the risen Christ can be described as with the faithful and supporting them.[80] Theologically, this idea may come as a surprise to modern readers. We may wonder why Christians, who in this period already sometimes find themselves obliged to explain to outsiders in what sense they have only one god, not three, feel it appropriate to cast faith as yet another form of God's presence with the faithful. Remarkably, writers of this period do not seem to regard this as a problem. One reason may be that the fourth century is an era in which intermediaries of various kinds proliferate between the divine and human spheres, notably in the cults of Mary the Bearer of God and the saints. Another reason may be that Faith never becomes a fully-fledged hypostasis of God, as Roman Fides is of Jupiter. I have yet to discover a Christian praying to her.[81] She acts like Christ or the Spirit *ad occasionem*, to suit a writer's immediate needs, and then reverts to her usual status as an attitude, a relationship, a virtue, the body of doctrine or 'the faith'. This, indeed, is surely one of the attractions of imagery. It is highly flexible: it can help writers and their audiences think about the role of a quality like faith in their relationship with God, without involving them in complex and controversial questions of essence or personhood.

[79] *Crowns of Martyrdom* 2.2.17–20.

[80] Noted by Smith, *Psychomachia*, 158–9, but without connecting the point with earlier Christian thinking. This idea is probably not confined to personifications: it makes explicit an idea which is implicit in the imagery of medicine, teaching and guidance.

[81] Pseudo-Severian of Gabbala, in a sermon on faith, describes *pistis* as 'to be honoured and bowed down to in silence', in terms (*timōmenon, proskynoumenon*) which can be used of worship, but may not be intended so strongly here: Kinzig, *Formulae*, 2: 22–4. St Faith originates as a human martyr of the late third or early fourth century, although later she is sometimes confused with personified Faith.

All these images and personifications testify to the central and honoured place of Christian faith in the divine-human relationship. It can be the sign and (in a non-technical sense) the substance of God's presence with the faithful. By having faith, the faithful have God, and God has them. In contrast with Christian thinking about belief, however, the imagery of faith, fluid and adaptable as it is, never becomes a focus of controversy in antiquity.

CONCLUSION

The idea of faith developed dramatically on several fronts between the second and fourth centuries, and it would be premature to draw firm conclusions about the concept and practice as a whole on the basis of this brief account of two of its strands. We can, however, offer some final reflections. It is tempting to infer a symbiosis between the increasing institutionalization of orthopisty (among many, if not all Christians) and the burgeoning imagery of faith. Certainly there is no sign that the wealth, variety and flexibility of the images we have explored constitute a rebellion against right belief, or a response to any perception of the imposition of orthodoxy as oppressive. Nor do these images, or their creators, show signs of wanting to challenge the structures or hierarchies of the church. Most of the writers who develop the most colourful imagery are also establishment figures: bishops, aristocrats and (from the fourth century) supporters of Nicene orthodoxy. Rather, the parallel development of orthopisty and imagery points to an element of spontaneous self-regulation in a complex, increasingly sophisticated and very successful cult. Christianity recognizes faith as standing at its heart, and, in a period in which the faithful are being held to increasingly stringent standards of propositional belief, they are also offered a wealth of imagery to develop and shape their awareness of all the other things faith simultaneously means and does. Images ensure that faith is always recognized as both a gift and a responsibility; something which the faithful enact and which acts for them; a power which is with the faithful and in them, comforting and feeding them, teaching and fighting for them, and – if they do not scuttle the ship – eventually bringing them safely into God's harbour.

A Clash Between *Paideia* and *Pneuma?* Ecstatic Women Prophets and Theological Education in the Second-century Church

Josef Lössl*

Cardiff University

*The second half of the second century saw the development of a more hierarchical institutionalized church and of a theology of the Holy Spirit (*Pneuma*) reflecting this development. A driver of this development was a higher educational level among church leaders and Christians participating in theological discourse. In fact, 'higher education' (*paideia*) became a guiding value of Christian living, including for the study and interpretation of Scripture and for theology and church leadership. Yet the same period also saw a new wave of 'inspired', 'pneumatic prophecy', later known as 'Montanism', which was perceived as a threat in an increasingly institutionalized church and attacked and suppressed. This article sees a paradox here, and asks how* Pneuma *could be promoted as a source of Christian leadership under the banner of* paideia, *when the Spirit (*Pneuma*) at work in the 'New Prophecy' was perceived as such a threat. One area of investigation which may provide answers to this question is the controversial role women played both as educated participants in theological discourse and leading figures in the Montanist movement.*

Rudolf Helm's edition of Jerome's translation of Eusebius's chronological tables for the years 2187 and 2188 (171 and 172 CE) contains, back to back, two entries which at first glance may not seem to have too much to do with one another: The first, the last entry for 171, refers to the 'pseudoprophecy which is called "according to the Phrygians" (*kata Phrygas*)'. This began with Montanus as its creator (*auctore*) and with Priscilla and Maximilla its insane prophets (*insanis uatibus*)'. The second, the first entry for 172, reads: 'Tatian has been recognized [i.e. been identified] as a

* School of History, Archaeology and Religion, John Percival Building, Colum Drive, Cardiff, CF10 3EU. E-mail: LosslJ@cardiff.ac.uk.

Studies in Church History 57 (2021), 32–53 © The Author(s), 2021. Published by Cambridge University Press on behalf of Ecclesiastical History Society.
doi: 10.1017/stc.2021.3

heretic. From him the Encratites take their beginning (*Tatianus haereticus agnoscitur, a quo Encratitae*)'.[1] Thus the 'outbreak', if that is the right word, of what modern scholarship knows as 'Montanism' (an expression that has been used only since the fourth century;[2] the more authentic designation is 'The New Prophecy'[3]) is noted here in Eusebius's *Chronicle* as the last event for the year 171. The same author's *Church History* 5.16.7, excerpting an earlier source, the so-called 'anti-Montanist Anonymous', adds that the events occurred under the proconsulate in Asia of a certain Gratus, which could be dated to 169/70 or 171/2.[4] The *Chronicle* entry refers to the 'movement' as a 'pseudo-prophecy', on grounds, or so it seems, of its ecstatic nature, and to the prophets involved as 'insane'. Jerome uses for 'prophet' an expression usually reserved for pagan seers, *uates*. The expression *insanis uatibus* can be understood as applying to the three persons who are named, Montanus, Priscilla and Maximilla, although from the way the sentence is structured the phrase seems to refer primarily to the two women. The understanding is, or so it seems, that they uttered 'dark' oracles in a manner similar to that of seers at pagan shrines.

---

[1] Eusebius, *Chronicle*, *s.aa.* 2187–8 (171–2 CE) (GCS 47, 206): 'pseudoprofetia, quae kata frygas nominator, accepit exordium auctore Montano et Priscilla Maximillaque insanis uatibus'; *s.a.* 171; 'Tatianus haereticus agnoscitur, a quo Encratitae': *s.a.* 172. All translations in this article are my own.

[2] The earliest known mention of οἱ Μοντανοί occurs in Cyril of Jerusalem, *Catecheses* 16.8.6 (*Cyrilli Hierosolymorum archiepiscopi opera quae supersunt omnia*, 2 vols, ed. W. C. Reischl and J. Rupp [Munich, 1860], 2: 214), where Montanus is called ἔξαρχος τῶν κακῶν and Priscilla and Maximilla προφήτιδες αὐτοῦ. The context is the Montanists' belief (rejected by Cyril as false) that the millenarian Jerusalem will at the end of time descend over Pepouza. Didymus refers to οἱ Μοντανισταί: *De trinitate* 3.18, 23, 41 (PG 39, 881B, 924C, 984B). Although Didymus does not refer explicitly to the Montanists as heretics, he ascribes to them a heretical position, namely a 'Sabellian-like' identification of 'the Father-Son and the Paraclete' (τὸν αὐτὸν υἱοπατέρα ὁμοῦ καὶ παράκλητον νοοῦντας). For further details and background on Montanism, see Christoph Markschies, 'Montanismus', *Reallexikon für Antike und Christentum* 24 (Stuttgart, 2012), 1197–1220, at 1197–8; also, still, William Tabbernee, *Prophets and Gravestones: An Imaginative History of Montanists and other Early Christians* (Peabody, MA, 2009).

[3] Cf. Eusebius, *Ecclesiastical History* 5.16.4 (GCS 9, 460.14–17): 'τῆς νέας … , ὡς αὐτοὶ φάσιν, προφητείας'; 5.16.18 (GCS 9, 466.27).

[4] Ibid. 5.16.7 (GCS 9, 462–3). There is otherwise no evidence for this name. But it has been suggested that he could fill existing gaps in the proconsular lists for the years 169–70 or, more likely, 171–2; for further discussion and literature, see Markschies, 'Montanismus', 1205.

The expression 'oracle' for Montanist prophecies is also still sometimes used in modern literature, especially when possible ties between Montanism and traditional, pre-Christian, Phrygian religion are explored,[5] an aspect of the topic that will not be considered here. The alleged oracle-like darkness of the prophecies was later used by heresiologists as evidence against their authoritative nature, although the extant *logia* do not strike one as overly dark. Alternatively, and somewhat in contradiction to the first charge, there was the suggestion that the prophecies came ultimately from 'evil spirits' or 'the adversary' (i.e. the devil). This charge, too, was inconsistent, for not only were the sayings by and large comprehensible, at the time they were not perceived as overly problematic doctrinally. Only from the fourth century was Montanism linked to heretical views, such as Sabellianism.[6] What did cause trouble, however, was the way in which they were delivered (involving ecstatic prophecy as a source of doctrine that could potentially undermine tradition) and who delivered them, namely women, who as pneumatically gifted prophets assumed the status and functions of ordained leaders, bishops, a role that was about to be defined in ways that definitely excluded women.

The entry in Eusebius's *Chronicle* alludes to these implications. Montanus, a man, is mentioned as 'originator' (*auctor*) of the movement. Yet according to other sources he too was an ecstatic prophet,[7] and the expression *insanis uatibus* can be understood as referring to him as well. But the real issue, as this article will argue, is the fact that women publicly acted as prophets and thereby assumed leadership roles and threatened structures that were developing in a different kind of theological and ecclesial discourse.[8]

---

[5] See the discussion in Christoph Markschies, *Christian Theology and its Institutions in the Early Roman Empire: Prolegomena to a History of Early Christian Theology* (Waco, TX, 2015), 92 n. 310.

[6] See n. 2 above (Didymus's view).

[7] For Montanus as an ecstatic prophet, see Eusebius, *Ecclesiastical History* 5.16.7 (GCS 9, 462.10–15). A third leading woman prophet, Quintilla, is mentioned in Epiphanius, *Panarion* 49.1.2 (GCS NF 13, 241.23–242.8). On her role, see also William Tabbernee, 'Recognizing the Spirit: Second-Generation Montanist Oracles', *SP* 40 (2006), 521–6, at 522–3.

[8] There can be no doubt that gender is a central issue in the Montanist controversy. However, there are nuances in the way it is, or can be, treated in modern scholarship. For instance, Christine Trevett, *Montanism: Gender, Authority and the New Prophecy* (Cambridge, 1996), 159–62, has argued that Anne Jensen, *Gottes selbstbewußte Töchter.*

Tatian, who is also known as author of the *Diatessaron*, was a pupil of Justin Martyr and author of an apology entitled *Oration to the Greeks*,[9] which he probably completed not long after 172.[10] The first known witness to accuse him of heresy and of being a leading theologian (if not the founder) of the Encratites is Irenaeus,[11] a contemporary. A few decades later Clement of Alexandria corroborated Irenaeus's charge, with additional evidence.[12] Both Irenaeus and Clement cite from works of Tatian which are no longer extant. The only extant work, the *Oration to the Greeks*, does not contain any material that would suggest that Tatian promoted Encratism.[13] Be that as it may, the comments of Irenaeus and Clement make it quite clear that the issue was about the interpretation of certain Pauline passages (1 Corinthians 7: 5–6, 39; 15: 22). According to Irenaeus and Clement, Tatian held that according to these passages

---

Frauenemanzipation im frühen Christentum (Freiburg im Breisgau, 1992), 268–326, may have gone too far by arguing that Montanus was falsely named as *auctor* and that precedence is due to Priscilla and Maximilla in every respect, as prophets *and* founders; cf. also Anne Jensen, 'Prisca-Maximilla-Montanus: Who was the Founder of "Montanism"?', *SP* 26 (1993), 146–50. Trevett, however, sees no reason why heresiologists should have invented the role of Montanus, who was himself 'feminized' and denigrated because of his ecstatic prophecy, and ultimately superseded in impact and influence by the two women prophets, Priscilla and Maximilla. Moreover, the two women were also hierarchically graded: Priscilla seems to be given precedence in the sources over Maximilla. But Trevett agrees with Jensen in emphasizing the fact that the women were not dependent on Montanus and that over time they emerged as leaders in their own right: *Montanism*, 162.

[9] See, most recently, Heinz-Günther Nesselrath, *Gegen falsche Götter und falsche Bildung. Tatian,* Rede an die Griechen, SAPERE 28 (Tübingen, 2016); Jörg Trelenberg, *Tatianos:* Oratio ad Graecos / Rede an die Griechen, Beiträge zur historischen Theologie 165 (Tübingen, 2012); Molly Whittaker, *Tatian:* Oratio ad Graecos *and Fragments* (Oxford, 1982). On Tatian's authorship of the *Diatessaron*, see most recently Matthew R. Crawford and Nicholas J. Zola, eds, *The Gospel of Tatian: Exploring the Nature and Text of the Diatessaron* (London, 2019).

[10] For the date, see Josef Lössl, 'Date and Location of Tatian's *Oratio ad Graecos*. Some Old and New Thoughts', *SP* 74 (2016), 43–56.

[11] Irenaeus, *Against Heresies* 1.28.1 (SC 264, 354–6; cited in Eusebius, *Ecclesiastical History* 4.29.2–3 [GCS 9, 390.6–20]), 3.23.8 (SC 211, 466–9).

[12] Clement of Alexandria, *Stromateis* 3.12.80–1 (GCS 15, 232–3).

[13] There is a tendency today to see those charges as trumped up by heresiologists; see, for example, Naomi Koltun-Fromm, 'Re-Imagining Tatian: The Damaging Effect of Polemical Rhetoric', *JECS* 16 (2008), 1–30; but compare Matthew R. Crawford, 'The *Problemata* of Tatian: Recovering the Fragments of a Second-Century Intellectual', *Journal of Theological Studies* 67 (2016), 542–75, who argues that Tatian's own inconsistency may have contributed to his being accused of various heresies.

Adam was not saved (15: 22) and that only those could possibly be saved who abstained radically and permanently from sexual activity, even in marriage, as well as from luxury food and drink.[14]

Views of this kind were also attributed to adherents of the 'New Prophecy'. Origen, invoking Psalm 5: 10 and Romans 3: 13, cites them as saying: 'Do not come near me for I am clean. I have taken no wife ... Like a Nazirite of God I am drinking no wine'.[15] Jerome attributed the same attitudes to the Encratites.[16] He, too, invokes the Nazirite oath from Numbers 6: 1–21, originally a temporary vow; but Amos 2: 12 was understood in Antiquity to have interpreted it as permanent and thus to have radicalized it. This is why Jerome can say that Tatian derived his heresy from this verse. Both Origen and Jerome are alluding to a second-century Pauline controversy. Getting married and drinking wine (1 Timothy 5: 23) were prominent themes in the Pastoral Epistles aimed specifically at refuting Encratite tendencies, perhaps during the time of Marcion,[17] perhaps earlier. Contemporaries therefore appear not to have seen a great difference between the ascetic practices of Encratites and those of Montanists. Tertullian, in later life an adherent of the 'New Prophecy', tried hard to highlight that difference,[18] but he appears to have been splitting hairs.[19]

---

[14] For Tatian's views in the context of early Christian Encratism more generally, see Henry Chadwick, 'Enkrateia', *Reallexikon für Antike und Christentum* 5 (Stuttgart, 1962), 343–65, at 352–3.

[15] Origen, *Commentarium in epistolam ad Titum apud Pamphilum* (PG 14/1, 1306A–B), cited in Markschies, *Christian Theology*, 111 n. 423.

[16] 'De hoc loco haeresim suam Tatianus, Encratitarum princeps, struere nititur, uinum asserens non bibendum, cum et in lege praeceptum sit, ne Nazaraei bibant uinum, et nunc accusentur a propheta, qui propinent Nazaraeis uinum': Jerome, *Commentary on Amos* 1.2 (CChr.SL 76, 354), on Amos 2: 12, which in Jerome reads: 'et propinabatis Nazaraeis uino et prophetis mandabatis dicentes non prophetetis'.

[17] See now Markus Vinzent, *Offener Anfang. Die Entstehung des Christentums im zweiten Jahrhundert* (Freiburg im Breisgau, 2019), 265–6.

[18] Tertullian, *On Fasting, against the Psychics* 8 (CSEL 20, 284.9), praises Paul's extreme asceticism as attested in 2 Cor. 11: 27 (frequent night vigils, hunger, thirst, cold and nakedness); but refutes 'those who order the abstinence of food' (1 Tim. 4: 3): ibid. 15 (CSEL 20, 293). Such people, says Tertullian, are 'with Marcion and with Tatian ... but not with the Paraclete'.

[19] The comprehensive comparative overview on fasting and marriage in Trevett, *Montanism*, 105–14, also gives the impression that Encratites and Montanists had much in common in these areas.

This combination of entries, the beginning of the Montanist, 'Kataphrygian', 'false prophecy' (note that Eusebius does not call it a heresy[20]) and Tatian's identification as a heretic and his role as founder of the Encratites, suggests the theme of the present article. However, they do so less in view of common ascetic practices and more in view of the interconnections between pneumatic prophecy and ascetic intellectualism, between *Pneuma* and *Paideia*, Spirit and Education, as possible driving forces in second-century Christianity towards stronger, tighter, more militant but also more sophisticated, institutional, ecclesiastical forms. During the ensuing decades these forms made Christianity more comprehensible, permeable and transparent to its cultural, social and political environment, forces to be reckoned with, but also persuasive forces. The phenomenon of ecstatic prophecy, the practical workings (so to speak) of the Holy Spirit in everyday decision-making, which suspended common sense and rationality and by its nature resisted institutional control and intellectual categorization, met with increasingly sophisticated efforts at achieving, paradoxically, precisely that, namely theological conceptualization and institutional (i.e. hierarchical) integration. As Hans von Campenhausen outlined some time ago in his monumental *Ecclesiastical Authority and Spiritual Power in the Church of the First Three Centuries* (1953),[21] the path from New Testament concepts of apostolic and Spirit-led authority (e. g. in the *Praxapostolos* and in the Pauline corpus) to second- and third-century concepts of tradition, apostolic succession and pneumatic leadership (as in the office of the bishop) led around the middle of the second century via a thorny, conflict-ridden but also in many ways fertile route of competition and engagement between prophets and teachers, those who represented or worked through 'the Spirit' *(Pneuma)* and those who worked through theological 'education' (*Paideia*), and put forward (among others) theologies of 'the Spirit', theologies which (so to speak) 'rationalized the irrational'. More often than not, such representatives of *Paideia*, that is teachers or educators, more intellectuals than spiritually inclined men (and the majority were men), were accused of heresy, sometimes after they had died, because they

---

[20] The expression 'false prophecy' is also used in the Armenian version of Eusebius's chronicle (GCS 20, 222).
[21] Hans von Campenhausen, *Ecclesiastical Authority and Spiritual Power in the Church of the First Three Centuries* (London, 1969).

were invoked as authorities by later heretical teachers. Leaders of prophetic movements, including women, were also condemned, not as heretics (initially at least) but as social rebels. Later, in the fourth century, they were anachronistically found to have held heretical views.[22] A neuralgic point of contact between these movements may be detected around the time of the formation of Montanism and the teaching activity of Tatian in the late 160s and early to mid-170s; it may not be entirely accidental that Eusebius linked these two items in his *Chronicle* by listing them next to one another. Exploring this link, we shall first revisit the early history of Montanism before turning to Tatian and his promotion of a distinct Christian concept of *paideia* labelled 'barbarian *paideia*' as opposed to (classical) Greek *paideia*, his association with the heresy of Encratism and his possible links to Montanism. We shall conclude with some tentative remarks concerning the possible wider significance of the apparent tensions between *paideia* and *Pneuma* in second-century Christianity.

We begin with the early history of Montanism: Eusebius's date of 171/2 is only one of several that were suggested in Antiquity.[23] Epiphanius of Salamis dates the beginnings of the movement to 156/7, referring to the 'nineteenth year of the emperor Antoninus Pius',[24] while the *Paschal Chronicle* dates it somewhat later, to 182.[25] This latter date is implausible, for reasons to be seen shortly; the earlier is worth examining. Of course, none of them are certain. That given by Epiphanius in particular is notoriously unreliable in several respects. To begin with, and interestingly, Epiphanius draws a causal link between the emergence of Encratites and Montanists where Eusebius's juxtaposition cautiously suggested mere coincidence. Epiphanius then refers to the Phrygians as the successors of the Encratites (διαδεχομένη) and dates the origin of the latter in the reign of the emperor Hadrian, which is well before the 140s (ὁ Μαρκίων δὲ καὶ οἱ περὶ Τατιανοῦ καὶ οἱ ἀπ' αὐτοῦ διαδεξάμενοι Ἐγκρατῖται ἐν χρόνοις Ἀδριανοῦ). Everything Epiphanius says here is dubious. In reality Marcion only became

---

[22] See n. 2 above.

[23] The Armenian version (n. 6) omits Tatian and dates the beginning of Montanism to 172.

[24] Epiphanius, *Panarion* 48.1.2 (GCS NF 13, 219).

[25] *Paschal Chronicle*, *s.a.* 182 (*Chronicon Paschale*, vol. 1, ed. L. Dindorfius, Corpus Scriptorum Historiae Byzantinae 16 [Bonn, 1832], 490.17–20).

active in Rome in the 140s. Tatian did not become active before the 160s, or even the 170s, when he was declared a heretic, left Rome and probably returned to Syria. If he really was the founder of the Encratites, as Eusebius and others seem to claim, he and his 'movement' cannot have predated the Montanists, for whom recently discovered archaeological and epigraphic finds suggest dates as early as the 140s,[26] although this evidence has also to be treated with caution. Since ecstatic prophecy was known and tolerated in early Christianity from the very beginning, the so-called 'outbreak' of Montanism only marks the point when it began to be attacked as schismatic, and even then only in some cases and in specific areas.

Thus a looser chronology, similar to the one suggested (for example) by the entry in Eusebius's *Chronicle*, is more probable. First Montanism emerged (150s), then Tatian appeared on the scene (160s). He was then accused of being the founder (or at least the leading theoretician) of Encratism, although more probably he provided material in his work (the *Oration to the Greeks*) which could later be invoked as authoritative by those promoting Encratism, or cited as damning evidence by those who rejected it and who looked for early authoritative writers on whom to pin the charge of Encratism.

We offer one more word regarding the possibility of reconstructing such sequences of events as are listed in sources such as Eusebius's *Chronicle* relatively precisely, (say) year by year. Markus Vinzent has recently drawn attention to what Rudolf Helm, editor of one of the authoritative editions of the *Chronicle*, says about this. Helm writes that not one of the chronological references in the chronicle is reliable; every single entry poses a problem in itself, for which the possibility of authorial error, authorial views regarding the reliability of the available sources, errors in the transmission of the sources and many further aspects need to be taken into account. From a purely historical-chronological standpoint, the project of forcing a world history of such a scope into a year-by-year framework such as this must

---

[26] For a date in the 140s, see Ilaria Ramelli, 'Tracce di Montanismo nel *Peregrinus* di Luciano?', *Aevum* 79 (2005), 79–94; for recent epigraphic discoveries, Heidrun Elisabeth Mader, *Montanistische Orakel und kirchliche Opposition. Der frühe Streit zwischen den phrygischen 'neuen Propheten' und dem Autor der vorepiphanischen Quelle als biblische Wirkungsgeschichte des 2. Jh. n.Chr.*, Novum Testamentum et Orbis Antiquus / Studien zur Umwelt des Neuen Testaments 97 (Göttingen, 2012); Stephen Mitchell, 'An Epigraphic Probe into the Origins of Montanism', in Peter Thonemann, ed., *Roman Phrygia: Culture and Society* (Cambridge, 2013), 168–97, at 191–2.

be deemed unfortunate.[27] Helm adds, however (and this is significant here), that Eusebius himself was not overly rigid in attributing individual events to precise years. Rather, he grouped events, which he had already preliminarily judged to be somehow connected, relatively loosely within spans of years marked, in the case of the second century, by the reign of particular emperors or dynasties. For example, he dated the martyrdom of Ignatius of Antioch to the reign of Trajan (98–117)[28] and the flourishing of the two apologists Quadratus and Aristides to the first decade of the reign of Hadrian (117–38), that is, around the mid-120s.[29] Interestingly, Eusebius says of the apologist Quadratus that according to tradition he shared with the daughters of Philip (Acts 21: 8–9) the gift of prophecy and that he belonged, besides them and many others, to the first rank of the apostolic succession.[30] Thus in the 120s prophecy seems not to have been an issue, whether the prophets were men or women. This makes any early dating of the beginnings of 'Montanism' (i.e. before Montanus) problematic, since before Montanus prophecy seems not to have been deemed controversial. Judging by Eusebius's remark, it may even have counted as a possible criterion of apostolicity.

For the outbreak of Montanism and the flourishing of Tatian, Eusebius reserved the last decade of the Antonine dynasty, or more precisely, the last decade of the reign of Marcus Aurelius (161–80), that is the 170s. To look at this from a historical perspective, this was long after the apparently positive and constructive 120s and after a first wave of heresies such as Marcionism (early 140s) and Valentinianism (150s), and also just after the death of Justin Martyr (c.165). Tatian, as we have heard, was a pupil of Justin Martyr and was accused of heresy shortly after his death. This period preceded the monumental works of Irenaeus (180s) and Tertullian

---

[27] Paraphrased according to Rudolf Helm, introduction to Eusebius, *Chronicon* (GCS 47, xlv), and following Vinzent, *Offener Anfang*, 69–70.

[28] In Helm's edition it is listed under the year 108 CE: GCS 47, 194. But this date has proved awkward for those who would like to relate Ignatius to contemporaries, especially in the context of his letter corpus. Modern researchers have therefore tended to date Ignatius's death towards the end of Trajan's reign, which is permissible according to Helm's understanding of the chronology.

[29] See Eusebius, *Chronicle*, *s.aa.* 124–9 (GCS 47, 199); and, generally, Helm's introduction (ibid., xliv).

[30] Eusebius, *Ecclesiastical History* 3.37.1 (GCS 20, 280). The fragment of Quadratus's *Apology* cited by Eusebius has therefore traditionally been included among the writings of the Apostolic Fathers.

(190s–210s), when a (lenient and even positive) stance towards Montanism and critical-polemical, although not completely convincing, voices against Tatian were first articulated.

For a better understanding, therefore, of the coming to a head of the impact of early Montanism alongside an intellectual teaching such as that of Tatian, a focus on the early to mid-170s may be more appropriate. The end-point of this phase would be *c.*180, the *terminus ad quem* of Tatian's *Oration to the Greeks* and the date given for the death of Maximilla.[31] This decade is often seen conventionally as a first period of 'catholic rejection of the Prophecy'. Christine Trevett, for example, refers to it in this manner.[32] However, it could also be perceived as a time of heightened dialectical tension, between a desire on the part of church leaders to achieve more theological and ecclesial integration and a readiness to put this integration at risk by suppressing movements that were perceived as obstacles to this process.

Earlier we mentioned Eusebius's distinction between Montanus as 'originator' (*auctor*) of the movement and Priscilla and Maximilla as 'mad prophets' (*insanae uates*).[33] A few decades after Eusebius, Didymus referred to Montanus as 'exarch'.[34] As Trevett has pointed out, Eusebius may be by and large reliable here and Anne Jensen's assertion that Montanus was introduced to reduce the role of the women agents in the drama may be unnecessarily revisionist.[35] The movement started with him but it was dominated by Priscilla and Maximilla. On the other hand, Didymus's use of the term 'exarch' may indicate that there was a tendency to ascribe to him a stronger role than he actually had. The notion that there simply had to be a man's guiding mind behind a movement of crazy women prophets or that such a movement could only be judged properly against the evidence of at least one male representative has even affected modern scholarship. Thus, in George Salmon's entry on Montanus in the *Dictionary of Christian Biography*, Trevett found this sentence: 'If Montanus had triumphed, Christian doctrine would have been

---

[31] According to the anti-Montanist Anonymous, paraphrased in Eusebius, *Ecclesiastical History* 5.16.18–19 (GCS 9, 466.27–468.6), 5.17.4 (ibid. 470.18–472.4).
[32] Trevett, *Montanism*, 14.
[33] See n. 1 above.
[34] See n. 2 above.
[35] See n. 8 above; generally, Trevett, *Montanism*, 151–98.

developed not under the superintendence of the Christian teachers most esteemed for wisdom, but of wild and excitable women'.[36]

As a matter of fact, however, the early heresiological sources treat Montanus no better than any of the women: 'Bent on being leader he allowed the adversary to possess him and ... fell into ... convulsions. He became ecstatic, ... spoke strangely and prophesied in a way that clearly contradicted the tradition ... of the church.'[37] Similarly, of Priscilla and Maximilla the sources say that they spoke 'crazily, indecently and strangely, just like the aforementioned Montanus'.[38] The word 'indecently' suggests that the source assumes that there is one specific aspect of the women's prophetic activity that differs from that of Montanus, but apart from this additional characteristic, Montanus and the two women are treated with equal disdain. There is nothing to suggest that the women behaved more irrationally than the man, or that their prophecies were 'less rational' than the man's. Even Salmon's account contains evidence that suggests the opposite.

Salmon's statement stands in a particular context: Tertullian's admission in *On the Soul* 9 that he derived certain aspects of his doctrine of the soul directly from the revelation proclaimed by a prophetic woman in his congregation. This makes Salmon's statement all the more poignant. What did he really think would have been the source of the Christian teaching derived from the wisdom of those male Christian teachers whom he invokes against those 'wild, excitable' women? Was it a kind of formal education, a form of Greek *paideia*, as opposed to the 'barbaric' lack of education of those women, who were prone to uncontrolled emotions and easily fell into ecstasy? Even Eusebius did not gender ecstasy like that. Moreover, for early Christians, how wisdom could emerge from folly presented a conundrum: how the supra-rational could enter into this world and transform it. They would have been careful not to dismiss reports of ecstatic prophecy as 'tittle-tattle', as von Campenhausen does,[39] nor would they have been tempted to reduce

---

[36] George Salmon, 'Montanus', in William Smith and Henry Wace, eds, *A Dictionary of Christian Biography*, vol. 3 (London, 1880), 935–45, at 941, cited in Trevett, *Montanism*, 151.
[37] Eusebius, *Ecclesiastical History* 5.16.7 (GCS 9, 462.10–15), cited in Markschies, *Christian Theology*, 100 n. 349.
[38] Eusebius, *Ecclesiastical History* 5.16.9 (GCS 9, 462.28–464.3), cited in Markschies, *Christian Theology*, 100 n. 350.
[39] Hans von Campenhausen, *The Formation of the Christian Bible* (Philadelphia, PA, 1972), 233, cited in Trevett, *Montanism*, 3.

it to an ultimately rationalist technique of discursive communication, like Karl Froehlich.[40] To be sure, however, ultimately the prophecies did have to be communicated through discursive techniques. They presented what we might call a media challenge.[41] They required literary and rhetorical skills, and civility: in short, *paideia*. Crucially, as the sources suggest, women such as Priscilla, Maximilla and Quintilla possessed those skills. They did not require, in Salmon's words, a Montanus to 'triumph'. We shall cite some examples.

In his *Church History* (5.18.13), Eusebius reports that a certain Zoticus of Cumane set out publicly to refute the spirit that worked in Maximilla. However, he was prevented from doing so by those agreeing with her.[42] One could interpret this passage in two ways: either Maximilla behaved like a possessed spirit medium and Zoticus tried to perform a kind of exorcism on her but was prevented by her supporters, or Zoticus tried to challenge Maximilla as she communicated her prophetic message in plain discursive language. The verb 'to refute' (διελέγξαι) used in the source to denote Zoticus's activity suggests at least some degree of rhetorical-dialectical exchange, not a purely ritual intervention. This view is further supported by the observation that all extant Montanist *logia* – though admittedly there are no more than fourteen of these – are discursive theological statements, not dark, obscure oracles or magical-ritual incantations.[43]

---

[40] Karl Froehlich, 'Montanism and Gnosis', in David Neimann and Margaret Schatkin, eds, *The Heritage of the Early Church: Essays in Honor of the Very Reverend Georges Vasilievich Florovsky* (Rome, 1973), 91–114, discussed by Markschies, *Christian Theology*, 101.

[41] Cf. Markschies, *Christian Theology*, 91; note also Sheila E. McGinn, 'The "Montanist" Oracles and Prophetic Theology', *SP* 31 (1997), 128–35; for Tertullian's use of Montanist oracles, see also Tabbernee, 'Recognizing the Spirit', 523–5.

[42] Eusebius, *Ecclesiastical History* 5.18.13 (GCS 9, 478.10–14); cf. 5.16.17 (ibid. 466.24–6), where in addition to Zoticus, Julian of Apamea is mentioned as a church leader who tried to 'exorcize' Maximilla by exposing the spirit speaking through her as a demon, which would have made it easier for her enemies to justify the banishment of herself and her followers.

[43] Markschies, *Christian Theology*, 101–2. Note also that in the context of the encounter with Zoticus (n. 42 above), Eusebius, *Ecclesiastical History* 5.16.17 (GCS 9, 466.19–20), cites Maximilla (or the spirit speaking through her) as follows: 'διώκομαι ὡς λύκος ἐκ προβάτων· οὐκ εἰμὶ λύκος, ῥῆμά εἰμι καὶ πνεῦμα καὶ δύναμις' ('I am persecuted like a wolf among sheep; [but] I am not a wolf. I am "a word that is spoken" and spirit and power'). The implication here may also be that a spirit that is ῥῆμα is not an evil spirit.

In another source, the *Dialexis*, depicting essentially a disputation between a Montanist and an orthodox Christian, the orthodox interlocutor accuses the Montanist women prophets of 'speaking publicly in the churches', 'assuming authority over men', 'writing books in their own name', 'praying and prophesying without covering up', and generally not subjecting themselves to their 'head', 'that is their husband'.[44] These latter phrases in particular, but in a certain sense the entire passage, allude to 1 Timothy 2: 12. We have already noted the significance of this in the light of the controversies about Pauline teachings since the 140s. The present passage, which may be as late as the fourth century, refutes, and by doing so attests, the fact that Montanist women prophets had assumed clerical status, as Trevett puts it.[45] If the *Dialexis* reflects a real (or at least realistic) scenario, they fulfilled the roles of bishops.

Such a level of leadership involving authoritative public speaking and especially the writing of books presupposes that such women had acquired a high degree of *paideia*. *Paideia*, we should also remember, had a practical purpose in Antiquity. It qualified citizens to speak in public, in councils and assemblies, and to be elected (or selected) to civic leadership roles and positions of power in the *polis* or the imperial administration. Another aspect of *paideia* in this more practical sense (of projecting an air of superiority and self-confidence) may lie behind the remark that the women prophets were not 'covering up' ('wearing a veil') when praying and prophesying. This could also refer more generally to the way the women dressed.

Eusebius's *Church History* (5.18.4, 6, 11) adds some further colour to this. It reports that Priscilla and Maximilla were from a well-to-do

---

An evil spirit (a 'wolf among sheep') would cause muteness (cf. Matt. 9: 32–3). But also, by linking ῥῆμα and δύναμις, Maximilla claims her voice as a woman. Here the implication might be that those who want to deny her that voice do so less for theological than for cultural reasons. See also Laura McClure, *Spoken like a Woman: Speech and Gender in Athenian Drama* (Princeton, NJ, 1999), 37, who notes that in classical Athenian drama women's public speech is depicted as dangerous because of a 'pervasive equation between speech and power'. The instinct therefore was to suppress women speaking in public. For a famous response to that tendency in classical and Hellenistic culture, see the case of Hipparchia of Maroneia below.

[44] Text in Ronald E. Heine, *The Montanist Oracles and Testimonia* (Macon, GA, 1989), 124; see also Ross Shepard Kraemer, *Women's Religions in the Greco-Roman World: A Sourcebook* (Oxford, 2004), 93–4.

[45] Trevett, *Montanism*, 185–96.

background. They had been married but had left their husbands. Nevertheless, as already noted, Priscilla was now accorded the title of virgin, to reflect her ecclesiastical status. Both presumably lived an ascetic life. Yet they continued to dress according to their social status, put on make-up, wore jewellery and hosted banquets. They maintained this lifestyle with proceeds from their work, gifts that they received from their followers.[46] Jerome refers to them in a very Roman turn of phrase as *nobiles et opulentes feminas* (noble and wealthy women).[47]

Yet again, the fact that Priscilla and Maximilla met the media challenge posed by their mission as they showed themselves to possess *paideia* in every sense of the word, in communicating their prophecies and assuming leadership roles as they did so, does not mean that their prophesying was 'only pretended', as some sources would like to suggest,[48] a charge that is not consistent with the simultaneous accusation that it was caused by evil spirits or the devil. Nor does it do justice to the sources if we depict the women's actions as motivated primarily by rational considerations such as a quest for power and influence. The extant *logia* set out quite credibly what is meant by ecstatic prophecy in the case of Priscilla and Maximilla, and also, of course, of Montanus. The charge that it involves a state 'out of one's mind', strange language (either foreign or completely incomprehensible) and convulsions, was mentioned earlier.[49] In what follows attention will be drawn to another aspect, the theological content of the prophecies.

Montanus is reported to have said that prophesying is like being played 'like a lyre' by the Lord, who removes the old heart and puts in a new one.[50] Maximilla described herself as one who 'is

---

[46] Eusebius, *Ecclesiastical History* 5.18.4, 6, 11 (GCS 9, 474.7–9; 474.20–476.2; 476.24–478.6).

[47] Jerome, *Epistle* 133.4 (CSEL 56, 248.5).

[48] Eusebius speaks of Maximilla pretending to prophesy: *Ecclesiastical History* 5.18.13 (GCS 9, 478.11–12).

[49] See nn. 37, 38 above. I have explored this aspect further in Josef Lössl, 'Between Hipparchian Cynicism and Priscillian Montanism: Some Notes on Tatian, *or.* 3.6', *VChr* 74 (2020), 84–107, at 99–106.

[50] Epiphanius, *Panarion* 48.4.1 (GCS NF 13, 224.22–225.2). In *Panarion* 48.11.1 (GCS NF 13, 233.18–19) God (or Christ) is cited as follows (with a view to Montanus): 'ἐγὼ κύριος ὁ θεὸς ὁ παντοκράτωρ καταγινόμενος ἐν ἀνθρώπῳ' ('I the Lord God Omnipotent am one who is indwelling in a human being'). Montanus's claim is comparable to that of Paul in Gal. 2: 20: 'ζῶ δὲ οὐκέτι ἐγώ, ζῇ δὲ ἐν ἐμοὶ Χριστός'.

compelled, willinging or unwillingly, to know the knowledge of God (γνωθεῖν γνῶσιν θεοῦ)'.[51] Thus what Montanus and Maximilla are reported to have experienced are theological truths, of such a kind as can also be found in works of Philo of Alexandria, who refers to the human soul as 'God's tool',[52] or in apologists such as Clement of Alexandria, who also uses the image of the lyre.[53] In Tatian, too, we find a philosophically grounded theology of the *Logos* and the *Pneuma* as a single power of God salvifically active in those few human beings who are connected with that power and proclaim that which is hidden.[54] Ecstatic prophets were live models of this reality. They experienced it and they communicated this experience. Any power they were to exert in the church emerged from an authority grounded in the authenticity of their experience.

This raises once more the question of gender. Theoretically, at a purely abstract philosophical level, it could perhaps be said that an ecstatic God-experience as the one described by Maximilla[55] is gender-neutral. This would be confirmed by an apologist such as Tatian, who understood himself as a philosophical teacher and whose authority was derived from that role. In consequence, the God-experience had hardly any effect on social relations. In other words, what gender-neutrality really meant in this case was gender-bias (against women). We can see this in Tatian, who proudly announces to his putative pagan audience the existence of Christian women philosophers[56] but then refers to these as 'modest ... virgins speaking with each other about utterances concerning God while spinning yarn from a distaff'.[57] Elsewhere he speaks of older women among his hearers, who probably belonged to the group of poorer people to whom he lectured for free.[58] He reports that he is ridiculed by his opponents for speaking nonsense to women in

---

[51] Epiphanius, *Panarion* 48.13.1 (GCS NF 13, 237.9–13).

[52] 'ὄργανον θεοῦ': Philo, *Who is the Heir?* 259 (*Philonis Alexandrini Opera quae supersunt*, vol. 3, ed. L. Cohn and P. Wendland [Berlin, 1897], 59.15–16), cited by Markschies, *Christian Theology*, 95 n. 321.

[53] Clement of Alexandria, *Paedagogus* 2.41.4 (GCS 12, 182.22–3).

[54] See, for example, Tatian, *Oration* 7.1, 13.5 (Nesselrath, *Gegen falsche Götter und falsche Bildung*, 49; 63).

[55] See n. 51 above.

[56] '[W]omen among us, who philosophize': Tatian, *Oration* 33.4 (Nesselrath, *Gegen falsche Götter und falsche Bildung*, 98).

[57] Tatian, *Oration* 33.5 (Nesselrath, *Gegen falsche Götter und falsche Bildung*, 98).

[58] Tatian, *Oration* 33.1 (Nesselrath, *Gegen falsche Götter und falsche Bildung*, 96).

general and to young and old women in particular. But here 'speaking nonsense' does not mean the same as 'speaking strangely' in the case of Priscilla and Maximilla. Tatian was not an ecstatic prophet. His pagan critics merely took aim at what they saw as the deficient quality of his philosophy. By insisting that what he taught was a 'barbarian philosophy' that (because of its prophetic power) was ultimately superior to Greek *paideia*, he (in a certain sense) aligned himself with the tradition to which Montanism also belonged, but unlike Tertullian two decades later he seems not to have drawn the conclusion that prophetic women should be accepted as prophets or teachers, despite his apparent sympathy for women, tainted as this also was by cultural prejudice.

Judging by Tatian's remarks, the situation of the Montanist women prophets was very different from Tatian's 'women philosophers'. The latter are presented as continuing to obey traditional role models. Socially, very little changes for them. Their working day is lightened up by some religious conversation. The former, in contrast, were breaking the mould, and with some success, as we have seen. I have explored elsewhere what Tatian might have thought about women prophets such as Priscilla and Maximilla, who were, after all, contemporaries of his: there could be traces of possible allusions in the *Oration*. At one point he takes a swipe against Cynic philosophers who engage in 'manic speech'.[59] This could have been aimed at a specific woman Cynic, Hipparchia of Maroneia, the wife of Crates, whom Tatian mentions, who lived in fourth to third-century BCE Athens. Her 'manic' and 'erotic' (meaning '*eros*-driven') approach to philosophy (and to life) has been compared by modern scholars to that of the Montanist women prophets,[60] as it also broke the mould and made a considerable impact on society, and made her into a leading, albeit controversial, figure. Tatian, as can be gathered, took a dim view of this type of womanhood, not only within Christianity but generally. His 'barbarian' kerygma did not go so far as to redefine the traditional pre-Christian status of women and to admit that women gifted

---

[59] Tatian, *Oration* 3.6 (Nesselrath, *Gegen falsche Götter und falsche Bildung*, 42); see the discussions in Lössl, 'Between Hipparchian Cynicism and Priscillian Montanism'.
[60] See Christopher Forbes, *Prophecy and Inspired Speech in Early Christianity and its Hellenistic Environment*, Wissenschaftliche Untersuchungen zum Neuen Testament, 2nd series 75 (Tübingen, 1995), 141 n. 43.

with pneumatic prophecy could on that basis assume ecclesiastical leadership positions.

Let us return to the topic of gender: The decisive characteristic of Hipparchia's philosophy (as of Montanist women prophecy) was that it was not derived from abstract principles but emerged from lived experience; and it is this characteristic that renders it irrefutably gendered. The ecstasy, the 'strange' ('manic') speech, the convulsions of the body, these were physical manifestations, no matter how abstract and lofty the spiritual content that was communicated, and the persons on whom they manifested themselves and who had to proclaim these messages and to stand up for them were women. There was on the one hand the intellectual content of the prophecy, gnosis and God, but there was on the other hand emotion, too, ecstasy, mania, physicality, suffering and pleasure, experiences of an erotic nature. The Neo-Platonist Iamblichus once defined prophecy as something divine and intellectual, yet not expressed in a state of reason but of mania.[61]

In Epiphanius's *Panarion*, Quintilla or Priscilla (the narrator is not certain which) is reported to have received her prophecy in her sleep. According to her own witness she was visited in her sleep by Christ, who lay beside her and (in a literal translation) 'slept with her'. In her own words the prophetess then continues: 'Christ came to me in the form (ἰδέα) of a woman, dressed in a shining robe, and imbued me with wisdom.'[62] One gets the impression that modern translators tend to defuse this passage and make it sound more anodyne (for example, saying that Christ chastely came to sleep beside the prophet, imbuing spiritual wisdom, in the [presumably inauthentic] disguise of a woman).[63] But it must be kept in mind that the text is about an ecstatic experience. The use of the Greek expressions 'to sleep (together) with' (συνυπνόω) and 'to imbue with' (ἐμβάλλω), perhaps even better, 'to inseminate with', clearly suggests sexual imagery. The phrase of Christ coming in the form (ἰδέα) of a woman suggests that this was meant in the sense that Christ revealed herself as a woman (in the sense of an identity of *Logos* and *Pneuma* which

---

[61] Iamblichus, *On the Mysteries* 3.8 (*Iamblichi de mysteriis liber*, ed. G. Parthey [Berlin, 1897], 322).

[62] Epiphanius, *Panarion* 49.1.2 (GCS NF 13, 241.23–242.8).

[63] See, for example, Frank Williams, *The Panarion of Epiphanius of Salamis, Books II and III. De Fide*, Nag Hammadi and Manichaean Studies 79, 2nd edn (Leiden, 2013), 22: 'slept beside her … imbued me with wisdom'.

could already be seen expressed in Tatian's *Oration*) and as such infused the prophetess with wisdom (σοφία), the spiritual fertility of the act not relying on Christ's masculinity. The fourth-century heresiologist dismisses this as absurd, but in its original second-century context this revelation could (and apparently did) make sense; for this written testimony is extant, which suggests that the tradition went some way, not only with female but also with male followers, as the example of Tertullian's *On the Soul* 9 cited earlier suggests. What is extant here may be a trace of a gendered (one might even say feminist) take on early Christian doctrine, which emerges from an ecstatic experience and is being communicated as a prophecy or revelation, thus contributing to Christian tradition, albeit in a context that was geographically and ecclesiastically contained, while after the second century the movement tended to be disowned in its entirety, although it later experienced repeated resurgence in various forms.[64]

What can be clearly observed, however, is how the heresiological strategy applied by Epiphanius is in this case different from that employed for Gnostic teachings (for example). The attitude of Tertullian also indicates that (and was subsequently perhaps a reason why) Montanist women prophet-teachers, despite the hostility directed against them, were later treated by heresiologists (to say the least) 'with caution'; for it was clear that they were no heretics.

---

[64] To mention just two somewhat obscure but nevertheless significant examples: in the late thirteenth century, a small group of Milanese Christians held that a recently deceased saintly woman believed to be Guglielma, daughter of King Ottokar I of Bohemia, was the Holy Spirit incarnate. They were led by an aristocratic nun, Maifreda da Pirovano, who claimed for herself the position of *vicaria* (understood at the time as a claim to the papacy) and performed priestly functions. The theological implications, which show a number of similarities to topics discussed in the present article, are explained excellently by Luisa Muraro, *Guglielma e Maifreda. Storia di un'eresia femminista* (Milan, 1985). The more recent study by Barbara Newman, 'The Heretic Saint: Guglielma of Bohemia, Milan, and Brunate', *ChH* 74 (2005), 1–38, focuses more on the later veneration of Guglielma as a saint. In the early to mid-nineteenth century, the Roman convent of Sant'Ambrogio became the centre of a scandal when the founder, Maria Agnese Firrao, and (after her death in 1854) her successor as *mater vicaria* (master of novices), Maria Luisa, claimed for themselves visionary experiences involving Christ, Mary and the Holy Spirit. Although discredited by a number of investigations on grounds of (among other things) sexual misconduct and conspiracy to murder, the remarkable 'theological accuracy' of the visions was noted at the time, especially since the women were known to have lacked any higher theological education. The visions also provided a basis for the spiritual authority wielded by Maria Agnese and Maria Luisa within, but also beyond, their convent: see the magisterial study by Hubert Wolf, *The Nuns of Sant'Ambrogio: The True Story of a Convent Scandal* (Oxford, 2015), especially 121–65, 291–310.

Moreover, the idea expressed by the likes of Salmon that Montanist women prophets were a bunch of wild and excitable and (by implication) uneducated women[65] and that there was therefore a hermeneutical gap opening up between ecstatic prophecy and an emerging ecclesiastical theology that relied on ever increasing levels of 'higher education' is not supported by the evidence either; nor are the findings of 'enlightened' church historians who interpret ecstatic prophecy merely as a communicative strategy.[66] There is a difference between the ecstatic experience and its communication, between *Pneuma* and *paideia*. However, the reason why this difference led to tensions in the course of the Montanist crisis lay not in the women prophets' level of education, which could be considerable, as is poignantly illustrated by the example of Zoticus of Cumane's abortive attempt to put down Maximilla,[67] or on the quality of the theological content of the prophecies (which is beyond doubt), but somewhere else: even though the emerging teaching on the Holy Spirit, as in the theology of the apologists, did allow for ecstatic prophecy, and an early apologist such as Quadratus in the early 120s was even credited with the gift of prophecy, conventional thinking among the mostly male theologians did not allow for women assuming public ecclesial roles such as the office of bishop on the basis of that gift. This kind of thinking can already be detected in Tatian, who, as has been shown, was in certain respects sympathetic and respectful towards, and supportive of, women,[68] but did not see them as teachers and leaders. The probably fourth-century *Dialexis* provides an even clearer picture, as it concedes on the basis of Acts 21: 8–9 that women can be prophets but insists that they cannot proclaim their prophecies in public in the church, let alone write them up and publicize them, and thereby assume the authority reserved for bishops.[69]

The real issue, therefore, was not a clash between *paideia* and *Pneuma*, two dimensions of early Christian life which in principle perfectly complemented one another, but the persistence of prejudice, of a pre-Christian social-cultural mould[70] that time and again

---

[65] See n. 36 above; Trevett, *Montanism*, 151.
[66] See the examples cited in nn. 39–40 above.
[67] See n. 42 above.
[68] See nn. 57–8 above.
[69] See n. 44 above.
[70] See, for example, n. 43 above.

resisted the pressures that were applied to it by the forces of pneumatic prophecy. It was this that caused the relationship between *paideia* and *Pneuma* in the mid- to late second-century church to be not only fruitful but at times also acrimonious and tense.

This article set out from the observation that for the years 171 and 172 Jerome's translation of Eusebius's chronicle lists two events in close proximity to one another, the 'outbreak' of Montanism and Tatian's identification as a heretic by the Roman church and his departure from Rome. It then discusses these dates and the question of whether there might be other aspects than this proximity of dates that link Tatian to Montanism. While the date regarding Tatian is not usually called into doubt, that regarding Montanism is. Alternative dates, mostly earlier, have recently been suggested. Arguing mainly on the basis of new archaeological and epigraphic evidence, the article critiques this recent trend to date the onset of Montanism earlier, even as early as the 140s. Of course, prophecy did exist as early as that, and even earlier, but it was then a mainstream feature and even considered indicative of apostolicity, as in the case of Quadratus. It may not have been prophecy that underwent a change in the decades running up to 170 but attitudes to prophecy, especially among a new type of church leaders, who increasingly saw the Spirit at work in the liturgical and doctrinal structures of the church, which they controlled, rather than in the activities of inspired prophets. Similarly, it seems that Tatian was able to remain in Rome and be active there as a theological teacher and leader of a school for several years after his teacher Justin's death around 165, but that in the early 170s a point was reached when he was eventually condemned and expelled. Sources potentially referring to this event suggest that schools and teaching in schools became suspect in the new climate in the same way as prophecy did.[71]

Cautiously, we therefore suggest that links might be drawn between Tatian's thought (as expressed in the *Oration*) and that of the 'New Prophecy': There is, for example, a common affinity to, or association with, Encratism. Such an affinity or association was

---

[71] Irenaeus, *Against Heresies* 1.28.1, in Eusebius, *Ecclesiastical History* 4.29.2–3 (GCS 9, 390.14–16), emphasizes that Tatian's leaving the church ('ἀποστὰς τῆς ἐκκλησίας') was linked with his claim to be a teacher ('οἰήματι διδασκάλου ἐπαρθεὶς καὶ τυφωθείς'), whose teaching had a distinct character of its own ('ἴδιον χαρακτῆρα διδασκαλείου συνεστήσατο').

perceived by critics of both Tatian and the Montanists, as the texts cited demonstrate. But ascetic rigour as a source of spiritual and intellectual authority and as a reflection of a fundamental theological perspective (for example, that humanity's fallen state requires sustained remedial ascetic action) may also be two things Tatian and the New Prophecy had to some degree in common anyway.

In *Oration* 5.1 and 7.1 and elsewhere, Tatian identifies *Logos* with *Pneuma*. Although he does not use this as a starting point for reflecting on the possibility of 'experiencing' or visualizing a mystical dream-encounter with a female Spirit-Christ imbuing Wisdom of the kind Priscilla is reported to have had in Epiphanius's *Panarion* 49.1.2, his *Logos-Pneuma* concept could have provided the theological framework for interpreting such an encounter precisely.

Tatian could also have considered the possibility of theological learning inspired by the divine *Pneuma*, when in connection with his conversion he refers to himself as one taught directly by God (θεοδίδακτος, *Oration* 29.3).[72] At the same time Tatian endorsed the philosophical activity of women in his community and defended it against mockery by pagan outsiders.[73] Also, what Tatian meant by 'philosophy' was serious 'God talk'.[74] His defence of women theologizing might equally have been directed against Christian polemics against such practices.

The references in Tatian's *Oration* remain fairly vague, however. By comparison, extant biographical data of women leaders of the New Prophecy suggest that at least some of them were formally educated and able to perform rhetorically in public, that their social status permitted them to do this, and that in doing so they exerted authority and commanded sizeable followings. The fact that they faced

---

[72] Miguel Herrero de Jáuregui, 'Tatian *Theodidaktos* on Mimetic Knowledge', in H. Gregory Snyder, ed., *Christian Teachers in Second-Century Rome: Schools and Students in the Ancient City*, VChr Supplements 159 (Leiden, 2020), 158–82, interprets this reference in terms of Tatian's rejection of conventional forms of education. In classical antiquity such a rejection might have implied the promotion of autodidacticism. But Tatian rejected that as well (*Oration* 3.1).

[73] 'μὴ χλευάζητε τὰς πάρ' ἡμῖν φιλοσοφούσας': Tatian, *Oration* 33.4. For the ambiguity of Tatian's references to women philosophizing in his community, see nn. 56–8 above. Still, when Tatian writes that the philosophizing of 'his' (παρ' ἡμῖν) women is more serious than that of the pagan women (σπουδαιότερον) he targets the entire Greek philosophical tradition; cf. in ibid. 2.1 the sarcastic reference to classical philosophers as 'τῶν πάνυ σπουδαίων' ('O so serious').

[74] 'τὰ κατὰ θεὸν λαλοῦσιν ἐκφωνήματα σπουδαιότερον': ibid. 33.5.

opposition and were later suppressed is secondary from the point of view of the present article. Here it is important to note that women such as Priscilla and Maximilla had both the pneumatic inspiration to envision, and the philosophical and rhetorical education to construct, alternative theologies: theologies, for example, that closely identified *Logos* and *Pneuma*, or conceived within such a framework of a female incarnation.[75] There is too little evidence from the second century to reconstruct any such theology in detail, but there is enough evidence to suggest that the struggle was not between *paideia* and *Pneuma*, at least not on the part of those who were (unjustifiably) accused of a lack of the former, for example Montanist women prophets. Rather, it was between cultures of theological discourse: an older culture of prophets and teachers, men and women, who produced a variety of original teachings, be it from prophecy, philosophical reflection or a combination of both, and a new culture emerging from around the middle of the second century, in which prophecy, in particular of women, was suppressed, or at least tightly controlled, and in which individual teachers and their schools were rejected for the apparent idiosyncrasy of their teaching.[76] We might almost get the impression that there was a tendency in the church not so much to choose *paideia* over *Pneuma* but to reject both in a move to assert authority, power and control.

---

[75] For the possibility of such a development, see n. 62 above.
[76] See n. 71 above.

From Institution to Inspiration: Why the Friars Minor Became *Francis*cans

Neslihan Şenocak*

Columbia University

Medieval religious institutions, such as the papacy or the religious orders, tend to designate a saint as their founding inspiration. For the papacy, this has been St Peter; for the religious orders, saints such as St Benedict, St Dominic or St Francis. While it might appear logical to think of these inspiring founders as preceding the establishment of such institutions, in reality the latter are almost entirely responsible for the making, maintaining and circulating of the image of a founding saint. Hence it is necessary to approach historiographical narratives with great caution in which an institution is thought to be diverging from the founder's path, falling short of the founder's ideals or deliberately distorting the image of a founder to justify their evolution. If such a discrepancy between the initial ideal and later practice is observed, the central point of investigation should focus on why the hagiographical and liturgical records regarding the founding saint included elements in conflict with the institutional practice. This article will investigate the medieval evidence and the historiographical narratives pertaining to the Order of Friars Minor.

When reflecting about inspiration and institution, it is natural to suppose that inspiration comes first. There is an event, an idea, or someone who inspires, and that inspiration, if the conditions are ripe, might turn into an institution. Jesus comes before the Roman Catholic Church, or Francis of Assisi comes before the Franciscan Order.

Yet belying that natural order of precedence, we should also acknowledge readily that many such individuals, known as 'fathers' or 'founders', are in great part products of the institutions themselves. Of course this does not mean that they did not exist or that they were entirely fabricated – although in some cases they might have been – but rather that we have come to know them predominantly not through what they themselves wrote but through the discourses

* 1180 Amsterdam Avenue, Fayerweather Hall 324, 10027, New York, NY 10027, USA. E-mail: ns2495@columbia.edu.

Studies in Church History 57 (2021), 54–73 © The Author(s), 2021. Published by Cambridge University Press on behalf of Ecclesiastical History Society.
doi: 10.1017/stc.2021.4

and images produced, almost always after their death, by the institution that associates itself with that inspirational figure. This is particularly the case with respect to the ancient and medieval institutions, since individuals in modern times tend to leave behind more record. Socrates, for example, has been credited as the 'founder of Western philosophy' and a deep inspiration to philosophers of all times, yet all we know about him comes from Plato and Xenophon: Socrates himself did not leave anything written, nor did he establish a school of philosophy. Anthony of Egypt is considered to be the father of Christian monasticism, yet his life was written by Athanasius, bishop of Alexandria, a representative of the institutional church. Perhaps the archetypal example is Jesus Christ, who also did not leave us any written record during his lifetime, although the accounts of his words and deeds written by the four evangelists became the holy books of the church. Whilst we call such individuals founders and by that word attribute to them the agency in making the institution that has come after, in reality we cannot know what their intention was since we have no, or very little, record left to us directly by them. Did they set out to found institutions? Or is it more the case that the institution, having once arisen due to a unique combination of many causes, then turns back and identifies a person or persons as its founder or its chief inspiration, and construes that person or those persons in literary work?

These questions bring the present article squarely into the domain of institutional memory studies. In recent decades, historians, anthropologists and sociologists have contributed greatly to the unpacking of the concept of memory, whether understood as individual, institutional, organizational or social.[1] These studies have made very useful incursions into the questions of why and how an institution shapes and controls a particular narrative of growth and evolution from its origins, and

---

[1] The number of published studies is too many to mention, but among works of medievalists, see: Cornelia Linde, *Working the Past: Narrative and Institutional Memory* (Oxford, 2009); Mary J. Carruthers, *The Book of Memory: A Study of Memory in Medieval Culture*, 2nd edn (Cambridge, 2008); James Fentress and Chris Wickham, *Social Memory* (Oxford, 1992). A few recent studies on Charlemagne have looked into aspects of how his memory has been shaped and employed towards certain political ends: Matthew Gabriele, *An Empire of Memory: The Legend of Charlemagne, the Franks, and Jerusalem before the First Crusade* (New York, 2011); Anne Austin Latowsky, *Emperor of the World: Charlemagne and the Construction of Imperial Authority, 800–1229* (Ithaca, NY, 2013).

how the institutional past should be remembered by present members. The need for an inspirational founding story becomes ever more necessary, even vital, when the institution goes through significant changes and consequently assumes an organization and goals different from those in its beginnings. A carefully woven memorial narrative connects the past to the present, providing continuity and a respected tradition.

When it comes to medieval religious institutions in particular, the inspirational discourse tends to be hagiographical. That is to say, often we find either a saint or a quasi-saint to be the chief founding or reforming inspiration behind an institution. The papacy, for example, from its early centuries onwards has identified the apostolic community with St Peter in particular as its chief founder and inspiration. In *The Invention of Peter: Apostolic Discourse and Papal Authority in Late Antiquity* (2013), George Demacopoulos called the cult of St Peter a most effective marketing campaign, through which the creation, evolution and subsequent promotion of the papal monopoly was made possible.[2] The most popular and enduring religious orders are those who championed a saintly founder: St Benedict and Benedictines, St Dominic and Dominicans, St Francis and Franciscans, St Clare of Assisi and Poor Clares, and so on. In what follows, I will examine this complex relationship between institution and inspiration in the medieval Franciscan order.

The Perceived Conflict between Inspiration and Institution

At the outset, it is worth remembering that the way modern historians usually study and teach the history of a religious order presents a barrier to understanding the true relationship between an institution and the story of its foundation. Historical thinking often privileges chronology of events, rather than chronology of the composition of sources. Modern histories of religious orders invariably begin with the founder, with that inevitable first chapter on Francis of Assisi or Dominic of Guzman.[3] To construct the image of the saint

---

[2] George E. Demacopoulos, *The Invention of Peter: Apostolic Discourse and Papal Authority in Late Antiquity* (Philadelphia, PA, 2013), 5.
[3] See for example, John R. H. Moorman, *A History of the Franciscan Order: From its Origins to the Year 1517* (Oxford, 1968), 1–9, 'Francesco Bernardone'; William A. Hinnebusch, *The Dominicans: A Short History* (Staten Island, NY, 1975), 3–11, 'Dominic the Founder'.

accurately, a historian gathers all the information currently available to her by skimming the hagiographical *vitae* for their historical truth content.[4] When the writings of the founder are extant, they are placed on a pedestal and deemed the most accurate source of all.[5] At this point, the scene is already set. An image of the founder is erected at the beginning, one considered as the most faithful to the actual, and as the embodiment of the initial inspiration. The reader is enlisted for the historian's journey. From this point, successive chapters recounting the development of the order are read in the light of that first chapter, in the light of the acts and intentions of the founder. As pages are turned, with each new statute, each new direction or hint of a new mentality, the historian feels compelled to establish for themselves and the reader whether that novelty is compatible with the original vision of the founder. Similarly, as they inform the readers dutifully of each new source concerning the life of the founder emerging in the medieval period, there seems to be an urgent necessity to establish the trustworthiness of that source, based on the degree to which its content agrees with the historian's depiction of the founder as revealed in the first chapter.[6]

[4] In *Social Memory*, Fentress and Wickham identify two modes in which historians have read the contemporary works of history, among which we can count the *vitae* and medieval histories of the order: 'For the positivist tradition of the nineteenth and twentieth centuries, it was enough to work out the sources and the "bias" of ancient and medieval writers, and to discount "obvious" errors and superstitions, in order to draw reasonably firm conclusions about the "truth content" of their writings. Such procedures were often naive, and, indeed, particularly in periods where the writers so analysed were the only sources, logically circular ... At the other extreme, particularly in the last two decades, we find a more textual approach, which, through literary analysis of structure, style, or the network of meanings inside a work, aims at restoring an understanding of the internal context of what a writer intended. The problem of this approach is that it sometimes tends to assume that it is pointless to use historians as sources for anything but themselves; it argues that Livy or Bede were so far from the events they described, and intervened in their material so much (whether for literary or ideological reasons), that we can analyse only their world-view, rather than their world': ibid. 144.

[5] At the beginning of his bestseller, Paul Sabatier presents a critical discussion of all sources regarding the life of Francis. Regarding Francis's own writings, he says that they are the most important ones to understand the saint and one cannot help but be surprised that his biographers neglected them: *Vie de S. François d'Assise*, 9th edn (Paris, 1894), xxxvi. This critical discussion of sources is missing in the English translation cited in n. 12 below.

[6] To give one example, we find Michael Robson calling the chronicle by John of Perugia composed in 1239–41 'partisan', and serving to justify the 'present orientation of movement with Haymo of Faversham at the helm': *The Franciscans in the Middle Ages* (Woodbridge, 2006), 7.

The historian's understanding of the history of a religious order with its neat chronological progression from inspiration to institution has no parallel in the experience of the medieval friar. No medieval Franciscan had access to the entire corpus of Francis's writings, as his writings, with the exception of the Rule and the Testament, did not circulate in the friaries, nor were they bound together in a single volume in the way they are available to today's historian in the modern editions.[7] The great majority of friars joined the order in lands far from Umbria, and their access to oral testimonies would also be limited. What Francis meant to these friars is difficult to establish, other than that he was the author of the Rule which they professed, and that his holiness had been formally sanctioned by the papacy. In fact, in the fellow mendicant order of Dominicans, Dominic himself was not initially an inspirational figure. When he died in 1221, the friars were not particularly interested in preserving his memory. During the twelve years until his canonization in 1233, he was largely ignored and forgotten by the Dominican friars, a fact that has been pointed out by historians of the order. The only work in this period containing information about Dominic was written in 1232–3 by Jordan of Saxony, the second master general of the order, and is titled *Little Book on the Beginning of the Order of Friars Preachers*.[8] The story of the foundation of the order was regarded more as a collective undertaking, rather than one about Dominic acting as founder. This narrative changed dramatically upon his canonization in 1233, and within twenty-five years of his canonization four *legendae* had been composed on St Dominic.[9]

Both Dominic and Francis left us very little that originated from their pens, and what we have are mostly letters or texts of a theological or devotional nature. Even when we have access to the original writings of the founding saint, these represent what the order chose to protect, circulate and preserve. We, as modern scholars, have no direct access to those oral testimonies, or to the words and deeds of founder saints that have not been created, controlled or mitigated by

---

[7] I have dealt extensively with the question of how much friars knew about Francis in *The Poor and the Perfect: The Rise of Learning in the Franciscan Order, 1209–1310* (Ithaca, NY, 2012), 96–105.

[8] Jordan of Saxony, *Libellus de Principiis Ordinis Praedicatorum*, ed. D. H.-C. Scheeben, Monumenta ordinis fratrum praedicatorum historica 16 (Rome, 1935).

[9] Kyle C. Lincoln, 'A Canon from Castile: The Early Life of St Dominic of Osma (1170/4–1207)' (MA thesis, Saint Louis University, 2012), 3.

the institution itself. Their lives were always written after their death. Thus, whatever is left to posterity concerning the founder is, in the majority of cases, only that which those at the helm of those institutions wanted people to know about that particular individual, whom they presented to the world as the inspiration behind their institution.

It is therefore rather surprising when historians sometimes point to a clash or conflict between the founder's ideals and the institution itself. This was, for example, the narrative arc of Paul Sabatier's famous book *La Vie de Saint François*, first published in 1893.[10] This book fundamentally changed the perception of Franciscan history, and has made such a powerful impact that even to this day its main argument remains influential: namely, that Francis was a truly Jesus-like, incorruptible revolutionary who wished to reform a rich and corrupt church, but whose movement was hijacked by a spiritually compromised papacy and by the intellectuals who became Franciscans. Collaborating with each other, in Sabatier's reading, the papacy and the administrators of the order suppressed the true memory of Francis to quash any dissent within the order, as they slowly transformed the Franciscan movement into a tool for the ecclesiastical power and machinery.[11]

In the preface to his book, Sabatier laid out the heart of his argument:

> The priest of the thirteenth century is the antithesis of the saint, he is almost always his enemy. Separated by the holy unction from the rest of mankind, inspiring awe as the representative of an all-powerful God, able by a few signs to perform unheard-of mysteries, with a word to change bread into flesh, and wine into blood, he appeared as a sort of idol which can do all things for or against you and before which you have only to adore and tremble. The saint, on the contrary, was one whose mission was proclaimed by nothing in his apparel, but whose life and words made themselves felt in all hearts and conscience; he was one who, with no cure of souls in the Church, felt himself suddenly impelled to lift up his voice.[12]

---

[10] Paul Sabatier, *Vie de S. François d'Assise*, 1st edn (Paris, 1893).
[11] For a more detailed analysis of Sabatier's argument and his influence on the subsequent histories of the Franciscan Order, see my *The Poor and the Perfect*, 9–11.
[12] Paul Sabatier, *The Life of Francis of Assisi*, trans. Louise Seymour Houghton (New York, 1928), xiv–xv.

A similar conspiratorial trend can also be observed in studies on the history of the Dominican Order. Akin to the charges levelled by Sabatier against the medieval Franciscan establishment, in 1997 Vladimir Koudelka argued that 'the historical image of Dominic was distorted soon after his death and adapted, especially by Dominicans, to suit current trends of fashion'.[13] This interpretation assumes that there are two images of Dominic. One is the image of him before his death that, according to Koudelka, is the true image, and the other his posthumous image that has been distorted. But how do we access Dominic's image before his death, let alone know that it is the true image, when we have only two formal letters written by Dominic himself, with the rest of the evidence comprising episcopal and papal charters and bulls?

Going back to Sabatier's words about the priest being the antithesis of the saint, the fault-line that renders such a statement problematic is Sabatier's failure to recognize that there are no saints without priests sitting down writing their lives, collecting their miracles and preparing thick dossiers of canonization to be sent to the Roman Curia. Of course there were local cults that sprang up amidst the people, and the writing of the saint's life in most cases followed the formation of a local cult, but those lives written by the clergy nevertheless preserved the eccentricities of the saint, and his extraordinary (in many ways supernatural) actions; it is through those texts that subsequent generations, including modern historians, learned about the saint. If, as Sabatier says, the saint appears to be the antithesis of the priest, it is because the priest described him so. If nothing in the saint's apparel proclaimed his mission, it is because the priest told us that the saint's clothing was plain and simple. Moreover, the priests not only wrote the lives of the saints, they also preserved, copied and circulated those texts; they extracted and used them in their sermons to the faithful, and in the readings at the refectory and chapterhouse. The truth is that educated medieval churchmen were not afraid to create hagiographical discourses that could be in blatant contradiction to what was actually happening in institutional practice.

Let us turn to the Franciscan evidence. The medieval Order of Friars Minor produced no less than four lives of Francis within fifty years of his death. The first three were all written by the same friar, Thomas of Celano. The *First Life* (*Vita Prima*) was

---

[13] Vladimir Koudelka, *Dominic*, ed., trans. and rev. Simon Tugwell (London, 1997), 3.

commissioned by Pope Gregory IX for the purpose of Francis's canonization. The second life, which was discovered by Jacques Dalarun in 2014, was written at the instigation of the second general minister of the order, Brother Elias.[14] The third, known as *Vita Secunda*, was commissioned by the general chapter of the order in 1244 and completed in 1246–7. A fourth life known as *Legenda Maior* was written by the great Franciscan theologian Bonaventure of Bagnoregio while he was minister general of the order, after having been commissioned by the general chapter. These are the so-called official lives of Francis. Then there are the unofficial lives, those which Sabatier thought to reflect the true Francis: these are *Anonymous of Perugia, Legend of the Three Companions* and *Assisi Compilation*, which are believed to have been authored by Francis's immediate companions.[15] However, the first two of these draw heavily on the first and second lives by Celano, while the third life by Celano draws on the *Legend of the Three Companions*. Accordingly, there are many anecdotes common to the official and unofficial lives and, as they borrow heavily from one another, in many instances it is almost impossible to say who has borrowed from whom. In fact, the question of authorship and date of composition of the unofficial lives has been termed 'the Franciscan Question' and has occupied considerable scholarly energy.[16]

Since Sabatier's work, it has been a running contention in Franciscan historiography that the unofficial and official lives describe Francis differently, with some scholars, such as Sabatier, believing that the latter distorted his image to conform to the order's contemporary position and vision. In fact, we need not look at the unofficial lives to see how Francis's image differed from what the institution had become. Celano's *Second Life* includes several instances where the contrast between the saint and the contemporary institution is

---

[14] Jacques Dalarun, *The Rediscovered Life of St Francis of Assisi*, trans. Timothy Johnson (Bonaventure, NY, 2016).

[15] For all the biographies of Francis mentioned here, except the recently discovered life, the critical Latin editions are found in Enrico Menestò and Stefano Brufani, eds, *Fontes Franciscani* (Assisi, 1995). Similarly, for the English translations of the Franciscan corpus mentioned here, see Regis J. Armstrong, J. A. Wayne Hellmann and William J. Short, eds, *Francis of Assisi: Early Documents*, 3 vols (Hyde Park, NY, 1999; hereafter: *FAED*).

[16] Jacques Dalarun, *Vers une Résolution de la question franciscaine. La légende ombrienne de Thomas de Celano* (Paris, 2007). See also the contributions of several scholars in a round table on Dalarun's book: Jacques Dalarun et al., 'The "Umbrian Legend" of Jacques Dalarun', *Franciscan Studies* 66 (2008), 479–508.

made quite explicit. By the time this work was written, in 1246, the order had already gone through a significant transformation with regard to learning. Schools had been established in many friaries and friars were being trained in theology; moreover, the entire administration of the order was chosen from among educated men. The order's 1239 constitutions even included a clause stating that no ignorant, illiterate person was to be accepted to the novitiate. Nonetheless, Thomas of Celano wrote about Francis:

> I did not choose you as an educated and eloquent man over my family, but I chose you as a simple man, that both you and others might know that I will watch over my flock. I put you as a sign to them, that the works which I work in you they ought to perceive in you, and do them.[17]

And again:

> It grieved him when brothers sought learning while neglecting virtue, especially if they did not remain in that calling in which they were first called. He said: 'Those brothers of mine who are led by curiosity for knowledge will find themselves empty-handed on the day of reckoning. I wish they would grow stronger in virtue, so that when the times of tribulation arrive they may have the Lord with them in their distress. For,' he said, 'a tribulation is approaching, when books, useful for nothing, shall be thrown into cupboards and into closets!' He did not say these things out of dislike for the study of the Scriptures, but to draw all of them back from excessive concern for learning, because he preferred that they be good through charity, than dilettantes through curiosity. Besides, he could smell in the air that a time was coming, and not too far away, when he knew learning would be an occasion of ruin, while dedication to spiritual things would serve as a support to the spirit. After his death he appeared in a vision to one of the companions who was once tending toward preaching, and he forbade it, commanding him to walk on the way of simplicity. As God is his witness, he felt such a sweetness after this vision that for many days it seemed the dew of the father's words was still dropping into his ears.[18]

---

[17] Thomas of Celano, *Vita Secunda*, in Menestò and Brufani, eds, *Fontes Franciscani*, §158 (my translation).

[18] Thomas of Celano, *The Remembrance of the Desire of a Soul*, §195, in Armstrong, Hellmann and Short, eds, *FAED*, 2: 372.

Though Thomas is quick to point out that Francis did not dislike the study of Scripture, these passages are quite condemnatory of books and the pursuit of learning. If a friar was a preacher before he joined the order, let him preach, but those who were not should not strive to become one, Francis says. But, as the order at the time was specifically training friars to become preachers, why include such a paragraph? One might propose that such statements might represent a personal intervention on the part of Thomas himself, but as Mary Carruthers reminds us authority only half belongs to the author, while the other half is the creation of the society or community that values the work.[19] The authority of Thomas's composition was bestowed on it by the general chapter as the representative body of the Franciscan community. If the general chapter of the order had seen a contradiction between the institutional practice and Francis's stand on books, studying and preaching as expressed by Thomas, they surely could have altered those words, or deleted them altogether.

Consequently, an important question for the historian is why a religious order chose to describe its founding saint in contradiction with institutional practice; so differently, in fact, that centuries later historians like Sabatier peering over these records could point to that difference and blame the institution for not being like its saint. If we, so removed from that age, can perceive in our minds the difference between a Francis with his patched habit, no property and living solely on alms, and the rich institutional church personified by the silk garments of popes and cardinals, or between an uneducated Francis and the eloquent friars holding chairs of theology at Paris and running the order, that difference must have been much more apparent to medieval men and women. Thus, we must question why the order behaved as it did, championing an image that would create such a rift. Why write and circulate the story of Francis's life, and declare him a saint with the greatest urgency? Why risk being blamed for abandoning the ideals of Francis?

Whilst this contradiction might appear problematic to the secularized modern historian, the medieval intelligentsia might have a different opinion. In the mental world of the medieval churchman, the apparent conflict, while real, does not necessarily mean that the institution fell short of what it set out to do, or failed in fulfilling the founder's inspiration. One does not need to reconcile the inspiration

---

[19] Carruthers, *Book of Memory*, 234.

and the institution, because the inspiration is divine and the institution is worldly; it is therefore expected and normal that they will differ in their methods of operation, but not in what they try to achieve. The contrast is in their means, but not in their ends.

In Christian theology, the divine often stands in stark contrast to what is worldly. According to Scripture, God works in mysterious ways; that is to say, we in this world recognize the divine, because the divine is unexpected and supernatural. The Christian divine realm is based on an inversion of all customary social value judgements, hence 'blessed are the poor' and 'the last shall be first'. It is where a man born in a stable becomes the king; where virgins give birth; where 'a poor, little, contemptible, ignorant' man, as the bishop of Terni described Francis of Assisi to the eager crowds at the town square, becomes one of the greatest saints. This contrast underpinned the hagiographical literature, as in many saints' lives, with the declaration of the saints' earthly status as noble, of wealthy families or learned is followed immediately by their voluntary self-abasement and humility as evidence of their holiness. The saints' subscription to an inversion of social values then becomes the true sign of their belonging to the divine realm.[20] The hagiographical tradition, going back to Gregory of Tours, depicted the saint as one who lived simultaneously in both divine and earthly realms.[21]

Those who were at the helm of medieval ecclesiastical institutions understood and seemingly accepted this inevitable difference between the divine model and its earthly embodiment. An institution associated with a saint imitates the ends of the deeds of the saint, but not the specific ways in which the saint operated. Accordingly, an institution should also be providing the worldly means and tools, the infrastructure, with which those virtues can be imitated and acquired.

Bonaventure of Bagnoregio, the minister general of the Franciscan Order from 1257–74, and one of its most important theologians, preached about Francis of Assisi on his feast day to the student friars at Paris in 1255:

---

[20] This reversal of values in hagiography has also been discussed recently by Jacques Dalarun, *Gouverner c'est server. Essai de démocratie médiévale* (Paris, 2012), 13–15. I am grateful to Sean L. Field for allowing me to read his forthcoming translation of this book, *To Govern is to Serve: An Essay in Medieval Democracy*.

[21] Thomas J. Heffernan, *Sacred Biography: Saints and their Biographers in the Middle Ages* (New York, 1988), 10.

One may well wonder at his teaching. How was he able to teach others what no man had taught him? Did he come to this knowledge by himself? Be assured he did not. The evidence of that is found in the account of his life. When he was instructed by another man or had to prepare something himself, he had absolutely nothing to say. In that, however, he is more to be praised and wondered at than imitated. Hence it is not without reason that his sons attend the schools. To arrive at knowledge without a human teacher is not for everyone, but the privilege of a few. Though the Lord himself chose to teach St. Paul and St. Francis, it is his will that their disciples be taught by human teachers.[22]

It has been often suggested that the main function of hagiographical literature is to provide a role model for the faithful. However, here, by inserting the comment, 'in that, he is more to be praised and wondered at than imitated', Bonaventure invites his audience to a different kind of engagement with Francis as saint. We are to recognize Francis's extraordinary wisdom, but cannot hope to acquire it the way he or St Paul did, that is, directly from God.[23] That particular gift of Francis had belonged to the realm of the divine, and as Bonaventure says, Francis's disciples will have to be taught by 'human' teachers. In fact, the Franciscan administration in the years between 1230 and 1260 worked quite diligently to achieve this particular end, establishing a school network in the order to teach the friars doctrinal wisdom.

If saints embody the inspiration, their special status as those who belonged to the divine realm creates a distinct gap between them and the institutions they inspired, as the latter firmly belongs to the earthly realm. This made the relationship between the founder and the order, between inspiration and institution, much more complex than linear thinking about the saint as a model.

---

[22] Eric Doyle, *The Disciple and the Master: St Bonaventure's Sermons on St Francis of Assisi* (Chicago, IL, 1984), 64.

[23] On the use of St Paul in Bonaventure's sermons, and the contextualization of this particular sermon within the polemical preaching at the University of Paris, see C. Colt Anderson, 'Polemical Preaching at the University of Paris: Bonaventure's Use of Paul as a Forerunner of Francis', in Timothy J. Johnson, ed., *Franciscans and Preaching: Every Miracle from the Beginning of the World came about through Words*, Medieval Franciscans 7 (Leiden, 2012), 91–113.

The Saint as the Sign of Divine Approval for the Order

If an important function of a saint's life is to educate the reader in virtues or vices, another and perhaps more important one is to demonstrate in the strongest possible terms the holiness of the saint. We are well aware that most of the saints' lives are accompanied by an account of their miracles, which may be woven into the main narrative of a saint's life, or may, as in the case of the lives of both Francis and Dominic, be recounted in a separate section on miracles. There is certainly more than one reason for these miracle stories to be attached to the lives. One is, of course, the case for canonization: without miracles, particularly post-mortem ones, no one can be canonized. For those lives which were intended not for the Roman Curia but for a different audience, such as the friars themselves or external critics of the order, there is another purpose. In the case of a religious institution, the miracles and the sanctity of its founder are simultaneously the proof of the order's claim to holiness and of the divine approval it enjoys. For Bonaventure, Francis's stigmata were not merely a sure sign of Francis's sanctity but also the strongest proof that his movement was divinely approved, since, by the time he had received the stigmata in 1224, the order was already well developed. Thus, Bonaventure preached to his fellow friars:

> Moreover, it pleased the Lord to endorse and confirm the teaching and Rule of St. Francis, not only by miraculous signs, but also by the marks of his own stigmata, so that no true believer could possibly call them into question on external or internal evidence ... His teaching could not have had its lasting character, in the eyes of others, from St. Francis himself, for he was an uneducated merchant and no learned doctor. Therefore, it was the Lord's good pleasure to confirm it by manifest signs in the form of an awe-inspiring seal from on high, so that none of the learned could dare despise his teaching and Rule as only the efforts of an uneducated man. This shows us clearly how we ought to marvel at the depth of God's judgments, which Christ indicates at the beginning of today's Gospel when he says: thank you, Father, Lord of heaven and earth, that you have hidden these things from the wise and understanding and revealed them to little ones. ... Consequently, anyone who doubts that the doctrine and Rule of St. Francis are a most perfect way to reach eternal life, when

these have been confirmed by such great signs, must be exceedingly hard of heart.[24]

This last sentence explains very well why friars sought to control the image of Francis. Bonaventure was preaching this sermon in October 1255, in the midst of the first great tribulation that would lead to the long secular-mendicant dispute in the University of Paris. As Bonaventure was preaching these words, a group of the secular masters was on its way from Paris to Rome to secure a condemnation of a work by a Franciscan friar, *Introduction to the Everlasting Gospel* by Gerard of Borgo San Donnino. This apocalyptic work claimed the friars as the new saviours, exalting the status of the friars to the top of the ecclesiastical hierarchy. From the events that followed, it can be deduced that there must already have been much discussion in Parisian circles of Gerard's work and of the friars' status in the church. Five months after Bonaventure's sermon to the friars, the secular master William St Amour, who headed the effort to condemn Gerard's work, published a long think-piece *On the Dangers of the Last Days*, in which he called into question the legitimacy of the mendicant movement as a whole.[25] What was also implicitly being called into question by William and other like-minded secular masters was the sanctity of Francis and of his Rule, adopted by the friars.

Sabatier has argued that Bonaventure's *Legenda Maior* focused disproportionately on Francis's miracles and God-given powers at the expense of the story of the real man himself who had to face many tragedies.[26] Following him, other historians have also assumed that Bonaventure, as a representative of the order's administrative body, and later a cardinal bishop, had distorted Francis's image, while the Spiritual discourse remained loyal to the true Francis.[27] However,

---

[24] Sermon 1 on St Francis, preached at Paris, 4 October 1255: Doyle, *The Disciple and the Master*, 66.
[25] For the turbulent story of the mendicant-secular dispute, see Penn R. Szittya, *The Antifraternal Tradition in Medieval Literature* (Princeton, NJ, 1986), 11–61. For the most recent edition and translation of William's work, see *William of Saint-Amour, De periculis novissimorum temporum*, ed. and trans. Guy Geltner (Paris, 2008).
[26] Sabatier, *Life of Francis of Assisi*, 394.
[27] John V. Apczynski, 'What Has Paris to do with Assisi? The Theological Creation of a Saint', in Cynthia Ho, Beth A. Mulvaney and John K. Downey, eds, *Finding Saint Francis in Literature and Art* (New York, 2009), 79–93, at 82. On the *Legenda Maior*, see also Susan J. Hubert, 'Theological and Polemical Uses of Hagiography: A Consideration of Bonaventure's *Legenda Major* of St Francis', *Comitatus* 29 (1998), 47–61.

Bonaventure's focus on Francis's miracles and in particular his stigmata should be understood within the polemical context of the times. One might think that the fact of Francis's canonization in 1228 would have quashed such disputes as those described above even before they started, but it did not. There was a renewed need to defend the Franciscan life and to rebrand it as an extension of the sanctity of Francis, which was much more important than his everyday actions or tribulations. By demonstrating forcefully to the world that their founder was among the divine *collegium* of saints, the friars would position themselves far more securely within the religious universe.

Nevertheless, Bonaventure borrowed heavily from Thomas of Celano's lives of Francis. He had good reason to do so as Thomas was evidently a gifted hagiographer, who had absorbed well the norms of this genre. Scholars who have studied Celano's lives of Francis have found that they contain elements from the Life of Martin of Tours, Gregory the Great's Life of St Benedict (among his *Dialogues*), and the Life of Bernard of Clairvaux (begun by William of St Thierry and completed by Geoffrey of Auxerre), as well as Athanasius's life of St Anthony of Egypt.[28] This heavy borrowing from other saints' lives should come as no surprise to the student of hagiography. As Heffernan has stated succinctly: 'For sacred biographers, there existed a veritable thesaurus of established approved actions which they could employ in their texts. The repetition of actions taken from Scripture or from earlier saints' lives (often this practice extended to appropriating the exact language) ensured the authenticity of the subject's sanctity.'[29] Francis was to be followed, not because of who he really was as a human being, but because he had been taught and sent by God, and no suspicion could be shed on Francis's Rule if it could be demonstrated beyond doubt that he was indeed one of the saints of the church.

Nevertheless, it is to a degree understandable that Bonaventure's biography has garnered special – or perhaps sceptical is a better word – attention in Franciscan historiography, and there is good

---

[28] Joshua Benson, 'Reflections on Memory in Thomas of Celano's *Vita Prima*', in Michael Cusato, Steven McMichael and Timothy Johnson, eds, *Ordo et Sanctitas: The Franciscan Spiritual Journey in Theology and Hagiography. Essays in Honor of J. A. Wayne Hellmann, O.F.M. Conv.*, Medieval Franciscans 15 (Leiden, 2017), 11–31, at 24–5.

[29] Heffernan, *Sacred Biography*, 6.

reason for that. It was the general chapter of Narbonne in 1260 that commissioned Bonaventure to write a new life of Francis, and Bonaventure was at that time the minister general of the order presiding over that chapter. He completed the *Legenda Maior* in three years and presented it to the general chapter of 1263, when it was decided that all previous lives of Francis written by Thomas of Celano should be removed from the friaries and replaced by the *Legenda* written by Bonaventure. This, of course, immediately begs the question of why this was done. Why were friars not allowed to keep Celano's lives, which had been approved by previous general chapters? After all, as has been seen above, Bonaventure draws heavily on Celano, and it would therefore be a stretch to say that the two works are all that different in terms of content. Indeed, the modern critical editions of the *Legenda Maior* demonstrate that Bonaventure had genuinely sought out all the testimonies on the life of Francis. He made extensive use not only of the official lives but also of the other extant testimonies, such as the *Legend of the Three Companions* and the *Assisi Compilation*.[30]

What Bonaventure does differently from Thomas of Celano is to keep direct citations from Francis to a minimum, choosing rather to paraphrase and tending to add passages at the end of each anecdote which draw a moral or spiritual lesson. For example, in chapter 11 of the *Legenda*, Bonaventure tells a story of how a wicked canon becomes crippled. This canon comes to Francis for healing, but Francis warns him that if he falls back into sin, God's wrath will be upon him. And indeed, once Francis has removed his ailment, the canon returns to his wicked ways. As a result, shortly thereafter, he dies when a room collapses. At the end of the narration of the story, Bonaventure adds a short commentary: 'Therefore, by a just judgment of God, the last state of that man became worse than the first because of his vice of ingratitude and his contempt for God. Since gratitude must be shown for forgiveness received, an offense repeated doubles displeasure.' Such examples, in which a tale about Francis ends with a moral lesson expounded by Bonaventure, abound in the *Legenda Maior*. In fact, it might be pertinent to call Bonaventure's work a *glossa ordinaria* to Thomas of Celano's *vitae* of Francis. Such a reframing of Bonaventure's work can indeed

---

[30] See the introduction to the *Legenda Maior* in Armstrong, Hellmann and Short, eds, *FAED*, 2: 500.

explain why the Franciscan Order wanted to remove the texts of Thomas of Celano. This was not so much an erasure of Thomas's work, since much of its content has been repeated in Bonaventure's life, but rather a means of conveying a particular moral message portrayed on the basis of Francis's words and deeds. As such, Bonaventure's work can be regarded as a mechanism of control, but this is certainly inherent in the nature of all medieval *glossae*, insofar as any commentary on a text is essentially an attempt to mix its meaning in accordance with the commentator's ideological framework. If the Bible, accepted as the most perfect of all inspirational and authoritative texts, could not be read in the schools without a commentary or gloss, how much more was there a need to read other inspirational religious texts such as hagiographical *vitae* with a similar aid. It is not hard to imagine that a scholastic theologian such as Bonaventure would look at the paragraph from Thomas which quotes Francis as saying 'books are useless' and interpret that in a completely different way. We can imagine him thinking that Francis could not possibly mean here any book, but only those books which do not in any way contribute to our knowledge or love of God, such as a book on medicine or magic that has no bearing on salvation. After all, the Bible itself is a book, so it is impossible that Francis meant all books. For Bonaventure then, just as the gospels needed the commentary of theologians, Francis's *vitae* also needed exposition, lest friars derive contradictory meanings from passages or proceed to understand it literally.

THE COMPLEXITY OF AN 'ORIGINS' NARRATIVE

In his influential work, *Metahistory: The Historical Imagination in Nineteenth-century Europe*, Hayden White famously argued that writing history is at the same time the construction of an artificial narrative story with a beginning and an end.[31] Historical narratives have a plot to support a particular argument or a moralistic purpose. This latter would also be determined by the ideological framework in which the historian operates, whether liberal, devoutly religious or Marxist. When we examine the history of a medieval religious institution with respect to its presupposed inspiration, we are dealing with

---

[31] Hayden White, *Metahistory: The Historical Imagination in Nineteenth-Century Europe* (Baltimore, MD, 1975), especially 7–11 for White's categories of emplotment.

a double layer of narrative construction. On one hand, we have the medieval friars constructing a narrative about their founder written in a medieval Christian ideological framework. Bonaventure, as an official representative of his order, unmistakably provides us with what White would call a Romantic plot, that is, a plot where 'the hero transcends the world of experience, gains victory over it' and achieves self-liberation and redemption.[32] Answering the question of how friars reconcile Francis's lack of education with the focus on education in the order, Bonaventure wrote: 'I confess before God, that this is what has made me love the way of life of St Francis: that it is like both the beginning and the perfection of the Church, which first started from fishermen and afterwards advanced to the most renowned and skilful doctors.'[33] Thus Francis's earthly journey is a story of triumph, and his order shares the same historical arc: its story too is triumphant.

On the other hand, we have modern historians operating in diverse ideological frameworks (Protestant, Catholic or non-religious), who read these hagiographical accounts and come up with an alternative story featuring a variety of plots, such a 'satirical' plot in the dramatic world of Sabatier, whereby Francis's movement passes through many tribulations chronicled by the likes of Angelo Clareno and in part falls a victim to grand ecclesiastical politics. The 'satirical' plot chronicles the tribulations of the hero and his inability to fulfil what he sets out to do, beaten by the forces of nature.[34] Sabatier's is a tortured Francis, doubtless himself a saint, who nevertheless failed to reform the church or even his own order, and died a bitter death.

---

[32] Ibid. 8–9.

[33] *Epistola de tribus quaestionibus ad innominatum magistrum*, in Bonaventura da Bagnoregio, *Opera Omnia*, ed. Patres Collegii S. Bonaventurae, 10 vols (Florence, 1882–1902), 8: 331–6, at 336. For a more recent edition of this letter, see F. M. Delorme, 'Textes Franciscains', *Archivio Italiano per la storia della pietà* 1 (1951), 179–218, at 212–18.

[34] 'The Romance is fundamentally a drama of self-identification symbolized by the hero's transcendence of the world of experience, his victory over it, and his final liberation from it – the sort of drama associated with the Grail legend or the story of the resurrection of Christ in Christian mythology. It is a drama of the triumph of good over evil, of virtue over vice, of light over darkness, and of the ultimate transcendence of man over the world in which he was imprisoned by the Fall. The archetypal theme of Satire is the precise opposite of this Romantic drama of redemption; it is, in fact, a drama of diremption, a drama dominated by the apprehension that man is ultimately a captive of the world rather than its master, and by the recognition that, in the final analysis, human consciousness and will are always inadequate to the task of overcoming definitively the dark force of death, which is man's unremitting enemy': White, *Metahistory*, 8–9.

By constructing the plot as such, Sabatier has no hesitation in seeing a chronological arc beginning with Francis and proceeding with the Franciscans. Having also written prior to the publication of Herbert Grundmann's *Religious Movements of the Middle Ages*, Sabatier largely ignored the influence on Francis of twelfth-century evangelical movements, which are now acknowledged to be the true forerunners of the mendicant orders.[35] In a recent article, Augustine Thompson, one of the most recent biographers of St Francis of Assisi, has shown how much the Franciscan movement as whole, considering its early aspects of mendicancy, manual labour, penance and evangelical preaching, was in debt to religious figures who preceded Francis.[36]

If we are to accept White's theory of emplotment, what or whom we usually consider a historical 'inspiration' is a necessary invention to provide an augural beginning to a narrative of progression. At times, an institution might have difficulty in locating an inspirational beginning, a foundational moment, in its history. It might choose to ascribe its beginning to a collective enterprise rather than to a single individual. However, in the particular case of a medieval religious order such as the Franciscans, it made a lot of sense to locate the inspiration in the person of Francis alone, who had already been declared a saint in 1228. His holiness having been sanctioned by the highest ecclesiastical authority, Francis was the perfect founder to serve as a means of legitimation and glorification of an institution that had its true origins in the twelfth-century evangelical movements.

Conclusion

Ultimately, this article is not about whether or not Francis was the inspiration for the Franciscan Order from the perspective of the modern historian, but more about ways in which the medieval friars' focus on the figure of Francis as the founder of their order shaped the narrative of Francis's hagiographical biographies, and how the earliest

[35] Herbert Grundmann, *Religious Movements in the Middle Ages: The Historical Links between Heresy, the Mendicant Orders, and the Women's Religious Movement in the Twelfth and Thirteenth Century, with the Historical Foundations of German Mysticism* (Notre Dame, IN, 1995).
[36] Augustine Thompson, 'The Origin of Religious Mendicancy in Medieval Europe', in Donald Prudlo, ed., *The Origin, Development, and Refinement of Medieval Religious Mendicancies* (Boston, MA, 2011), 3–30.

vitae written by Thomas of Celano have been read both by later friars such as Bonaventure and by historians such as Sabatier to create certain narratives about the order's historical development. The variation or contradiction in such narratives has less to do, therefore, with differences in the sources, and much more to do with the way these sources were used to serve a particular ideological or polemical purpose. This holds true even when we move to the fourteenth century and look at the Spiritual friars such as Angelo Clareno. His *Chronicle of the Seven Tribulations of the Franciscan Order*, which Sabatier cherished as an authentic account of the order's history, similarly draws largely on the accounts of Thomas of Celano.[37] Angelo and other Spiritual friars who wrote lives and *legendae* of Francis in the fourteenth century, and the modern historians who championed their narrative of a 'fall from the ideals of Francis', would have been well served if they were reminded that Celano's stories were all commissioned and eventually sanctioned by the order's governing body. The image of Francis, as we know it, is a legacy of the thirteenth-century friars. Since this is so, and given also the fact that it is highly difficult to establish how from his own writings Francis saw his movement's future, a historical presentation of the order's history as a narrative of triumph or failure with respect of its founder's wishes becomes the proof of an assumption rather than the presentation of a genuine argument.

---

[37] The two most recent editions are Angelo Clareno, *Liber chronicarum; sive, Tribulationum ordinis minorum*, ed. G. M. Boccali (Assisi, 1999); *Historia septem tribulationum ordinis minorum*, ed. O. Rossini (Rome, 1999).

Trinitarian Hagiography in Late Medieval England: Rewriting St Robert of Knaresborough in Latin Verse

Hazel J. Hunter Blair*

University of Lausanne

The Order of the Holy Trinity for the Redemption of Captives (or Trinitarian Order) is one of the least studied continental religious groups to have expanded into thirteenth-century England. This article examines shifting notions of Trinitarian redemption in late medieval England through the prism of the order's writing about Yorkshire hermit St Robert of Knaresborough (d. 1218). Against the Weberian theory of the routinization of charisma, it demonstrates that Robert's inspirational sanctity was never bound too rigidly by his Trinitarian hagiographers, who rather co-opted his unstable charisma in distinct yet complementary ways to facilitate institutional reinvention and spiritual flourishing in the fourteenth and fifteenth centuries.

Recent scholarship on late medieval cultural institutions has shown an increased interest in a diversity of religious orders. Once seen as belonging to an era of monastic decline, following a 'golden age' of twelfth- and thirteenth-century expansion, late medieval English religious houses have been reframed by modern scholars as sites of intellectual and spiritual vitality and creativity.[1] Rarely, however,

* Section of English, Faculty of Letters, Bâtiment Anthropole, University of Lausanne, CH-1015 Lausanne-Chamberonne, Switzerland. E-mail: hazel.blair@unil.ch.
Thank you to Christiania Whitehead, Denis Renevey, Alasdair Grant, John Jenkins, Robin Hughes and the editors and reviewers for their suggested revisions, and to Alasdair for correcting my Latin and transcriptions (any errors remain my own). This research was funded by the Swiss National Science Foundation (project no. 100015_166133) and was presented in 2019 at the conference 'Northern Lights: Late Medieval Devotion to Saints from the North of England' (Lausanne), the Leeds International Medieval Congress and the Summer Conference of the Ecclesiastical History Society (Durham).
[1] See, for example, James G. Clark, ed., *The Religious Orders in Pre-Reformation England* (Woodbridge, 2002); Janet Burton and Karen Stöber, eds, *Monasteries and Society in the British Isles in the Later Middle Ages* (Woodbridge, 2008).

Studies in Church History 57 (2021), 74–95 © The Author(s), 2021. Published by Cambridge University Press on behalf of Ecclesiastical History Society.
doi: 10.1017/stc.2021.5

has the English history of the Order of the Holy Trinity for the Redemption of Captives (hereafter: the 'Trinitarian Order' or 'Trinitarians') received sustained academic focus.[2] Where the order's English province has been made a subject of academic enquiry, archaeological and antiquarian writers have focused on the establishment of individual foundations or on their roles as hospitals.[3] Without a full history of the order to refer to, it is unsurprising that modern scholarship has often perpetuated narratives of English Trinitarian unlearnedness, obscurity and decline following the Black Death.[4] Nevertheless, Karen Stöber has noted that the order was 'popular with lay patrons and benefactors' in late medieval England, while R. N. Swanson has drawn attention to industrious Trinitarian engagement with the fourteenth- and fifteenth-century indulgence trade, suggesting that there is yet more to uncover about the nature of English Trinitarian life.[5]

---

[2] Starting points for Trinitarian history include Giulio Cipollone, *Cristianità-Islam. Cattività e liberazione in nome di Dio. Il tempo di Innocenzo III dopo 'il 1187'*, Miscellanea Historiae Pontificiae 60 (Rome, 1992); James W. Brodman, *Charity and Religion in Medieval Europe* (Washington DC, 2009), 150–62; Yvonne Friedman, *Encounter between Enemies: Captivity and Ransom in the Latin Kingdom of Jerusalem* (Leiden, 2002), 189–206.

[3] Nicholas Orme, 'Warland Hospital, Totnes and the Trinitarian Friars in Devon', *Devon and Cornwall Notes and Queries* 36 (1987), 41–8; Margaret Gray, *The Trinitarian Order in England: Excavations at Thelsford Priory*, ed. Lorna Watts and Phillip Rahtz, British Archaeological Reports, British Series 226 (Oxford, 1993); Neil R. Aldridge, 'The Trinitarian Priory of Motynden at Headcorn', *Archaeologia Cantiana* 115 (1995), 177–212; Tim Pestell, 'Of Founders and Faith: The Establishment of the Trinitarian Priory at Ingham, Norfolk (England)', in Guy de Boe and Frans Verhaeghe, eds, *Papers of the 'Medieval Europe Brugge 1997' Conference*, 6: *Religion and Belief in Medieval Europe* (Zellik, 1997), 65–78.

[4] Paul Deslandres said the English Trinitarians 'played no role in the order', due to their 'isolated situation': *L'Ordre des Trinitaires pour le Rachat des Captifs*, 2 vols (Paris, 1903), 1: 187 (translation mine). The English Trinitarians were dubbed 'a small and unlearned order' by John B. Friedman, 'The Cipher Alphabet of John de Foxton's *Liber Cosmographiæ*', *Scriptorium* 36 (1982), 219–35, at 234. It has been suggested that in England, '[f]or the Trinitarians in general, the later fourteenth and fifteenth centuries were a time of decline and even of crisis': Orme, 'Warland Hospital', 44; cf. Gray, *Trinitarian Order in England*, 14. The Trinitarians are termed 'marginal' and 'not particularly favoured in England' in Brodman, *Charity and Religion*, 158; and 'obscure' in Richard W. Pfaff, *The Liturgy in Medieval England: A History* (Cambridge, 2009), 383. There is a sense that there may be too few written sources to support English Trinitarian history: Charles Cornish-Dale, '"A Pint of these Maiden Cuthburga Oats": The Cult of St Cuthburga at Thelsford Priory, Warwickshire, October 1538', *Midland History* 42 (2017), 183–93, at 184.

[5] Karen Stöber, *Late Medieval Monasteries and their Patrons: England and Wales, c.1300–1540* (Woodbridge, 2007), 13, 52–3; R. N. Swanson, *Indulgences in Late Medieval England: Passports to Paradise* (Cambridge, 2007), especially 63–4.

This article highlights developments in the literary and spiritual lives of late fourteenth- and fifteenth-century English Trinitarians, concentrating on Trinitarian writing about Yorkshire hermit St Robert Flower (d. 1218), patron saint of the order's priory at Knaresborough (founded *c.*1252).[6] It makes comparative reference to all extant lives of Robert (three of which are Trinitarian and one of which may be Cistercian), but is focused on analysing the Trinitarian Latin verse life, the anonymous *De nobilitate vite Sancti Roberti confess[oris]* (hereafter: *De nobilitate*).[7] This text deviates from other narratives of Robert's sanctity, which centred on his supreme charity, but despite this distinctiveness it remains the least referenced of the Trinitarian hagiographies, all of which are preserved in a single manuscript in the British Library, MS Egerton 3143.[8] Examining the Latin verse life in its manuscript, literary and historical contexts, the article delineates a key contradiction in the way Robert's inspirational charisma was institutionalized and memorialized by later medieval Trinitarians, arguing that this can be resolved by observing that Robert's late medieval hagiographers wrote to inspire different groups of his devotees in distinct yet complementary ways.

[6] *CPReg*, 1: *1198–1304*, 277. On Robert, see Brian Golding, 'The Hermit and the Hunter', in John Blair and Brian Golding, eds, *The Cloister and the World: Essays in Medieval History in Honour of Barbara Harvey* (Oxford, 1996), 95–117; Joshua Easterling, 'A Norbert for England: Holy Trinity and the Invention of Robert of Knaresborough', *Journal of Medieval Monastic Studies* 2 (2013), 75–107; Ralph Hanna, '"So to interpose a little ease": Northern Hermit-lit', in Anita Auer et al., eds, *Revisiting the Medieval North of England: Interdisciplinary Approaches* (Cardiff, 2019), 73–90; Laura Slater, 'Recreating the Judean Hills? English Hermits and the Holy Land', *JMedH* 42 (2016), 603–26; Tom Licence, *Hermits and Recluses in English Society, 950–1200* (Oxford, 2011), 173–6; Christopher Holdsworth, 'Hermits and the Powers of the Frontier', *Reading Medieval Studies* 16 (1990), 55–76.

[7] Two Latin prose lives of St Robert (one of which is Trinitarian) are edited in Paul Grosjean, 'Vitae S. Roberti Knaresburgensis', *Analecta Bollandiana* 57 (1939), 364–400. These are partly reproduced, alongside Middle English and Latin verse versions of Robert's legend (both of which are Trinitarian), in Joyce Bazire, ed., *The Metrical Life of St Robert of Knaresborough; Together with the other Middle English Pieces in British Museum Ms. Egerton 3143*, EETS 228 (London, 1968). ET of the Trinitarian prose life in Frank Bottomley, trans., *St Robert of Knaresborough* (Ilkley, 1993). All translations from *De Nobilitate* (in Bazire, ed., *Metrical Life*, Appendix C, 134–44) are my own.

[8] Easterling discusses Robert's Trinitarian hagiography (Latin prose and Middle English) in 'A Norbert for England', examining the Latin verse life briefly in '*Singulare Propositum*: Hermits, Anchorites and Regulatory Writings in Late Medieval England' (PhD thesis, Ohio State University, 2011), 136.

ADOPTING THE CULT

The Trinitarian Order was founded in 1198 in northern France by one John, variously called 'de Matha' and 'de Provence' by medieval writers. Active in the diocese of Meaux, he first appears in the documentary record as head of a religious foundation at Cerfroid. This house was primarily committed to the redemption of Christians held captive by 'enemies of the cross', and Innocent III granted it his protection by papal bull in May 1198.[9] Innocent issued another letter that December, describing John as the driving force behind the new Order of the Holy Trinity, which was established to pursue the release of Christians imprisoned for their faith while on crusade.[10] The *Trinitarian Rule*, appended to Innocent's December letter, stated that this was an activity for which one third of the order's income should be reserved, the other two thirds being earmarked for local poor relief and for the maintenance of the brothers.[11] The new order, which was committed to poverty, charity and redemption, first expanded into southern France and Spain, but came to establish houses across medieval Christendom, including ten in England.

The Trinitarians penned at least three versions of Robert Flower of Knaresborough's life in the Middle Ages (one in Latin prose, one in Latin verse, and one in Middle English verse), all of which are preserved in single copies, alongside histories of the Trinitarian Order and further devotional materials pertaining to Robert, in a late fifteenth-century manuscript from Knaresborough Priory, MS Egerton 3143. Despite this juxtaposition of material, Robert was not a Trinitarian himself. There is a dearth of evidence relating to Robert and dating from his lifetime, but his eremitism is confirmed in a royal grant: in February 1216, King John issued a letter to his Brian de L'Isle, Constable of Knaresborough in the West Riding of Yorkshire, instructing him to confer half a carucate of woodland upon 'brother Robert the Hermit', as close as possible to his hermitage

---

[9] '*Cum a nobis petitur*', 16 May 1198; edited in Cipollone, *Cristianità-Islam*, 489 (no. 18; quoted in translation in Friedman, *Encounter between Enemies*, 189).

[10] '*Operante divine dispositionis*', 17 December 1198; edited in O. Hageneder et al., *Die Register Innocenz' III.*, 1/1: *Pontifikatsjahr 1198/99* (Graz and Cologne, 1964), 703 (no. 481; translated in Anthony O. D'Errico, *The Trinitarians: An Overview of their Eight Hundred Year Service to God and Humanity* [Rome, 2002], 54–62).

[11] *Trinitarian Rule* (I), edited in Joseph Gross, *The Trinitarians' Rule of Life: Texts of the Six Principal Editions* (Rome, 1983), 9–15 (ET online at <http://www.trinitari.org/Inglese/L'ordine/Costituzioni%20-%20Regola.html>, accessed 7 September 2019).

(*hermitago*).[12] No further documentary references to Robert survive from his lifetime and he left no writings to posterity. Yet this grant suggests that he was an independent actor in the eremitic revival of the High Middle Ages, embraced elsewhere institutionally by Cistercians, Carthusians and other reformers who sought comparable returns to Christianity's desert roots.[13]

Nevertheless, Robert seems to have been dissatisfied with contemporary clerical and monastic institutions. According to his hagiographers, he was born in York and began an ecclesiastical career before entering the Cistercian abbey of Newminster, in Northumberland. Excelling there spiritually, he departed and took up residence with a Knaresborough hermit who later abandoned him. After a year alone mortifying his flesh in a chapel dedicated to St Hilda of Whitby, Robert moved to Spofforth, where his zealous devotions gave rise to rumours of his extraordinary holiness. Crowds gathered to praise him, causing the holy man, fearful of vanity, to flee and take up residence with the Benedictines at Headley Priory. Rejected by them on account of his austere way of life, however, Robert returned to the wilderness and St Hilda's chapel. Here he engaged in devotional activity while managing a small eremitic community consisting of four servants dedicated to agricultural work and poor relief. Despite these meritorious works, Robert found himself fending off demonic attacks and resisting the persecutions of landowner William de Stuteville. In the end, William's men destroyed his hermitage, and Robert fled to a new site: a cave on the northern bank of the River Nidd by Knaresborough. His brother Walter financed the building of a chapel adjoined to this new hermitage, where Robert continued to attract a following on account of his devotions, miracles, prophecies and charitable activities. Here, Robert caught the attention of King John, in whose presence the saint brazenly demonstrated the limits of royal authority. The Cistercians at nearby Fountains Abbey, impressed by his sanctity, tried to recruit Robert into their community and, later, to inter him at their monastery. Both attempts failed, and Robert was buried in his hermitage upon his death in

---

[12] *Rotuli litterarum clausarum in Turri Londinensi asservati*, ed. Thomas Duffus Hardy, 2 vols (London, 1833–4), 1: 249.

[13] Henrietta Leyser, *Hermits and the New Monasticism: A Study of Religious Communities in Western Europe*, 1000–1150 (New York, 1984); Gert Mellville, *The World of Medieval Monasticism: Its History and Forms of Life*, trans. James D. Mixon (Collegeville, MN, 2016), especially 89–124, 'Return to the Desert'; Licence, *Hermits and Recluses*.

1218. The cave-chapel became a site of pilgrimage, although Robert's relics were later translated to the nearby Trinitarian priory of Knaresborough, which inherited the site in the middle of the thirteenth century, along with all the land King John had given to Robert during his lifetime.[14] Henceforth, Robert's cult was managed by the Knaresborough Trinitarians, who adopted him as their spiritual patron.

In many ways, Robert was not an obvious candidate for Trinitarian veneration: he did not found any Trinitarian houses and does not appear to have had contact with the order during his lifetime. Unlike his eremitic predecessor St Godric, he did not venture abroad to areas of Trinitarian interest such as the Holy Land or the Iberian peninsula. Nor was he famed for releasing captives or working other liberation miracles, like St Foy or (more locally) St Cuthbert. Moreover, whilst the majority of Robert's extant cult literature bears marks of Trinitarian authorship, the Trinitarians were not the first order to venerate him: a fragmentary version of Robert's life is preserved in British Library MS Harley 3775 and was perhaps authored by the Cistercians.[15] It is not within the scope of this article to provide a full analysis of Cistercian influence on the development of Robert's hagiographic persona, but the most distinctive aspect of the hermit's sanctity according to this early text was his charity: the nature (*substancia*) of this saintly or holy man (*sancti viri*) is defined in the prologue in relation to his tendency to extend his generosity towards the poor (*manus largas extendendo pauperibus*).[16] The same text also focuses on Robert's eremitism, not only in its title (*Vita sancti Roberti heremite*), but also through depicting him heroically as a soldier (*miles*) and athlete (*athleta*) of Christ who dwelt in the wilderness (*heremo*) amid numerous persecutions, some of them self-inflicted.[17] It seems plausible that the Cistercians penned this life while seeking acquisition of Robert's relics or hermitage, and that in so doing they emphasized elements of his spirituality with

---

[14] William Dugdale, *Monasticon Anglicanum: A New Edition*, ed. John Caley, Henry Ellis and Bulkeley Bandinel, vol. 8 (London, 1846), 1566 (no. II).

[15] *Vita sancti Roberti heremite* [hereafter: *VA*], ed. Grosjean, 365–74 (all translations mine); Licence, *Hermits and Recluses*, 193–4.

[16] *VA* 1 (ed. Grosjean, 367). Robert is also said to have stored food for the poor: ibid. 5 (ed. Grosjean, 369).

[17] Ibid. 1, 3, 5 (ed. Grosjean, 366, 368, 369).

which their order empathized most, particularly his desert spirituality.[18]

Robert's charitable reputation as recorded in this early life was embraced by his first Trinitarian hagiographer. This is particularly pertinent, considering that northern European Trinitarians were rarely involved in active ransom missions, instead performing other good works while supporting their order's titular redemptive cause financially, via alms-collecting.[19] Indeed, although royal protections were granted to English members of the 'Order of the Holy Trinity and the Ransom of Captives of the Holy Land' so that they might collect alms 'for the ransom of such captives', early English Trinitarians are more commonly recognized as having cared primarily for the local poor and sick and those who visited their hospitals.[20] Robert's shrine surely attracted many such individuals to Knaresborough, and so it is perhaps unsurprising to find that when writing about him the Trinitarians elaborated upon his charitable tendencies: the Trinitarian author of the saint's prose life in the Egerton manuscript implies Robert's direct involvement with the collection of alms for poor relief, for example, whereas the Harley *vita* suggests that Robert delegated alms-collecting to one of his servants, distancing the saint somewhat from day-to-day charity work despite his generous spirit.[21] Thus, while comparison of the two *vitae* is limited by the fragmentary state of the Harley text, Robert's work on behalf of the poor is emphasized in the Trinitarian prose *vita*, which, as Joshua Easterling has demonstrated, simultaneously presents the hermit as a devotee of the Trinity and (through clever rhetoric and compilation) as a natural spiritual patron and point of origin for the Trinitarian community at Knaresborough.[22]

---

[18] Tom Licence, 'The Benedictines, the Cistercians and the Acquisition of a Hermitages in Twelfth-Century Durham', *JMedH* 29 (2003), 315–29.

[19] James Brodman, 'Trinitarian and Mercedarian Orders: A Study of Religious Redemptionism in the Thirteenth Century' (PhD thesis, University of Virginia, 1974), 157.

[20] *Calendar of the Patent Rolls preserved in the Public Record Office of Great Britain: Edward I*, 3: *1292–1301* (London, 1897), 253 (issued 18 June 1297). Similar references can be found in royal correspondence covering the period 1242–1336. On account of their charitable activity, Brodman groups the Trinitarians under 'The Hospitaller Orders': *Charity and Religion*, 126–77.

[21] *Vita Sancti Roberti iuxta Knaresburgum* [hereafter: *VR*] 6 (ed. Grosjean, 375–400, at 381); cf. *VA* 6 (ed. Grosjean, 372).

[22] Easterling, 'A Norbert for England', 75–107. As Easterling notes, the dating of this text is uncertain: ibid. 77 n. 9. Holdsworth, 'Hermits and the Powers of the Frontier', 73

The literary strategies that Easterling argues the Trinitarian prose hagiographer used to legitimize Knaresborough Priory's connection to its patron saint might usefully be articulated by analogy with what Max Weber called the 'routinization of charisma', summarized as 'a process through which the enthusiasm generated by the prophet and his followers might be channelled into the foundation of a community or religious order'.[23] Robert's charisma is suggested by his miracles and the excitement his sanctity inspired in his contemporaries, but also by his rejection of contemporary church institutions and monastic rules, coupled with his disdain for secular authority, which reflects Weber's observation that charismatics are inherently disruptive figures. According to Weber, charisma is both transitory and unstable, such that attempts to grant it permanence necessarily result in changes to its nature which diminish the purity of its nascent form. When charismatic authority is routinized by an institution, then, it loses some of its unruly potency, becoming 'a component of a concrete historical structure'.[24] Thus the Harley *vita* emphasizes the eremitic tradition to which Robert belongs, which would certainly have been of interest to a Cistercian audience ideologically invested in that same lineage, while the Trinitarian prose hagiographer chooses to emphasize Robert's entrepreneurial spirit and active charity at the expense of his eremitic purity. As C. Stephen Jaeger has observed, however, texts (and especially hagiographies) can themselves 'exercise charismatic effects', spurring devoted readers past simple admiration for their subjects and on to imitation.[25] Indeed, Robert's Trinitarian prose hagiographer arguably 'textualizes' his charisma (to borrow Jaeger's terminology) in such a way as to preserve the energetic momentum of its nascent instability: as Easterling argues, the text

---

n. 12, suggests the mid-thirteenth century, which would accord with the earliest known reference to Knaresborough Priory as the house 'of St Robert' (see n. 6 above), and with Easterling's reading of the *VR* as a text focused on constructing *pater Robertus*.

[23] Andrew Brown, 'Charisma and Routine: Shaping the Memory of Brother Richard and Joan of Arc', *Religions* 3 (2012), 1162–79, at 1164; Max Weber, *Economy and Society: An Outline of Interpretative Sociology*, ed. Guenther Roth and Claus Wittich, 2 vols (Berkeley, CA, 1978), 2: 1111–57.

[24] Weber, *Economy and Society*, 2: 1121.

[25] C. Stephen Jaeger, 'The Saint's Life as Charismatic Form: Bernard of Clairvaux and Francis of Assisi', in Brigitte Miriam Bedos-Rezak and Martha Dana Rust, eds, *Faces of Charisma: Image, Text, Object in Byzantium and the Medieval West* (Boston, MA, 2018), 181–204, at 175–6.

encourages readers to imagine Robert in 'elastic and indeterminate' ways, respecting local history and literary tradition by never quite labelling Robert a Trinitarian founder while nevertheless engaging 'the powers of uncertainty' in order to imply Robert's authority as Knaresborough Priory's spiritual initiator.[26] Therefore, while the Trinitarian prose *vita* routinizes Robert's charisma to some extent, it also embodies that charisma in such a way as to encourage wishful thinking on the part of Trinitarian readers and to inspire them to action in Robert's image.[27]

Nevertheless, while Trinitarian institutionalization of Robert's charisma in the thirteenth century depended on clever crafting of Robert's life, it was also necessarily predicated upon securing a stable connection between Robert's holy reputation and the wider Trinitarian mission.[28] Indeed, Robert's alms-collecting and care for the poor retained a key place in Trinitarian expressions of his sanctity into the later Middle Ages: the Middle English translation of Robert's life (MS Egerton 3143, fols 39v–60v), produced around the turn of the fifteenth century, thus makes frequent reference to Robert's charitable concerns, even emphasizing that the saint's principal purpose was 'to begge an brynge pore men of baile'.[29] It is striking, then, that the Trinitarian author of Robert's life in Latin verse minimizes this aspect of the hermit's sanctity in his rewriting of the saint's legend: indeed, based on the Latin verse text alone one would never suspect that Robert had once been renowned for alleviating poverty.[30] How should we explain this radical departure from the established narrative of Robert's holiness and its juxtaposition with competing images of his sanctity in a late medieval Trinitarian manuscript?

De nobilitate: St Robert in Latin Verse

Robert's Latin verse life is an alliterative poem in 116 stanzas of four lines each with rhyming pattern aaab cccb; it is the first item in the

---

[26] Easterling, 'A Norbert for England', 104–5, 84.

[27] 'It appears as though certain brothers at Knaresborough wished to believe him their order's founding hermit': ibid. 105.

[28] The Trinitarian prose hagiographer 'finds in Robert an author of Trinitarian ideals': ibid. 93.

[29] Bazire, ed., *Metrical Life*, line 295.

[30] Robert's charity is implied only once in *De nobilitate* (stanza 41), where the hagiographer references the hermit's 'destitute' (*egenis*) guests.

Egerton manuscript, where it is followed immediately by an account of the foundation of the Trinitarian Order, *De innovatione Ordinis Sancte Trinitatis* (hereafter: *De innovatione*).[31] This second text is also in Latin verse and has a rhyme scheme identical to the hagiography preceding it. The two texts are distinct, and yet they are a pair, bound together materially, metrically and linguistically in the form of a textual diptych. They have not been dated formally, but may have been produced in the fourteenth or fifteenth centuries: A. G. Rigg has dated a similar textual pairing concerning another Yorkshire saint (a Latin verse life of St Hilda of Whitby, which survives coupled with a Latin verse account of the refoundation of Whitby Abbey) to this period.[32] Indeed, as Rigg has noted more generally, the fourteenth and fifteenth centuries witnessed 'a rise in literary interest in Northern saints and antiquities', with the production of a Latin metrical chronicle of the church of York in the late fourteenth century, as well as composition of a Latin verse poem on the archbishops of York to 1455, and further fifteenth-century Latin poetry sanctifying Richard Scrope, archbishop of York (d. 1405).[33] Given the form and Yorkshire provenance of the Latin verse diptych in the Egerton manuscript, it would not be unreasonable to suggest that the Latin verse hagiography and its attached history were written at around the same time, so that the pairing might be dated, roughly, to the late fourteenth or fifteenth centuries. Indeed, as demonstrated below, the decision to rework Robert's life in Latin verse might fruitfully be read in relation to institutional and spiritual changes taking place in the English Trinitarian province at around this time.

By comparison with the Trinitarian prose and Middle English texts, Robert's verse *vita* is a reshuffled and heavily edited version of his life story.[34] The text is front-loaded with lengthy descriptions of the saint's eremitism, labelling Robert a hermit from the moment he is introduced in the sixth stanza.[35] The Trinitarian prose hagiographer, by contrast, took care to stress Robert's institutional ties and,

---

[31] In Bazire, ed., *Metrical Life*, Appendix D, 144–8.

[32] A. G. Rigg, 'A Latin Poem on St Hilda and Whitby Abbey', *Journal of Medieval Latin* 6 (1996), 12–43.

[33] A. G. Rigg, *A History of Anglo-Latin Literature, 1066–1422* (Cambridge, 1992), 293–4, 311.

[34] Bazire, ed., *Metrical Life*, Introduction, 33.

[35] *De nobilitate*, stanza 6.

long before narrating the saint's eremitic turn, informed readers that Robert:

> ... was in the habit of frequenting churches and even more often spending time in monasteries and the chosen youth [*electus adolescens*] had the intention of serving God more fervently in the office of the priesthood. I am totally ignorant of what made him withdraw from this initial intention. ... Anyway, this devout man, turning to the bishop, persistently asked for ordination to the subdiaconate and the bishop willingly agreed to his request. However, when he had been raised to this minor order by the hand of the bishop, he withdrew from proceeding to major orders.[36]

The Middle English *Life* does feature an early celebration of Robert's eremitism (lines 17–24) but nevertheless emphasizes his youthful ties to schools ('scoles', line 77), the priesthood (line 90) and the subdiaconate (line 92). Indeed, where the *Life* and the Trinitarian prose hagiography present readers with an images of a young churchgoer keen on an ecclesiastical career, the Latin verse text omits much of this information, instead covering Robert's parentage and background briefly, before narrating his embrace of the wilderness:

Domus dapis declinavit,
Knaresburgo festinavit,
Ibi carnem conculcavit
    Miris [ab]stinenciis.

Adherebat heremite
Valde virtuose vite,
Latitanti sine lite,
    Presso penitenciis.

Inspiratus sponte sprevit
Voluptatis facta; flevit,
Et sub rupe requievit
    Fretus in foramine.

---

[36] VR 1 (ed. Grosjean, 378; Bottomley, trans., *St Robert of Knaresborough*, 3).

Hic Robertus residebat,
Dum prodire proponebat
Herimata quem habebat
    Secum pro solamine.[37]

Similarly, further episodes from the Trinitarian prose and Middle English texts in which Robert experiments with monasticism at Newminster and Headley are reduced to only a stanza or two in Latin verse.[38] Robert's initial journey into the wilderness is elaborated in the Latin verse before either of these monastic episodes is related, and Robert also seems lonelier: we learn little of his earliest eremitic companion and nothing of the four assistants at his early community at St Hilda's.[39] Thus, by comparison with the Trinitarian prose and Middle English lives, which stress the saint's care for the poor and his ties to the established church, the monastic, institutional and charitable moments in Robert's life are diminished in the Latin verse. What remains is an image of Robert in which his sanctity seems predicated on asceticism and devotional activity, rather than on ecclesiastical community-building or care for the poor. But to what extent was this extra-institutional and prayerful eremitism of interest to a community like the Trinitarians, who had once written to bind their patron saint's reputation for charity to their corporate emphasis on active works of mercy in honour of the Trinity?

As François Dolbeau has demonstrated, Latin verse *vitae* in devotional manuscript contexts were often produced as aids to meditation and individual piety.[40] From much of the secondary literature, however, one gets the impression that the English Trinitarians were unlearned, practical men, and that, moving into the later Middle

---

[37] 'Declining household feasts, he hurried to Knaresborough where he spurned meat with remarkable abstinence. He adhered vigorously to the virtuous life of a hermit, secluded without smear, suffering self-inflicted penitence. Inspired [by God], he voluntarily scorned deeds of pleasure; he wept and rested beneath the cliff, protected by a cave. Here Robert lived until the hermit whom he had with him for comfort proposed to leave': *De nobilitate*, stanzas 13–16. Robert's ordination as subdeacon is referred to in passing in stanza 17.

[38] Newminster: ibid., stanza 18, cf. *VR* 2 (ed. Grosjean, 378–9); *Life*, lines 97–126. Headley: *De nobilitate*, stanzas 23–4; cf. *VR* 5 (ed. Grosjean, 380–1); *Life*, lines 215–38.

[39] See *VR* 2 (ed. Grosjean, 378–9); *Life*, lines 134–72, where details of Robert's initial embrace of the wilderness near Knaresborough follow the narration of his entry into Newminster.

[40] François Dolbeau, 'Un Domaine négligé de la littérature médiolatine. Les Textes hagiographiques en vers', *Cahiers de Civilisation Médiévale* 45 (2002), 129–39, at 134.

Ages, the English province was in decline; that it struggled financially to operate its hospitals, the Black Death having been felt acutely by the Trinitarians due to their relatively small number in England by comparison with better established religious orders.[41] Nevertheless, as Carole Rawcliffe and others have highlighted, medieval hospitals (unlike their modern equivalents) were essentially religious houses, 'chiefly concerned with the promotion of spiritual rather than physical health', and they frequently facilitated liturgical, devotional and meditative activity, perhaps even more so in the period after the Black Death, when financial difficulties meant that the survival of hospitals depended on their ability to minister to the spiritual health of patrons and their deceased relatives.[42] Thus there is a degree of contradiction in the literature pertaining to Trinitarian life in England. It is true that in 1402 the English Trinitarian province stated that it could not afford to contribute the 'ransoming third' of its income towards the order's founding goal of the redemption of captives, instead petitioning for continued payment of a smaller quota.[43] In particular, during the period after 1350, financial and staffing difficulties seem to have affected the Trinitarians in Oxford, Hertford, Easton and Totnes.[44] But to view this period as one of general decline for the English Trinitarians, or as a period in which they had drifted away from their order's founding redemptive purpose, does not do justice to the complexity of the institutional transformations taking place in the late medieval English province.

As W. G. Clark-Maxwell and R. N. Swanson have shown, among the religious orders of late medieval England, the Trinitarians were some of the most prolific producers of letters of confraternity in the fifteenth century.[45] Examples of these documents survive from Knaresborough, Hounslow, Mottenden, Ingham, Thelsford and

---

[41] See n. 4 above.

[42] Carole Rawcliffe, *Medicine for the Soul: The Life, Death and Resurrection of an English Medieval Hospital, St Giles's, Norwich, c.1249–1550* (Thrupp, 1999), 103–8; Nicholas Orme and Margaret Webster, *The English Hospital, 1070–1570* (New Haven, CT, 1995), 49, 139.

[43] Lateran Regesta 109 (1402–3), in *CPReg*, 5: *1398–1404*, 543–57, online at: British History Online, <http://www.british-history.ac.uk/cal-papal-registers/brit-ie/vol5/pp543-557>, accessed 10 September 2019; Brodman, *Charity and Religion*, 158; idem, 'Trinitarian and Mercedarian Orders', 239.

[44] Orme, 'Warland Hospital', 44.

[45] [William Gilchrist] Clark-Maxwell, 'Some further Letters of Fraternity', *Archaeologia* 79 (1929), 179–216, at 192–3; see also n. 5 above.

Walknoll. They certified the extension of spiritual privileges to lay associates of the order in return for financial patronage. Trinitarian letters generally offered the recipient remittance of several years' penitential punishment, thereby reducing the amount of time the recipient would spend in purgatory, alongside the privilege of choosing a deathbed confessor capable of granting plenary remission of sins and particular burial privileges, while also promising the holder posthumous prayers for their soul on a par with those offered to full members of the order.[46] Reading these sources from a post-Reformation standpoint or in the context of anti-fraternal sentiment, one might be tempted to view later Trinitarians as desperate pedlars of spurious promises, but as Robert W. Shaffern and others have stressed, the image of the corrupt pardoner has been frequently exaggerated, both in the medieval sources themselves and in modern historiography.[47] While there certainly was a financial aspect to Trinitarian confraternity, the order was plainly invested in late medieval England's spiritual economy, and arguably interested less in crude fundraising than in stimulating and rewarding lay charity.[48] Moreover, drawing on the theory of 'cultural capital' outlined by sociologist Pierre Bourdieu, Nicole R. Rice has emphasized that laypeople in late medieval England treated letters of confraternity as a means by which they might 'accrue *spiritual* capital'.[49] Spiritual capital, like cultural capital, can exist in many forms, and thus in procuring letters of confraternity (the objectified form), the laity could, by way of association, benefit from (and thereby embody) some of the institutional spiritual capital that had been produced and conserved by the house and order issuing the letters.[50] The relatively high number of surviving English Trinitarian letters may therefore imply that the brethren were famed and valued in England not only for their redemptive crusading

---

[46] Swanson, *Indulgences*, 64–72.

[47] Robert W. Shaffern, 'The Pardoner's Promises: Preaching and Policing Indulgences in the Fourteenth-Century English Church', *The Historian* 68 (2006), 49–65; Swanson, *Indulgences*, 278–348.

[48] Swanson, *Indulgences*, 350–1, 522.

[49] Nicole R. Rice, *Lay Piety and Religious Discipline in Middle English Literature* (Cambridge, 2008), xii, 7 (italics mine); Rawcliffe, *Medicine*, 106–7; Sheila Sweetinburgh, *The Hospital in Medieval England: Gift-Giving and the Spiritual Economy* (Dublin, 2004).

[50] Rice, *Lay Piety*, xii, 7. On the forms of 'spiritual capital' (embodied, objectified and institutionalized), see Bradford Verter, 'Spiritual Capital: Theorizing Religion with Bourdieu against Bourdieu', *Sociological Theory* 21 (2003), 150–74, at 159–60.

heritage and active charitable work, but also as conduits of spiritual deliverance.

The English Trinitarian province was certainly attending to the maintenance and development of its own 'spiritual capital' in the late fourteenth and fifteenth centuries, as suggested by patterns of book ownership. There are no extant Trinitarian library catalogues from medieval England, but a late fourteenth-century copy of the Middle English spiritual guidance poem *Speculum vitae*, attributed to William of Nassington, survives from Knaresborough and is signed by John Kylyngwyke, minister of the house from *c*.1380 to 1400.[51] Moreover, there was, at the Trinitarian house in Hounslow, an early printed copy of Michael Francisci's *Quodlibet de veritate fraternitatis rosarii* (*An Academic Disputation on the True Character of the Brotherhood of the Rosary*), published in 1480, which belonged first to brother John Sa[n]dys(?) of Hounslow, and then his colleague Ralph Beckwyth.[52] This text promoted the Rosary prayer, an elaborate series of meditations on Mary's joys and sorrows featuring Paternosters and Aves, said to have been received direct from the Virgin by St Dominic and promoted by his followers.[53] Meanwhile, among the Trinitarians at Mottenden in Kent, minister Richard Lancing possessed a manuscript containing several texts by the noted Parisian theologian Jean Gerson (1363–1429), including an affective tract entitled *De oratione et valore eius* (*On Prayer and its Value*), which draws meditative parallels between prayer and pilgrimage.[54] Indeed, this last book may well have been sent to Mottenden from Knaresborough.[55] Knaresborough Priory thus

---

[51] Oxford, Bodleian Library, MS Eng. Poet. d.5. The scribal identification is noted in Richard Sharpe and James Willoughby, eds, *Medieval Libraries of Great Britain*, online at: <http://mlgb3.bodleian.ox.ac.uk>, accessed 31 July 2020.

[52] Richmond, VA, Library of Virginia, BX890.G3, listed in Sharpe and Willoughby, *Medieval Libraries*.

[53] Anne Winston-Allen, *Stories of the Rose: The Making of the Rosary in the Middle Ages* (University Park, PA, 1997), 65–8.

[54] Gouda, Stichting Openbare Bibliotheek, no shelfmark. This text was held in high esteem by Thomas More: see More, *De tristitia Christi*, 1: *The Valencia Manuscript: Facsimiles, Transcription, and Translation*, ed. and trans. Clarence H. Miller, CWTM 14/1 (New Haven, CT, 1976), 765.

[55] Library of Virginia, MS BX890.G3, 78. The book contains a late fifteenth-century inscription indicating that it was gifted to Richard Lancing by one Robert Bolton, 'magistri domus de'. According to Sharpe and Willoughby, *Medieval Libraries*, the remainder of the sentence is illegible and the house remains unidentified. We know, however, that a Robert Bolton was minister of Knaresborough from at least 1461 until as late as 1494, so

seems to have existed within a network of houses with demonstrable enthusiasm for the types of meditative devotion and affective literature in vogue during the late fourteenth and fifteenth centuries.

The Egerton manuscript, moreover, contains original Trinitarian prayers designed to promote meditative reflection on Robert's holy life. Thus folio 11 features an alliterative Latin verse text entitled 'The five joys of St Robert', which is immediately followed by an extensive 'Fifteen joys of St Robert'.[56] Enumerating, meditating on, and sharing in the spiritual joys of a holy individual, usually key moments from their life, is a form of Marian devotion that enjoyed circulation in England in the form of Middle English lyrics.[57] While these Marian-esque prayers to Robert are nowhere near as complex as those circulating in texts such as Francisci's Rosary, they do suggest an increased interest at Knaresborough in contemplative meditation as a legitimate Trinitarian activity.[58] Robert is even honoured in the Egerton manuscript with a set of hours; here, both the collect, which traditionally summarizes the central theme of the day's liturgy and was repeated throughout the day, and the prayer at the most solemn hour of vespers, are suggestive of the spiritual interests and ambitions of this Trinitarian house. The collect reads:

> We pray, almighty God, that you might pour the heat of your charity (*calorem caritatis*) into our minds, and that by intercession of your saint Robert, your confessor, we might become deserving to taste the

---

there is a strong chance that he is the *magister* to whom the inscription refers. Bolton seems to have been Lancing's predecessor as English provincial. Bolton is also styled minister of Thelsford in letters up to 1474, and one letter of 1465 refers to him as minister of both Thelsford and Knaresborough. Lancing's ministerial career does not appear to have taken off until the 1480s, by which time one Roger Lyntton had taken over from Bolton as minister of Thelsford. Bolton continues to be styled minister of Knaresborough up to 1494: David M. Smith, ed., *Heads of Religious Houses: England and Wales, 3: 1377–1540* (Cambridge, 2008), 609–15.

[56] *Quinque gaudia beati Roberti*, London, BL, MS Egerton 3143, fols 11r–v; *Quindecim gaudia beati Roberte*, ibid., fols 11v–12v.

[57] Karen Saupe, ed., *Middle English Marian Lyrics* (Kalamazoo, MI, 1998). For Latin forms of the devotion, linked to further universal (predominantly female) saints, see BL, MS Sloane 2471.

[58] Claire Macht has drawn parallel conclusions in the context of her study of historical writing in late medieval England. I thank Claire for sharing with me sections of her recently defended thesis, 'The Changing Nature of Monastic Historical Writing in Late Medieval England' (PhD thesis, University of Oxford, 2020).

sweetness of your love (*dulcorem dilectionis*) in heaven, which he [Robert] desired with all the longing of his heart to grasp in the wilderness.[59]

Then, at vespers, the text instructs the speaker to pray: 'Give me the power, O flower of hermits, to avoid sin at the hour of Vespers. Cure sicknesses of the flesh and of souls, offering to me the bright fire of love (*amoris incendium clarum*).'[60]

Alongside the conspicuous pun on Robert's surname (Flower), there are parallels between the vocabulary used here and the writings of fourteenth-century Yorkshire hermit Richard Rolle (*c.*1300–49), who wrote in his widely read *Incendium Amoris* about his experience of God's love, which he first felt in the wilderness through mystical encounters with heat (*calor*), sweetness (*dulcor*) and song (*canor*).[61] Moreover, a prayer worded very similarly to the collect can be found in one of the manuscripts of Rolle's *Officium*.[62] There are no Rollean texts listed among the books extant from English Trinitarian libraries, but certain fifteenth-century Trinitarian brothers may have had access to this literature through their membership of York's Corpus Christi Guild.[63] We are, then, perhaps glimpsing here Knaresborough Priory's creative engagement with Rollean

[59] 'Mentibus nostris quesumus omnipotens deus calorem tue caritatis infunde et intercessione beati Roberti confessoris tui dulcorem tue dilectionis in celis mereamur degustare: quem toto cordis desiderio comprehendere in herimo concupivit': *Matutine de sancto Roberto ex devocionem dicende*, BL, MS Egerton 3143, fols 10v–11r, at fol. 10v (translation, including expansion of abbreviations, and transcription mine, including 'mereamur' for MS 'meriamur').

[60] 'Opem michi porrege, flos herimitarum, / Ad vitanda vicia hora vesperarum. / Carni ac contagia cura animarum, / Amoris incendium prebens michi clarum': ibid., fol. 11r (transcription, including expansion of abbreviations, and translation mine).

[61] Richard Rolle, *The* Incendium Amoris *of Richard Rolle of Hampole*, ed. Margaret Deanesly (New York, 1915).

[62] Uppsala, UL, MS Uppsala C. 621, fol. 103v (a fragment of the *Officium*), transcribed as an appendix in Harald Lindkvist, ed., 'Richard Rolle's "Meditatio de Passione Domini" according to MS. Uppsala C. 494', in *Skrifter ut-gifna af Kungl. Humanistika Vctenskaps* 19 (Uppsala, 1917), 73–8, at 78.

[63] Eleven Knaresborough Trinitarians are recorded as guild members, with clusters of registrations in the 1430s and 1460s: see *The Register of the Guild of Corpus Christi in the City of York*, ed. R. H. Skaife, Surtees Society 57 (Durham, 1872), 13, 28, 33, 34, 62, 63, 83. Carmelite friar Richard Misyn translated Rolle's *Incendium Amoris* into Middle English in 1435 for anchorite Margaret Heslington; both may have been guild members in 1461–2: see Johan Bergström-Allen, 'The Whitefriars' Return to Carmel', in Liz Herbert McAvoy and Mari Hughes-Edwards, eds, *Anchorites, Wombs and Tombs: Intersections of Gender and Enclosure in the Middle Ages* (Cardiff, 2005), 77–91.

material during a period of increased interest in contemplative activity in the later Middle Ages. Indeed, the concluding prayer set for compline explicitly asks St Robert to instruct the speaker in eremitic contemplation, and the text concludes with the words: 'make me, I entreat (*flagito*), a brother to you in the struggle (*tibi in agone fac me fratrem*) ... so that, with contemplation of heaven, I might delight in extraordinary things here in this house (*contemplacione sic ut poli perfruar mira mansione*)'.[64] Moreover, the intensely alliterative form of further Latin prayers in the Egerton manuscript is reminiscent of the sort of ecstatic mystical writing for which Rolle is well known.[65] Knaresborough Priory thus seems to have come to associate an interest in Rollean contemplative spirituality with the spirituality it envisaged its patron saint having practised centuries before in the wilderness.

By the end of the medieval period, through their copying of spiritual guidance poetry and their composition of new devotional texts linked to Robert's cult, the Knaresborough Trinitarians seem to have increased and diversified the amount of meditative and devotional literature at their disposal. Might Robert's eremitic charisma, as textualized in Latin verse, have been designed to sustain and further inspire new literary and contemplative directions in the spiritual life of English Trinitarians in this period? This is the impression one gets from reading the history of the Trinitarian order appended to the Latin verse hagiography: while describing the order's tripartite financial structure (stanza 15) and historical redemptive purpose (stanzas 16–26) in some detail, the text also features an early petition that Trinitarian brothers might be able to explore a less active, more devotional way of life within the walls of their church: 'May the objective of this monastery be sincerely to please the Creator; and to practice in the monastery acts nourishing to the soul.'[66] The next stanza references the liturgical life of the priory and its hymns and hours, and the author then describes Trinitarian brothers engaged in meditative

---

[64] *Matutine de sancto Roberto*, fol. 11r (transcription, including expansion of abbreviations, and translation mine, including 'perfruar' for MS 'perfruer').
[65] See ibid., fols 12v–14r (a poem about Robert made up of words beginning with 'p'), 14r–v (an acrostic in which the alliteration is structured around the letters of Robert's name). On Rolle's alliteration, see Nicolas Watson, *Richard Rolle and the Invention of Authority* (Cambridge, 1991), 178–9.
[66] 'Causa celle sit scincere / Plasmatori complacere, / Et in cella exercere / Almos actus anime': *De innovatione*, stanza 2.

practice: 'The brothers bear the cross of Christ for meditating with contrite heart on the Redeemer, through whom they have been saved by [his] blood.'[67] The text then goes on to describe the Trinitarian habit (stanzas 6–14) and introduces the legend that the order was founded by two hermits who went to Rome and received papal approval for their redemptive project (stanzas 32–8).[68] Prior to this, *De innovatione* had celebrated the Trinitarian order in superlative terms as a model of fraternity: 'The Order of the Holy Trinity is the flower of brotherhood, which like the sun of serenity will shine forth to the brothers.'[69]

In epitomizing Trinitarian eremitism as 'the flower of brotherhood', *De innovatione* calls to mind the life of the hermit Robert Flower, who, as seen above, is addressed elsewhere in the Egerton manuscript as 'flower of hermits'.[70] Indeed, the juxtaposition of the Latin verse life of Robert with a complementary history of the legendary, anonymous but decidedly eremitic roots of the Trinitarian order writes Robert into Trinitarian history and simultaneously imbues that history with the exemplary eremitic values espoused in the attached hagiography. In what sense, however, could Robert's individualistic, prayerful eremitism, rather than his active charity and community-mindedness, be celebrated as a quasi-foundational tenet of Trinitarian life?

The answer, perhaps, lies in changing notions of Trinitarian redemption during the late medieval period. As Brodman has observed, Trinitarian ransom work was in decline in the fourteenth and fifteenth centuries, and 'the Trinitarians of England and Scotland display the same lack of interest in the liberation of captives as we have encountered in northern France'.[71] This reading corresponds well to the fact that during the early fifteenth century the English province appeared resistant to paying a third of its income towards the redemption of captives, claiming instead that the English houses were accustomed to payment of a ransoming quota smaller than the 'third part' mandated by their order's *Rule*. On

---

[67] 'Fratres ferunt crucem Cristi, / Meditando mente tristi / Redemptorem, per quem isti / Sunt salvati sanguine': ibid., stanza 5.
[68] Brodman, 'Trinitarian and Mercedarian Orders', 132–46.
[69] 'Ordo Sancte Trinitatis / Flos est fraternitatis, / Qui ut sol serenitatis / Prefulgebit fratribus': *De innovatione*, stanza 27.
[70] See n. 60 above.
[71] Brodman, *Charity and Religion*, 162.

the other hand, *De innovatione* describes Christian captivity in the Holy Land (stanzas 18–21) and Trinitarian ransoming activity (stanzas 39–40) in some detail, reinforcing the expectation that all Trinitarian brethren should be committed to the redemption of captives: 'If all who are professed Trinitarians do not take account of this obligation of the cross, they will end in the devil's house.'[72] This suggests that the English brethren were not as straightforwardly uninterested in redemptive activity as Brodman implies. Moreover, and contrary to Brodman's assertion that the Trinitarians refused 'here as elsewhere to broaden the definition of captivity beyond those held in Muslim lands', Jan Luc Liez has argued convincingly for an increasingly metaphorical interpretation of captivity and ransom among the Trinitarians, for whom redemptive activity, he argues, probably came to encompass the liberation of souls.[73] At one point *De innovatione* suggests that the order facilitates the rescue of sinners.[74] I wish to complement Liez's argument, then, by proposing that the centralization of Robert's prayerful eremitism in *De nobilitate* (combined with, and partly constituted by, the same text's de-emphasis of that hermit's famed poor relief), was a conscious literary strategy designed to inspire later medieval Knaresborough Trinitarians to pray and meditate on Robert's life and in his image. This would enable the order to accrue sufficient spiritual capital to facilitate a wider Trinitarian goal of liberating sinful Christians from purgatorial suffering.

If this holds, then the Latin verse pairing speaks to a much altered institutional vision of Trinitarian life in England at the end of the medieval period, which recognized that English Trinitarian brethren were no longer so closely aligned to active redemptive work as they once might have been, and reflected the new literary, contemplative and spiritual interests that the Trinitarians were developing at the turn of the fifteenth century. This is not to say that the Trinitarians of later medieval England had necessarily become

---

[72] 'Huic omnes obligati / Sunt professi Trinitati; / Si non curent cruciati, / Erunt domo demonis': *De innovatione*, stanza 41.

[73] Brodman, 'Trinitarian and Mercedarian Orders', 239; Jan Luc Liez, 'L'Esclavage comme métaphore religieuse dans l'iconographie de l'ordre des Trinitaires', in Elizabeth McGrath and Jean-Michel Massing, eds, *The Slave in European Art: From Renaissance Trophy to Abolitionist Emblem* (London and Turin, 2012), 63–81.

[74] 'Ordo sanus est inceptus / Per quem reus est ereptus' ('A healthy order has been started, by means of which the guilty [person] has been rescued'): *De innovatione*, stanza 31.

detached from their commitment to local charity or physical care. Rather, it is to highlight that the province had developed concomitant spiritual and contemplative interests alongside its traditional institutional focus on redemptive and corporal works of mercy, in a period when English ties to traditional Trinitarian ransom work had lessened. These interests coalesced with the late medieval spiritual economy and essentially revived – but also rewrote – the founding purpose of the order in such a way that it could continue to be celebrated and mandated in late medieval England.

A CONFLICTING MODEL OF INSPIRATIONAL SANCTITY? THE MIDDLE ENGLISH *LIFE*

In contrast to the image of Robert presented in *De nobilitate*, the hermit's active charity is given particular emphasis in the near-contemporary Middle English translation of his legend, the fifth-to-last item in the Egerton manuscript.[75] Written in octosyllabic couplets, this text opens in the style of a romance and is addressed to a fictional audience of (apparently noble) feasting 'frendes' (line 35), who may be synonymous with literate gentry or upper mercantile members of the Trinitarian confraternity.[76] The text's narrator appears to hope to cajole his audience into parting with their 'bred' for the benefit of the poor: 'Partte a porcioun vnto the pore / Sway dyd Sayntt Robert att hys dore', perhaps a metaphorical petition for charitable donations to the Trinitarian cause.[77] Here in the vernacular, however, Robert's eremitic charisma is expressed not simply according to the traditional trope of the *miles Christi*, but also in the language of secular heroism, such that the saint is presented in chivalric terms as a figure who outshines 'Arthure, Ector, and Achilles' (line 39). Robert is even labelled 'Cheftane and chefe of charite' (line 74) and thus his charity is presented in secular terms as something worthy of lay imitation.

---

[75] Dated to the late fourteenth or fifteenth centuries in Bazire, ed., *Metrical Life*, 15.

[76] *Life*, lines 35–46. Trinitarian confraternity letters were obtained by members of these social strata. See the list of individuals mentioned in Clark-Maxwell, 'Some further Letters', 212–13; Raluca Radulescu, 'Literature', in eadem and Alison Truelove, eds, *Gentry Culture in Late Medieval England* (Manchester, 2005), 100–18.

[77] *Life*, lines 285–96 (quotation at lines 291–2); Matthew Woodcock, 'Crossovers and Afterlife', in Sarah Salih, ed., *A Companion to Middle English Hagiography* (Cambridge, 2006), 141–56.

The Egerton manuscript thus seems to be bookended by two radically different late medieval versions of Robert's life: one in Latin verse, which minimizes Robert's care for the poor and seems to have been intended for internal consumption at Knaresborough Priory, offering a more spiritual interpretation of the Trinitarian *raison d'être*; the other written in the vernacular, also in verse, and intended for circulation outside the priory, to elaborate Robert's story for a secular audience of would-be patrons who might be inspired to imitate Robert's exemplary active charity and to support the Trinitarian cause financially. While the depictions of Robert in these texts exist, ostensibly, in tension with one another, when read in the context of English Trinitarian investment in the late medieval spiritual economy they can also be considered complementary narratives, both designed to support and add spiritual value to secular engagement with St Robert's cult and his Trinitarian shrine-keepers. Despite an early Trinitarian impulse to bring Robert's life in line with order's corporate and charitable values, then, the hermit's borderline transgressive (but nevertheless inspirational) holy legacy was never bound too rigidly by his hagiographers. Indeed, Trinitarian institutionalization of Robert's charismatic authority at Knaresborough was inherently and continuously unstable, a quality that allowed the inspirational and generative force of his spirit to continue exercising itself textually during the fourteenth and fifteenth centuries, in contending yet complementary ways in both sacred and secular spheres. In sum, among the Trinitarians at Knaresborough, Robert's charisma facilitated a spiritual flourishing and a late medieval institutional reinvention of redemption that is quite at odds with narratives of English Trinitarian marginality and decline.

A Church 'without stain or wrinkle': The Reception and Application of Donatist Arguments in Debates Over Priestly Purity

Helen Parish*

University of Reading

This article examines the reception and application of arguments developed during the Donatist controversy in later debates over clerical celibacy, marriage and continence in the medieval and early modern church. It explores the collision of inspiration and institution in this context, arguing that the debates over sacerdotal celibacy in the medieval Latin church and Reformation controversy over clerical marriage and continence both appropriated and polemicized the history of Donatism. The way in which the spectre and lexicon of Donatism permeated the law and practice of the medieval and early modern church, particularly when it came to the discipline of clerical celibacy, is a prime example of the process of imbrication by which the history of heresy and the history of the church were constructed. As such, it exemplifies the ways in which forms of religious inspiration that manifested as dissent, such as Donatism, became embedded in the histories and self-fashioning of the institutional church.

The history and meaning of 'Donatism' in the later Western church were not the result of direct encounter with a community of believers who used such a vocabulary to describe themselves. Rather, the use of this term represented the outworking of a language that originated in the condemnation of Donatism by its opponents, and in the appropriation of that same condemnation by subsequent generations of theologians and history-writers who sought to polemicize an increasingly unfamiliar language to their own ends. This process was at work both during the period of the Gregorian reform in the Latin church and in the construction of an evangelical history of the medieval church at the hands of Reformation polemicists and martyrologists.

* Department of History, University of Reading, Whiteknights, Reading RG6 6AH. E-mail: h.l.parish@reading.ac.uk.

Studies in Church History 57 (2021), 96–119 © The Author(s), 2021. Published by Cambridge University Press on behalf of Ecclesiastical History Society. This is an Open Access article, distributed under the terms of the Creative Commons Attribution licence (http://creative commons.org/licenses/by/4.0/), which permits unrestricted re-use, distribution, and reproduction in any medium, provided the original work is properly cited.
doi: 10.1017/stc.2021.6

The search for an answer to the question 'Where was your church before Luther?' was the driver behind the reimaging of the history of heresy in order to provide a location for evangelicalism within what Bruce Gordon has described as 'the expanse of Christian history'.[1] The creation of a chain of 'godly witnesses' to the faith was a vital component in the construction of a history, identity and collective memory for the nascent evangelical churches, bringing the past into the present and the present into the past.[2] This was a narrative of history that was distinctive in its anchor in doctrine, testimony to the long ancestry of true belief. In John Foxe's *Acts and Monuments*, each martyr was a link in a chain, a member of a community that existed in past and present and within which there was a commonality of belief. Those individuals who had been condemned by the church as heretics were 'the bricks and mortar with which he construct[ed] an image of the church and the lives of faithful Protestants'.[3] The writing of medieval heresy was contoured by the confessionalized histories of the church produced in the same period. Representations of heresy, schism and dissent in such a schema were simultaneously more nuanced and more normative, dependent upon the exploitation of surviving sources (themselves far from objective) to enable the polemicization of the past.[4]

---

[1] Bruce Gordon, 'The Changing Face of Protestant History and Identity in the Sixteenth Century', in idem, ed., *Protestant History and Identity in Sixteenth-Century Europe*, 2 vols (Aldershot, 1996), 1: 1–22, at 3; S. J. Barnett, 'Where was your Church before Luther? Claims for the Antiquity of Protestantism Examined', *ChH* 68 (1999), 14–41.

[2] John R. Knott, 'John Foxe and the Joy of Suffering', *SCJ* 27 (1996), 721–34.

[3] I. Ross Bartlett, 'John Foxe as Hagiographer: The Question Revisited', *SCJ* 26 (1995), 772; Susan Royal, 'English Evangelical Histories on the Origins of "the Reformation"', *Études Épistémè* 32 (2017), [online journal], at: <https://doi.org/10.4000/episteme. 1859>, accessed 15 November 2020.

[4] Luke Racaut, *Hatred in Print: Catholic Propaganda and Protestant Identity during the French Wars of Religion* (Aldershot, 2002); Yves Krumenacker, 'The Use of History by French Protestants and its Impact on Protestant Historiography', in Bernd-Christian Otto, Susanne Rau and Jörg Rüpke, eds, *History and Religion: Narrating a Religious Past* (Berlin and Boston, MA, 2015), 189–202; Bertrand van Ruymbeke, 'Minority Survival: The Huguenot Paradigm in France and the Diaspora', in idem and Randy J. Sparks, eds, *Memory and Identity: The Huguenots in France and the Atlantic Diaspora* (Columbia, SC, 2003), 1–25; Bethany Hume, 'The Idea of Medieval Heresy in Early Modern France' (PhD dissertation, University of York, 2019); Deborah Shulevitz, 'Historiography of Heresy: The Debate over "Catharism" in Medieval Languedoc', *History Compass* 17/1 (2019), [online journal], at: <https://doi.org/10.1111/hic3. 12513>, accessed 15 November 2020; Antonio Sennis, ed., *Cathars in Question*

In this context, it is hard to separate the early history of Donatism, or indeed any heresy, from the inescapable tendency of doctrinal deviance to become first a label and then a pejorative slur. Ali Bonner's recent analysis of the history of Pelagianism treats that heresy as a construct of Augustine rather than Pelagius; the same process is also seen at work in the construction of Arianism and Gnosticism.[5] Any history of Donatism and its legacy is similarly non-linear and untidy, but despite (or perhaps because of) that, it provides an illuminating illustration of the ways in which a rhetoric of dissent, opposition and separatism could become embedded in the structures of the visible, institutional church. The existence or otherwise of a fundamental connection between doctrinal and sacramental purity was a critical component in the solidification of the Donatist schism. In the eyes of the Donatists, those bishops and clergy who during periods of imperial persecution had renounced their faith and handed over the Scriptures to the authorities (and were therefore criticized by the Donatists as *traditores*) had been rendered impure by their actions; to allow such impurity to intermingle with the purity of the Donatist sect was to tolerate sin, and the presence of sin in the sacraments that lay at the very heart of the true church. If the ordination of clergy by the *traditor* bishops was invalid, then their errors also permeated the sacraments of baptism and the eucharist, casting doubt upon their validity and efficacy. In the Donatist schism (and the responses to it) we can see elements of what was to become an enduring debate about the relationship between the sacraments and the personal moral and spiritual standing of the celebrant, a debate that was eventually to crystallize around the assertion that the validity

---

(Woodbridge, 2016); R. I. Moore, *The War on Heresy: Faith and Power in Medieval Europe* (London, 2012).

[5] John Arnold, *Inquisition and Power: Catharism and the Confessing Subject in Medieval Languedoc* (Philadelphia, PA, 2001); Caterina Bruschi, '"Magna diligentia est habenda per inquisitorem": Precautions before Reading Doat 21–26', in eadem and Peter Biller, eds, *Texts and the Repression of Medieval Heresy* (Woodbridge, 2003), 81–110; Shulevitz, 'Historiography'; Monique Zerner, *Inventer l'hérésie? Discours polémiques et pouvoirs avant l'Inquisition* (Turnhout, 1998); Ali Bonner, *The Myth of Pelagianism* (Oxford, 2018); David M. Gwynn, 'From Iconoclasm to Arianism: The Construction of Christian Tradition in the Iconoclast Controversy', *Greek, Roman and Byzantine Studies* 47 (2007), 225–51; idem, *The Eusebians: The Polemic of Athanasius of Alexandria and the Construction of the 'Arian Controversy'* (Oxford, 2006), 169–244, 'The "Arianism" of the "Eusebians"'.

of the sacraments was not anchored in the conduct and conscience of the priest, but existed rather *ex opere operato*, by virtue of the work carried out.[6] The debates unleashed both within Donatism and between Donatists and their critics were woven into the fabric of the medieval Catholic Church, providing a language of priestly purity and pollution that remained with the church in the centuries that followed.[7]

But if the debate was enduring, its origins remained opaque. References to Donatism in medieval and Reformation sources demonstrate the extent to which the term 'Donatist' could be imbued with a meaning that was far from specific. The Donatism that existed within the pages of medieval and early modern controversy was far broader than that which had been described by St Augustine, indicating that the term had become a polemical shorthand for a set of beliefs that were far from consistent. The heresy was known and recognized, but rarely encountered first-hand, by those who exploited its multiple messages. Was it the case that Donatism influenced later debates over priestly purity because the Donatist controversy was still, centuries later, common theological currency? Or (perhaps more likely) did subsequent generations devise their own definition of Donatism in order to press a familiar name into service in order to condemn their opponents, as, for example, in the debates over clerical marriage in the mid-sixteenth century? The history of Donatism was repeatedly (re)written and (re)applied by those who had had no direct contact with the movement, and that seemingly flawed and fluid history is a rich example of the manipulation of the narratives of the past in the service of the needs of the present.

---

[6] Jesse Hoover, 'They bee Full Donatists', *Reformation & Renaissance Review* 15 (2013), 154–76.

[7] For fuller discussion of the early history of Donatism, and particularly its construction at the hands of St Augustine, see Paul Keresztes, *Imperial Rome and the Christians: From the Severi to Constantine the Great*, 2 vols (Lanham, MD, 1989), 2: 67–83; Eusebius of Caesarea, *The Ecclesiastical History*, trans. Kirsopp Lake, 2 vols, Loeb Classical Library (London, 1926), 447–61; W. H. C. Frend, *The Early Church* (London, 1965), 116; Brent D. Shaw, *Sacred Violence: African Christians and Sectarian Hatred in the Age of Augustine* (Cambridge, 2011); Maureen A. Tilley, trans., *Donatist Martyr Stories: The Church in Conflict in Roman North Africa* (Liverpool, 1997); eadem, 'Dilatory Donatists or Procrastinating Catholics: The Trial at the Conference of Carthage', *ChH* 60 (1991), 7–19; eadem, 'Sustaining Donatist Self-Identity: From the Church of the Martyrs to the Collecta of the Desert', *JECS* 5 (1997), 21–35; eadem, 'Redefining Donatism: Moving Forward', *Augustinian Studies* 42 (2011), 21–32; Richard Miles, ed., *The Donatist Schism: Controversy and Contexts* (Liverpool, 2016).

It is in the debate over the connection between the purity of the priesthood and the efficacy of the sacraments that the shadow of Donatism and other such heresies, real or imagined, in the later medieval church is most visible. As Henry C. Lea observed in his (albeit rather polemical) history of clerical celibacy, 'the hateful name of Manichaean acquired a sinister notoriety which maintained its significance for a thousand years'.[8] Like Donatism, Manicheanism exerted a substantial influence over the growth of asceticism and the rhetoric of priestly purity in the institutional church. Similar connections between the repression of dissent in the early church and the subsequent construction of histories of heresy have been raised more recently in Ali Bonner's discussion of what she describes as the 'myth' of Pelagianism. Simply put, Bonner argues, Pelagius was not Pelagian; the moral and theological tenets attributed to Pelagianism were acquired rather later in its history, and as part of a conscious desire to invent heresy in order to define and relocate orthodoxy.[9] We can observe the same evolutionary trajectory in the punctual and systemic presence of Donatism within the dialogues of the medieval and early modern churches. Whether or not Donatism existed with a historical reality, the 'intuitive practicality' of even the most inconsistent narratives of heresy rendered them real in the language of doctrinal debate. Bonner's contention that the term 'Pelagian' should be abandoned altogether 'because it introduces a faulty paradigm into every sentence in which it is used' is certainly compelling, and applies not only to Pelagianism but also to Donatism.[10] But even if the model of the nature and impact of heresy is erroneous, there is still much that we can learn from the perpetual and polemical (re)construction of that error.

The way in which the spectre and lexicon of Donatism permeated the law and practice of the medieval church, particularly when it came to the discipline of clerical celibacy, is a prime example of the process of imbrication by which the history of heresy was constructed. Debates over the purity of the priesthood were embedded in the reforming culture of the eleventh-century church. In the mid-eleventh century, the Patarines of Milan launched a violent campaign

---

[8] Henry C. Lea, *History of Sacerdotal Celibacy in the Christian Church*, 2 vols (London, 1904), 1: 33.

[9] Bonner, *Pelagianism*, 26–8.

[10] Ibid. 305.

to expel simoniacal and married priests from the church, a campaign that culminated in the deposition of the bishop of Milan on grounds of simony. The Patarines, as Janine Larmon Peterson has observed, argued that only the virtuous and morally pure had the right to judge other Christians, a belief that resonated with early Donatist ideas that the catholic church had condemned, but which had not entirely disappeared. The label Patarine, like Donatist, came to designate a loosely defined form of heresy, although its arguments became largely ineffectual in the face of inquisitorial process. As Lucy Bosworth has demonstrated, catalogues of heresies that had their roots in the early church were a mainstay of medieval writing on the history of heresy, and encouraged a tendency to see the roots of all heresy in the nascent Christian church.[11] The actions of the Patarines did not have papal sanction, but the language that they used to denounce clerical simony and unchastity certainly chimed with the voices and vocabulary of the ecclesiastical reformers of the eleventh century. Cardinal Humbert's *Three Books against the Simoniacs* called on princes and laymen to address the damage that the sale of offices had caused to the church, and encouraged the faithful to absent themselves from masses celebrated by simoniac priests. In the first instance, the debate over sacramental obligation was confined to its connection with simony, but by the end of the century the focus had shifted to the sacraments of the 'schismatics' who had backed the emperor and the antipope against Gregory VII.[12] Here, in the views of the imperialist party expressed by Wibert of Ravenna, we see language akin to Augustine's defence of the validity of the sacraments of the *traditor* clergy against the objection of the Donatists. Denouncing the views of Hildebrand (Gregory VII), Wibert complained that it was the pope who was schismatic, precisely because he 'taught that the sacraments of unworthy and excommunicate priests were polluted ... [and] commanded that they were not to be received and indeed forbade them to be called sacraments'.[13]

---

[11] Janine Larmon Peterson, *Suspect Saints and Holy Heretics: Disputed Sanctity and Communal Identity in Late Medieval Italy* (Ithaca, NY, 2019), 155–6; Lucy Bosworth, 'Perceptions of the Origins and Causes of Heresy in Medieval Heresiology' (PhD thesis, University of Edinburgh, 1995).

[12] I. S. Robinson, 'Reform and the Church, 1073–1122', in David Luscombe and Jonathan Riley-Smith, eds, *New Cambridge Medieval History*, 4: *c.1024–c.1198*, Part 1 (Cambridge, 2004), 268–334, at 307–10.

[13] *On the Schism of Hildebrand*, quoted in Robinson, 'Reform', 310.

The link with Donatism here was far from fully formed, but the exchanges provide evidence of the appropriation of earlier heresies, and the condemnation of such beliefs, to prove the error inherent in the opposing view.

Gregory was swift to reject such allegations, but we can hear echoes of that same connection between moral error and sacramental participation in demands that priests, deacons and subdeacons who were guilty of the 'sin of fornication' should not be permitted to enter churches without first doing penance, and the accompanying instruction that the laity were to withdraw from the sacraments of such priests, 'because their blessing is turned into a curse and their prayer into a sin'. The language of this debate was resonant with references to the heresies of the early church. Humbert referred to married priests as 'Nicolaitans', a sect characterized by moral depravity (Revelation 2),[14] while Peter Damian described both clerical marriage and incontinence as fornication and a 'foul commerce', asserting that 'they are rightly called Nicolates when they defend their death-bringing plague as though by authority'. The genealogy of the debate over clerical marriage was not yet fully formed, but the desire to locate the controversy firmly within the history of the early church is evident.[15]

This connection between theological corruption and carnal concupiscence was neither novel nor unique to the debate over clerical marriage; such language punctuated the denunciations of other medieval heresies, including Waldensianism, the Cathars, the Beguines and even the Publicani.[16] Indeed the proliferation of such judgements contributes to the challenge of identifying the precise origins of such ideas. And as recent historians of medieval heresies have reminded us, the force and impact of such accusations was not simply to justify the persecution of morally depraved heretics, but also to define and enforce a normative pattern of belief and behaviour within Western Christendom and orthodox Christian society. The consequence – and perhaps even the intention – was the compilation of a profile of dissent that, once defined, served either to define orthodoxy and protect it from the pollution of doctrinal and moral error or

[14] C. N. L. Brooke, *Medieval Church and Society* (London, 1971), 72–3.
[15] H. E. J. Cowdrey, *Pope Gregory VII, 1073–1085* (Oxford, 1998), 283.
[16] Walter Wakefield and Austin Evans, *Heresies of the High Middle Ages* (Columbia, SC, 1969), 220, 101.

to create a fear of such pollution that then became a means of impos-
ing order and defending the boundaries of Christian orthodoxy.[17]

How high was the step from the instructions in conciliar legislation
to depose simoniacs and withdraw from the sacraments of married or
unchaste priests to a more iconoclastic assertion that those clergy who
were tainted with the sins of simony and fornication were capable of
spreading that pollution via their sacramental celebration? The articulation of connections between clerical unchastity and the efficacy or
value of the eucharistic celebration deployed a language that was common to the leaders of reform and to other forms of devotional and
pastoral writing, as well as the literature of complaint.[18] Humbert's
denunciation of the married clergy of the Eastern Church is a case
in point: these priests, he argued, were so 'completely enervated
and exhausted by the recent pleasures of the flesh and thinking in
the midst of the holy sacrifice about how to pleasure their wives,
they handle the immaculate body of Christ and distribute it to the
people. Immediately afterward they turn their sanctified hands to
touch the limbs of women.'[19] The horrifying image of the priest
whose hands touched both the body of Christ and the body of a
whore was exploited to the full by Peter Damian in his assertion
that bodily purity was a necessary part of priestly function.[20]
However, even Peter Damian stopped short of asserting that the
validity or efficacy of the sacrament was connected to the moral standing of the celebrant.[21] Nonetheless, as Louis Hamilton has argued,
the debates over simony and nicolaitism in the eleventh century
did not result in a triumph for the Augustinian view. The controversy
placed Donatism at the centre of the debate, and the outcome was in
fact a practical triumph for the 'Donatist' position. Damian was a

---

[17] Robert I. Moore, *The Formation of a Persecuting Society: Power and Deviance in Western
Europe, 950–1250* (Oxford, 1987); Mary Douglas, *Purity and Danger: An Analysis of the
Concept of Pollution and Taboo* (London, 2002).
[18] Phyllis G. Jestice, 'Why Celibacy? Odo of Cluny and the Development of a new Sexual
Morality', in Michael Frassetto, ed, *Medieval Purity and Piety: Essays on Medieval Celibacy
and Religious Reform* (New York, 1998), 81–115.
[19] Humbert of Romans, *Contra Nicetam* (PG 143, 1000), quoted in Amy Remensnyder,
'Pollution, Purity and Peace: An Aspect of Social Reform between the Late Tenth Century
and 1076', in Thomas Head and Richard Landes, eds, *The Peace of God: Social Violence
and the Religious Response in France around the Year 1000* (Ithaca, NY, 1992), 280–307, at
301.
[20] Remensnyder, 'Pollution, Purity and Peace', 301.
[21] R. I. Moore, *The Origins of European Dissent* (Oxford, 1985), 60–1.

perceptive reader of Augustine, but still capable of confusing the issue of sacramental efficacy by fluctuating between the assertion of a link between the validity of the sacrament and priestly purity and the denial that such a link existed. In the Patarine affair, moderation triumphed, but after Damian's death the Donatist position re-emerged, particularly in debates over the dedication of churches.[22]

In general it was agreed that incontinent priests committed sacrilege, but did not diminish the sacrament.[23] In 1382, the Blackfriars Council condemned explicitly the proposition that 'a bishop or priest in mortal sin does not ordain, consecrate or baptize', derived from the writings of John Wycliffe.[24] The propositions that were condemned at that council informed the more general condemnation of Wycliffe's theology at the Council of Constance in 1415 as part of its proceedings against Jan Hus. The condemnation at Constance did not reflect the entirety, or the nuances, of Wycliffe's thinking on the connection between the morality of the priest and the ministration of the sacraments, but by using this particular phrasing, the council clearly recognized the potency of the language and its implications.[25] The demand that priests should forsake the corruption of worldly concerns in order to focus on the spiritual concerns of the *lex Christi* was not tied to the efficacy of the eucharist alone; Wycliffe's commentary on the 'mortal sin' of bishops and priests extended into a broader denunciation of the nature and impact of corruption as a disease that infected the church, and which should excised in the same way as a surgeon would remove a tumour. Such language, in the eyes of his critics, echoed the assertions that had been condemned in Donatism.[26] Wycliffe adopted a more conciliatory tone in *De Ecclesia* and the *Sermones*, in which he argued that priests in a state of mortal sin might indeed minister to the faithful, but 'damnably'. The *Decretum* was invoked by Wycliffe to defend the proposition that

[22] Louis Hamilton, 'Sexual Purity, "the Faithful" and Religious Reform in Eleventh Century Italy: Donatism Revisited', in John Doody, Kevin Hughes and Kim Paffenroth, eds, *Augustine and Pollution* (Oxford, 2005), 237–60.
[23] Helen Parish, *Clerical Marriage and the English Reformation: Precedent, Policy and Practice* (Aldershot, 2000), 167–8.
[24] Peter Marshall, *The Catholic Priesthood and the English Reformation* (Oxford, 1994), 48.
[25] Walter W. Shirley, ed., *Fasciculi Zizaniorum magistri Johannis Wyclif cum tritico*, RS 5 (London, 1858), 277–82.
[26] Ian Levy, 'Was John Wyclif's Theology of the Eucharist Donatistic?', *Scottish Journal of Theology* 53 (2000), 137–53.

God's grace could be conferred through 'both good and evil ministers, without imperilling the faithful'.[27] However, his continued
and vehement criticism of clerical immorality did not establish a
clear distance between Wycliffe's understanding of the connection
between priestly morality and sacramental efficacy, and that of the
Donatist heresy, or at least the historical construction of that heresy.
In England, the persecution of Lollard heresies exposed the extent to
which anxieties about the connection between clerical morality and
sacramental efficacy had come to punctuate the rhetoric of anticleri-
calism and anti-sacerdotalism. In 1426, the Franciscan Thomas
Richmond was required to retract the opinion that 'a priest in mortal
sin does not consecrate the body of Christ'.[28] This assertion certainly
featured prominently in the Lollard heresy trials. Even considering
the extent to which such comments were elicited by specific question-
ing that imposed the concerns of the institutional church upon a
more disparate set of beliefs, sacramental efficacy was not only a matter for the theologians. That much was recognized in the vernacular
polemic of the early sixteenth century. Thomas More, in the *Dialogue
Concerning Heresies*, launched a spirited attack on the assertion that
the sacramental ministry of a priest in sin might be ineffective.
'That sacred sacrifice and sweet oblation of Christ's holy body offered
up by his office, can take none impairing by the filth of his sin,' More
argued against the Messenger, 'and is to God as acceptable and to us
as available for the thing itself, as though it were offered by a better
man.'[29] That such a discussion took place within the structure of the
Dialogue is perhaps indicative of the extent to which the opinion
articulated by the Messenger was assumed to reflect a more widely
held belief.

Such imagery and narratives used the same language as had been
used by the Donatists, but, it is important to note, without the same
intent to assert that the sacraments of immoral clergy were tainted
and rendered invalid. However, the issue could be emotive. Priestly
incontinence, it was suggested, was not just morally indefensible, but
capable of ripping apart or even crucifying the body of Christ, who

---

[27] John Wycliffe, *De Ecclesia* 19; *De Antichristo* 48. For a fuller discussion, see Anthony
Kenny, *Wyclif* (Oxford, 1985), 71–3.
[28] '[S]acerdos in peccato mortali lapsus, non est sacerdos': D. Wilkins, *Concilia Magnae
Britanniae et Hiberniae*, 2 vols (London, 1737), 2: 488.
[29] Thomas More, *A Dialogue concerning Heresies*, ed. Thomas M. C. Lawler, Germain
Marc'hadour and Richard C. Marius, CWTM 6 (New Haven, CT, 1981), 299.

appeared with torn clothes or bleeding wounds in the visions of unchaste clerics who had chosen to celebrate mass.[30] As the cult of the eucharist became embedded in popular devotional practice, a genre of *miracula* in which Christ appeared physically on the altar could readily accommodate eucharistic miracle stories in which the transformation of the bread and wine became a trope for assessing the moral purity, or otherwise, of the priest. Unworthy priests who celebrated mass were reminded of their obligation to lead a pure and chaste life by a consecrated host that turned to coal in their mouth, or by the appearance of a human finger that removed the host from the unclean hands of the priest at the moment of consecration.[31]

In particular, eucharistic visions experienced by female saints at the elevation became, in Caroline Walker Bynum's phrase, 'a kind of litmus test for clerical immortality or negligence', from which the inescapable (if still theologically controversial) conclusion was that any unusual occurrences could be attributed to the incontinence of the priest who approached the altar with unclean hands.[32] A eucharistic miracle recorded in the Cistercian *Exordium Magnum* described the experience of a monk present at a mass celebrated by an 'unchaste and dissolute' priest: the monk observed that whenever the priest turned to face the congregation, a holy child would appear upon the altar, and then rush to hide behind the chalice 'as if avoiding the priest's unclean breath' when the celebrant turned to the altar.[33] *Miracula* of this type were not reserved for the clergy alone. Lay men and women who received the eucharist while in a state of sin were reported to have choked, witnessed the host fly out of their mouths, experienced demonic torture or observed the host bleed.[34] How much more telling were these miracles if they involved priests?

There is a question to ask here about the extent to which the theoretical distinction between defects in the chastity of the priesthood and defects in sacramental ministry was recognized and understood

[30] Remensnyder, 'Pollution', 297 n. 65.

[31] Miri Rubin, *Corpus Christi: The Eucharist in Late Medieval Culture* (Cambridge, 1991), 125.

[32] Caroline Walker Bynum, *Holy Feast and Holy Fast: The Religious Significance of Food to Medieval Women* (Berkeley, CA, 1987).

[33] Stephen Justice, 'Eucharistic Miracle and Eucharistic Doubt', *Journal of Medieval and Early Modern Studies* 42 (2012), 307–32.

[34] Rubin, *Corpus Christi*, 125–6.

by the laity, particularly given instructions such as those issued at the Lateran Councils of the early twelfth century that the faithful should absent themselves from the masses of unchaste and simoniac priests. To do so on the basis that such sacraments were invalid looked very much like latent Donatism, but if that was not the intention, how widely was this understood?[35] Conciliar decrees and miracles of moral judgement may well have underpinned the kind of language that Peter Marshall observed in lay demands that a priest who prayed for their soul should be an 'honest man', a shorthand for an insistence on clerical continence.[36] Such anxiety and language was itself tied inextricably to the vocabulary that defined the priesthood in the late medieval church. As Marshall notes, the priest, and the priest alone, was permitted to '*touch* the body of Christ Jesus', and that distinction both described and imposed the separation of the priest from the laity.[37]

Dionysius the Carthusian's summary of the qualities demanded of the clergy was informed by this assertion that priests alone enjoyed such proximity to the most sacred. If purity was expected of all who would devote themselves to the service of God, how much more vital was it, Dionysius argued, to recognize that the true servants of Christ were those who 'ponyshed theyr fleshe' with abstinence from vice and concupiscence.[38] Priests, whose duty and vocation was to serve God with a pure heart and a chaste body, committed a grievous sin by conceding to the temptations of the flesh, 'for in the synne of the fleshe is the moste great & manifest turpitude bestlynes / dishonestie / and fylthynes', all of which distracted and detracted from the holy.[39] 'Wanton prestes' who continued in such living presented a poor example to the laity, but more importantly failed in their obligations towards that which was most sacred:

> In so much as that that holy ministerye of the altare is most pure / and the sacramentes of the churche be most clene and ghostly (especially the sacrament of the blessyd body of our lord) it is most vicyous and

---

[35] Malcolm Lambert, Medieval *Heresy: Popular Movements from Bogomil to Hus* (New York, 1977), 37.
[36] Marshall, *Catholic Priesthood*, 51–3, 161–2.
[37] Ibid. 44.
[38] Dionysius Carthusianus, *The lyfe of Prestes* (London, 1533), sigs B5r–v.
[39] Ibid., sigs C4v–5r.

inconuenie[n]t that the minystres of the church and altare / should so
precyous sacramentes defyle and corrupt.[40]

Dionysius invoked the authority of Levitical law to argue that the
injunction 'be ye holy for I am holy' was a necessary instruction to
the Catholic priesthood. In the sacrifice of the mass, priests encountered an obligation to 'be ware of all unlawful actes / that we may lyft
by clene handes unto almyghty god (which sayth) be you holy for
I am holy'.[41] The same passage was exploited by Thomas Martin
in his denunciation of clerical marriage in England in the middle of
the sixteenth century. Priests, he argued, were subject to the same
demands as those imposed in Levitical law.[42] If the priests of the
Old Testament abstained from their wives, the priests of the new
law were under an even greater obligation to chastity, not least
because while the law of Moses referred to the sacrifice of animals,
the discipline of the church referred to the sacrifice of the mass and
therefore Christ himself. In these circumstances, Thomas Martin
argued it was only right that 'Christian priestes which muste offer a
more worthy, a more noble, a more divine sacrifice, then all the
priestes of the olde lawe shoulde liue in perpetual chastitye'.[43]

Such language did not contradict the insistence that the validity of
the sacraments was not impaired by the imperfections of the clergy,
but it is clear that condemnations of the failure of the clergy to keep to
their obligation to celibacy was frequently couched in terms of the
dishonour which it caused to the sacrament, and to God. Priests
who were guilty of breaching their vows were accused of committing
sacrilege, as the author of *The Lyfe of Prestes* explained: 'It is callyd
sacrylege / for that it corruptyth holy ordre / by unworthy handelynge
and myscheuous abusyng that thyng that to god is consecrate'.[44] The
bodies of priests should have been the temples of God, but had
become instead the temples of the devil.[45] Such charges of

---

[40] Ibid., sigs C8r–v, G4v, C5r.

[41] Ibid., sig. F8r.

[42] Thomas Martin, *A Traictise declaring and plainly prouyng that the pretensed marriage of priestes, and professed persones, is no marriage but altogether unlawful* (London, 1554), sigs Ll4v, Mm1r.

[43] Ibid., sig. B4v, cf. Bb2v.

[44] Dionysius, *Lyfe of Prestes*, sigs D1r, G2v.

[45] Ibid., sig. H2r; a similar argument is made at sig. G7r using St Bernard's condemnation of a priest who should have been the 'sepulture of the blessyd body of Chryst', but
had fallen from purity.

profanation were repeated elsewhere. In *Dives and Pauper*, the character of Pauper explained that while there were many different degrees of lechery, clerical immorality was the one most worthy of particular opprobrium on the grounds that those who broke their chastity were guilty not only of adultery, but also of sacrilege and treachery.[46] The fact that Christ was still present in the elements consecrated by such priests did not lessen the serious nature of their transgression; indeed the sin was worsened by the fact that Christ was present and thus dishonoured.

As we have seen, potent intersections existed between such rhetoric, a burgeoning lay eucharistic piety and the visibility of narratives of unchaste clergy who presumed to handle the sacraments. The image of the concubinary priest who touched the consecrated elements with 'unclean' hands was a common theme not only in medieval Catholic, but also in later, evangelical, literature. Thomas Brunton, the bishop of Rochester, commended a priest who had refused to celebrate mass because he had slept with a concubine the previous night. The immoral conduct of the priest was not in question, but his decision to avoid handling the eucharistic elements while in a state of sin presented a pious but perhaps pastorally challenging message, given that the 'unclean' hands of the celebrant should not affect the sacrament itself. In pre-Reformation literature, the object of derision was the concubinary priest, but the image was later applied by Catholic polemicists to contact between married priests and their wives. Thomas Martin protested that the sacraments were treated with disdain in England, and had few doubts as to why this had situation had arisen. 'The cause of the which contempt', he argued, 'issued forth partly of the unreuerent and vncleane handling of the holy sacramentes by the old priestes, partlye also, & that most especially by the unlawful and most wicked marriages of the new ministers.'[47] The dishonour done to the sacraments by impure priests was matched, if not exceeded, by that inflicted by married clergy. But whether such concern about the 'honesty' or continence of a priest was genuinely indicative of a spirit of lay Donatism is a more complex question. In the centuries after its effective suppression, Donatism had become a convenient shorthand, or term of abuse, that was not always deeply rooted in the clash between Augustine and those

[46] Anon., *Dives and Pauper* (London, 1534), fol. 226r.
[47] Martin, *Pretensed Marriage*, sig. A4v.

that he defined as Donatists. The meaning of the heresy had become more broadly applicable, tied to concerns about clerical immorality, rather than to the specific challenges posed by Donatus and his followers to the structures of the church.

In their defence of the validity of the sacraments of incontinent priests, neither the councils of the church nor Catholic polemicists and pastoral writers proposed that clerical misconduct and immorality should be condoned, or that it was inconsequential. It was possible for a Corpus Christi sermon to assert that the character of the priest had no influence upon the efficacy of the sacraments, while at the same time reminding priests that they had received a gift from God 'þat he gaf neuer to no angele in Heuen: þat is forto make Godis body'.[48] The Council of Toledo (1302) had instructed that concubinary priests were to be deprived of the fruits of their benefices and suspended from office. In England, the Winchester Synod of 1308 took similar action against incontinent priests, and that same concern and language can be seen in the decrees of councils in Ravenna (1314), Toledo (1324), Florence (1346), Prague (1355) and Magdeburg (1370). By this point, any distinction between clerical marriage and clerical incontinence had been eroded; the language used was that of *concubine*, *focaria*, *solute* or *pedisseca*, suggesting that the focus of the problem had shifted to priestly immorality rather than illicit marriage per se.[49] The Franciscan preacher William Staunton denounced the behaviour of unchaste priests who had 'become most fowl in the Devil's service'.[50] John Colet condemned the 'abhominable impiety'of the multitude of the clergy, 'who fear not to rush from the bosom of some foul harlot into the temple of the church, to the altar of Christ, to the mysteries of God'.[51] Thomas More defended

---

[48] *Mirk's Festial: A Collection of Homilies by Johannes Mirkus*, ed. T. Erbe, EETS extra series 96 (London, 1905), 169.

[49] Jennifer Thibodeaux, 'Man of the Church or Man of the Village? Gender and Parish Clergy in Medieval Normandy', *Gender and History* 18 (2006), 380–99, at 388; J. Gaudemet, 'Le Celibat Ecclesiastique. Le Droit et la practique du XIe au XIIe siècle', *Zeitschrift der Savigny-Stiftung fur Rechtsgeschichte, Kanonistische Abteilung* 68 (1982), 1–31, especially 4–5; B. Schimmelpfennig, '*Ex Fornicatione Nati*: Studies on the Position of Priests' Sons from the Twelfth to the Fourteenth Century', *Studies in Medieval and Renaissance History* n.s. 2 (1980), 3–50, at 33–6.

[50] G. R. Owst, *Literature and Pulpit in Mediaeval England: A Neglected Chapter in the History of English Letters & of the English People* (Oxford, 1961), 247, 267.

[51] Dionysius, *Lyfe of Prestes*, sig. G7v; Christopher St German, *The Debellation of Salem and Bizance*, ed John Guy et al. (New Haven, CT, 1987), 379; Marshall, *Catholic Priesthood*, 46.

the efficacy of the sacraments of unchaste priest, but that defence was accompanied by the blunt judgement that although such sacraments were still channels of God's grace, 'yet he is with that priest's presumption highly discontented', because in such circumstances 'Christ is also betrayed into the hands of sinners'.[52] Priests who celebrated mass and handled the consecrated elements with unclean hands were, in a broad consensus, acting in a way that invited criticism that was of necessity more simplistic than any response. Into that gap between the outward character of the priest and their sacerdotal function, satire might readily intrude. Desiderius Erasmus, for example, complained that it was all too easy for a priest to adjourn to parties, gambling, hunting, idleness and other refuges of mankind only moments after standing at an altar at which 'angels wait upon' him.[53] The language of Erasmus was far from impotent, but was certainly more measured than that of some polemicists.

The malleability of the language that connected the theology of the eucharist with the moral standing of the priest was exploited ruthlessly by evangelical polemicists in the middle decades of the sixteenth century. Evangelical polemicists repeatedly invoked the idea that theological and moral corruption were coterminous, but it was in the discussion of the eucharist that the link was most clearly defined, precisely because the requirement to celibacy for the priesthood was so inextricably tied to the theology of the mass. In the (admittedly not entirely objective) eyes of John Bale, the theology of transubstantiation was itself fundamentally flawed by its association with Peter Lombard, a child of a nun, a suggestion that has the ring of fiction rather than fact.[54] Anthony Gilby asserted that transubstantiation was prima facie an erroneous doctrine because immoral priests could not be agents of the miraculous. God, Gilby argued, although omnipotent, 'wyll not be chaunged into any newe formes, by the mu m]bling and breathing of an whoremo[n]ger or sodomiticall priest'.[55] John Ramsey demanded that his Catholic opponents justify

[52] More, *Dialogue*, 299; More, *De Tristitia Christi*, 1: *The Valencia Manuscript: Facsimiles, Transcription, and Translation*, ed. Clarence H. Miller, CWTM 14/1 (New Haven, CT, 1976), 351.

[53] Marshall, *Catholic Priesthood*, 46 n. 70.

[54] John Bale, *A Mysterye of Iniquyte Contayned within the Heretycall Genealogy of Ponce Pantolabus* (Antwerp, 1545), fol. 33v.

[55] Anthony Gilby, *An Ansvver to the Deuillish Detection of Stephane Gardiner* (London, 1547), sigs 56v–57r.

their claims that 'horemasters prestes, by their ministracio[n] so com / to alure Christ out of heaue[n] as me[n] do byrdes to twigges'.[56] Such views were common in the flurry of anti-mass tracts printed in England early in the reign of Edward VI. The anonymous author of *The v. abhominable Blasphemies conteined in the Masse* argued that blasphemy was embedded in any assertion that the mass was a true sacrifice and oblation by which the priest and the participants could obtain forgiveness for their sin *ex opere operato*, because such a claim denied the merits of the sacrifice of Christ. Anti-sacerdotalism fuelled an argument that the nature of the Roman Catholic priesthood detracted from the eternal priesthood of Christ, not least in its implicit assumption that the death of Christ was not a sufficient atonement, but one which it was necessary to repeat daily.[57] The precedent enshrined in Levitical law that required priests to retain their ritual purity in order that they might offer sacrifices presented no justification for the existence of a celibate, sacrificing New Testament priesthood; with no material sacrifice to offer, and the abrogation of the old law and ministry by the priesthood of Christ, there was no need for such ritual cleanness. The question was less the extent to which priestly incontinence profaned the sacred, and more whether the doctrine of transubstantiation itself was a pollutant, a doctrinal error which defiled the holy.[58] A new relationship was posited between the morality of the priest and the actual theology of the eucharist; the unchaste priest did not impair the efficacy of the sacrament, but rather indicated the extent to which the very definition of the sacrament was flawed. Luke Shepherd used the name 'Philogamus', 'lover of women', to set the tone of *Pathose*, in which the base language and the supposed lascivious thoughts of the priest contributed to the mockery of both the mass and the celibate ideal. Idolatry and failed chastity were linked, with the allegation that unmarried priests were not only morally corrupt, but set up Priapus as their god.[59]

---

[56] John Ramsey, *A Plaister for a galled horse* (London, 1548), unpaginated.

[57] Anon., *The v. abhominable blasphemies conteined in the Masse* (London, 1548), sigs A2r, A5r–B7v; Nicholas Pocock, 'The Condition of Morals and Religious Belief in the Reign of Edward VI', *English Historical Review* 10 (1895), 417–44, at 419–21.

[58] Gilby, *Deuillish Detection*.

[59] 'Quod non estis Nupti / Eo plus Corrupti / Castum profitentes / Non custodientes / … Incestui cedentes / Lupi Existentes / Priapo servientes / In Deum statuentes': Luke Shepherd, *Pathose, or an Inward Passion of the Pope* (London, c.1548), sigs B1r–v; see

The character of 'Mistress Missa' featured prominently in evangelical polemic; a personification of the mass, frequently as a debauched woman, who condemned herself by her words and actions, and those of the unchaste priest in whose hands she was held. The feigned chastity of the priests supported the very deception contained within the mass itself, instituted 'vnder shadow and colour of holynesse, the more easely to seduce & deceyue the worlde'.[60] In Hugh Hilarie's work, the personification of the ass expressed indignation that she was denounced as 'a thefe and a God robber, An harlot and a spirituall whore'. In the same vein, William Turner suggested that the pope and the mass had then begotten several children, including 'missa de pro defunctis, missa pro pluuia, masse de nomine Jesu',[61] and a multitude of others. The sins of which the clergy were accused – avarice, idolatry and concupiscence – were present at the heart of Catholic eucharistic theology, as both the cause and the fruit of its theological error.

Predictably, evangelical polemicists were swift to exploit any putative connection between clerical misconduct and the theology of transubstantiation precisely because of the debates over the connection between the purity of the priesthood and sacramental efficacy. However, the use of the image of the mass as a debauched woman ensured that the mass emerged from the pages of polemical pamphlets as the root cause of the immorality of the clergy. It was the mass that encouraged, or even required that priests forswear marriage in favour of adultery and depravity. A pamphlet in 1528 depicted clergy lamenting the fall of the mass in Strasbourg, where it had been 'The chief vpholder of our liberte / whereby our whores a[n]d harlots euerychone / Were maytayned in ryche felicite.'[62] In Hugh Hilarie's tract, the mass openly admitted that although she had the power to make people marry, and 'gyue you housebands and wyues at my pleasure', she preferred her 'smered shauelynges' to remain unmarried.[63] Rather than being dishonoured by unchaste clergy,

---

also John N. King, *English Reformation Literature: The Tudor Origins of the Protestant Tradition* (Princeton, NJ, 1982), 269–70.

[60] Anthony Marcourt, *A Declaration of the Masse* (London, 1548) sigs A6v–7r.

[61] William Turner, *A Briefe Recantacion of maystres Missa* (London, 1548), sig. A3r.

[62] William Roy, *Rede me and be nott Wroth* (London, 1528), sigs A7r–A8v.

[63] Hugh Hilarie, *The Resurreccion of the Masse / with the wonderful vertus of the same* (Wesel, 1554), sigs A3r–v, Marcourt, *Declaration*, sig. E7r, cf. G4r.

the figure of the mass claimed that 'Nothyng defyleth me / but honest marryage', and took delight in the number of idle and immoral clergy that were raised 'to be makers of christes'.[64] Clerical immorality could be attributed directly to the Catholic theology of the eucharist, not only in the suggestion that it was the prohibition of clerical marriage which led priests to keep concubines, but also in the depiction of a personification of the mass that positively demanded that priests behave in this manner. From this point, it was argued that the mass should be abolished, not because the impurity of the priesthood impacted upon the efficacy of the sacrament, but because such a corrupt sacrament, as the root cause of clerical immorality, could not be a true vehicle of salvation.

It is possible to perceive here the legacy of that 'latent' Donatism that seemed to reside in the concerns of the faithful about the purity of the priesthood. But the persistence of those concerns is not in itself explicit evidence of the survival of Donatism into the era of the Reformation. However, it is clear that Donatism, and with it other early church heresies such as Montanism, Manichaeism and Pelagianism, still had a pivotal role to play in the polemical literature of the English Reformation, on both sides. That stalwart of the genre, Thomas More, in the second part of his doggedly determined and detailed *Confutation of Tyndale*, for example, appealed to the authority of the old Augustine to pass judgement on the evangelicals as new 'Donatystes ... such heretykes then in Affryke as these be now in Almayne'.[65] Stephen Gardiner, bishop of Winchester, turned to the condemnation of the Donatists in the early church in his defence of the Roman Catholic theology of the eucharist:

> ... accordyng herevnto S. Augustine againste the Donatistes geueth for a rule, the sacramētes to be one in all, although they be not one that receiue & vse them. Sainct Augustine hath these formal wordes in Latyn. *Corpus Domini, & sanguis Domini nihilominus erat etiam illis, quibus dicebat Apostolus: qui manducat indigne iudicium sibi māducat & bibit.* Which wordes be thus much in English. It was neuertheles the body of our Lorde, & the bloud of our Lorde also vnto them, to

---

[64] Hilarie, *Resurreccion*, sigs A3r, A8r.

[65] Thomas More, *The second parte of the co[n]futacion of Tyndals answere in whyche is also confuted the chyrche that Tyndale deuyseth. And the chyrche also that frere Barns deuyseth* (London, 1533), 331.

whom thappostel sayde, he that eateth vnworthely, eateth and drynketh iudgement to himselfe.[66]

Richard Smyth or Smith, Oxford's Regius Professor of Divinity, in his defence of traditional religion in the reign of Mary Tudor, compared evangelicals to Donatists, citing Augustine's condemnation of Donatist iconoclasm: 'here, & in many other places of alters, whiche our new brethren did cast down, as the heritikes called Donatistes did, which neuer christiā good man did'.[67] Robert Caly's 1554 edition of Vincent's *Way home to Christ* invoked the example of the Donatist schism and the division of the church that it threatened to create, this time as a judgement on the spread of evangelicalism. 'In the tyme of *Donate* that heretike of whom suche as maintaine his heresies be called Donatistes, what time a great part of Affricke ... forgettinge their religion and profession, preferred the cursed and blasphemous temeritie of one vayne man, before the vnitie of the churche'.[68] In a similar vein, John Churchson's *Brefe Treatise* asserted a connection between the divisions within the North African church caused by Donatus and the state of the English church in the 1550s.

> The scysmatycall churches be but partyculer multytudes in partyculer places, as the donatystes in Affryke, the hussytes in beame, the Lutherans in some certeyne prouinces of Germany, and the Sacramentaryes of late heare in Englande, wherfore it is most certaine, that our late particuler church, was not the church of Chryst, whyche is catholike that is to saye, vnyuersal thoroughoute all the vnyuersall world, as ye may perceyue by the promyse of God.[69]

The invocation of the dangers of Donatism was not the preserve of Catholic polemicists alone. John Bale situated the Donatist heresy

---

[66] Stephen Gardiner, *An explicatiō and assertion of the true Catholique fayth, touchyng the moost blessed Sacrament of the aulter with confutacion of a booke written agaynst the same* (Rouen, 1551), 78, 82.

[67] Richard Smith, *A bouclier of the catholike fayth of Christes church, conteynyng diuers matters now of late called into controuersy, by the newe gospellers* (London, 1554), 26. He was Regius Professor 1536–48, 1554–6 and during 1559.

[68] Robert Caly, *The waie home to Christ and truth leadinge from Antichrist and errour, made and set furth in the Latine tongue, by that famous and great clearke Vincent, Frenche man borne, aboue .xi. hundred yeres paste, for the comforte of all true Christian men, against the most pernitious and detestable crafte of heretikes* (London, 1554), unpaginated.

[69] John Churchson, *A brefe treatyse declaryng what and where the churche is, that it is knowen, and whereby it is tryed and known* (London, 1556), unpaginated.

firmly within the internal structure of his apocalyptic history of the age-old struggle between the true church and the false in the *Image of Both Churches*, listing the heresies unleashed at the opening of the third seal. 'Then arose heresies and scismes, sectes, and deuisions, and were spred the world ouer, lyke as ye histories mencioneth', Bale claimed, and 'the Donatistes helde it necessarie to bée rebaptised'.[70] 'The Papists agree also with the heretiques / named Donatistes', Bale argued in his *Apology*, citing the history of Donatism as evidence that the Roman Catholic Church had usurped the name of the apostles. The Catholic priesthood, he protested, adopted a lifestyle which was itself a form of Donatism, while at the same time using the language of Donatism to condemn the sacraments of married priests.[71] John Ponet, in his response to Stephen Gardiner, declared that 'the Papists agree also with the heretiques / named Donatistes'. scourging and punishing their flesh, and opposing clerical marriage.[72] Thomas Cranmer's *Confutation of Unwritten Verities* warned against the practice of withdrawal from communion and seeking the church in man's own righteousness, describing it as a Donatist heresy which had been condemned.[73] Cranmer was also willing to use the example of the Donatists to draw comparisons with sixteenth-century radicalism and sacramentarianism; as Jesse Hoover's work has shown, significant connections were made between Donatists (or at least the Donatists as they were constructed by their opponents) and religious radicalism in post-Reformation Europe, including Anabaptism and English separatism.[74] The Donatist epithet acquired multiple meanings in the debates of the Reformation, anchored in its doctrinal characteristics,

---

[70] John Bale, *The Image of both Churches, after the most wonderfull and heauenly Reuelation of sainct Iohn the Euangelist, contayning a very fruitfull exposition or Paraphrase vpon the same* (London, 1548), 74; Richard Bauckham, *Tudor Apocalypse: Sixteenth-Century Apocalypticism, Millenarianism, and the English Reformation* (Sutton Courtenay, 1978), 58; Leslie Fairfield, *John Bale, Mythmaker for the English Reformation* (Eugene, OR, 2006), 171.

[71] John Bale, *The apology of Iohan Bale agaynste a ranke papyst answering both hym and hys doctours, that neyther their vowes nor yet their priesthode areof [sic] the Gospell, but of Antichrist* (London, 1550), 108, 118, 127.

[72] John Ponet, *An apologie fully answering by Scriptures and aunceant Doctors / a blasphemose Book gatherid by D. Steph. Gardiner* (Strasbourg, 1556), 20, 45, 108.

[73] Thomas Cranmer, *A Confutatiō of vnwrittē verities / both bi the holye scriptures and moste auncient autors* (Wesel, 1556), unpaginated.

[74] Hoover, 'They bee Full Donatists'.

but exploiting the subversive and dangerous implications that the heresy had acquired in its long written history.

The vigour of such polemical language did not override the under-lying pastoral problem. Any reformed church that preserved a sacra-mental theology could not ignore entirely the connection between sacrament and ministry, and could no more allow the existence of con-cerns about the impact of clerical morality on sacramental efficacy than could its Roman Catholic opponents. As a result, arguments about the institutionalization of theological corruption were difficult to divorce from the kind of vocabulary used in Donatist objections to what they deemed to be the *traditor* church. Visitation articles from the mid-sixteenth century provide tantalizing glimpses into a lay anxiety that the character of the clergy might affect the validity of their sacra-ments. The specific question of 'whether any sayeth that the wicked-ness of the minister taketh away the effect of Christ's sacraments' suggests the existence of an anxiety that such beliefs existed.[75] As Hoover and Marshall have observed, such anxiety is likely to have been associated with broader concern about the presence of Anabaptism in the English church, rather than the existence of Donatism in sixteenth-century England. Nonetheless, the connection between the vocabulary used in Anabaptism, and in the condemnation of it, does provide some indication of the ways in which the history of the Donatist heresy was readily invoked in the context of such concerns about doctrinal diversity and separatism. Article 26 of the Thirty-Nine Articles certainly engages both with the language of the Donatist con-troversy and with the ongoing challenge presented by Anabaptism:

> Although in the visible Church the evil be ever mingled with the good, and sometimes the evil have chief authority in the Ministration of the Word and Sacraments, yet forasmuch as they do not the same in their own name, but in Christ's, and do minister by his commission and authority, we may use their Ministry, both in hearing the Word of God, and in the receiving of the Sacraments. Neither is the effect of Christ's ordinance taken away by their wickedness, nor the grace of God's gifts diminished from such as by faith and rightly do receive the Sacraments ministered unto them; which be effectual, because of Christ's institution and promise, although they be ministered by evil men.

[75] W. H. Frere, *Visitation Articles and Injunctions of the Period of the Reformation*, 2 vols (London, 1907), 2: 239.

The perpetual intermingling of the evil with the good in the community of the visible church was core to Augustine's argument against the Donatists, and the assertion that the sacraments administered by imperfect clergy were still received and effectual for the laity is indicative of an engagement with a much longer debate, and its lexicon, in the history of the church.[76]

In practical terms, the Donatist controversy and schism were, by the sixteenth century, a chronologically far distant period of discord from which the institutional Roman Catholic church had long since recovered. The inspiration that underpinned Donatist criticism of, and separation from, the North African church was the product of a particular political, social and devotional context in the region, conditions that did not pertain in other parts of Christian Europe in the centuries that followed. By the time of the Gregorian reform movement in the twelfth century, and even more so by the sixteenth century, Donatism was present in the institutional church not in a physical sense, but as a memory, as a vocabulary and as a convenient shorthand for dissent that was moralizing in its tone. It is at that level that the most obvious and interesting connections between institution and inspiration existed. The Donatist vision of the church was rich with a language of purity and holiness, rigorism and a deeply rooted desire to avoid contact with all, priests and practice, that had been tainted or polluted by accommodation with sin. That language resonated with the reforming impulses of the Gregorian papacy, but its use was effective, and possible, only because its connections with early Donatism were tenuous, rather than embedded in a heretical community that was visible in the eleventh-century church.

The original Donatist controversy was shaped by the rhetorical and theological construction of the priest as saint or sinner, a process of shaping that continued in discussions of purity and priesthood in the centuries that followed. That fraught relationship between inspiration and institution came to the fore in debates over the imposition of clerical celibacy and the escalation of expectation of clerical continence in the eleventh and twelfth centuries, but also in the debates over clerical marriage in the sixteenth. Debates over priestly purity in the medieval

---

[76] E. J. Bicknell, *A Theological Introduction to the Thirty-Nine Articles of the Church of England*, 3rd edn (London, 1955), 353; the same statement is made in Article 27 of the 42 Articles (1553).

and early modern church were informed by the same assumptions about the priesthood as the physical embodiment of the holiness of the church that had characterized Donatist thought. But the early history of Donatism was, to a large extent, written by those who had argued it out of existence, and then further polemicized by those who encountered the written record, not the material heresy. If the history of Donatism works at all as an example of the collision of inspiration and institution in the history of Christian priesthood, it is precisely because so much of its origins and early meaning had been distorted or lost. But in some ways, that makes its history all the more illuminating. Humbert, Damian, Hildebrand, the Waldensians, the collectors and promulgators of eucharistic miracle stories, lay testators who requested the services of honest priests, Bale, Gilby and Ramsay were not Donatists, but were all too aware of the polemical potential – and pitfalls – in invoking the language and legacy that had inspired that heresy in order to transform the institutional church.

The Institutionalization of the Congregational Singing of Metrical Psalms in the Elizabethan Reformation

Andrew Poxon*

Durham University

Previous scholarship has often employed the categories of 'voluntary' and 'established' religion when studying lay involvement in parish religion; yet these categories do not provide adequate space for the vitality of lay religious initiatives during the English Reformation. Through a study of the singing of metrical psalms, this article argues that the categories of 'inspiration' and 'institution' provide a more nuanced understanding of lay religious initiatives during the English Reformation. It outlines the ways in which the singing of metrical psalms, taken from the Sternhold and Hopkins Whole Booke of Psalmes, *moved from its origins in domestic devotions, through inspirational initiative, to become an institutionalized part of the worship of English congregations. This process developed over many years, coming to the fore during the reign of Elizabeth I, yet even once institutionalization had occurred, inspiration could still arise, providing fresh direction and development.*

In October 1559, the clergy of Exeter Cathedral complained to the royal visitors that a group from London who had travelled to attend a fair, along with some local sympathizers, had marched into the cathedral daily to sing psalms. The clergy protested about two things: their own worship was being disrupted, and (worse still) men and women were singing alongside one another, even sitting in the seats of the

* Department of Theology and Religion, Durham University, Abbey House, Palace Green, Durham, DH1 3RS. E-mail: andrew.r.poxon@durham.ac.uk. I would like to thank all those who asked questions or offered comments when the paper was first delivered. I also wish to thank the two anonymous reviewers and the editors, who offered criticisms and comments which have, I hope, made the article much stronger. I would like to thank in particular Christopher Marsh and Andrew Spicer for valuable comments and advice, and Alec Ryrie for reading through numerous drafts and offering sage guidance. I also wish to thank AHRC Northern Bridge for the funding which allowed the research in this article to take place.

Studies in Church History 57 (2021), 120–141   © The Author(s), 2021. Published by Cambridge University Press on behalf of Ecclesiastical History Society. This is an Open Access article, distributed under the terms of the Creative Commons Attribution licence (http://creativecommons.org/licenses/by/4.0/), which permits unrestricted re-use, distribution, and reproduction in any medium, provided the original work is properly cited.
doi: 10.1017/stc.2021.7

vicars choral. They did not, however, secure their desired outcome, since the lead visitor was none other than bishop-elect, John Jewel, who, rather than condemn the visitors, praised the laity for their desire 'to sing a Psalm for their greater comfort and better stirring up of their hearts to devotion ... according to the use and manner of the Primitive Church'. In turn, Jewel secured a letter from Archbishop Parker giving the psalm-singers his blessing.[1]

To the clergy of Exeter Cathedral, and no doubt many locals too, the singing of metrical psalms was a significant disruption to their normal order; an example of inspirational practices in conflict with the institutional worship to which the cathedral had become accustomed. Their complaints demonstrate that they viewed the singing as unacceptable and impulsive and assumed that the royal visitors would agree. Unfortunately for them, the singing of metrical psalms by men and women, in both congregational and domestic settings, had developed as a significant element in the worship of English exiles on the Continent during the reign of Mary I, and would increase in popularity and prominence throughout the reign of Elizabeth I.[2]

Previous scholarship has often employed the categories of 'voluntary' and 'official' religion when discussing such conflicts or lay religious initiatives more generally. Yet it is the argument of this article that the categories of 'institution' and 'inspiration' provide a more nuanced framework for understanding the English Reformation. Throughout this article 'inspirational' will be applied to practices, rituals or outworkings of faith which took place both in church and outside it, which may be performed or participated in by individuals or

---

[1] Herbert Reynolds, ed., *The Use of Exeter Cathedral* (London, 1891), 54, cited in Alec Ryrie, 'The Psalms and Confrontation in English and Scottish Protestantism', *ARG* 101 (2010), 114–37, at 125.

[2] Ian Green, *Print and Protestantism in Early Modern England* (Oxford, 2000), 503–52; idem, '"All people that on earth do dwell, Sing to the Lord with cheerful voice": Protestantism and Music in Early Modern England', in Simon Ditchfield, ed., *Christianity and Community in the West* (Aldershot, 2001), 148–64; Christopher Marsh, *Music and Society in Early Modern England* (Cambridge, 2010), 405–53; Jonathan Willis, *Church Music and Protestantism in Post-Reformation England: Discourses, Sites and Identities* (Farnham, 2010), 121–8; Beth Quitslund and Nicholas Temperley, *The Whole Book of Psalms, Collected into English Metre by Thomas Sternhold, John Hopkins, and Others: A Critical Edition of the Texts and Tunes*, 2 vols (Tempe, AZ, 2018), especially 2: 505–621. While her concern is principally with Scotland, see also Jane Dawson, '"The Word did everything": Readers, Singers and the Protestant Reformation in Scotland *c*.1560–*c*.1638', *Scottish Church History* 46 (2017), 1–37, especially 31–5.

groups, and which are not dependent on the leadership or approval of church authorities. 'Institution(al)' will be taken to refer to practices which were a regular, assumed part of the worship or religious experience of early modern people. The absence of such an institutionalized practice may disturb those who think this practice to be a normal part of their involvement and interaction with their religion and its outworking, whether individual or collective, parish-focused or not. Such practices may not have been officially mandated by the relevant authorities, yet nevertheless assumed a role in worship or religious experience which was akin to those practices which did receive this mandate. In this sense, an 'inspirational' practice could arise and over time become institutionalized, a process which is distinct from when, and whether, the practice was ever officially permitted or mandated.

Christopher Haigh's categories of Reformation from above and from below provide a helpful lens through which we can begin to understand the categories of 'inspiration' and 'institution'. In Haigh's account, the 'Reformation from above' model argued that the English Reformation was 'enforced from the centre by deliberate governmental action'.[3] While local government and authorities could provide the impetus for the imposition of these policies, or a block on them, and while 'Reformation from below' may subsequently have taken over, the Reformation was first and foremost directly mandated by those at the centre who held political power. This argument is regularly implied through the use of the term 'official' (as opposed to 'voluntary'), referring to those religious activities which received a mandate and were thus implemented in the localities, in theory if not necessarily in practice. Meanwhile the alternative perspective, namely 'Reformation from below', 'means that the new religion soon seized the imaginations of artisans and peasants'.[4] Haigh's terminology opens up the categories of inspiration and institution helpfully, and particularly the congruence between 'inspiration' and 'Reformation from below', in which the key impetus for reform comes from the common people, rather than through politically mandated changes.

---

[3] Christopher Haigh, 'The Recent Historiography of the English Reformation', in idem, ed., *The English Reformation Revised* (Cambridge, 1987), 19–33, at 20.
[4] Ibid. 24.

In the Exeter example above, we see inspiration operating for the clergy, since their view is that there is no official mandate for the practice of psalm singing, but also for the group from London since they nevertheless choose to sing psalms, in spite of the lack of official direction. We see the category of institution in the approach of the clergy who feel that the singing of metrical psalms does not fit with the form of worship to which they are accustomed, and yet for the group from London the singing of psalms has become institutionalized so that they now see it as an essential expression of worship. Haigh's categories are helpful here because we see the interaction of 'Reformation from above' in the cathedral's disrupted worship and 'Reformation from below' in the singing of psalms by the group from London. The latter category here reflects an inspirational practice – which is to say, not officially mandated – which had become institutionalized in the group's understanding of worship.

This article will use the singing of metrical psalms as a means of critiquing older categories of 'voluntary and 'established' and demonstrating that a framework based on 'inspiration' and 'institution' allows us to see that lay religious initiatives could develop and flourish, even in a period of religious uncertainty and strict control, eventually becoming institutionalized as practices which later came to be considered central parts of the worship of English congregations.

The Historiography of 'Voluntary' Religion

A full account of voluntary religion is offered in volume 23 of Studies in Church History. The editors, Bill Sheils and Diana Wood, define 'voluntary religion' as referring to those 'societies and associations which brought together groups of like-minded individuals for a religious purpose either within or without the life of the broader church', yet which, as Patrick Collinson noted in the introduction, 'at no time *claimed* to be churches, but professed to perform a role which their leaders and adherents understood to be complementary to that of the Church or churches, providing additional emotional satisfaction, social support and fellowship'.[5] Indeed, much of Collinson's work could be seen as an attempt to define and document the differences and similarities, as well as the relationship between voluntary and

---

[5] W. J. Sheils and Diana Wood, 'Preface', to eidem, eds, *Voluntary Religion*, SCH 23 (Oxford, 1986), viii; Patrick Collinson, 'Introduction', ibid. xii.

involuntary or compulsory religion during the English Reformation.[6] In particular, we may note his work on the differences between those 'groups' or 'communities' with separatist potential, whom historians loosely think of as 'puritans'.[7] It is, however, in the context of his work on the English conventicle that Collinson's assertions regarding voluntary religion are articulated most clearly.[8] Conventicles, he observes, were a form of voluntary religion in that members would meet together and learn, repeat, discuss, sing or hear what they wanted, or travel to other communities or parishes, enjoying fellowship alongside their attendance at the parish church.[9]

For all the power of Collinson's framework, it leaves open a number of questions which are important when we consider metrical psalmody. In particular, it does not allow us to address the kind of process by which the singing of metrical psalms moved from inspiration to become an institutionalized part of the worship of English congregations. Nor does it allow for the fluidity that characterized the singing of metrical psalms, as the practice moved from domestic, private devotions into parish worship – and back again – in the way that most other beliefs and practices of conventicles and puritans did not. And while voluntary religion for Shiels, Wood and Collinson is focused on 'groups' and 'communities' who met alongside their attendance at church, the singing of metrical psalms was equally a part of individual, private devotion, which then also attained a collective role in the worship of English congregations after the accession of Elizabeth I and the return of the Marian exiles.

---

[6] For the use of the term 'involuntary', see Collinson, 'Introduction', xii; Beat Kümin, 'Voluntary Religion and Reformation Change in Eight Urban Parishes', in Patrick Collinson and John Craig, eds, *The Reformation in English Towns, 1500–1640* (Basingstoke, 1998), 175–89, at 176. Kümin also uses the term 'compulsory': ibid.

[7] See Patrick Collinson, *The Religion of Protestants: The Church in English Society 1559–1625* (Oxford, 1982), 268 (on 'community'); idem, *The Elizabethan Puritan Movement* (Oxford, 1990), 27 (on 'the hotter sort of Protestants'); idem, 'Night Schools, Conventicles and Churches: Continuities and Discontinuities in Early Protestant Ecclesiology', in Peter Marshall and Alec Ryrie, eds, *The Beginnings of English Protestantism* (Cambridge, 2002), 209–35, at 215 (on 'semi-separatist'); idem, *Religion of Protestants*, 274–83 (on 'separatist', 'semi-separatist' and 'quasi-separatist').

[8] For definitions of conventicle, see Collinson, 'Night Schools', 214; compare Patrick Collinson, 'The English Conventicle', in Sheils and Wood, eds, *Voluntary Religion*, 223–59, at 230.

[9] Collinson argues that they are thus 'better termed semi-separatist' or 'quasi-separatist': 'Night Schools', 215; idem, *Religion of Protestants*, 274; see also idem, 'English Conventicle'.

Beat Kümin has offered the clearest statement of the 'voluntary religion' hypothesis as applied to practice rather than to mere association, looking at both the pre- and post-Reformation periods. Kümin charts the high levels of lay involvement in the medieval period, demonstrating that the religious transformations of the mid-Tudor period ushered in a dramatic stripping of many of the opportunities for lay expressions of 'voluntary religion'. He defines 'voluntary religion' as 'collective spiritual activities pursued in addition to or instead of those prescribed by the Church'.[10] Through rigorous analysis of the financial transactions found in the churchwardens' accounts of eight urban parishes, Kümin suggests that the Tudor Reformation removed the majority of the medieval parish's opportunities for 'voluntary religion', as certain forms of lay devotion were stripped away, or their role dramatically altered with a 'general trend towards a more restrictive religious atmosphere'.[11] He concludes that these religious changes of the mid-Tudor decades 'were enforced too quickly, too uniformly, too comprehensively, and also reversed too frequently to reflect genuine grass-roots developments. In fact, any divergent parochial initiative would have been stifled by the flood of meticulous guidelines and the intensive supervision.'[12]

Eamon Duffy has also made a significant contribution regarding the impact of the English Reformation on voluntary religious activities. In *The Stripping of the Altars*, Duffy argues that the high level of lay commitment and investment in traditional religion was largely destroyed by the Reformation.[13] However, the framework offered by Duffy does not allow for the sort of inspirational lay initiative we see during the English Reformation, such as the singing of metrical psalms; moreover he does not fully address the means through which inspirational practices become institutionalized.

Instead, examination of the singing of metrical psalms demonstrates that what Kümin calls 'genuine grass-roots developments' did take place during the English Reformation,[14] and that, over time, the practice flourished and became institutionalized in public worship. The singing of metrical psalms in England originated during

---

[10] Kümin, 'Voluntary Religion', 176.
[11] Ibid. 185.
[12] Ibid. 186.
[13] Eamon Duffy, *The Stripping of the Altars: Traditional Religion in England, c.1400–c.1580* (New Haven, CT, 2005; first publ. 1992).
[14] Kümin, 'Voluntary Religion', 186.

the reign of Edward VI and at the initiative was originally directed towards the young king and his entourage.[15] Indeed, Thomas Sternhold's first edition of metrical psalms, published around 1549 under the title *Certayne Psalmes chose[n] out of the Psalter of Dauid, and drawe[n] into Englishe Metre by Thomas Sternhold*, contained a dedicatory preface addressed to the boy king.[16] In it, Sternhold praised Edward for the fact that his 'tender and Godly zeale doethe more delyghte in the holye songes of veritie than in anye fayned rimes of vanitie'.[17] Sternhold urged Edward 'to se[e] & read them your selfe, but also to com[m]and them to be song to you of others'.[18] Yet while its origins lay in the Tudor court, the singing of metrical psalms soon spread into domestic devotions. By the death of Edward VI, it seems likely that some ten thousand copies of English translations of metrical psalms by Sternhold and Hopkins had been printed, and those that survive reveal that the singing of metrical psalms developed alongside other devotional practices facilitated through primers and catechisms (which are often bound with copies of metrical psalms), all of which were viewed as fully in keeping with the Edwardian Reformation.[19] The significance of metrical psalmody in the Edwardian period may have been significantly underestimated.

Yet while the practice of singing psalms seems to have been relatively common in private devotions during the reign of Edward VI, its migration into public worship was by no means an obvious transition. Crucial to this process was the time spent by English exiles on the Continent, where congregational singing of metrical psalms was relatively well established. It was only following the return of English exiles that the congregational singing of metrical psalms became established in English parishes, and I would argue that this was a result of the inspirational initiative of ordinary parishioners. Central to this practice was the publication in 1562 of *The Whole Booke of Psalmes*, which contained at least one metrical version of each of

[15] Marsh, *Music and Society*, 406–7; Beth Quitslund, *The Reformation in Rhyme: Sternhold, Hopkins and the English Metrical Psalter, 1547–1603* (Aldershot, 2008), especially 19–20.

[16] On the dating of this first edition see Quitslund, *Reformation in Rhyme*, 27–8.

[17] Thomas Sternhold, *Certayne Psalmes chose[n] out of the Psalter of Dauid*, RSTC 2419 (London, *c*.1549), preface, fol. Aiiir.

[18] Sternhold, *Certayne Psalmes*, sig. Aiiir.

[19] My doctoral research, due for completion in September 2021, will investigate this further.

the hundred and fifty Psalms, along with sixty-five tunes to which they could be sung. Evidence for the quick uptake and use of the *Whole Booke of Psalmes* is found in the purchasing of metrical psalms as recorded in churchwardens' accounts.[20] As will be discussed below, the purchasing of these books for use in congregational worship was not mandated by the Elizabethan regime, and thus relied on the initiative of ordinary members of the congregation. Further, the process of purchasing for inclusion in congregational worship would have been doomed to failure had the whole congregation not approved, and so establishing the practice must also have involved more than a few individuals. This inclusion of metrical psalmody into worship, and the support necessary for it, counter Kümin's conclusion that the religious changes of the mid-Tudor decades suppressed 'genuine grass-roots developments'.

Further, by claiming that the religious changes of the mid-Tudor period 'were enforced too quickly, too uniformly, too comprehensively, and also reversed too frequently to reflect genuine grass-roots developments', Kümin assumes that genuine grass-roots movements can only develop slowly.[21] Yet we can see that the singing of metrical psalms spread rapidly from its inspirational origins to occupy a more institutionalized place in the worship of English congregations and in private devotions, particularly following the accession of Elizabeth I and the return of the Marian exiles. While in exile, English Protestants were influenced by congregational psalm singing, particularly in Wesel, Strasbourg and (most importantly) Geneva, developing further the corpus of texts and tunes which had been produced by Sternhold and Hopkins.[22] In England during Mary I's reign, John Foxe records Protestant martyrs singing psalms. For example, on 8 August 1555, John Denley of Maidstone sang a psalm while being burnt for heresy, stopping only when a burning log was thrown at his head, and then finally to '[yield] his spirit into the hands of God'.[23]

[20] On purchasing of metrical psalms as recorded in churchwardens' accounts, see the discussion and n. 26 below.

[21] Kümin, 'Voluntary Religion', 186.

[22] Marsh, *Music and Society*, 407; Robin A. Leaver, *'Goostly psalms and spirituall songes': English and Dutch metrical psalms from Coverdale to Utenhove* (Oxford, 1991), 175–237; Timothy Duguid, *Metrical Psalmody in Print and Practice: English 'Singing Psalms' and Scottish 'Psalm Buiks'*, c.*1547–1640* (Aldershot, 2014), especially 14–48.

[23] John Foxe, *The Unabridged Acts and Monuments Online* (1570) or *TAMO* (Digital Humanities Institute, Sheffield, 2011), 1906, online at: <https://www.dhi.ac.uk/foxe/>. Other examples can be found in the online edition: ibid. 2162, 2303, 2253, 2004, 2142. These will be considered in my forthcoming thesis.

Following the accession of Elizabeth I, exiles returned to England with editions of metrical psalms they had compiled, singing from which had become an institutionalized part of their church services, complementing the domestic, devotional role psalm-singing had played before Mary's accession. These versions provided the basis for the *Whole Booke of Psalmes* (1562), the edition from which all other collections of metrical psalms would develop over the following century-and-a-half. With the publication of this collection and the growing number of parishes incorporating the singing of psalms into their worship, the practice moved from the domestic to the congregational sphere for the first time in England. In so doing, it shifted from an 'inspirational' movement towards institutionalization. Initially, its inclusion was initiated by individuals as well as groups such as congregations, and while the singing of metrical psalms did not receive an official mandate – in contrast to, for example, the requirement that parishes purchase and use the *Book of Common Prayer* – the practice established itself as a central element of congregational worship. In this early phase, to use Haigh's terminology, the process of institutionalization occurred 'from below' in that individual parishes decided to adopt it, as opposed to 'from above' as a requirement for all parishes.[24] Indeed, as early as April 1559, the London chronicler Henry Machyn recorded how 'boyth prychers and odur [others], and [women,] [sang] of a nuw fassyon'.[25] He followed this up that September, recording that at 'mornyng prayer at sant Antholyns in Boge-row, after Geneve fassyon … men and women all do syng, and boys', and 1561 he recorded the singing of a psalm in church during a funeral.[26] We can see, therefore, that, even from the beginning of Elizabeth's reign, the singing of metrical psalms was ceasing to be a purely inspirational practice and was beginning to find institutional expression in the public worship of certain parishes.

This parish initiative can be seen in a brief survey of churchwardens' accounts from the early decades of Elizabeth's reign.[27] In

[24] Haigh, 'Historiography', 19–21.
[25] J. G. Nichols, ed., *The Diary of Henry Machyn, Citizen and Merchant-Taylor of London, 1550–1563* (London, 1848), 193.
[26] Ibid. 212, 247.
[27] This is only a preliminary survey and much more work needs to be done, but the accounts outlined here provide a sample of a larger trend. For a more comprehensive account of churchwardens' accounts in Elizabethan parishes, see Willis, *Church Music*, 121–8, for metrical psalmody; see also Quitslund and Temperley, *Whole Book of*

1560, the parish of St Stephen Walbrook purchased 'a service bok with the psalter and the homilies', and two psalm books, while the parish of St Mary Woolnoth purchased 'ii psalme books in myter for the churche' for the price of 16 pence.[28] In 1559, the parish of St Margaret Pattens bought 'iiii salme books of Awstyne' and 'v Jenova bokes', and an inventory of 1567 reveals that the church also owned 'a psalter bocke in prose and also in myter with homilies'.[29] Finally, in 1570 the parish of St Ethelburga the Virgin, Bishopsgate, bought 'two psalters and twoo bookes of Jeneva psalmes'.[30] The evidence from churchwardens' accounts (covered broadly here, but more thoroughly by Jonathan Willis) suggests that throughout the reign of Elizabeth I the singing of metrical psalms as a congregational as well as a domestic practice moved from inspirational origins at the beginning towards a more institutionalized place in the worship of English congregations.[31] As will be explored further below, the Elizabethan regime eventually recognized this development by prescribing metrical psalms for the annual service to celebrate the queen's accession.

Finally, the singing of metrical psalms demonstrates that not all lay religious initiatives were suppressed by the various guidelines, visitations and court proceedings. This particular practice developed in part due to the ambiguity of the Elizabethan Injunctions with relation to music or singing in worship. The injunctions of 1559 provided that:

... for the comforting of such as delight in music, it may be permitted that in the beginning or in the end of common prayers, either at

---

Psalms, 2: 1023–7. When reviewing churchwardens' accounts, it is important to note that metrical psalms are described variously as 'Psalms books', 'in metre', 'Jeneva psalms' and 'singing psalms', while the prose versions are typically referred to as 'psalters': Jonathan Willis, 'Ecclesiastical Sources', in Laura Sangha and Jonathan Willis, eds, *Understanding Early Modern Primary Sources* (Abingdon, 2016), 58–77; John Craig, 'Psalms, Groans and Dogwhippers: The Soundscape of Worship in the English Parish Church, 1547–1642', in Will Coster and Andrew Spicer, eds, *Sacred Space in Early Modern Europe* (Cambridge, 2005), 104–23, at 106.

[28] London, LMA, St Stephen Walbrook, 1551–1738, P69/STE2/B/008/MS00593/002, fol. 44r; St Mary Woolnoth, 1539–1641, P69/MRY17/B/006/MS01002/001A, fol. 96r.

[29] LMA, St Margaret Pattens, 1555–1760, P69/MGT4/B/004/MS04570/002, pp. 3–4, 12; St Mary Woolnoth, P69/MRY17/B/006/MS01002/001A, fol. 96r.

[30] LMA, St Ethelburga the Virgin, Bishopsgate, 1569–1681, P69/ETH/B/006/MS04241/001, fol. 69.

[31] Willis, *Church Music*, 121–8.

morning or evening, there may be sung an hymn or suchlike song, to the praise of Almighty God, in the best sort of melody and music that may be conveniently devised, having respect that the sentence of the hymn may be understanded and perceived.[32]

The phrase 'or suchlike song' opened up the possibility that music other than hymns sung by choirs or music provided by an organ could be used in the service, leaving a gap which allowed the congregational singing of metrical psalms.[33] Indeed, this instruction could also be read as suggesting that the Elizabethan authorities recognized that the process of institutionalization of psalm singing had already begun in the parishes. Again, it challenges Kümin's analysis by demonstrating how the singing of metrical psalms moved from inspirational origins towards a more institutionalized role in the worship of English congregations.

We have noted that the first complete edition of metrical psalms was published in 1562 under the title *The Whole Booke of Psalmes*.[34] From the outset, the book declared that it could be used first in a domestic, then in a congregational, setting. The title page declared that it was '[v]ery mete to be vsed of all sortes of people priuately for their solace & comfort', while that of editions printed from 1566 onwards stated that the psalms were 'to be sung in all churches, of all the people together ... and moreover in private houses, for their godly solace and comfort'.[35] In this change we can see how the singing of metrical psalms was developing from its Edwardian origins as a domestic devotional practice, through the Marian exile and the lessons regarding adaptation for congregational use learnt by English congregations on the Continent, and now, through inspirational initiative, was slowly developing an institutionalized role in the worship of English congregations. The following sections will examine three strands of evidence which allow us to trace the process by which this practice became institutionalized during the first two decades of Elizabeth's reign.

[32] Gerald Bray, ed., *Documents of the English Reformation* (Cambridge, 2004), 345.
[33] Marsh, *Music and Society*, 401–2, 407. Marsh explains that '[t]he term "hymn" referred to any song of praise, whether or not its text was based squarely on a Scriptural passage': ibid. 407.
[34] *The Whole Booke of Psalmes, collected into Englysh metre*, RSTC 2430 (London, 1562).
[35] Ibid., sig. †1r; *The Whole Boke of Psalmes, collected into English metre*, RSTC 2437 (London, 1566), sig. A1r.

PREFATORY MATERIAL AND THE MOVEMENT INTO WORSHIP

Alongside metrical versions of the psalms and tunes to which they could be sung, the *Whole Booke of Psalmes* contained additional prefatory material, whose function was to explain the texts and tunes and offer direction for individuals and congregations on how best to utilize the contents. The first item, 'A Treatise made by Athanasius the great', elevates the importance of the Psalms within Scripture and outlines over ninety circumstances in which psalms may be sung. For example, the treatise suggests: 'If thou hast need of prayer for them which withstand thee and compass thy soul about, sing the 17th Psalm and 86th, 89th, and 142nd Psalm'; and 'If thou wilt sing particularly of the saviour, thou hast of him in every Psalm, but specially in the 25th and 110th Psalm.'[36]

After the Athanasian treatise there is a second item, 'The vse of the rest of the Psalmes not comprehended in the former Table of Athanasius'. This second list has two functions which root the use of the psalms in an Elizabethan setting. First, the list provides direction for individuals: 'If thou desirest to be just and virtuous, use the 33rd Psalm'; 'If thou be afflicted with any sickness and wouldst fain live and see good days and Christ's glory to be increased, use the 39th Psalm'.[37] Second, the list offers directions which could be applied more readily to the Elizabethan church, as well as the wider world: 'If thou seest the nobility, the Council, the magistrates, and princes not given to religion nor to the praising of God, use the 29th Psalm'; 'If thou neither wouldst have idolatry neither any licentious lusts reign in Christ's commonwealth, thou must give God thanks, if thou be persuaded he both will and can take them away, using the 81st Psalm'; 'To sing praises to God for his mercies, use the 134th Psalm.'[38] These latter examples in particular could readily be applied in a congregational setting, and they may have made the transition from private to institutionalized corporate worship more fluid.

This second, shorter preface did not appear in editions of the *Whole Booke of Psalmes* printed after 1577.[39] Beth Quitslund has argued that the reason for this is because its tone was 'so close to what would come to be called "puritan"', although she does not

---

[36] *Whole Booke of Psalmes*, RSTC 2430, sigs †6v–A2v.
[37] Ibid., sigs A3r–v.
[38] Ibid.
[39] Quitslund and Temperley, *Whole Book of Psalms*, 2: 575, 627.

provide any clear rationale for this judgement.[40] In 1577 both 'the use of the rest' and the 'Athanasian Treatise' were replaced by a different translation of the latter by Archbishop Parker.[41] Quitslund and Temperley suggest a link between Richard Day's renewal of the patent to print the *Whole Booke of Psalmes* and the removal of the original 'Athanasian Treatise' and 'the use of the rest' (with their 'rather pointedly political occasions and uses') and their replacement with Parker's translation.[42] While this does seem possible, the removal of the original prefaces could also imply that the singing of metrical psalms was becoming increasingly central to congregational worship in this period, so that there was less need for these prefatory texts outlining how and when to sing specific psalms. There is no guarantee that the Parker preface was studied in detail, and his directions could apply to either individual or congregational use, particularly if the singing of metrical psalms was institutionalized in the worship of congregations. It seems plausible that by 1577, congregations were singing metrical psalms as an important part of their public worship, and that they knew the texts and tunes they wanted to sing (as discussed further below) and understood the directions which had been given in 'The vse of the Rest of the Psalmes'; presumably they could refer to an edition of the *Whole Booke of Psalmes* which contained it should they require additional direction.

The two original prefaces functioned as a bridge between the origins of the singing of metrical psalms in domestic devotions and their increasingly widespread inclusion in the worship of English congregations. Their removal by the late 1570s suggests that the singing of metrical psalms had moved from its inspirational origins in private devotions, through a stage of inspirational inclusion in the service, towards a more institutionalized role in worship. This institutionalization can also be seen in the purchasing recorded in churchwardens' accounts and the increasing number of references by contemporary commentators to the popularity of the practice.[43] Moreover, this

[40] Quitslund, *Reformation in Rhyme*, 228. This suggestion is carried into Quitslund and Temperley, again without any clarity on which elements are controversial: *Whole Book of Psalms*, 2: 551–2, 574–5.
[41] While the author is not named, the text was first published in Parker's *Whole Psalter Translated into English Metre* (1567): Quitslund and Temperley, *Whole Book of Psalms*, 2: 574, 882.
[42] Ibid. 2: 574–5.
[43] Marsh, *Music and Society*, 406–11, 435–53.

institutionalization was cemented only a year later with the publication of the service to celebrate the accession of Elizabeth I (outlined in detail below), which acted as an important marker in the move of congregational singing of metrical psalms from inspiration to institutionalization. If the removal of the prefaces and the move of congregational singing towards a central place in parish worship were taking place together, they may provide evidence both for the influence that the singing of metrical psalms was exerting on the population and Elizabethan policy, and also for the extent to which the regime was beginning to take seriously the place of congregational singing of metrical psalms in public worship and to recognize the possible influence that might be exerted through it.

In the 1562 *Whole Booke of Psalmes*, alongside these prefatory treatises on the texts, a musical preface was printed: 'A short Introduction into the Science of Music'.[44] This outlines the widespread practice of solmization known as the *Gamut*: the most widespread system of musical learning in Europe from the Middle Ages until the late sixteenth and early seventeenth century.[45] The preface was intended '[f]or that the rude and ignorant in Song, may with more delight[,] desire, and good will: be moved and drawn to the godly exercise of singing of Psalms, as well in common place of prayer, where all together with one voice render thanks and praises to God, as privately by themselves, or at home in their houses'.[46] It explained that individuals who did not know how to pitch the six notes, 'must learn to tune aptly of some one that can already sing, or by some Instrument of music, as the Virginals'.[47] The suggestion that tunes be learnt through using musical instruments is particularly interesting, since instruments accompanied the singing of the psalms in *Al Suche Psalmes*, both in the Edwardian court and in domestic devotions.[48] The implication here could be that metrical psalms were still being performed in domestic settings, so that individuals could learn the psalms at home (either through their own musical abilities or those

---

[44] *Whole Booke of Psalmes*, RSTC 2430, sigs †2r–7r.

[45] Andrew Hughes and Edith Gerson-Kiwi, 'Solmization', in *Grove Music Online*, 20 January 2001, at: <https://doi.org/10.1093/gmo/9781561592630.article.26154>, accessed 2 May 2019.

[46] *Whole Booke of Psalmes*, RSTC 2430, sig. †2r.

[47] Ibid., sig. †4r.

[48] See my forthcoming thesis. For a discussion of Edwardian musical accompaniment, see Quitslund and Temperley, *Whole Book of Psalms*, 2: 510–27.

of others) and, once the tunes were familiar, could use them in congregational worship. Quitslund suggests that the presence of this preface 'demonstrates considerably more confidence about the role of psalm-singing during or at least immediately before and after Prayer Book services than the title page' of the *Whole Booke of Psalmes*.[49] From 1569, however, a shorter preface entitled 'To the Reader' often replaced the longer 'Introduction', and the longer treatise does not appear in any surviving copy after 1583.[50] The shorter preface developed a system of placing sol-fa letters before the notes used for the tunes in the *Whole Booke of Psalmes*, so those who were reading the music understood the pitching of each note: essentially a visual aid for the solmization explained in the longer 'Science of Music' preface.[51] Samantha Arten suggests that the printing of these letters may have been 'intended to accommodate those with less formal education' and in this way, 'the [*Whole Booke of Psalmes*] advocated musical literacy for the common people, not just those formally trained in music'.[52] Arten, however, implies that the key impetus in this shift towards solmization syllables comes from the publishers of the *Whole Booke of Psalmes* and so does not fully address the role of the 'common people' in this shift. In particular, she does not consider the possibility that the singing of metrical psalms had become an institutionalized, central element in public worship, and that the preface thus had limited utility once congregations knew which tunes they wanted to sing and how to sing them. As Timothy Duguid has shown, the evidence for such congregational understanding is seen in the printing of tunes which contained variations from those printed by the original printer of Sternhold and Hopkins in England, John Day. These variations seem to be based on variations in performance practice, and suggest the possibility that congregations were 'increasingly comfortable mixing and matching tunes and texts based on singers' knowledge, preferences, and abilities'.[53] The possibility is instructive, and suggests that the relationship between the printers (especially John Day) and those using the *Whole Booke of Psalmes* was fluid, with each party responding to

---

[49] Quitslund, *Reformation in Rhyme*, 204.
[50] Quitslund and Temperley, *Whole Book of Psalms*, 2: 872, 881.
[51] *Whole Booke of Psalmes* (1569), sig. A1v.
[52] Samantha Arten, 'The Origin of Fixed-Scale Solmization in *The Whole Booke of Psalmes*', *Early Music* 46 (2018), 149–65, at 159.
[53] Duguid, *Metrical Psalmody*, 116–17.

and directing the changes of the other.[54] In this process we see the fluidity which the categories of 'inspiration' and 'institution' bring: while the singing of metrical psalms had established itself as a central element in the worship of English congregations, inspirational innovation and development, whether directed by individuals, congregations or printers, was still present, although it too could become institutionalized over time.

The earlier, longer 'Introduction' demonstrates that by 1562, English congregations were incorporating the singing of metrical psalms as a central part of their worship services. This preface had not appeared in editions printed before the Marian exile; nor was it part of editions used by English congregations in continental exile. Its appearance in 1562 gives us a snapshot of changing patterns of metrical psalmody in the Elizabethan period. The omission of the longer musical preface and the addition of the shorter sol-fa version would have been a risky move for John Day if individuals or congregations still required direction in how to understand and utilize the music. We can, therefore, surmise that individuals using the *Whole Booke of Psalmes* in private devotions understood how they wanted to use the texts and tunes, possibly learning the melodies through instrumental accompaniment, while congregations who were singing metrical psalms had someone who understood how to read the music and lead the congregation, or who knew the tunes and could lead the congregation through singing or with musical accompaniment, or else congregations had developed a limited corpus of tunes (possibly incorporating 'common tunes') and did not require direction. These possibilities should also be considered alongside Christopher Marsh's assertion that '[e]arly modern people were thoroughly accustomed to picking up melodies by ear, and the evidence from balladry suggests that they could hold hundreds of tunes in their memories.'[55] Thus, as with the textual treatises discussed above, the presence of these two prefaces on the music in the *Whole Booke of Psalmes* demonstrates that the singing of metrical psalms was becoming institutionalized and moving away from its inspirational origins as individuals and congregations grew more familiar with the texts and tunes found in the work.

One final indication of the presence of the singing of metrical psalms in the services of English congregations is the binding of

[54] Ibid., especially 111–18.
[55] Marsh, *Music and Society*, 426.

the *Whole Booke of Psalmes* together with the *Book of Common Prayer*, the Bible or both. My initial survey of twenty-three surviving copies of the *Whole Booke of Psalmes* dated 1562–79 revealed that nine (i.e. 39 per cent) of the surviving copies of the *Whole Booke of Psalmes* were bound with a prayer book between 1562 and 1579, and that the practice was particularly prominent during the 1570s.[56] This phenomenon demonstrates the intersecting movement of these two texts: the institutional Prayer Book being increasingly used in domestic devotion, where the singing of metrical psalms had originated and still continued, as outlined above, while the inspirational *Whole Booke of Psalmes* moved towards a more established role in public worship. It seems highly unlikely that domestic owners or churches would have bound the two texts together unless they were using both in both contexts. We can see, therefore, in these shared bindings, the movement of the singing of metrical psalms from its inspirational origins towards a more established, institutionalized place in the worship of English Protestant congregations and individuals, particularly during the 1570s.

THE SINGING OF METRICAL PSALMS IN OCCASIONAL SERVICES

The singing of metrical psalms by English congregations was further institutionalized when, in 1576, Elizabeth's government ordered all congregations to participate in a special service on 17 November to celebrate the anniversary of the queen's accession. The conclusion of *The Fourme of Praier with Thankes Giuing* includes the instruction: 'The xxi psalm in meter before the sermon, unto the end of the vii verse. And the c psalm after the sermon.'[57] This was the first time that the singing of metrical psalms had been officially required by

---

[56] I examined 23 copies of the *Whole Booke of Psalmes* published between 1562 and 1579, held by four repositories. Of these, 8 were printed in the 1560s, of which 2 were also bound with the Book of Common Prayer [hereafter: BCP] (or 25%), while 15 were printed in the 1570s, with 7 of these bound with the BCP (46%). In total, 9 of the 23 were bound with a BCP. The first edition of the *Whole Booke of Psalmes* to be bound with a BCP from the copies I examined was from 1566. Those editions of the *Whole Booke of Psalmes* bound with a BCP were located as follows: three in the British Library, two in the Bodleian Library, three in Cambridge University Library, and one in the library of Christ Church, Oxford.

[57] *The Fourme of Praier with Thankes Giuing, to be Used Every Yeere, the 17 of November*, RSTC 164795 (London, 1576).

the Elizabethan authorities and it is interesting that no mention is made in the *Fourme of Praier* as to which version of the metrical psalms is to be sung, or to which tune, much less a text provided. This reflects the widespread use of the *Whole Booke of Psalmes* by this date and the familiarity of English Protestants with this version. Both these psalms have music printed alongside them in the *Whole Booke of Psalmes*, so congregations would not have had difficulty integrating them into the service. We can also, however, see intention in the prescription of these two psalms. Psalm 21 speaks of God's blessings upon 'the king', declaring: 'Thou didst preuent him with thy giftes, and blessinges manifolde' (v. 3); 'great is his glory by thy helpe, thy benefite and ayde' (v. 5); 'Thou wilt geue him felicitye, that neuer shall decay' (v. 6).[58] Additionally, Psalm 21 is prescribed in the preface discussed above, 'The vse of the rest of the Psalmes', where it is asserted: 'If thou wouldst prayse God because he hath geuen vs a good prince, which will and dooth punish the enemies of Christes religion. vse the 21. Psalme.'[59] It seems highly likely that congregations and individuals who were familiar with the *Whole Booke of Psalmes* would have been familiar with the use of this psalm in the same context as that directed in the *Fourme of Praier*; thus prescribing it for that service would not have been a dramatically new use of it for Elizabethan congregations.

Psalm 100, on the other hand, is simply a hymn of praise, exhorting 'All people that on earth do dwell,' to 'Sing to the Lord with cherefull voyce'.[60] Another version of Psalm 100, sometimes set to music (though not that in the *Whole Booke of Psalmes*), would have been known to English congregations since it had been prescribed in the 1552 and 1559 Prayer Books as the *Jubilate Deo*, to be sung after the second lesson of Morning Prayer, 'as an alternative canticle ... because the *Benedictus* is sometimes the lesson or Gospel of the day'.[61] Additionally, the Athanasian treatise at the beginning of the *Whole Booke of Psalmes* directed: 'If thou markest the providence of the Lord in all things, and the Lord of the same, and wouldst instruct any with the faith and obedience thereof, when thou hast persuaded

[58] *The Whole Booke of Psalmes, collected into Englishe metre*, RSTC 2447 (London, 1576), sigs B4r–v.

[59] *Whole Booke of Psalmes*, RSTC 2430, sig. A3r.

[60] *Whole Booke of Psalmes*, RSTC 2447, sig. F1v.

[61] Brian Cummings, ed., *The Book of Common Prayer: the texts of 1549, 1559, and 1562* (Oxford, 2011), 109–10, 724–5.

them first to acknowledge, sing the 100th Psalm.'[62] While this is a less explicit direction than that for Psalm 21, it is possible that this had resonance with congregations and individuals, and, again, the order to sing it in the service to celebrate the queen's accession may have fitted with a common interpretation of this direction. By choosing both these psalms, therefore, those who created the *Fourme of Praier* presumably recognized that in doing so they were satisfying the desire of those who wanted the singing of metrical psalms to be acknowledged by the Elizabethan state and accepted officially as an integral part of public worship, but they also understood that the singing of psalms could be used to serve their own purposes, as in this service.[63]

It is also worth noting that the preface on 'The vse of the Rest of the Psalmes' (discussed above) ceased to appear in editions of the *Whole Booke of Psalmes* published in the late 1570s, around the time that *The Fourme of Praier with Thankes Giuing* was published. It is possible that the publishing of this liturgy marked the point at which congregations were settling into fixed habits and customs regarding which psalms could or should be sung for different purposes and how they wanted to utilize the texts and tunes within the *Whole Booke of Psalmes*, and also a point at which the Elizabethan authorities began to utilize the practice for their own ends, instructing congregations to sing metrical psalms for particular purposes. This direction by the authorities would continue throughout the remainder of Elizabeth's reign, as discussed below.

Returning to our dichotomy of 'inspiration' versus 'institution', we note that the direction to sing psalms in metre marks the movement of the singing of metrical psalms from its 'inspirational' origins towards a mandated institutionalization. Yet even by this date, there was no explicit direction that the singing of metrical psalms was to form a regular part of the worship of English parishes. Its institutionalization came about as it became a regular part of the worship of English congregations, developing initially as a grassroots initiative, but then being reinforced and given official approval in the direction for congregations to sing metrical psalms during the annual service to celebrate Elizabeth's accession. This process of institutionalization advanced further in 1580 when, following an

---

[62] *Whole Booke of Psalmes*, RSTC 2430, sig. A2r.
[63] Marsh, *Music and Society*, 409.

earthquake, the Elizabethan authorities published a liturgy to be used 'vpon Wednesdayes and Frydayes, to auert and turne Gods wrath from vs'.[64] This liturgy provided an order which included psalms, readings from Joel and Isaiah, a prayer, and Psalm 46 in metre, which reminds the singer that 'The Lord is our defence and aid … Though thearth remoue, we will not feare, though hils so high and steepe: Be thrust and hurled here and there, within the sea so deepe.'[65] In this liturgy, unlike that devised to celebrate the queen's accession, both the words and a tune are printed for people to use; however, whilst the words are the same as those found in the *Whole Booke of Psalmes*, the tune is different. Moreover, this tune does not appear in the *Whole Booke of Psalmes*; neither is it one of the 'Common Tunes'. It is possible, therefore, that this tune was devised specifically for this service, suggesting that Elizabeth's government understood the power of uniting congregations in one text and tune.

In addition, key moments in English history throughout this period were marked by psalm-singing. In 1586, after the Babington plot to kill the queen was foiled, John Strype reported that 'the city of London made extraordinary rejoicings, by public bonfires, ringing of bells, feastings in the street singing of psalms, and such like'.[66] Two years later, on 19 November 1588, John Stowe recounted that a holiday was kept 'throughout the realme, with sermons, singing of Psalmes, bone-fires. &c. For ioy, and a thanks giuing unto God, for the ouerthrow of the Spanyards our enimies on the sea'.[67] Strype also recorded that '[t]here was a prayer and psalm, appointed to be used duly in the parish-churches on this joyful occasion'.[68] This was not a metrical psalm, but rather a cut-and-paste psalm made up of various references from Scripture and the psalter, rearranged to make a 'psalm'.[69] Yet the psalm singing which Strype

---

[64] *The Order of Prayer, and Other Exercises upon Wednesdayes and Fridayes*, RSTC 16512 (London, 1580), title page.
[65] Ibid., sig. 3v.
[66] John Strype, *Annals of the Reformation and Establishment of Religion*, 4 vols (Oxford, 1824), 3/i: 607.
[67] John Stowe, *The Annales of England*, RSTC 2334 (London, 1592), sig Ppppi.r.
[68] Strype, *Annals*, 3/ii: 28.
[69] *A Psalme and Collect of Thanksgiuing, not vnmeet for this present time: to be said or sung in Churches*, RSTC 16520 (London, 1588), sigs A2r–A3v. For a discussion of cut-and-paste psalms, see Ryrie, 'Psalms and Confrontation', 116–18.

records seems most likely to have been singing of metrical psalms, demonstrating further how they had become institutionalized: now, the singing of metrical psalms had become a natural celebratory response for the nation. This practice, and the *Whole Booke of Psalmes* itself, developed over the course of the following century and a half, though not dramatically. The melodies slowed, and the corpus of regularly sung psalms seems to have diminished, yet the singing of metrical psalms continued to form an important part of the worship of English congregations, to be used by individuals in domestic devotion, and to be appointed during times of national celebration, until it encountered competition from new forms and settings of metrical psalms in the late seventeenth and early eighteenth centuries, and was later replaced by hymns in the late eighteenth and early nineteenth centuries.[70]

CONCLUSION

Through the lens of the *Whole Booke of Psalmes*, this article has argued that the dichotomy of inspiration versus institution provides a nuanced and fruitful framework for understanding lay religious devotion during the English Reformation. The 'voluntary' versus 'official religion' framework outlined at the beginning does not provide space for the singing of metrical psalms, a practice which was not the sole preserve of 'groups' or 'communities', and was neither explicitly prescribed nor proscribed by the Elizabethan authorities but emerged through inspirational lay initiative. A framework constructed around the relationship between institution and inspiration makes it possible to study a larger web of lay religious activity, but also the diverse ways in which inspirational practices became institutionalized. Additionally, this new framework reveals the interaction between institution and inspiration (seen in the prefatory material in the *Whole Booke of Psalmes*) as the latter became more established and thus embedded in the former. In the opening example from Exeter, we see institutionalization at work in the approval of Bishop-elect Jewel and Archbishop Parker for the laity to continue singing psalms, despite there being no explicit direction for them to do so in the

---

[70] For the slowing of melodies, and possible reasons for this, see Marsh, *Music and Society*, 430–4. For the longevity of Sternhold and Hopkins see Marsh, *Music and Society*, 405–53, especially 435–53; Green, "'All people that on earth do dwell'".

Elizabethan settlement, while inspiration is evident in the singers and (by reaction) the clergy who viewed such singing as unwelcome and unlawful. As the Exeter example shows, inspiration could still arise during the process of institutionalization, as in the rise of the common tunes, particularly in the mid-to-later Elizabethan period, and in the practice of binding the metrical psalms with the Book of Common Prayer and Bible. This latter point also demonstrates the two phases of institutionalization, within both of which inspiration continued to operate, so that there was a fluid movement of metrical psalm singing between the domestic and congregational settings. The framework proposed may contribute towards renewing our understanding of the interplay between inspiration and institution in the English Reformation.

Inspiration and Institution in Catholic Missionary Martyrdom Accounts: Japan and New France, 1617–49

Rhiannon Teather*

University of Bristol

This article focuses on the martyrdoms of the French Jesuit Antoine Daniel in New France and the Spanish friars Alonso Navarrete and Hernando Ayala in Japan. Drawing upon the accounts written by the missionaries Paul Ragueneau and Jacinto Orfanel, it shows how they adapted apostolic teaching and the Tridentine vision of the priesthood to interpret the acts of their brethren as sources of inspiration and models of renewed institutional identity. It argues that martyrdom was viewed as a pastoral responsibility in the missions to New France and Japan. Martyrs were portrayed as divinely inspired to lay down their lives for their communities, while the act of martyrdom was viewed as a literal, semi-liturgical sacrifice imbued with the sacramentality of the priesthood. Martyrdom was perceived both to fulfil an urgent pastoral need within communities and to model the apostolic vision of the Roman Catholic Church.

On the eve of Corpus Christi 1617, Alonso Navarrete, the vicar provincial of the Dominicans in the Japan mission, announced his intention to travel from the relative safety of Nagasaki to Omura, a hotspot of recent executions.[1] Navarrete's friend and fellow missionary, Hernando Ayala, the lone Augustinian in Japan and vicar

* I am very grateful for the feedback, support and encouragement of my doctoral supervisors, Kenneth Austin and Fernando Cervantes. They nurtured the ideas in this article and helped to bring them to fruition. The research was made possible by a PhD scholarship funded by the University of Bristol Alumni. I am also grateful to the two reviewers for their helpful suggestions for improvement. Scripture quotations in this article are taken from the Revised Standard Version. E-mail: rt1702@my.bristol.ac.uk.

[1] Alfonso Navarrete Benito was born on 21 September 1571 in Logroño, Spain. A Dominican missionary priest originally based in the Philippines, Navarrete arrived in Japan in August 1611. He remained after the edict of expulsion in 1614 and was made vicar provincial in 1615. For these biographical details, see J. S. Cummins and Charles Boxer, *The Dominican Mission in Japan (1602–1622) and Lope de Vega* (Rome, 1963), 71; Juan G. Ruiz de Medina, *El martirologio del Japón, 1558–1873* (Rome, 1999).

Studies in Church History 57 (2021), 142–162 © The Author(s), 2021. Published by Cambridge University Press on behalf of Ecclesiastical History Society
doi: 10.1017/stc.2021.8

provincial of that order, volunteered to accompany him.[2] Traditionally the year 1614 marks the beginning of the end of Japan's 'Christian Century' (*c.*1549–1649) with a gathering storm of persecution.[3] Edicts were published across the country mandating the expulsion of missionaries and influential Japanese converts. It became a capital offence for European missionaries to operate or to proselytize for their religion.[4] By 1617, the enforcement of anti-Christian measures had gained pace, with fresh executions of European missionary priests, and so the friars' trip to Omura was fraught with danger.[5] When challenged about the risks, Navarrete and Ayala explained that they felt moved to offer pastoral support to the bereft Christians of Omura. On arrival, Navarrete and Ayala tonsured themselves, donned their habits and were swiftly arrested. They were then taken to the island of Koguchi (Takashima) in Omura Bay, where they were beheaded on 1 June

---

[2] Hernando Ayala (also Hernando de San José) was born in 1575 near Toledo, Spain. He entered the Augustinian order in 1593 and made his profession on 19 May 1594. He was chosen to go to the college of the order at the university of Alcalá de Henares. As a missionary, Ayala arrived in Japan in 1605. He founded an Augustinian monastery in Nagasaki in 1612 and was nominated as its prior. Ayala remained in Japan after the edict of expulsion in 1614. For a detailed biography and account of his martyrdom, see Arnulf Hartmann, *The Augustinians in Seventeenth-Century Japan* (Marylake, ON, 1965), 43–73.

[3] For a recent overview of the Catholic mission to Japan, see M. Antoni J. Ucerler, 'The Christian Missions in Japan in the Early Modern Period', in Ronnie Po-chia Hsia, ed., *A Companion to Early Modern Catholic Global Missions* (Leiden, 2018), 303–43. The standard works in English on the development of anti-Christian policy and the mission to Japan remain George Elison, *Deus Destroyed: The Image of Christianity in Early Modern Japan* (Cambridge, MA, 1973); Charles R. Boxer, *The Christian Century in Japan 1549–1650* (Lisbon, 1951).

[4] Prior to 1614 there had been sporadic episodes of anti-Christian violence, of which the most famous is the martyrdom of twenty-six Christians in Nagasaki in 1597. For a recent analysis of this episode, see Hélène Vu Thanh, 'The Glorious Martyrdom of the Cross: The Franciscans and The Japanese Persecutions of 1597', *Culture & History Digital Journal* 6 (2017) [online journal]), at: <https://doi.org/10.3989/chdj.2017. 005>, accessed 19 May 2020; eadem, *Devenir japonais. La Mission jésuite au Japon (1549–1614)* (Paris, 2016). Also see Rady Roldán-Figueroa, 'Father Luis Piñeiro S.J., the Tridentine Economy of Relics and the Defense of the Jesuit Missionary Enterprise in Tokugawa Japan', *ARG* 101 (2010), 209–32; Timon Screech, 'The English and the Control of Christianity in the Early Edo Period', *Japan Review* 24 (2012), 3–40.

[5] The Franciscan Pedro de la Asunción (b. *c.*1570) and the Jesuit João Baptista Machado de Távora (b. *c.*1580) were executed in Omura on 22 May 1617.

1617. Leo Tanaka (b. *c*.1590), a Japanese lay catechist, was executed alongside them.[6]

On other shores, the Jesuit missionary Antoine Daniel was killed in the mission to the Huron (also *Wendat*, meaning 'Islanders' or 'Dwellers on a Peninsula') in New France, North America.[7] In the 1640s, this remote French mission had been devastated by escalating inter-tribal conflict.[8] With weapons supplied by the Dutch, the neighbouring Iroquois League (also *Haudenosaunee*, or 'people of the Longhouse'), had been waging war against the Huron with increasing intensity.[9] In early July 1648 at the village of Teanaostaiaë, Daniel had just celebrated mass with his congregation

[6] Tanaka is introduced in the account as a *Dojuku* (a term used in the Japan mission to refer to a type of lay catechist and preacher) to the martyred Jesuit João Baptista Machado de Távora; Tanaka was captured with João Baptista Machado on the Goto Islands but was not executed with him in May 1617. Tanaka's actions, including at the moment of his death, are not reported in detail in Orfanel's account which focuses principally on Navarrete and Ayala. Tanaka is referred to as 'blessed Leon', and from the time he is brought to be executed with Navarrete and Ayala is presented (albeit fleetingly) as a willing evangelist alongside the missionaries. For example, Tanaka was recorded as mirroring the actions of Navarrete and Ayala in his treatment of his executioners ('y el bendito Leon con sus dos verdugos'): Jacinto Orfanel and Diego Collado, *Historia eclesiástica de los sucesos de la Christiandad de Japón, desde el año de 1602* (Madrid, 1633), 78r. However, his actions are not given the same narrative weight or symbolism, given the focus of Orfanel's account: Orfanel and Collado, *Historia*, 77v–78r, 79r–v.

[7] Antoine Daniel was born on 27 May 1601 in Dieppe, France. He entered the Jesuit novitiate at Rouen on 1 October 1621, later studied theology at Clermont College in Paris, and was ordained in 1631. He crossed the Atlantic in the spring of 1632, joined the mission to the Huron in 1634 and began work the following year. In 1647, he was assigned to the village of Teanaostaiaë (also Teanaustayé): Joseph N. Tylenda, *Jesuit Saints & Martyrs* (Chicago, IL, 1998), 200–1; Léon Pouliot, 'Daniel, Antoine', in *Dictionary of Canadian Biography*, 1: *1000–1700* (Toronto, ON, and Laval, QC, 2003; first publ. 1966), online at: <http://www.biographi.ca/en/bio/daniel_antoine_1E.html>, accessed 19 May 2020.

[8] New France was a vast territory claimed by the French Crown which stretched from north-eastern Canada down to what is now the mid-western United States of America. This article uses the historical names 'Huron' and 'Iroquois' to retain a clear connection to the source material. For a substantive account of the Huron and their history, see Bruce G. Trigger, *The Children of Aataentsic: A History of the Huron People to 1660* (Montreal, QC, 1976). For a recent overview of the mission in New France, see Dominique Deslandres, 'New France', in Hsia, ed., *Companion to Early Modern Catholic Global Missions*, 124–47; Dominique Deslandres, *Croire et faire croire. Les Missions françaises au XVIIe siècle (1600–1650)* (Paris, 2003).

[9] For an account of the Iroquois and their history, see Daniel K. Richter, *The Ordeal of the Longhouse: The Peoples of the Iroquois League in the Era of European Colonization* (Chapel Hill, NC, 1992).

when he found himself in the midst of an Iroquois raid. He urged the Christians to flee and went forward to meet the raiders. Moments later Daniel was slain and his body was thrown into the burning church.

Navarrete, Ayala and Daniel were swiftly recorded as martyrs in the writings of their brethren. For Navarrete and Ayala, this article focuses on the account written by the Spanish Dominican missionary Jacinto Orfanel (1578–1622), in his *Historia eclesiástica de los sucesos de la Christiandad de Japón* (1633).[10] In comparison to their Jesuit and Franciscan contemporaries, the Dominicans and Augustinians in Japan have received little detailed attention since the accounts of Boxer, Cummins and Hartmann in the 1960s, so this article seeks to incorporate their stories into the global picture of Catholic missions.[11] The death of Antoine Daniel was recorded by the Huron mission superior and French Jesuit Paul Ragueneau (1608–80) in his private correspondence to the superior general, published in the *Jesuit Relations* for 1648–9. The latter were popular serialized annual letters, published almost continuously in Paris at the printing house of Cramoisy between 1632 and 1673.[12] The martyrdom accounts from these *Relations* have not been compared systematically with those from other missions or regions.[13] This article will demonstrate that the interplay between the themes of inspiration and institution in

---

[10] Jacinto Orfanel (also Pedro Orfanell Prades) was himself executed a few years later, during the 'Great Martyrdom' of Nagasaki on 10 September 1622: Orfanel and Collado, *Historia*. I am grateful to Fernando Cervantes and Diego Navarro-Tapia for their advice and assistance with my translations. I have modernized the original spelling for clarity.

[11] Cummins and Boxer, *Dominican Mission*; Hartmann, *Augustinians*. For full references, see nn. 2 and 3 above.

[12] Reuben Gold Thwaites, ed., *The Jesuit Relations and Allied Documents: Travels and Explorations of the Jesuit Missionaries in New France, 1610–1791*, 73 vols (Cleveland, OH, 1896–1901; hereafter: *JR*). For a more recent transcription of the original texts, see Lucien Campeau, ed., *Monumenta Novæ Franciæ*, 9 vols (Rome, 1967–2003).

[13] For a recent analysis of these 'North American Martyrs', see Emma Anderson, *The Death and Afterlife of the North American Martyrs* (Cambridge, MA, 2013). While martyrdom was not the focus of his work, Takao Abé has usefully compared the evangelization strategies and methods of the missions to New France and Japan in *The Jesuit Mission to New France: A New Interpretation in the Light of the earlier Jesuit Experience in Japan* (Leiden, 2011); idem, 'What Determined the Content of Missionary Reports? The Jesuit Relations Compared with the Iberian Jesuit Accounts', *French Colonial History* 3 (2003), 69–83.

these martyrdom accounts is brought into sharp relief by the use of a global comparative approach.

Traditionally martyrs represent one of the most ancient synergies of inspirational faith and institutionalized religion. With the Passion at the heart of Christianity, martyrdom functioned as a conduit that conveyed the central teachings of the Scriptures in a simple evocative form. Martyrs served as a fulfilment of Christianity's promises of transformation and resurrection, as well as a manifestation of its principal spiritual gifts of faith, hope and love.[14] The word 'martyr' in the original Greek meant 'witness', and in the period of persecution between the first and the fourth centuries, martyrs came to embody Christianity's distinctive identity.[15] The heroic stories of early martyrs bore witness to the religion's unique claim to divine revelation through Jesus Christ. The essential role of the martyr in bonding inspiration and institution was even formalized by a decree of the Fifth Council of Carthage (401), which specified that two relics (of a martyr and of a saint) must be buried in the altar of every church building, institutionalizing the maxim famously attributed to Tertullian that 'the blood of martyrs is the seed of the church'.[16] From the early church, right through to the sixteenth century (and indeed beyond), institutional expression evolved to accommodate the role of martyrs. Likewise the concept of martyrdom, be it 'white' (spiritual) or 'red' (with bloodshed), continued to be a source of inspiration that was adapted by the Christian community.[17]

[14] 1 Cor. 13: 13; Josef Pieper, *Faith, Hope, Love* (San Francisco, CA, 2012; first publ. Munich, 1986).

[15] The literature on this subject is vast, but key authorities include W. H. C. Frend, *Martyrdom and Persecution in the Early Church* (Oxford, 1965); Theofried Baumeister, *Die Anfänge der Theologie des Martyriums* (Münster, 1980); Hans von Campenhausen, *Die Idee des Martyriums in der alten Kirche* (Göttingen, 1936); G. W. Bowersock, *Martyrdom and Rome* (Cambridge, 1995); more recently, Candida R. Moss, *Ancient Christian Martyrdom: Diverse Practices, Theologies, and Traditions* (New Haven, CT, 2012).

[16] Tertullian actually wrote: 'The oftener we are mown down by you, the more in number we grow; the blood of Christians is seed': *Apology* 55 (ANF 3: 50).

[17] St Cyprian of Carthage (d. 258) first suggested that God provided two 'crowns' of martyrdom, 'white' for the physical and spiritual suffering of confessors, and 'crimson' for bloodshed: see Cyprian, *Ep.* 10.5 (CSEL 3: 494–5); Clare Stancliffe, 'Red, White and Blue Martyrdom', in Dorothy Whitelock, Rosamond McKitterick and David Dumville, eds, *Ireland in Early Mediaeval Europe* (Cambridge, 1982), 21–46, at 32. For a helpful general introduction to the rich Christian tradition of martyrdom and its development over time, see Diana Wood, ed., *Martyrs and Martyrologies*, SCH 30

The sixteenth and seventeenth centuries witnessed a bloody resurgence of martyrs. The traditional focus of studies has been on the martyrological revival in Europe, where some five thousand Christians of all confessions were killed and commemorated as martyrs.[18] In contrast, the martyrs from the missions to Asia and the Americas have been treated as a 'third distinct group', separate from Protestant and Catholic martyrs within Europe, and distinguished by the 'remote theatre' of their executions and the 'different' relationship with perpetrators, who tended to be non-Christians rather than adherents of a rival confession.[19] However, in the seventeenth century, Japan was the site of one of the most systematic persecutions of Christians in any country anywhere in the early modern era: the lower estimates are that 2,128 were recorded as having died during the persecutions, including 71 Europeans who were executed or died in prison; the higher figures suggest that almost double this number were killed.[20] Some scholars have likened the scale of the martyrdoms in Japan to that under the Roman Empire.[21] This suggests that, in terms of numbers and historical significance, a principal centre for Christian martyrdom was located beyond Europe rather than within it.[22]

(Oxford, 1993); also Danna Piroyansky, 'Thus may a man be a martyr': The Notion, Language and Experiences of Martyrdom in Late Medieval England', in Thomas S. Freeman and Thomas F. Mayer, eds, *Martyrs and Martyrdom in England, c.1400–1700* (Woodbridge, 2007), 70–87.

[18] For a comprehensive approach to Christian martyrdom in this context, see Brad S. Gregory's seminal *Salvation at Stake: Christian Martyrdom in Early Modern Europe* (Cambridge, MA, 1999), 6; also Susannah Brietz Monta, *Martyrdom and Literature in Early Modern England* (Cambridge, 2005). For a detailed analysis of Catholic martyrs in Tudor England, see Anne Dillon, *The Construction of Martyrdom in the English Catholic Community 1535–1603* (Aldershot, 2002).

[19] Gregory, *Salvation at Stake*, 252.

[20] Boxer, *Christian Century*, 448; Ronnie Po-chia Hsia, *The World of Catholic Renewal 1540–1770*, 2nd edn (Cambridge, 2005; first publ. 1998), 208. More recent studies tend to cite higher estimates, including some 4,000 martyrs, from a baptized *Kirishitan* population of between 200,000 and 300,000 in the period 1614–40; for these figures, see Haruko Nawata Ward, 'Women Martyrs in Passion and Paradise', *World Christianity* 3 (2010), 47–66, at 52–3.

[21] Ucerler, 'Christian Missions in Japan', 334; Liam Brockey, 'Books of Martyrs: Example and Imitation in Europe and Japan, 1597–1650', *Catholic Historical Review* 103 (2017), 207–23, at 210.

[22] Simon Ditchfield has argued for a 'decentering' of Eurocentric perceptions of the Christian world and a reorientation of our historical frames of reference: 'De-centering

This article explores how the martyrs Navarrete, Ayala and Daniel, and their martyrologists Orfanel and Ragueneau, interpreted acts of martyrdom in their missions. The first part contextualizes these martyrdom accounts briefly, emphasizing both the significance of apostolic precedent and the Tridentine view of the priesthood as providing important interpretative frameworks for missionaries. The second part explores how the missionaries applied Christ's teaching to their own circumstances and argues that they viewed martyrdom as an aspect of pastoral responsibility. The third part shows how martyrdom was interpreted in light of the sacramentality of priestly identity as well as confessional beliefs about relics and the intercessory role of saints.[23] The article argues that martyrdom was interpreted as a literal, semi-liturgical sacrifice, a gift of self-sacrificing love to meet the specific needs of mission communities and advance the Roman Catholic Church.

Interpreting Martyrdom in Missions

Martyrdom accounts by missionaries such as Ragueneau and Orfanel were raw material in, as well as products of, a vast martyrological culture within and beyond the Society of Jesus and the mendicant orders. The *indipetae* letters, or petitions to be sent abroad, were full of expressions of a willingness to die in the mission vineyard and included references to Christ himself, early martyrs and missionary saints as their inspiration.[24] Martyrs were the subject of annual letters (*cartas annuas*), private correspondence, histories, art and

---

the Catholic Reformation: Papacy and Peoples in the Early Modern World', *ARG* 101 (2010), 186–208, at 191, 187.

[23] These themes appear in other contexts, for example the letters and writings of the English Cardinal William Allen, especially *An apologie and true declaration of the institution and endeuours of tvvo English colleges* [Rheims, 1581]; see also Rhiannon Teather, 'Traitors, Invaders and Glorious Martyrs: Attitudes toward the Execution of Catholics in England, Japan, Paraguay and New France (*c.*1580–1650)' (PhD dissertation; University of Bristol, 2019), 153–81.

[24] Camilla Russell, '"Imagining the "Indies": Italian Jesuit Petitions for the Overseas Missions at the Turn of the Seventeenth Century', in Massimo Donattini, Giuseppe Marcocci and Stefania Pastore, eds, *L'Europa divisa e i nuovi mondi. Per Andriano Prosperi*, vol. 2 (Pisa, 2011), 179–89, at 182.

plays.[25] Martyr relics, too, were a form of currency across the 'horizontal networks' of missions.[26] A prominent example of the scale and global reach of Catholic martyrdom in the early modern era is the *Societas Jesu usque ad sanguinis et vitæ profusionem militans*, by the Jesuit Mathias Tanner (1630–92), published in Prague in 1675.[27] This martyrology was organized by continent, and recorded the stories of some 304 Jesuits who died in the Catholic mission fields in Europe, Africa, Asia and the Americas during the sixteenth and first half of the seventeenth centuries.[28] Tanner's patchwork of martyr stories reflects a matured perception of missionary martyrs that was well established toward the end of the seventeenth century. Martyrs

[25] A play loosely based on the story of Alonso Navarrete was penned by Lope de Vega: Cummins and Boxer, *Dominican Mission*, 28–46, 60–70; see also Carmen Hsu, 'Martyrdom, Conversion and Monarchy in *Los primeros mártires del Japón* (1621)', in Julia Weitbrecht, Werner Röcke and Ruth von Bernuth, eds, *Zwischen Ereignis und Erzählung. Konversion als Medium der Selbstbeschreibung in Mittelalter und Früher Neuzeit* in (Berlin, 2016), 217–34. On Jesuit martyrological culture, see Luke Clossey, *Salvation and Globalization in the Early Jesuit Missions* (Cambridge, 2008), 81–3, 120–7; Liam Brockey, *Journey to the East: The Jesuit Mission to China, 1579–1724* (Cambridge, MA, 2007), 7, 227–32; Ines G. Županov, *Missionary Tropics: The Catholic Frontier in India (16th–17th Centuries)* (Ann Arbor, MI, 2005), 147–71.

[26] Luke Clossey, *The Early-Modern Jesuit Missions as a Global Movement*, UC Berkeley: UC World History Workshop, Working Papers (2005), online at: <https://escholarship. org/uc/item/0h45m0jw>, last accessed 3 January 2021; Simon Ditchfield, 'Martyrs on the Move: Relics as Vindicators of Local Diversity in the Tridentine Church', in Wood, ed., *Martyrs and Martyrologies*, 283–94. Many relics were sourced from the Roman catacombs, as well as the 'Golden Chamber' of Cologne which contained those of St Ursula and her 11,000 Companions. The cult of the latter was spread around the world by the Jesuits in the 1540s; for a detailed account, see Hermann Crombach, *Vita et martyrium S. Ursvlæ et sociarum undecim millium virginum*, 2 vols (Cologne, 1647). For recent analysis, see Scott B. Montgomery, *St Ursula and the Eleven Thousand Virgins of Cologne: Relics, Reliquaries and the Visual Culture of Group Sanctity in Late Medieval Europe* (Oxford, 2010); Jaime Ferreiro Alemparte, *La leyenda de las once mil vírgenes. Sus reliquias, culto e iconografía* (Murcia, 1991); Simon Ditchfield, 'St Ursula and her 11,000 Companions: A Global Microhistory of the making of Roman Catholicism as a World Religion', in Wietse de Boer, Vincenzo Lavenia and Giuseppe Marcocci, eds, *La ghianda e la quercia. Saggi per Adriano Prosperi* (Rome, 2019), 125–34.

[27] Mathias Tanner, *Societas Jesu usque ad sanguinis et vitæ profusionem militans, in Europa, Africa, Asia, et America contra gentiles, Mahometanos, Judæos, Hæreticos, impios, pro Deo, fide, ecclesia, pietate* (Prague, 1675), especially 278–81, 531–3, for accounts of the martyrs featured in this article.

[28] For a recent brief discussion of this work and its place in Jesuit martyrological discourse, see Ronnie Po-chia Hsia, 'Mission Frontiers: A Reflection on Catholic Missions in the Early Modern World', in Alison Forrestal and Seán Alexander Smith, eds, *The Frontiers of Mission: Perspectives on Early Modern Missionary Catholicism* (Leiden, 2016), 180–93, at 182–5.

were seen as embodiments of the apostolic spirituality and mission of religious orders, reflecting a missionary world view as well as an increasingly global Tridentine church.[29]

Ragueneau and Orfanel, like many other missionary martyrologists, drew upon ancient traditions to interpret their experiences and those of their brethren. The apostolic example in Scripture and the early church was critical to their perception of the role of martyrdom. In the gospels, Christ himself had emphasized the relationship between love and sacrifice, and in particular its expression in laying down one's life for others: 'I am the good shepherd. ... The good shepherd lays down his life for the sheep' (John 10: 11, 16). This was underlined by his later teaching that '[n]o one has greater love than this, to lay down one's life for one's friends' (John 15: 13), and reinforced by his own Passion. In addition to Christ's example, the apostle Paul, who was himself martyred, articulated the clear importance of self-sacrifice in his exhortation in his letter to the Romans, instructing all Christians 'to present your bodies as a living sacrifice, holy and acceptable to God, which is your spiritual worship' (Rom. 12: 1). Thus the reality of martyrdom as an act of spiritual or physical sacrifice was inherent to this apostolic example. The Scriptures offered a 'biblical blueprint' for martyrdom.[30]

The example of the sacrificial, apostolic life found in the New Testament was a primary inspiration for the founders of the Franciscan and Dominican orders in the thirteenth century, and for their vows of poverty, chastity and obedience.[31] This was also true of the early Jesuits, who believed that the establishment of their own order, like that of earlier religious orders, was the result of divine inspiration and an institutional vocation which was truly an 'imitation and revivification of the lifestyle of the first disciples of Jesus'.[32] The apostolic model, combined with these

---

[29] Teather, 'Traitors, Invaders and Glorious Martyrs', abstract. For an analysis of the martyrological views of the early Jesuits, see also Girolamo Imbruglia, '"*Ad militandum*": Sacrifice and the Jesuit Mode of Proceeding', in Vincenzo Lavenia et al., eds, *Compel People to come in: Violence and Catholic Conversion in the Non-European World* (Rome, 2018), 29–48.

[30] Gregory, *Salvation at Stake*, 105–11 (quotation at 109).

[31] *Francis and Clare: The Complete Works*, ed. and trans. Regis J. Armstrong and Ignatius C. Brady (New York, 1982), 17–20; *Early Dominicans: Selected Writings*, ed. and trans. Simon Tugwell, Classics of Western Spirituality (Mahwah, NJ, 1982), 1–47.

[32] John W. O'Malley, *The First Jesuits* (Cambridge, MA, 1993), 66–7.

institutionalized vocations, had an intensified application on the early modern frontiers of mission. Andrew Redden has shown, with reference to Jesuits in Chile, that the New Testament 'Good Shepherd' and 'Lost Sheep' parables combined with the 'Great Commission' (Matt. 28: 19–20) to form a 'step-by-step' biblical 'blueprint for missionary work' in Catholic missions.[33] This involved imitating Christ's example by going out into the world to seek 'the lost sheep' (unbelievers), to convert and baptize them, thereby offering them salvation.[34] These activities were works of charity which also prepared the missionaries for death and furthered their own salvation.[35] The role of martyrs in the creation of these new churches was pivotal in how the missions were viewed. The Jesuits frequently 'made a direct causal link between martyrdom and missionary success', in enterprises from England to Chile.[36] As we shall see, martyrdom was seen as a necessary, purified act of sacrificial love, and one which articulated the deepest aspirations of mission.

Similarly the papal apostolic succession had long institutionalized Christ's commission: bishops were believed to be the successors of the apostles, and the pope the successor of Peter, 'the rock' upon which the Church was to be built; who was given the keys to the kingdom.[37] The belief that Christ's evangelizing mission was assigned to 'Mother Church' could not have been more important during the intensive missionary activity of the sixteenth century and beyond.[38] In particular, it was the Catholic vision of the priesthood that would also shape the way in which missionaries viewed themselves and their martyrs. The priest, through the power vested in him during ordination, was believed to be able to stand in the place of Christ at the mass and in his administration of the other sacraments. In addition, the Council of Trent reaffirmed clerical celibacy and standardized professional

---

[33] Andrew Redden, 'Not-So-Good Shepherds: Reluctant Jesuit Martyrs on the Seventeenth-Century Chilean Frontier', in Forrestal and Smith, eds, *Frontiers of Mission*, 90–114, at 98–9.

[34] Ibid. 99.

[35] Catherine Ballériaux, *Missionary Strategies in the New World, 1610–1690: An Intellectual History* (New York, 2016), 12; Clossey, *Salvation and Globalization*, 246; *The Canons and Decrees of the Sacred and Ecumenical Council of Trent*, ed. and trans. James J. Waterworth (London, 1848), 35.

[36] Redden, 'Not-So-Good Shepherds', 100.

[37] Matt. 16: 18–19; John W. O'Malley, *Trent: What happened at the Council* (Cambridge, MA, 2013), 19–20.

[38] Ibid. 20–1.

training in the seminary, which combined with traditional views to make the priesthood a vocation set apart in service and reasserted priests' importance as paternal leaders of the laity.[39] Missionary priests were seen as a special apostolic task-force, sanctified through ordination and the missionary oath, for the assignment of converting the non-Catholic world.

MARTYRDOM AS A PASTORAL RESPONSIBILITY

The martyrologists Orfanel and Ragueneau emphasized the importance of the relationship between missionaries and their communities as the primary concern for the would-be martyrs. Orfanel included in his account the letter the Dominican missionary Alonso Navarrete had written to his superiors, which highlighted his anxiety about the spiritual welfare of Omura's Christians. Navarrete told his superiors: 'Already Your Reverences see how this Christian community is being gradually extinguished, and so it is necessary to set a good example ... I will go to Omura to confess, and comfort those Christians, because now is a good time, since with the fresh blood of the martyrs they will be more encouraged'.[40] Ayala's letter, also included by Orfanel, further elaborated on the situation and noted the current attitudes of Japanese Christians towards the missionaries: 'some Christians have complained that the Fathers persuade them to become martyrs, while they themselves shun the opportunities'. He argued that he and Navarrete must go to Omura to prove that they, like their Jesuit and Franciscan counterparts, would fulfil their pastoral obligations regardless of personal risk.[41]

This was an acknowledgement of the fact that, until the martyrdom of two European missionaries in May 1617, almost all the recent

---

[39] Michael Mullett, *The Counter-Reformation and the Catholic Reformation in Early Modern Europe* (London, 1984), 16–22.

[40] 'Ya vuestras Reverendísimas ven como esta Cristiandad se va acabando poco a poco, y así es menester dar buen ejemplo a estos Cristianos ... Yo voy a Omura a confesar, y consolar aquellos Cristianos, porque ahora es buen tiempo, pues con la sangre fresca de los Mártires estarán más animados': Orfanel and Collado, *Historia*, 70v.

[41] '[A]unque yo estaba determinado de no decir ninguna razón de las que nos movieron a ir (porque la principal que a mí me movió fue la obediencia que digo tengo dada en este caso) pero quiero dar una, y es, que algunos Cristianos habían murmurado que los Padres les persuadían a ellos que fuesen Mártires, y ellos huían las ocasiones': ibid. 72r.

martyrs had been lay Japanese.[42] In the account this is presented as a point of contention between converts and priests, with the laity seen as taking on a disproportionate burden of sacrifice in the community. This tension was only resolved by the priestly martyrdoms of Navarrete and Ayala.[43] The symbolic importance of the martyrdom of priests was grounded in Christ's teaching about leadership (the greatest among believers as the one who serves), combined with the institutionalized vision of the priesthood as acting *in persona Christi*.[44] While lay Christians could certainly be martyrs, it was the priesthood who were believed to be consecrated for the purpose of paternal leadership and were endowed with the pastoral function of following Christ in ministry (and, if required, martyrdom). Without priests, Japanese Christians were described as 'sheep in the midst of wolves'.[45]

In this context, Navarrete and Ayala viewed martyrdom as nothing less than a pastoral obligation defined by the specific political and religious context in Omura. The act of martyrdom would boost morale and would also make the commitment of the priesthood indisputable. Later in the account, when the moment came for their arrest, Orfanel compared the scene to that of the apostle Paul's goodbye to the Christians at Ephesus (Acts 20: 36–8): there was 'great feeling and weeping among the Christians, similar to the Christians of Ephesus, to whom Saint Paul bid farewell in walking to martyrdom, and said to them, that he would not see them any more'.[46] This parallel served to reinforce the message of the missionaries' apostolic self-sacrifice for the community, reflecting the roots of their inspiration as well as their hopes for the missions.

In 1640s New France, with the rise in violence against Huron villages, Paul Ragueneau's account emphasized the loving sacrifice of missionaries for their community even more explicitly. Ragueneau first reported the death of the Jesuit missionary Antoine Daniel in a letter to the Jesuit superior general Vincent Caraffa. He wrote that as the attack began, Daniel 'hastened wherever he saw the danger

---

[42] Prior to 1617, six Europeans (four Spaniards and two missionaries from Mexico and India) had been numbered among the twenty-six martyrs of Nagasaki in 1597.

[43] Orfanel and Collado, *Historia*, 72r, 79r.

[44] Luke 22: 24–30.

[45] '[C]omo ovejas en medio de los lobos': Orfanel and Collado, *Historia*, 72v.

[46] '[E]ra el sentimiento y llanto grandísimo, semejante al de Los Cristianos de Epheso, cuando san Pablo se despidió dellos caminando al martirio, y diciéndoles, que no le habían de ver mas': Orfanel and Collado, *Historia*, 76r.

most threatening ... intent upon the gain of souls, – mindful of the safety of others, but forgetful of his own, – he hurried into the cabins to baptize the sick, the aged, and children'.[47] Daniel also took a leading role in the evacuation of the village. Ragueneau recorded his final moments:

> That he may delay the enemy, and, like a good shepherd, aid the escape of his flock, he blocks the way of the armed men and breaks their onset; a single man against the foe ... At last he fell, mortally wounded by a musket-shot; and pierced with arrows, he yielded to God the blessed life which he laid down for his flock, as a good Shepherd, calling upon the name of Jesus.[48]

Ragueneau thus termed Daniel 'a good Shepherd' who 'laid down' his own life for the flock to aid their escape, sacrificing his own life to delay the raiders. Later, in the published account of the year 1648–9, Ragueneau emphasized Daniel's twofold sacrifice: he behaved 'truly as a good Pastor, who exposes both his soul and his life for the salvation of his flock'.[49]

Both accounts stressed that missionaries were inspired to sacrifice themselves in, and for, their respective communities. Orfanel's references to Paul, and Ragueneau's to Christ as the Good Shepherd, asserted that the missionaries were divinely inspired in the act of martyrdom. It was a traditional belief, stemming from the earliest accounts in the church, that in their suffering and dying, Christians manifested the real presence of Christ himself: the martyr became 'a sacrifice in the one sacrifice of Christ'.[50] The presence of the Holy Spirit enabled priestly martyrs to behave as model 'good shepherds' during the hour of need in their communities. In line with Christ's teaching that the greatest act of love was to lay down one's life for one's friends, the suffering and death of missionary priests were

---

[47] Paul Ragueneau to General Vincent Caraffa, 1 March 1649, in *JR*, 33: 261.
[48] Ibid. 263.
[49] Ragueneau, 'Relation of 1648–9', in *JR*, 34: 91; on the importance of 'good shepherd' imagery as applied to priests after the Council of Trent, see Richard Atherton, 'The Catholic Priesthood: From Trent to Vatican II and beyond' (PhD thesis, Durham University, 1996), especially 29; available at Durham E-Theses Online: <http://etheses.dur.ac.uk/5269/>, accessed 20 December 2020.
[50] Geoffrey Preston, *The Faces of the Church: Meditations on a Mystery and its Images* (Edinburgh, 1997), 239.

presented as acts of martyrological, sacrificial service to, and on behalf of, their flock.

BODILY SACRIFICE AND PRIESTLY IDENTITY

In missionary accounts the scriptural model of sacrifice and the liturgical role of the priesthood combined to present the act of martyrdom as a form of quasi-eucharistic sacrifice. This reflected the overlapping identities of the missionary priest as leader and servant, and the perceived sacramentality of the role. The focus on worship also encapsulated the deeper functions of the act of martyrdom, which included spiritual warfare, voluntary sacrifice and consecration. For missionaries, worship not only included prayer, the singing of psalms and the preaching of Scripture (all of which were shared with Protestants) but also the use of devotional items (crosses, rosaries) and specific forms of prayer and behaviours which echoed the mass. In Orfanel's account of the execution of Navarrete and Ayala, when they were finally brought to an island known as the place of 'thorns', they were shown as sanctifying the space with devotional objects and prayer. Navarrete bid a spectator, a Christian who had disguised himself as a sailor and earlier received the missionary's crucifix for a future relic, to make him a cross from a stick to hold when he died.[51]

Orfanel described how 'the guards placed them in order for the sacrifice, Father Fray Alonso in the middle, and on either side his saintly companions [Ayala and Tanaka], and the three of them kneeled'. This evoked Christ's crucifixion at Calvary between two thieves, although in this case, all three were Christians.[52] Ayala, the Augustinian, held a rosary in one hand and a candle in the other, and turned toward the *katana* with which he was to be executed in order to kiss it.[53] The kissing of the *katana* was itself highly significant, since in the early church it was not only the remains of martyrs which were revered but the objects with which they had made contact, including possessions or instruments of execution.[54] This *katana*

---

[51] Orfanel and Collado, *Historia*, 78v.
[52] '[L]a qual el hizo, y luego les pusieron en orden para sacrifico, al Padre fray Alonso en medio, y a los dos lado sus santos compañeros, y los tres hincados de rodillas': ibid.
[53] Hartmann, *Augustinians*, 70.
[54] Peter Brown, *The Cult of Saints: Its Rise and Function in Latin Christianity*, 2nd edn (Chicago, IL, 2015), 3.

was later purchased from the executioner and, together with a cloth soaked in Navarrete's blood, was sent to the Dominican priory of San Pablo de Valladolid, Spain.[55] From a liturgical perspective, Ayala's kiss evoked the practice, dating back to the fourth century, of kissing the altar at mass. The altar was the focus of the eucharistic ritual, symbolic of Jesus and of the supernatural family of the church represented by the relics contained therein. In this case, the martyr's body was to become an altar, of both physical and spiritual sacrifice.

After a brief speech in which Ayala outlined their evangelizing mission, declared his 'hope to deserve eternal life' and promised the advent of more missionaries from Europe, he asked for some time for meditation.[56] In what seems an extraordinary request, indicating his control over events, and as if presiding over his own semi-liturgical sacrifice, he instructed his executioner to strike him once he had indicated that his prayer was finished by raising his hand. He was beheaded with one blow and 'in this way triumphant he entered heaven'.[57] Similarly, Navarrete held 'a cross in one hand, and in the other a rosary, and a candle, and from the beginning he had been quietly in a very deep contemplation, and then he raised his hand'; the first blow missed his neck and he fell to the ground and 'looked at the sky, as if he was praying'.[58] The candle evoked the traditional meaning of the light of Christ and at least two were commonly placed on the altar; in this case the martyr's body. Traditionally a candle was also given at baptism and so the martyrs' holding a candle at the point of their deaths likewise indicated a cyclical fidelity to their faith. The rosary, too, referenced the Dominican's Confraternity of Our Lady of the Rosary (established in Nagasaki in 1609), as well as being symbolic of the private devotion of both men.[59]

---

[55] For details, see Cummins and Boxer, *Dominican Mission*, 32 and n. 43.

[56] '[E]stimamos la vida sobre todas las cosas, y el perderla ahora de nuestra voluntad es, porque por este camino esperamos alcanzar los bienes eternos': Orfanel and Collado, *Historia*, 78v–79r.

[57] '[Y] hecho así, de un golpe le cortaron la cabeza, con que entró triunfante en el cielo': ibid. 79r.

[58] 'El Padre fray Alonso tenía en una mano una Cruz, y en la otra el Rosario, y candela, y desde el principio había estado muy recogido en una profunda contemplación, y en levantando el la mano, levanto el verdugo la catana, y errando el golpe del pescuezo, se le dio tan terrible en la cabeza, que se la partió desde el colodrillo hasta las orejas; del cual, aunque cayó en tierra, levanto los ojos al cielo, como quien esta orando': ibid. 79r.

[59] On this confraternity, see Reinier H. Hesselink, '104 Voices from Christian Nagasaki: Document of the Rosario Brotherhood of Nagasaki with the Signatures of its Members

In New France, the act of martyrdom was also presented as a direct extension of the priest's role in the mass. This was made clear in the language of liturgical sacrifice used to describe Daniel's death as well as the circumstances of his death, which occurred during the raid shortly after the conclusion of mass. Ragueneau described the disposal of Daniel's body after he was shot with arrows and an arquebus:

> The fire meanwhile was consuming the cabins; and when it had spread as far as the Church, the Father was cast into it, at the height of the flames, which soon made of him a whole burnt-offering. Be this as it may, he could not have been more gloriously consumed than in the fires and lights of a *Chapelle ardente*.[60]

The fact that Daniel's body was literally thrown into the burning church was clearly dramatic in its symbolism, with his body consumed in the sacred space where the eucharist had been celebrated. His burning body was a vivid extension of the daily sacrifices of prayer and thanksgiving conducted there. These examples show that in the representation of the act of martyrdom itself, there was a fusion of inspired apostolic tradition and the institutional vocation of the priesthood.

Significantly, the reference to Daniel's death as a 'burnt-offering' was an expansion of Ragueneau's reflections in his private correspondence, where he wrote: 'his naked body cast into the midst of the flames was so completely consumed that not even a bone was left: indeed, he could not have found a more glorious funeral pyre'.[61] Ragueneau's later comparison to a *Chapelle ardente* elaborated Daniel's martyrdom on the frontier not only as a 'burnt offering' to God but also as a more glorious commendation than was possible at the most exalted funerals of popes and monarchs.[62] Both accounts also recorded the effect of the sacrifice of their missionary martyrs. In

---

(February 1622): An Analysis and Translation', *Monumenta Nipponica* 70 (2015), 237–83; João Paulo Oliveira e Costa, 'The Brotherhoods (Confrarias) and Lay Support for the Early Christian Church in Japan', *Japanese Journal of Religious Studies* 34 (2007), 67–84.

[60] *JR*, 34: 93.

[61] *JR*, 33: 263.

[62] A *Chapelle ardente* was an elaborate wooden structure decorated with many candles and coats of arms, which was frequently the focal point at a funeral. It also had the liturgical function of being the site where the deceased was granted absolution: Minou Schraven, *Festive Funerals in Early Modern Italy: The Art and Culture of Conspicuous Commemoration* (Farnham, 2014), 1–2, 264.

this, the doctrinal assumptions that distinguished the Catholic confession become more apparent. The emphasis on the role of works in justification, saints and relics, echoed points of confessional dispute and asserted the Catholic perspective. For Catholics, salvation was a project of the universal communion of saints, with each individual, living and dead, playing a reciprocal part in God's plan of reconciliation. This belief helped to shape the way Catholics interpreted the role of the martyrs in missions.

Ragueneau viewed Daniel's martyrdom as a gift which would provide the mission with an intercessor: 'He is the first of our Society who has died in this Mission of the Hurons ... We hope that in Heaven all this country will have in him a powerful intercessor before God.'[63] This was especially significant in a mission which had previously had few 'red' martyrs. In 1639, some nine years prior to Daniel's martyrdom, the then superior of the Jesuits at Quebec, Paul Le Jeune, expressed his concern that it would appear a 'sort of curse if this quarter of the world should not participate in the happiness of having contributed to the splendour of this [God's] glory'.[64] In addition to Daniel's role as an intercessor for the mission, the merits inherent in the act of martyrdom were also seen as having benefited souls in purgatory. In an apparition after his death, Daniel appeared 'in a state of glory' and was asked by the individual who saw him how 'the divine goodness had permitted the body of his servant' to be reduced to even less than ashes. The martyr replied that God had given beauty for his ashes in death, and by way of reward had 'given me many souls which were in Purgatory, – who have accompanied my entrance into Heaven and my triumph there'. In his second apparition, Daniel 'was seen to be present at an assembly that we held in regard to means for advancing the Faith in these countries, when he appeared, strengthening us with his courage, and filling us with his light, and with the spirit of God with which he was completely invested'.[65] According to Ragueneau, then, Daniel's martyrdom had a twofold supernatural power. In heaven, the suffering of his martyrdom merited the reward of freeing souls from purgatory,

---

[63] *JR*, 34: 97; Robert Kolb, 'God's Gift of Martyrdom: The Early Reformation Understanding of Dying for the Faith', *ChH* 64 (1995), 399–411.
[64] Le Jeune, 'Relation, 1639', in *JR*, 17: 13.
[65] *JR*, 34: 97.

while on earth his intercessory role strengthened the missionaries in the evangelizing cause.

The references to relics and the burial of the martyrs' bodies articulated the central meanings and purposes ascribed to the physical sacrifice. Traditionally relics were significant as symbols of the miraculous powers of healing and, in the wake of the Reformation, came even more to embody Catholic confessional identity. Trent affirmed that relics, like images, were physical representations of the intercessory powers available through the saints in heaven.[66] As we have already seen, Tertullian's maxim that the blood of martyrs is seed had a literal application, with all newly established church altars requiring the relics of both a martyr and a saint. The actual killing of Christians on terrain yet to be christianized therefore had a symbolic equivalence: it was a first step in establishing an altar on new ground.

The events which followed such martyrdoms were reportedly dramatic in their immediate effect on spectators. These effects were believed to reflect phenomena in the spiritual realm: the martyrs' blood unlocked spiritual strongholds in missions, staking out the territory for Christ and dealing a tangible blow to the devil's dominion over the people previously in 'darkness'. After the martyrdoms of Navarrete and Ayala, Orfanel recorded that Christian spectators, the executioners and 'the renegades' were all affected by the martyrdom of the missionaries: '[They] bathed their handkerchiefs and many papers in the blessed blood; and they cut their habits from them, and kept everything as great relics, saying, that by them one day they would be converted to the Lord.'[67] Even a sea burial did not prevent boats coming from Nagasaki 'with hooks and nets to try to obtain the bodies', an initially unsuccessful operation by local Christians which reportedly lasted for days.[68]

---

[66] O'Malley, *Trent*, 243–4; Erik R. Seeman, *Death in the New World: Cross-Cultural Encounters, 1492–1800* (Philadelphia, PA, 2010), 114.

[67] 'Sus mismos matadores también con ser renegados bañaron los pañizuelos, y muchos papeles en la sangre bendita; y cortándoles de los hábitos, lo guardaron todo por grandes reliquias, diciendo, que por ellas algún día se habían de convertir al Señor': Orfanel and Collado, *Historia*, 79v.

[68] '[Y] de Nangasaqui fueron muchas embarcaciones con garfios, y redes a procurar sacar los cuerpos, que les duro muchos días': ibid. For a discussion of the importance of relics in Jesuit narratives, see Roldán-Figueroa, 'Father Luis Piñeiro', 209–32.

In the case of the martyrdom of Navarrete and Ayala, the fate of their bodies was interpreted as a providential message from God about his vision for the church.[69] It was viewed as the fulfilment of a blood-red lunar eclipse the previous year, which Orfanel believed had signalled the beginning of the persecution of the priesthood in Japan.[70] The Jesuit and Franciscan martyrs executed in May 1617 had been disinterred in order to prevent their bodies being stolen by the Christians. Orfanel considered it an act of Providence that a martyred member of each order would be buried at sea together:

> When the martyrs died, they opened the coffins of the other two martyrs, that as it was said before the guards had brought, and they put the body of the blessed Father fray Alonso Navarrete [Dominican] with that of the blessed Father Juan Bautista [Jesuit], and the body of Father fray Hernando [Augustinian] with that of Father fray Pedro de la Asunción [Franciscan]; And tying many stones to the coffins, they threw their bodies into the sea, where it seems God wanted to make a close fraternity between these four Orders.[71]

The mission had been plagued at its outset with jurisdictional battles between the religious orders. The martyrdom of the four men, one from each order, was, in Orfanel's view, a message that underpinned God's vision for the church in Japan, in which missionaries overcame 'the world' and 'the flesh' of inter-religious pride and rivalry. Navarrete's body was paired with the Jesuit João Baptista, while Ayala's was paired with the Franciscan Pedro. In stressing the permanence of this collective sea burial, Orfanel was able to make the point that God had shown his people that he wanted to make a 'close fraternity' between the four religious orders. In a comparable way to Daniel's example in New France, the martyrdom of Navarrete and

---

[69] Tanaka, who was martyred alongside Navarrete and Ayala, was also given a sea burial but this act was not afforded the same symbolism, which focused specifically on the martyrdom of the priesthood in Japan and the relationship between religious orders: see Orfanel and Collado, *Historia*, 79v.

[70] Ibid. 80r.

[71] 'Muertos los Mártires abrieron los ataúdes de los otros dos Mártires primeros, que (como queda dicho) había traído, y pusieron el cuerpo del bendito P. fray Alonso Navarrete con el del bendito Padre Juan Bautista, y el del Padre fray Hernando con el del Padre fray Pedro de la Asunción; y amarrando a los ataúdes muchas piedras los arrojaron en la mar, donde parece que el Señor quiso hacer una estrecha hermandad entre estas cuatro Religiones': ibid. 79v.

Ayala allowed them to join the church triumphant in heaven and benefit the church militant on earth.

CONCLUSION

Martyrdom represented not only one of the most ancient synergies of inspiration and institution but one of the most enduring. In the ideal, martyrs distilled the most fundamental of Christ's teachings on love, faith, leadership and sacrifice. Martyrs also modelled for other Christians, at the moment of their death, the fulfilment of the biblical promises about God's love, redemption and salvation. Through the examples of Navarrete, Ayala and Daniel, this article has demonstrated the influence of scriptural teaching on the way missionary martyrologists explained and interpreted the act of martyrdom. Missionary martyrs were presented as inspirational because they embodied the principle of sacrifice for others as the ultimate act of love, made new for a new generation. They were seen as good shepherds, reflecting a renewed apostolic model for the priesthood, relived in the context of early modern frontiers.

This article has also shown that the act of martyrdom was imbued with the meaning and symbolism associated with the Tridentine priestly vocation. The themes of their ministry shaped the accounts and infused their deaths with a sacramentality characteristic of their role. By the seventeenth century, the priesthood also reflected a distinctive force in the wider reformed Roman Catholic Church; combined with its expanding missions, this highlights the missionary character of the age. It was these themes that made them a still deeper source of inspiration for their brethren. Missionaries viewed martyrdom as a literal, semi-liturgical sacrifice, a logical extension of the priest's administration of the sacraments. In the case of Daniel, his body became a burnt offering in the very same church where he had just celebrated mass. The acts of worship and prayer which characterized the final moments of Navarrete and Ayala likewise prepared them for the final sacrifice of their lives to God.

The act of martyrdom was believed to have transformative effects which fulfilled specific needs in the mission communities. In New France, Daniel was seen as a much-needed intercessor. In Japan, Navarrete and Ayala were two examples of a long-awaited priestly constancy. The men were joined with their Jesuit and Franciscan counterparts in the permanence of a sea burial. In both cases, Orfanel and Ragueneau viewed the missionaries as inspirational for their respective missions and religious orders. In the still wider context of confessional conflict, the sacrifice of missionary martyrs likewise underlined the central contention of the Roman Catholic Church that it alone could lay claim to an unbroken apostolic lineage, made manifest in contemporary sacrifices across the world. These martyrs have since received institutional recognition in the Roman Catholic Church. Alonso Navarrete and Hernando Ayala were among the 205 Martyrs of Japan beatified by Pope Pius IX in May 1867, and Antoine Daniel was canonized by Pope Pius XI in June 1930. He was one of eight Jesuits killed in Canada who received this status. Thus these men were seen as martyrs; divinely inspired and worthy representatives of their institutional church.

The Jesuitesses in the Bookshop: Catholic Lay Sisters' Participation in the Dutch Book Trade, 1650–1750

Elise Watson*

University of St Andrews

The institutional Catholic Church in seventeenth-century Amsterdam relied on the work of inspired women who lived under an informal religious rule and called themselves 'spiritual daughters'. Once the States of Holland banned all public exercise of Catholicism, spiritual daughters leveraged the ambiguity of their religious status to pursue unique roles in their communities as catechists, booksellers and enthusiastic consumers of print. However, their lack of a formal order caused consternation among their Catholic confessors. It also disturbed Reformed authorities in their communities, who branded them 'Jesuitesses'. Whilst many scholars have documented this tension between inspired daughter and institutional critique, it has yet to be contextualized fully within the literary culture of the Dutch Republic. This article suggests that due to the de-institutionalized status of the spiritual daughters and the discursive print culture that surrounded them, public criticism replaced direct censure by Catholic and Reformed authorities as the primary impediment to their inspired work.

Among the devoutly Reformed in seventeenth-century Amsterdam, a woman named Hendrikje Kool had developed a reputation for perpetuating blasphemy. Though she lived mere metres from the Oude Kerk, the oldest church in the city and one of the centres of Reformed life, she became notorious for selling printed material as egregiously heretical as hagiography, Roman Catholic liturgy and anti-Reformed polemic from the bookshop in her home. This

* School of History, University of St Andrews, 71 South St, St Andrews, KY16 9QW. E-mail: egw2@st-andrews.ac.uk.

Studies in Church History 57 (2021), 163–184 © The Author(s), 2021. Published by Cambridge University Press on behalf of Ecclesiastical History Society. This is an Open Access article, distributed under the terms of the Creative Commons Attribution-NonCommercial-ShareAlike licence (http://creativecommons.org/licenses/by-nc-sa/4.0/), which permits non-commercial re-use, distribution, and reproduction in any medium, provided the same Creative Commons licence is included and the original work is properly cited. The written permission of Cambridge University Press must be obtained for commercial re-use.
doi: 10.1017/stc.2021.9

house, nicknamed 'the Golden Compass', after the sign outside the shop, had been home to multiple generations of her illustrious Catholic printing and publishing family.[1] On 30 September 1697, Hendrikje died, and the local bailiff Adriaan van Paddenburg recorded and valued an inventory of her estate, including a separately labelled section for the contents of her bookstore. This probate inventory, logged in the book of the notary Joannes Commelin and certified on 19 October, records more than two hundred titles in her possession, with many more parcels of unnamed pamphlets and tracts bound or packaged together. Hendrikje's prominent position as sole bookseller and the overseer of her household was unusual. This was especially true as her family's printing press had shut down years before and she had a brother, Andries, still living. However, by involving herself in the Catholic book trade, she was participating in an important shared phenomenon for women of her stature in seventeenth-century Amsterdam.[2]

Hendrikje belonged to a particular group of women in the Dutch Republic who called themselves 'spiritual daughters'. Although Catholic women in a publicly Reformed country did not have the option of joining a conventional religious order, they could live chaste, prayer-filled, contemplative lives, although they could not commit to a formal rule. While these women would have faced the normative dichotomy of marriage or the cloister elsewhere, the scarcity of formal Catholic organization in the Dutch Republic gave spiritual daughters significant autonomy. Concerned by this dearth of recognized structure, both Catholic and Reformed institutional authorities employed mechanisms of print to constrain and criticize spiritual daughters. Their Catholic confessors, usually missionary priests, were troubled by spiritual daughters' self-directed devotional practices. In response, they wrote rules of life for them to follow in the form of published devotional prayer manuals. Reformed magistrates,

---

[1] This golden compass was probably a reference to the iconic Plantin-Moretus printing house in Antwerp. Catholic printers and booksellers in the Dutch Republic regularly borrowed imprints and iconography from their co-religionists to the south: Andrew Pettegree and Arthur der Weduwen, *The Bookshop of the World: Making and Trading Books in the Dutch Golden Age* (New Haven, CT, 2019), 343–4. My own forthcoming doctoral thesis, which investigates printing for the Catholic community in the seventeenth-century Dutch Republic, will explore this phenomenon more comprehensively.

[2] Amsterdam, Amsterdam City Archives, Archief van de Notarissen ter Standplaats Amsterdam (5075), Johannes Commelin (226), Minuutacten no. 5619, fols 542r–566r.

perturbed by their active work in education and bookselling, castigated them in pamphlets, broadsheets and other forms of public print. This material labelled them 'Jesuitesses' and portrayed them as dangerous tools of the papacy, motivated by 'papist impudence'.[3]

By the seventeenth century, Amsterdam had grown into a pre-eminent global capital of printing and bookselling. Its urban population became accustomed to seeing the printed word in every form: in elaborately bound volumes, mass-printed pamphlets and broadsheet ordinances posted on buildings. The city's diverse and sprawling urban markets and relative lack of censorship cultivated an uncommon level of freedom. An interested party could find any kind of confessional book, whether printed locally or imported from foreign printing firms and sold at local bookshops. The Dutch Republic, and the province of Holland in particular, also boasted an unusually large reading population for the era. This constant production of printed material created new forms of public discourse, in which political and confessional groups could compete for public opinion using propaganda and polemic.[4] For members of the minority Catholic community, common access to religious books and the printed words of their co-religionists provided spiritual solace, as well as a means to educate their children and proselytize their neighbours. As a result, Catholic books made up a significant part of the Amsterdam book trade. The lack of institutionalization that characterized this trade made it an ideal world in which spiritual daughters could participate.

Recent scholarship has increasingly acknowledged the instrumental role of spiritual daughters in the work of the missionary Catholic Church in the Dutch Republic. Since Eugenia Thiessing's foundational work in the 1930s, more recent generations of scholars such as Marit Monteiro, Joke Spaans and Marieke Abels have addressed

---

[3] The accusation of 'papist' or 'popish impudence' was frequently employed by Reformed critics to condemn a variety of Catholic practice. My forthcoming thesis will discuss the political use of this term in greater detail. See also Christine Kooi, 'Popish Impudence: The Perseverance of the Roman Catholic Faithful in Calvinist Holland, 1572–1620', *SCJ* 26 (1995), 75–85.

[4] Pettegree and der Weduwen, *Bookshop of the World*, 9–17; see ibid. 321–44 (for Catholic books), 153–9 (for literacy). For more on print and public discourse, see Jan Bloemendal and Arjan van Dixhoorn, 'Early Modern Literary Cultures and Public Opinion', in Jan Bloemendal, Arjan van Dixhoorn and Elsa Strietman, eds, *Literary Cultures and Public Opinion in the Low Countries, 1450–1650* (Leiden, 2011), 1–35.

new aspects of the spiritual daughters' extraordinary existence. These studies have branched into regional investigations, published transcriptions of the spiritual daughters' writings and inquiries into their role in religious controversy.[5] While these studies do discuss the reading habits of spiritual daughters, these have yet to be placed into the wider context of the critical role print played both in Catholic minority culture and in mechanisms of public discourse in the Dutch Republic. It is within this literary context, this article proposes, that tensions between inspired women and the dual institutional critiques from Catholic confessors and Reformed authorities found their fullest expression.

Using the probate inventory of Hendrikje Kool and the print culture of Amsterdam as exemplars, this article will discuss the spiritual daughters' participation in the Dutch book trade as educators, readers and booksellers. It will also detail the resulting criticism of this work by Catholic and Reformed authorities in manuscript and print. While Reformed ministers and magistrates used polemical writing to criticize spiritual daughters in their roles as educators and booksellers, their Catholic confessors attempted to exercise oversight over what their confessants read through published prayer manuals. Despite these efforts, spiritual daughters such as Hendrikje could pursue inspired spiritual work in the book trade and gain access to a wide variety of reading material. Public criticism became the primary, and sometimes exclusive, impediment to this work. This lack of effective oversight was due to two central and interconnected factors: the ambiguity of the spiritual daughters' roles in church and society as

---

[5] Eugenia Thiessing was the first to argue for the consideration of spiritual daughters on their own terms in her doctoral thesis, *Over klopjes en kwezels* (Utrecht, 1935), defending their active religious lifestyle as something chosen rather than a result of pressure by missionary clergy. Marit Monteiro complemented this with her study of representations of spiritual daughters in contemporary literature, *Geestelijke maagden. Leven tussen klooster en wereld in Noord-Nederland gedurende de zeventiende eeuw* (Hilversum, 1996). For regional studies, see Marieke Abels, *Tussen sloer en heilige. Beeld en zelfbeeld van Goudse en Haarlemse kloen in de zeventiende eeuw* (Utrecht, 2010); Joke Spaans, *De Levens der Maechden. Het verhaal van een religieuze vrouwengemeenschap in de eerste helft van de zeventiende eeuw* (Hilversum, 2012), a study of the De Hoek community in Haarlem. The latter study also includes a monumental transcription of a manuscript book of *vitae* written by a seventeenth-century spiritual daughter, Catharina (Trijn) Jans Oly. For spiritual daughters' role in the religious schisms that characterized the Dutch Catholic Church in this period, see Gerrit vanden Bosch, 'Pionnen op een schaakbord? De rol van klopjes in de belangenstrijd tussen jezuïeten en seculiere priesters in de Republiek omstreeks 1609–1610', *Trajecta* 3 (2000), 252–83.

semi-religious women, and a broader culture in which the widespread availability of print created a de-institutionalized public space for polemic and persuasion.

Being Catholic in the Dutch Republic

Like many seventeenth-century states, the Dutch Republic maintained a strict dichotomy between legal discrimination against, and the practical toleration of, minority religious groups. While every province of the Dutch Republic proscribed the public practice of Catholicism at its inception, the newly dominant Reformed Church did not institute a mandatory policy of conformity.[6] The Union of Utrecht (1579) guaranteed to every individual freedom of religion and the right not to face persecution for private beliefs. While it allowed Catholics to remain Catholic in private, the States General banned any form of public worship, which in 1581 expanded with the so-called 'Book Edict'. This new policy banned 'offensive and seditious' books, pamphlets, news, songs, ballads or any other written or spoken word that could bring 'the common [person] into error, schism and sedition'.[7] Though this neither extended to private belief nor mentioned any confession explicitly, the implication for Catholics was clear.

Remaining Catholics developed ways of life and methods of coping with their new status. Though newly a minority, less than a third of the population in Amsterdam, Catholic adherents tended to be more affluent and well connected than other confessional groups.[8]

[6] Alastair Duke, *Reformation and Revolt in the Low Countries* (London, 1990), 207; K. W. Swart, *William of Orange and the Revolt of the Netherlands*, 2nd edn (Aldershot, 2003), 34–6; James D. Tracy, *The Founding of the Dutch Republic: War, Finance, and Politics in Holland, 1572–1588* (Oxford, 2008), 119–20.

[7] Quoted and translated in Marianne Roobol, *Disputation by Decree: The Public Disputations between Reformed Ministers and Dirck Volckertszoon Coornhert as Instruments of Religious Policy during the Dutch Revolt (1577–1583)* (Leiden, 2010), 172–3; see also Christine Kooi, *Calvinists and Catholics during Holland's Golden Age: Heretics and Idolaters* (Cambridge, 2012), 16–43, 'War and Peace'.

[8] The precise number of faithful Catholics in cities and rural areas of the Netherlands is notoriously difficult to ascertain, not least because of the fluidity of confessional labels in this period: see Carolina Lenarduzzi, *Katholiek in de Republiek. De belevingswereld van een religieuze minderheid 1570–1750* (Nijmegen, 2019), 17, for a recent and useful synthesis of scholarship. For further estimates, see also Willem Frijhoff and Marijke Spies, *1650: Hard-won Unity* (Assen, 2004), 354; Jonathan Israel, *The Dutch Republic: Its Rise, Greatness and Fall, 1477–1806* (Oxford, 1995), 379–80; Hans Knippenburg, *De*

Since they could not worship publicly, they developed house churches (*huiskerken*), also known as clandestine churches (*schuilkerken*), for sacramental gatherings. By the end of the century, these had developed into ostentatious and elaborate sanctuaries capable of accommodating organs, choirs and rich decorations imported from the Catholic Southern Netherlands.[9] This regular flamboyance meant that no resident of the town, Catholic or Protestant, could be in any doubt about where these 'secret' churches were. By the middle of the seventeenth century, the city of Amsterdam housed at least twenty-six private Catholic house churches, with forty missionary priests to service the spiritual needs of the lay population.[10] Catholics at all levels were obliged to pay regular bribes to the local sheriff to turn a blind eye to their conventicles and other private religious gatherings.

Even then, they still ran the risk of occasional raids by municipal authorities. In one remarkable case in Utrecht, recorded by Catholic-born diarist and humanist Arnoldus Buchelius, government authorities raided a late-night mass. One woman in the congregation stepped forward, claiming that she had arranged for the mass to take place and was willing to pay a fee if the authorities promised that the eucharistic bread consecrated in the service would not be violated or destroyed. The sum she offered was 20,000 gulden, about forty times the annual salary of a small-town Reformed minister.[11] Buchelius, who had since converted to Protestantism, did not record the outcome of this lavish offer. Instead, he bemoaned the tenacity and self-sacrificing blindness of his former faith.

---

religieuze kaart van Nederland. Omvang en geografische spreiding van de godsdienstige gezindten vanaf de Reformatie tot heden (Assen, 1992), 23–4.

[9] J. L. M. de Leer, 'De schuilkerk in bedrijf', *Jaarboek de Oranjeboom* 24 (1971), 95–125; F. X. Spiertz, 'Liturgie in de periode van de schuilkerken', in J. A. van der Ven, ed., *Pastoraal tussen ideaal en werkelijkheid* (Kampen, 1985), 121–32; Benjamin J. Kaplan, 'Fictions of Privacy: House Chapels and the Spatial Accommodation of Religious Dissent in Early Modern Europe', *American Historical Review* 107 (2002), 1031–64.

[10] Xander van Eck, *Clandestine Splendor: Paintings for the Catholic Church in the Dutch Republic* (Zwolle, 2008), 111–12.

[11] Anecdote from the diary of Buchelius, described by Judith Pollmann, *Religious Choice in the Dutch Republic: The Reformation of Arnoldus Buchelius, 1565–1641* (Manchester, 1999), 149.

The Active Apostolate of Spiritual Daughters

This bribe-offering woman probably belonged to the spiritual daughters. In the latter decades of the sixteenth century, as the ecclesiastical Dutch missionary organization *Missio Hollandica* or *Hollandse Zending* took shape, women who wanted to live as chaste contemplatives began to petition missionary priests to act informally as their confessors. A few communities of beguines remained, and some women elected to join tertiary religious orders. In parallel, a new and separate identity also emerged, with a corresponding plethora of new labels. On the whole, their confessors and ecclesiastical superiors referred to these women as spiritual virgins (*geestelijke maagden*), emphasizing their virtue. In placards and official decrees, Reformed authorities called them *kloppen* or *klopjes*. However, in many legal documents, such as wills and testaments, as well as instances where their own hands survive, such as book inscriptions, these semi-religious women usually referred to themselves as spiritual daughters (*geestelijke dochters* or *filiae spirituales*). Though Hendrikje Kool's probate inventory was compiled by a Reformed bailiff and a Reformed notary, they maintained this identification, calling her 'Hendrikje Kool, spiritual daughter, who lately resided in her house on the Warmoesstraat under the sign of the compass'.[12] While some women who were beguines or tertiaries also called themselves spiritual daughters, generally the term served as a catch-all for women who wanted to lead active and chaste religious lives but had no formal institutional affiliation.[13]

By the seventeenth century, spiritual daughters had become a ubiquitous part of the religious landscape. Marit Monteiro estimates that five thousand such women lived in the Dutch Republic during

---

[12] Amsterdam City Archives, Minuutacten no. 5619, fol. 543r. While scholars usually refer to these women as spiritual virgins or *klopjes* or *kloppen*, this language reflects terms largely used by their critics. Since this article aspires to set out differences between institutional expectations of these women and their actual ministry, it seems most appropriate to follow the internal identification of 'spiritual daughter'. For more on the potentially pejorative etymology of *klop*, see Evelyne Verheggen, *Beelden voor passie en hartstocht. Bid- en devotieprenten in de Noordelijke Nederlanden, 17de en 18de eeuw* (Zutphen, 2006), 95.
[13] Ibid. 100. While most spiritual daughters in the Dutch Republic did not identify as beguines (i.e. women who belonged to and lived in a beguinage), most women who were beguines also identified as spiritual daughters. Therefore, I use beguine and spiritual daughter interchangeably when I am talking about women who were also beguines, but this dual label fits only a small minority of spiritual daughters.

the seventeenth century. Some communities had fifty or a hundred members, such as De Star in Amsterdam and De Hoek in nearby Haarlem. These communities had a resident priest who was responsible for hearing confessions and administering sacraments to all the sisters.[14] Like beguines or members of tertiary orders, spiritual daughters who lived on their own found confessors, to whom they made informal vows of chastity and obedience. Both secular and regular clergy were tasked with administering sacraments to hundreds if not thousands of congregants in a wide geographic area, leaving their confessants to provide spiritual solace to those they could not reach. As a result, spiritual daughters frequently shouldered the responsibility in their own parishes for setting up the altar and maintaining house churches and liturgical spaces. They also made house calls and performed emergency baptisms.[15] The community in Haarlem even resurrected pre-Reformation musical traditions, both sung and played on a variety of instruments, including the organ.[16] The reduced scrutiny offered to them by the institutional ambiguity of their position, and the family networks in which they traditionally moved, allowed spiritual daughters to pursue an active apostolate. This would not have been possible had they been able to join a formal monastic order, or been as visible in society as ordained clerics such as their confessors.

Spiritual Daughters as Educators

In the absence of overburdened missionary priests, the roles of evangelist and catechist quickly fell to spiritual daughters. In Amsterdam, a famously diverse and close-quartered city, spiritual daughters needed only to step outside their homes to enter the classroom and the mission field. Legally, the Reformed Church maintained a monopoly on primary school education in order to promote

---

[14] Marit Monteiro, 'Power in Piety: Inspiration, Ambitions and Strategies of Spiritual Virgins in the Northern Netherlands during the Seventeenth Century', in Laurence Lux-Sterritt and Carmen M. Mangion, eds, *Gender, Catholicism and Spirituality: Women and the Roman Catholic Church in Britain and Europe, 1200–1900* (Basingstoke, 2010), 115–30, at 115.

[15] Charles H. Parker, *Faith on the Margins: Catholics and Catholicism in the Dutch Golden Age* (London, 2008), 44, 142–3.

[16] Lenarduzzi, *Katholiek in de Republiek*, 215–24.

maximum literacy and educate children in the faith of the public church.[17] However, as with so many other aspects of life in the Dutch Republic, the intention of these laws differed significantly from the degree of their execution. While Catholics could not legally be schoolteachers, many flouted these regulations and taught anyway, hoping that the bribe system and the lax implementation of anti-Catholic legislation would continue.[18] Catholic education aimed to counter the narratives of the history books mandated in Reformed schools, which portrayed the Dutch Revolt as a heroic uprising against the oppressive rule of the Catholic Habsburgs. Outside the formal classroom, spiritual daughters recruited through familial and religious networks. They hosted informal schools for Catholic children, gathering and teaching groups in the homes of individuals under the guise of private education. In Amsterdam and Haarlem, the larger communities of spiritual daughters even established residential schools for girls (*maagdenhuizen*).[19]

The absence of confessional infrastructure meant that Catholic education was largely provided in private, whether in the home or in house churches. Catechisms, spiritual songbooks and basic educational books allowed for the education in a private setting of children and adults new to the faith. A large body of literature was printed for this purpose, especially in Amsterdam, by families such as the Kools. Catechizing children and educating them in the basic precepts of Catholic theology formed a critical part of overarching missionary strategy. Hendrikje Kool's probate inventory contains a much higher proportion of educational texts such as catechisms and canticle books than a personal Catholic library would: of the titled books, more than a quarter are labelled as one of these types of educational texts. Apart from pamphlets, they are also the least expensive, rarely exceeding one gulden apiece.[20] The most frequently appearing title is Heyman Jacobsz, *Sondaeghs schole, ofte Uytlegginge op de euangelien van de sondagen* (*Sunday School, or Description of the Sunday Gospels*),

---

[17] Leendert F. Groenendijk, 'The Reformed Church and Education during the Golden Age of the Dutch Republic', *DRChH* 85 (2005), 53–70.
[18] Kooi, *Calvinists and Catholics*, 207–9.
[19] Joke Spaans, 'Orphans and Students: Recruiting Boys and Girls for the Holland Mission', in Benjamin J. Kaplan et al., eds, *Catholic Communities in Protestant States: Britain and the Netherlands* (Manchester, 2009), 183–99.
[20] Amsterdam City Archives, Minuutacten no. 5619, fols 543r–555r.

which had been printed in many editions by the Kool family.[21] This title retells basic Bible stories through simple rhymes designed for schoolchildren, accompanied by didactic woodcut illustrations. These Bible stories reflect the Sunday lectionary, allowing families to learn alongside the liturgical calendar. This book even includes a note to teachers, reminding them that their students are impressionable 'white paper' and what they teach may remain with them forever.[22] The basic tenets of Catholic doctrine were packaged into catechisms small and large, educational songs in songbooks and short explanatory treatises. These resources allowed spiritual daughters to catechize and educate children and the poor in their communities.

Unsurprisingly, these activities invited a significant critical response from the wider community. While this educational work was generally encouraged by their confessors and other clerics in the Dutch mission, Reformed consistories protested at the aggressive catechizing of the spiritual daughters. They did so both in internal reports and through printed complaints. The classis of Gouda in 1632 alleged that the missionary efforts of the spiritual daughters in their community were so aggressive that they would sneak into the houses of Reformed neighbours and minister to them on their sickbeds. In 1651, a former nun in Delft reported that she had been jeered at in the street and even physically barricaded in her home by a band of spiritual daughters, who would not let her leave to attend a Reformed service.[23] Their dark, well-worn clothing and visible signs of piety such as rosaries and decorated liturgical books made spiritual daughters easily identifiable. As a result, they faced criticism from consistories and Reformed ministers in their communities for their ostentatious and aggressive strategies of seeking catechumens.[24] The synod of South Holland complained bitterly of the 'popish impudence' of these efforts.[25]

---

[21] Heyman Jacobsz, *Sondaeghs schole, ofte Uytlegginge op de euangelien van de sondagen* (Louvain [Amsterdam], 1675).

[22] Ibid. [383].

[23] Kooi, *Calvinists and Catholics*, 162.

[24] See Lenarduzzi, *Katholiek in de Republiek*, 150–8, for a discussion of the spiritual daughters' visibility in their communities, sometimes in intentional contrast with the garb of priests.

[25] W. C. Knuttel, ed., *Acta der particuliere synoden van Zuid-Holland 1622–1700*, 6 vols ('s-Gravenhage, 1908), 1: 277; Kooi, *Calvinists and Catholics*, 76.

Catholic schools for children run by spiritual daughters also achieved enough success to attract controversy. In one case the local lord, unable to eliminate the schools or the women themselves completely, had to insist that they at least include some Reformed books in their curriculum.[26] Reformed consistories protested that spiritual daughters were aggressively circulating catechisms and flouting the established laws on the education of children. A series of edicts in the 1630s and 1640s by the States of Holland castigated the spiritual daughters specifically, as well as their teaching of 'papist superstition'.[27] The synod of Gelderland lamented in 1658 that '*kloppen* schools will cause papist impudence to awaken superstition'.[28] These complaints about spiritual daughters' teaching and catechizing increased in frequency until well into the eighteenth century, when Catholic schools became a more established and accepted part of the Dutch landscape.[29]

Whilst their Catholic confessors and ecclesiastical authorities were supportive of these efforts, they also worked to exercise oversight. In Amsterdam, the *maagdenhuis* grew to the extent that in 1685, the priest-confessor of the Begijnhof, David van der Mye, compiled a list of new rules for its operation.[30] This included supervision by himself and four other priests, as well as their insistence on catechizing the male students. New procedures also regulated the collection of alms for the poor, set out guidelines for family visits and limited how many children could join. The proliferation and importance of the printed Catholic catechism also caused significant controversy; this focused on the use of certain editions in teaching, generating dozens of editions adding to, correcting or criticizing their explication of Catholic doctrine.[31] Altogether, schools run by spiritual daughters caused dismay among Reformed authorities, who accused them in print and manuscript of corrupting impressionable youth. Missionary clerics supported the spiritual daughters as an instrumental part of

---

[26] Arnhem, Gelders Archief, Het archief van de Heeren en Graven van Culemborg (0370), no. 3058.

[27] Cf. Parker, *Faith on the Margins*, 142; see also Monteiro, *Geestelijke Maagden*, 89.

[28] Gelders Archief, Synode van Gelderland (0336), no. 2, Article 10 (1658).

[29] Kooi, *Calvinists and Catholics*, 166.

[30] Haarlem, North Holland Archives, Oud-Katholiek Bisdom Haarlem (225), no. 377.

[31] For example, the controversy set out in Utrecht, Utrecht Archives, Apostolische Vicarissen van de Hollandse zending (1003), no. 407. My thesis will address this topic in greater detail.

Catholic mission strategy, so long as they followed the regulations laid down by their confessors.

SPIRITUAL DAUGHTERS AS READERS

Extant personal and library inventories show that literate, affluent spiritual daughters had significant interests in reading and collecting religious books. Hendrikje Kool's bookshop and its contents demonstrate the spiritual importance and profitability of inexpensive devotional and liturgical prayer books. Spiritual daughters found their religious pedigree in the medieval Brothers and Sisters of the Common Life, who had seen the integration of reading and prayer as sacrosanct. This culminated in the creation of *rapiaria*, personal notebooks that functioned as repositories of prayers, quotations and notes. The most famous of these was Thomas à Kempis's *Imitation of Christ*, which became a bestseller in the seventeenth century among both Reformed and Catholic readers.[32] The spiritual daughters in Amsterdam and the other populous cities of Holland often belonged to noble or upper-class merchant families. This gave them access to books and the education needed to read them from an early age. Many female members of influential Catholic printing families in seventeenth-century Amsterdam, such as the Aeltsz, Kool, Hartoghvelt and van Metelen families, became spiritual daughters.[33]

Spiritual daughters had been active consumers of Catholic books since the early days of the Republic. When a spiritual daughter died, she would often leave books to her spiritual sisters, sometimes accompanied by requests to pray for her soul. In one such example in the Radboud University Special Collections, the giver, Catharina Simons, gifted the book to her spiritual sister Maria van Heel 'as a reminder, so that whoever gets this book after us will pray for the love of God for the two of us'.[34] Especially within established communities such as

---

[32] For more on *rapiaria* and the *Imitatio Christi* as well as its sixteenth- and seventeenth-century publishing record, see Maximilian von Habsburg, *Catholic and Protestant Translations of the* Imitatio Christi, *1425–1650: From Late Medieval Classic to Early Modern Bestseller* (Farnham, 2011), 31–48, 'The *Imitatio Christi* and the *Devotio Moderna*', especially 32–3.

[33] This is well documented in Lienke Paulina Leuven, *De boekhandel te Amsterdam door katholieken gedreven tijdens de Republiek* (Epe, 1951), 28.

[34] Nijmegen, Radboud University Library, Hs 325 no. 1, *Het Gebedenboek van Maria van Heel* (n.pl., 1666). For more analysis of this text, see Verheggen, *Beelden voor passie en*

De Hoek in Haarlem, books like these could pass through generations of spiritual daughters, given as gifts with similar promises to pray for the salvation of their previous owners.[35] Claertje Pieters Breevliet, Hendrikje's cousin, was one of thirty women who attended the services of priest Willem Schep in a house church on the Nieuwezijds Voorburgwal, just down the street from the Begijnhof in Amsterdam. When she died in 1670, she remembered each individual sister in her will with the bequest of a devotional book and a 'little print'.[36]

Giving books as gifts could be both personal and institutional. In her will, made in 1676, Maria van Brakel, a noblewoman and spiritual daughter from Utrecht who spent most of her adult life in Haarlem, left twenty-five gulden for the improvement of the choir and the repair of the organ for her funerary mass, which specifically included the mending of songbooks for the choir.[37] In 1687, Amsterdam beguine Anna Vechters donated a sizeable collection of texts to the Begijnhof. This included a Blaeu atlas, one of the most expensive books of the seventeenth century, a thirty-seven-volume history of the ecumenical councils and several richly illustrated travel books. She gave these books in memory of her brother Jan, a Jesuit priest, on the condition that a mass be read for his soul every year.[38] The rector of the Begijnhof, David van der Mye, used this donation to found an institutional library. Vechters's donation was an exceptional one; in most cases, like the large De Hoek community in Haarlem, women retained their own private book collections, with the exception of common-use liturgical books.[39] A catalogue made of the Begijnhof library in 1891 records more than eight hundred sixteenth- and seventeenth-century religious books.[40] In this way,

---

hartstocht, 82–3; Feike Dietz, 'Gedrukte boeken, met de pen gelezen. Sporen van leesinterpretaties in de religieuze manuscriptcultuur', *De Zeventiende Eeuw* 26 (2010), 152–71.

[35] Verheggen, *Beelden voor passie en hartstocht*, 156.

[36] Jan Piet Filedt Kok, Erik Hinterding and Jan van der Waals, 'Jan Harmensz. Muller as Printmaker: II', *Print Quarterly* 11 (1994), 351–78, at 352.

[37] Gelders Archief, Huis de Doornenburg (0382), no. 246, no. 3, fol 2r. Though Maria did not specify where this mass was to be held, it is possible if not likely that it would have been in the chapel of De Hoek in Haarlem, which had both an organ and a regular choir made up of spiritual daughters: Spaans, *De Levens der Maechden*, 92–3.

[38] Amsterdam City Archives, Archief van het Begijnhof (740), no. 30.

[39] Spaans, *De Levens der Maechden*, 133–5.

[40] Antoine Flament, *Catalogus der Bibliotheek van het rectoraat des Beggijnhofs te Amsterdam* (Amsterdam, 1891).

books passed from sister to sister, laden with enormous personal and sacred significance.

This well-documented relationship between spiritual daughters and books means that, according to Evelyne Verheggen, the cities in Holland that produced the best-known devotional engravings were also home to the largest populations of spiritual daughters. Primarily this included Haarlem and Amsterdam, but also Gouda and Delft.[41] In their contemplation, spiritual daughters read and meditated on images and lives of saints, prayer books, printed pilgrimage literature and other kinds of simple devotional material. Some were praised by their sisters for their pious reading: Maritgen Isbrants, a spiritual daughter in de Hoek, 'read so many spiritual books that her heart was filled with sacred lessons', according to one of her sisters.[42] Claes Braau, a seventeenth-century Catholic printer and bookseller based in Haarlem, printed a large variety of devotional books, pamphlets and broadsheets. Like most Catholic printers in the Dutch Republic, he misrepresented the city of publication in his imprints, claiming to be located in Antwerp or Louvain, but these same imprints also contain the genuine location of his shop in Haarlem, on the same street as the beguinage.[43] The close proximity of Catholic printers and booksellers, as well as the familial connections of many spiritual daughters to the industry, provided avenues for them to acquire religious and devotional material.

While spiritual daughters' confessors and ecclesiastical superiors exercised some oversight over the daughters' educational efforts, they dedicated much more time and energy to addressing the women's devotional pursuits. Spiritual daughters had neither a formal rule nor any kind of institutionally codified informal rule. Priests in both the Northern and Southern Netherlands wrote and published devotional manuals providing instructions for their contemplation and religious practice, intending this genre to serve instead of a rule.[44] These books were almost always printed in vernacular

[41] Verheggen, *Beelden voor passie en hartstocht*, 244.

[42] According to a *vita* by her religious sister Trijn Jans Oly: Monteiro, *Geestelijke Maagden*, 136.

[43] Gabrielle Dorren and Garrelt Verhoeven, 'De twee gezichten van Claes Braau (circa 1636–1707). Een katholieke drukker en boekverkoper in Haarlem', *Holland* 26 (1994), 235–73.

[44] Parker, *Faith on the Margins*, 130.

Dutch in an accessible octavo format; they were produced in large quantity in Amsterdam and also imported from Antwerp, the print capital of the Catholic Southern Netherlands. While lack of a formal rule enabled the active work of the spiritual daughters in the book trade, their confessors and superiors in the mission sought to use these devotional manuals to address every aspect of a spiritual daughter's life, including daily offices, methods of contemplation, reading, eating and even sleeping.[45] In the early decades of the seventeenth century, some also emphasized the importance and value of work as an expression of piety and holiness. However, in later decades this changed to a focus on private devotion, as the demographic of spiritual daughters shifted increasingly towards aristocratic and noble women.[46]

In these manuals, confessors encouraged spiritual daughters to read, although only in a capacity that emphasized humility and obedience. Most writers agreed on the value of reading as a supplement to prayer. The leader of the Dutch Mission, Vicar Apostolic Johannes van Neercassel, argued in his 1670 treatise *Bevestigingh in 't Geloof en Troost in Vervolgingh* (*Confirmation in Faith and Comfort in Persecution*) that prayer and the reading of devotional texts were tools needed to maintain the faith and survive Reformed repression.[47] The availability of a huge variety of devotional books, whether printed locally in Amsterdam or imported from Antwerp and Cologne, was regarded as a spiritual benefit to the souls of the Catholics living *in partibus infidelium*, in the lands of the unbelievers. In his prayer manual *De Weg der Suyverheyt van d'Hollantse maegden* (*The Way of Purity of the Dutch Virgins*), Jesuit Willem Schoenius devoted an entire chapter to the 'spiritual reading of the virgins'. He exhorted them to read 'daily and half-hourly', noting that 'the reading of spiritual books is a sister to prayer, and a great helper to the self'. He even included a prayer to be said before commencing to read a

---

[45] Monteiro discusses this at length in *Geestelijke Maagden*, especially 122–204.

[46] Joke Spaans, 'Time for Prayer and Time for Work: Rule and Practice among Catholic Lay Sisters in the Dutch Republic', in R. N. Swanson, ed., *The Use and Abuse of Time in Christian History*, SCH 37 (Woodbridge, 2002), 161–72, at 166–9. For more on spiritual daughters and nobility, see Jaap Geraerts, *Patrons of the Old Faith* (Leiden, 2018), 190–249, 'Shaping the *Missio Hollandica*', especially 203–5.

[47] Joannes Baptista van Neercassel, *Bevestigingh in 't Geloof en Troost in Vervolgingh* (Brussels, 1670), 357–67.

spiritual book.[48] However, Schoenius also cautioned that reading should be done not in a spirit of curiosity but rather out of obedience and a desire to submit to what the book dictated. In a similar manual, *De leeder Jacobs* (*Jacob's Ladder*, 1670), dedicated to the holy lives of the virgins in Holland, secular priest Joannes Lindeborn wrote that literature was an essential part of contemplation: 'reading follows prayer, and prayer follows reading'.[49] Both authors restricted their readers to a corpus of acceptable texts, mostly classics such as St Augustine's *Confessions*, *The Imitation of Christ* by Thomas à Kempis, and the *Introduction to the Devout Life* by St Francis de Sales. To stray beyond texts already established by the church as canonical and instructive, they cautioned, violated the readers' or daughters' pledges of obedience to their confessors.[50]

Ironically, in the extant registers and library records for communities of spiritual daughters it is not clear that these manuals were widely owned and read. In her monograph, Marit Monteiro outlines a central corpus of thirty-four devotional manuals published before 1710, all intended for use by spiritual daughters. Of these, whilst all but two were published in Hendrikje's lifetime, her inventory includes only two: Schoenius's *Way of Purity* and the *vita* of a spiritual daughter, Joanna van Randenraedt, written by a Jesuit.[51] The Begijnhof library, in almost eight hundred sixteenth- and seventeenth-century titles, contains only one of these thirty-four, Lindeborn's text in both Latin and Dutch editions, although it includes several dozen other titles by authors on the list.[52] Of course, copies of these could have been owned by individuals but not sold in bookshops run by spiritual daughters or preserved in institutional libraries. However, the absence of these manuals dedicated to the spiritual daughters from their own

---

[48] 'Oh Holy Spirit, light my mind and my heart with your divine grace, so that I will want to know and accomplish your will': Willem Schoenius, *De Weg der Suyverheyt van d'Hollantse maegden* (Antwerp [Haarlem], 1685), 294–8 (prayer at 296).

[49] Joannes Lindeborn, *De leeder Jacobs* (Antwerp [Amsterdam], 1670), 219.

[50] Spaans, *De Levens der Maechden*, 133–40; Verheggen, *Beelden voor passie en hartstocht*, 51–2.

[51] Amsterdam City Archives, Minuutacten no. 5619, fols 544v (Schoenius), 547v, 548r (Joanna van Randenraedt); Monteiro, *Geestelijke Maagden*, 355–60.

[52] Flament, *Catalogus*, 89. Since this library was used continuously after the seventeenth century, it is impossible to know for sure how soon after publication sixteenth- and seventeenth-century titles entered the collection. However, it is still interesting to note the lack of this particular kind of devotional book.

bookshops and collections is conspicuous, especially given the presence of many other small-format devotional titles.

SPIRITUAL DAUGHTERS IN THE BOOK TRADE

While spiritual daughters invested in the book trade as readers and collectors from an early stage, the prosperous Amsterdam market offered a new opportunity for the industrious: participation as printers and booksellers. These women's involvement in the book trade was in and of itself not extraordinary in the seventeenth-century Dutch Republic. Women had worked as printers, publishers and booksellers since the introduction of the printing press, and it was not unusual for the widow of a male printer to inherit the family business after his death, continuing to print and sell new editions under either her husband's name or her own.[53] Spiritual daughters sold theological works, devotional engravings and even religious paraphernalia such as rosaries. They worked from their family homes, at book stalls or door-to-door as itinerant vendors.

Although most spiritual daughters in the Amsterdam book trade worked as booksellers, those with families in the industry could sometimes pursue exceptional opportunities as printers and publishers. Geertruy, Maria and Catharina Aeltsz, daughters of the Amsterdam Catholic printer Herman Aeltsz, probably became spiritual daughters in the last years of the seventeenth century. When their father died in 1696, they, along with their brother Allard, inherited his sprawling and profitable business. Over the decades that followed, they continued to print liturgical and devotional Catholic books under the name 'the heirs of Herman Aeltsz'.[54] According to the Short-Title Catalogue Netherlands, their output in the early years of the eighteenth century included folio missals and lives of saints intended for use in the missionary diocese of Utrecht. It also included an

---

[53] For a useful summary, see Paul Hoftijzer, 'Women in the Early Modern Dutch Book Trade', in Suzanna van Dijk, Lia van Gemert and Sheila Ottway, eds, *Writing the History of Women's Writing: Toward an International Approach* (Amsterdam, 2001), 211–22.
[54] Leuven, *De Boekhandel te Amsterdam*, 28, 60, 65. It is difficult to know exactly for how long Geertruy, Maria and Catharina worked in this business; the Short-Title Catalogue Netherlands, at: <https://www.kb.nl/en/organisation/research-expertise/for-libraries/short-title-catalogue-netherlands-stcn>, records sixteen titles printed by the 'heirs of Herman Aeltsz' between 1697 and 1786, implying that multiple generations of printers in the Aeltsz family used this designation.

educational play about the life of St Elizabeth of Hungary, written by a woman, Anna Maria Krul.[55] However, it was much more common for spiritual daughters, supplied by local print shops or booksellers importing religious texts from the Catholic Southern Netherlands, to sell the books themselves.

Hendrikje Kool's role as sole bookseller in her family's shop was unusual, especially given the previous prominence of her family in the print industry. Although near to the Reformed Oude Kerk, her home on the Warmoesstraat was also very close to several other Catholic printers and bookbinders. The Kool family had printed a high volume of Catholic works throughout the seventeenth century, including elaborate devotional engravings and a series of almanacs, although the family press had been closed down and the woodcut blocks and copper plates sold many years before Hendrikje's death. However, the presence of several unused reams of valuable paper in her probate inventory suggest that she still possessed and sold the family's leftover wares.[56] This stock reflects the family's long-standing interest in producing small-format devotional and prayer books, including almanacs, books of hours and rosary books.

These books, usually either printed in Amsterdam under a false imprint or imported from the Southern Netherlands, sold for an average of less than a gulden apiece. This was a manageable investment for a Catholic family of some means. Unfortunately, the compiler of the probate inventory, bailiff van Paddenburg, had no interest in nuanced distinctions between different types of liturgical and devotional prayer books, probably because he was Reformed. Many entries consist simply of phrases like 'A Latin prayer book', a 'prayer book for vespers', or 'a communion book', estimated at different values due to factors such as size and binding which are not made explicit in the description. This makes these books difficult to match to known editions. However, van Paddenburg does note carefully the worth of the books, especially those with valuable material aspects like clasps, gilded pages, French bindings and shagreen, all of which increased their value.[57] Altogether the value of Hendrikje's bookshop totalled

---

[55] [Anna Maria Krul], *De werken van barmhartigheid, vertoond in 't leeven van den heiligen Elizabeth … van Hongaryen … Leerzaam zinspel* (Amsterdam, 1721).

[56] Kok, Hinterding and van der Waals, 'Muller as Printmaker', 352–4; Amsterdam City Archives, Minuutacten no. 5619, fols 542r–566r.

[57] Amsterdam City Archives, Minuutacten no. 5619, fols 552r–555r.

four hundred gulden, a little less than the average annual salary of a Reformed minister, alongside further possessions and household goods worth more than a thousand gulden. While the bailiff's descriptions are tantalizingly vague, the size of the bookshop's inventory and the genres of the listed entries cover a wide variety of subjects and formats. These range from small packets of catechisms and tracts to large illustrated liturgical books.

Hendrikje Kool's family bookshop was exceptional among the population of spiritual daughters selling books in Amsterdam. In most cases, these women operated stalls and small shops in areas known for high concentrations of Catholics, especially near house churches.[58] A number of especially popular book stands became well known in Amsterdam during the second half of the seventeenth century, many of which are known to have been run by spiritual daughters even if their names were not preserved. One of these stands was located outside the Franciscan church nicknamed *'t Boompje* ('the tree'), and was run by a spiritual daughter, Anna Keyser. Another was located in the Jewish neighbourhood outside the Mozes en Aäronkerk, and a third stood outside the Augustinian church (nicknamed *de Ster*, 'the star'). These stands sold or were stocked with not only theological and devotional books, but also almanacs, popular prints and devotional images.[59] Catholic books were also particularly suited to informal networks of distribution. This made the itinerant sale of religious and devotional books profitable and rewarding for spiritual daughters, who could sell their wares more inconspicuously than could Jesuits or other members of the clergy, and as a result were very effective in this trade.[60]

Spiritual daughters' success as booksellers perturbed the Reformed majorities in their communities. However, this rarely translated into direct action against their work. Instead, as the classis of Amsterdam wrote in a resolution to its ministers in 1639, it was better to 'preach against popery, disprove thoroughly its principal arguments, refute completely its circulated books, visit households often, and if possible, confront the priests or at least the papists'.[61] Authors of

[58] Hoftijzer, 'Women in the Early Modern Dutch Book Trade', 215; Leuven, *De Boekhandel te Amsterdam*, 42.

[59] Verheggen, *Beelden voor passie en hartstocht*, 241; Leuven, *De Boekhandel te Amsterdam*, 28.

[60] Jeroen Salman, *Pedlars and the Popular Press: Itinerant Distribution Networks in England and the Netherlands 1600–1850* (Leiden, 2013), 196–204.

[61] Resolution translated and cited in Kooi, *Calvinists and Catholics*, 78.

Elise Watson

all confessions regularly used polemical pamphlets and broadsheets to evangelize and persuade readers in the Dutch Republic.[62] These published materials from Reformed ministers and magistrates portrayed spiritual daughters as both insidious papists and also ridiculous objects of satire, using deeply gendered anti-Catholic rhetoric.[63] Samuel Ampzing, a Reformed minister in Haarlem, wrote a polemical pamphlet against the actions of the spiritual daughters, referring to them by the ultimate pejorative, 'Jesuitesses'. 'Other cities and areas', he wrote, 'are not beset with a swarm of crawling ants ... in a dirty papist anthill, yes, even in a formal cloister, nesting and decaying at the same time'.[64] In 1617, a pamphlet entitled *Favlse position ofte Valschen regel van practijcke der Paepscher Kramers ende Koop-lieden* (*The False Position, or False Rules of the Practice of Popish Pedlars and Merchants*) conflated the stereotypical pushiness of the itinerant salesperson with the aggressive conversion strategy of evangelistic Catholics.[65] Hendrikje's family came under particular fire for their production of almanacs. In one pamphlet published in Amsterdam, Reformed minister Caspar Coolhaes complained bitterly about the proliferation of 'papist almanacs' that would cause the common people to believe falsehoods.[66]

This controversy and the success of spiritual daughters as booksellers attracted criticism not only from Reformed authorities but

[62] The importance of pamphleteering in both religious and political discourse in the Dutch Republic has been thoroughly discussed. Among many excellent texts, see Joep van Gennip's study on polemical pamphlets written by Jesuits, *Controversen in Context. Een comparatief onderzoek naar de Nederlandstalige controversepublicaties van de jezuïeten in de zeventiende-eeuwse Republiek* (Hilversum, 2014); Joke Spaans, *Graphic Satire and Religious Change: The Dutch Republic 1676–1707* (Leiden, 2011); Alastair Duke, *Dissident Identities in the Early Modern Low Countries*, ed. Judith Pollmann and Andrew Spicer (Farnham, 2009).

[63] For many anti-Catholic polemicists, women were particularly dangerous figures, representing the most illogical, superstitious and immoral aspects of Catholicism, suited especially to luring away children: Kooi, *Calvinists and Catholics*, 162–4, 209. For a useful comparative analysis of Catholic women in England, see Frances E. Dolan, *Whores of Babylon: Catholicism, Gender, and Seventeenth-Century Print Culture* (Ithaca, NY, 1999), especially 16–44, '"Home-bred Enemies": Imagining Catholics'.

[64] Samuel Ampzing, *Suppressie vande vermeynde vergaderinge der iesvuyteszen door Vrbanus VIII* (Haarlem, 1632), 4.

[65] *Favlse position ofte Valschen regel van practijcke der Paepscher Kramers ende Koop-lieden* (Middelburg, 1617), cited in Salman, *Pedlars*, 33–4.

[66] Caspar Coolhaes, *Christelycke ende stichtelycke vermaningen* (n.pl., 1607); Jeroen Salman, *Populair drukwerk in de Gouden Eeuw. De almanak als lectuur en handelswaar* (Zutphen, 1999), 305.

182

also from local guilds. The bookkeeper's guild was only founded in Amsterdam in 1662, and whilst Catholics did join they may have faced internal forms of ostracism and repression. Working more informally through family and religious networks, spiritual daughters rarely if ever appeared on guild registers. As a result, they were frequently accused of disrupting the market illegally with their effective bookselling. Spiritual daughters Anna Keyser and Maria de Vries in Amsterdam faced arrest for their illicit retail.[67] In one case, the guild called for the seizure of a spiritual daughter, Alida Liefring, for selling too many books without a guild membership. She was fined and obliged to join the guild, but afterwards permitted to continue her business.[68]

HENDRIKJE'S MISSION

While Reformed authorities had little interest in the reading practices of spiritual daughters, they used polemic to criticize the daughters' educational efforts and their success at selling and distributing print. Conversely, while Catholic priests had minimal issues with spiritual daughters' work as catechists and booksellers, they used devotional prayer manuals to warn against, and seek to curtail, their too-extensive reading habits. In the cases of both these institutions, however, these complaints, made through print or manuscript, rarely translated into actual censure or punishment for the spiritual daughters. Some Reformed authorities tried to prevent the consecration of any new spiritual daughters, and some issued edicts attempting to constrain their dress and behaviour. However, the lack of a hierarchical institution of spiritual daughters made it nearly impossible to discipline or eliminate them.[69] The survival of Hendrikje Kool's probate inventory, and the extant evidence of spiritual daughters' efforts as educators, readers and booksellers testify to their participation in the print world as part of their inspired vocation. Their work and devotion took place in the context of a culture that

---

[67] Leuven, *De boekhandel te Amsterdam*, 11–14.

[68] Amsterdam, Bibliotheek van het Boekenvak, no. 62 11a–h, Allard Pierson, letter to the officers of the book guild, online at: <http://cf.hum.uva.nl/nhl/marskramers/archivalia_18e_eeuw.htm>, accessed 20 June 2020.

[69] The 1581 Book Edict, for example, contained some of these prohibitions: see Roobol, *Disputations by Decree*, 172–3; Spaans, *De Levens der Maechden*, 23–5.

prioritized literary discourse, as did the criticism of them by both internal and external institutions. Though not recorded in her own hand, Hendrikje's probate inventory is a unique preserved example of this phenomenon.

On 5 November 1697, a newspaper in Haarlem, just outside of Amsterdam, publicized the auction of Hendrikje Kool's household effects. 'On Tuesday, 12 November', the advertisement read, 'the posthumous books and goods of Hendrickje Kool will be sold in her bookshop, on the Warmoesstraat in Amsterdam.'[70] While many private Catholic libraries were sold in exactly this way through an advertised sale, for a woman so intimately involved in the book trade this carried a particularly poignant meaning. In a fitting end to her textual ministry, the mechanism of the public auction made her stock available to her friends, customers and co-religionists in Amsterdam. Inspired spiritual daughters such as Hendrikje maximized the ambiguity of their de-institutionalized roles to work actively in their communities as evangelists, teachers, readers and tradeswomen. The text-oriented public discourse of the Dutch Republic meant that the dual criticism they faced from Catholic and Reformed religious institutions remained in the realm of public critique. Their participation in this world, as well as their semi-religious existence, allowed them to pursue their inspired vocation as members of a vocal minority, mediated through the trade of confessional books.

[70] *Oprecht Haerlemse Dingsdaegse Courant* no. 45, 5 November 1697.

Seeking the Seekers

Alec Ryrie*

Durham University

The Seekers, a supposed sect which flourished in late 1640s England, have generally been neglected by historians, with the exception of Quaker historiography, in which the Seekers play a pivotal but supporting role. This article argues that the Seeker phenomenon is worth attending to in its own right. Perhaps deriving from spiritualist, radical and Dutch Collegiant roots, it also represents the logical outcome of English Baptists and other radicals trying and failing to find ecclesiological certainty, and being driven to the conclusion that no true church exists or (for some Seekers) can exist. The article concludes by examining how the Seeker life was lived, whether as austere, apophatic withdrawal; a veering into libertinism; or by forming provisional communities, communities which did, in some cases, serve as a gateway to Quakerism.

The zoo of religious exotica which proliferated across England in the years of the Civil War and Revolution of the 1640s and 1650s has always attracted plenty of attention, but neither evenly nor even-handedly. There has been a good deal written on the phenomenon as a whole: how a Protestant culture which had formerly kept its disputes within relatively narrow bounds suddenly exploded into such exuberant, radical variety, and how the majority who did not join these religious adventures responded.[1] And there has been much scholarship on individual sects, whether the enduringly significant, such as the Baptists and the Quakers; the evanescent but eye-catching, such as the Ranters and the Fifth Monarchists; or the small-scale but indisputably fascinating, such as the Diggers and the Muggletonians.

* Department of Theology and Religion, Durham University, Abbey House, Palace Green, Durham, DH1 3RS. E-mail: alec.ryrie@durham.ac.uk.

[1] Most recently David Como, *Radical Parliamentarians and the English Civil War* (Oxford, 2018); see also the indispensable Ann Hughes, *Gangraena and the Struggle for the English Revolution* (Oxford, 2004).

Studies in Church History 57 (2021), 185–209

doi: 10.1017/stc.2021.10

Yet one of the supposed sects which was and is regularly listed in the catalogues has largely escaped attention. There is only a modest amount of modern scholarship on the Seekers, and, as we will see, the bulk of it represents a very particular, and problematic, way of framing this movement's history. The only substantial published exceptions to that are an article from 1948,[2] which actually spends most of its length discussing a group the author calls the 'Finders', a label the author admits having invented; and a rather better article from 1984,[3] which gives a proper nod in the Seekers' direction but nevertheless looks mostly at the Ranters, who have a much more developed historiography.

One might conclude from this that the Seekers were an inconsequential curiosity. But this is what Thomas Edwards, the obsessive Presbyterian chronicler of 1640s sectarianism, had to say about them in 1646:

> The Sect of Seekers growes very much, and all sorts of Sectaries turn Seekers; many leave the Congregations of Independents, Anabaptists, and fall to be Seekers. ... Whosoever lives but few yeers (if the Sects be suffered to go on) will see that all the other Sects ... will be swallowed up in the Seekers. ... Many are gone already, and multitudes are going that way.[4]

Nor was that simply a momentary panic. Over a decade later, Richard Baxter was asking 'how come so many called *Seekers*' doubt orthodox Protestant doctrine? His conclusion that Seekers are in fact a catspaw for the Jesuits is paranoia rather than reportage, but he added that it was the '*Seekers* ... among whom I have reason to believe the Papists have not the least of their strength in *England* at this day': he plainly saw them as a significant movement. And indeed he went on to list six different varieties of Seekers he had met, with detailed descriptions and examples of each.[5]

---

[2] G. A. Johnson, 'From Seeker to Finder: A Study in Seventeenth-Century English Spiritualism before the Quakers', *ChH* 17 (1948), 299–315.

[3] J. F. McGregor, 'Seekers and Ranters', in idem and B. Reay, eds, *Radical Religion in the English Revolution* (Oxford, 1984), 121–39.

[4] Thomas Edwards, *The first and second part of Gangraena, or, A catalogue and discovery of many of the errors, heresies, blasphemies and pernicious practices of the sectaries*, Wing E227 (London, 1646), 11.

[5] Richard Baxter, *A key for Catholicks, to open the jugling of the Jesuits*, Wing B1295 (London, 1659), 320, 332–4.

This article's starting-point, then, is simply that the Seekers appear to deserve a little more historical attention than they have received. It will argue that, as well as being a group of interest in their own right, they are an unusually extreme – and therefore unusually revealing – case of the relationship between institution and inspiration in the history of Christianity; and also that if we look at the world of radical religion in the English Revolution through their eyes, they give us a different view of radicalism's origins and of its possible trajectories.

WHAT WAS A SEEKER?

Unlike most of the sectarian labels used in this period, 'seeker' was not an inherently pejorative term. It had a long and rather banal pre-history of being used to refer to Christians striving towards God. So it was simple praise for a tract defending the work of the Westminster Assembly in 1643 to say that 'the whole *Assembly* are … *Seekers* unto God night and day'.[6] Only in the mid-1640s, not long before the publication of Edwards's *Gangraena*, did the word become a label for a certain kind, or kinds, of radicalism. That anodyne prehistory is significant, because it meant that the notion of fearlessly seeking after God was already seen in a positive light, and indeed it continued to be used in that way. In 1648 a posthumous collection of sermons by the Congregationalist preacher Jeremiah Burroughs was published under the title *Jacobs seed, or the generation of seekers*, and it used the word in a wholly positive and traditional sense, in praise of 'the Saints of God that have ever sought God truly'.[7] Whether Burroughs's editors were ignoring or playing with the new layer of meaning the word had now acquired, they show that there was still room for ambiguity here, an ambiguity which was open to exploitation. The most famous example of this comes from Oliver Cromwell in October 1646 – just on the terminological cusp – writing to his daughter Bridget Ireton about her younger sister, Elizabeth Claypole:

> Your Sister Claypole is (I trust in mercy) exercised with some perplexed thoughts. She sees her own vanity and carnal mind, bewailing it; she seeks after (as I hope also) that which will satisfy. And thus to be a

[6] *Powers to be resisted, or, A dialogue arguing the Parliaments lawfull resistance of the powers now in armes against them*, Wing P3111 (London, 1643), 48.
[7] Jeremiah Burroughs, *Jacobs seed or The generation of seekers*, Wing B6090 (Cambridge, 1648), 11.

seeker is to be of the best sect next to a finder; and such an one shall every faithful humble seeker be at the end. Happy seeker, happy finder![8]

This passage is cited by every scholar of the Seekers: it was this which set Johnson, in 1948, on the trail of the supposed sect of 'Finders'. Yet it is a very slippery text. It could be taken, perfectly plausibly, to mean that Cromwell was merely talking about simple Christian questing, with 'sect' being no more than a playful metaphor. That is certainly more credible than making him, on the basis of these remarks, into a Seeker fellow-traveller. More likely, however, Cromwell was making use of the space which the word's ambiguity afforded: trying to downplay his daughter's spiritual adventures, and so using the anodyne, generic sense of 'seeker' to smother the new, dangerous sense, which others were even then trying to bring to the fore.

Before we can understand this new sense of the word, a historiographical detour is necessary, for if most scholars have neglected the Seekers, one field has given them sustained and misleading attention. The Seekers have long had a very definite place in Quaker historiography, and most studies of them come from that perspective, including the only monograph dedicated to the subject.[9] There is a great deal of excellent scholarship in this tradition, and I am indebted to it, but it does also represent a distinctively Quaker tradition. Its bare bones were laid out clearly by William Penn in the 1690s. Penn provided a summary history of Christianity as a repeating process of successive holy withdrawals. So the Protestant reformers broke free from the Babylonian captivity of Rome, but they swiftly grew *Rigid* in their *Spirits* ... more for a *Party* then for *Piety*. This led separatists, who were *yet more retired* and select', to withdraw in their turn; only to be seduced by power, such that they *outlived* and *contradicted* their own *Principles*, leaving some who worried that they

[8] *The Writings and Speeches of Oliver Cromwell: With an Introduction, Notes and a Sketch of his Life*, 1: *1599–1649*, ed. Wilbur Cortez Abbot (Oxford, 1988), 416.
[9] Douglas Gwyn, *Seekers Found: Atonement in Early Quaker Experience* (Wallingford, PA, 2000). The most important scholar of the subject, however, was the American Quaker Rufus M. Jones, who returned to the Seekers in several works, in particular *Studies in Mystical Religion* (London, 1909), 452–67; and *Mysticism and Democracy in the English Commonwealth* (Cambridge, MA, 1932), 58–104. See also the pioneering work of the nineteenth-century English Quaker Robert Barclay, *The Inner Life of the Religious Societies of the Commonwealth* (London, 1876).

were not correctly baptized to withdraw from them once more. These Baptists 'for a time ... seemed like *John* of Old, a *Burning* and a *Shining Light*', and yet all too soon 'worldly *Power* spoiled them too. ... They grew *High, Rough* and *Self-righteous*.' Therefore:

> Many left them and all visible *Churches* and *Societies*, and *Wandred* up and down, as *Sheep* without a *Shepherd* ... seeking their *Beloved* but could not find *Him*, as their *Souls* desired to know *Him*. ... These *People* were called *Seekers* by some, and the *Family of Love* by others; because, as they came to the knowledge of one another, they sometimes met together, not *formally* to *Pray* or *Preach*, at appointed times or *Places*, in their own *Wills*, as in times past they were accustomed to do; but waited together in *Silence*, and as any thing rose in any one of their *Minds* that they thought *Savoured* of a *Divine Spring*, so they sometimes *Spoke*.

Some of these Seekers, lacking humility and '*exalted* above *Measure*', became Ranters and were ensnared in pride and debauchery. But it was when the rest stood firm that God chose

> ... to Honour and Visit this benighted and bewildred *Nation* with his *Glorious Day-spring from on High*; yea with a *most sure* and *certain sound of the Word of Light and Life*, through the Testimony of a *Chosen* Vessel. ... What People had been vainly seeking without, with much *Pains* and *Cost*, they by this Ministry found *within*.

By this he meant that eventually George Fox met them and persuaded them that what they had been seeking was Quakerism.[10] This is accurate enough to be misleading. It is true that many Seekers did become Quakers, and much of what we know about the Seeker experience comes from Quaker autobiographies. But the Seekers Penn describes are in effect proto-Quakers, anticipating Quaker forms of worship with suspicious precision. It is, as J. F. McGregor recognized, a sign of a deeper problem: for Penn and for most Quaker commentators since, the Seekers do not really signify as a phenomenon in their own right.[11] Penn tells us nothing about their specific convictions or concerns. They are merely links in

---

[10] William Penn, ed., *A journal or historical account of the life, travels, sufferings, Christian experiences and labour of love in the work of the ministry, of ... George Fox*, Wing F1864 (London, 1694), sigs B2r–C1r.
[11] McGregor, 'Seekers and Ranters', 128–9.

the chain, Quakers who have not yet realized that they are Quakers, supporting actors in someone else's drama. Later Quaker treatments were more sophisticated, but still tended to treat the Seekers as a sectarian version of Schrödinger's cat: mere suspended potentialities, waiting to be resolved by the historian's gaze into either Ranters or Quakers.[12] From the perspective of Quaker studies, it is still natural to speak of 'the gathered Seeker churches from which the Quaker movement emerged'.[13] From Seekers' own perspective, as we shall see, the very notion of a gathered Seeker church is somewhere between an irony and an impossibility.

In accounts of Quaker origins, we frequently read narratives of a Quaker preacher who comes upon a meeting of Seekers – or something like Seekers – and convinces them of the Quaker message. If the Quaker movement has a single recognized point of origin, it is George Fox's encounter in 1652 with the group whom Quaker historians have dubbed the Westmorland Seekers: the great Quaker historian William C. Braithwaite described them as 'a people in white raiment, waiting to be gathered'.[14] If these accounts are read closely, however, a recurrent feature begins to stand out. For example, at Mobberley in Cheshire in 1652, a Quaker preacher visited a group 'whose Custom was when met Together neither To preach nor pray vocally butt to Read the Scriptures & Discourse of Religion, Expecting a farther Manifestation'. He addressed them, and 'many of them were Convinced'. Again, at Nailsworth, Gloucestershire, in the mid-1650s, a Quaker evangelist heard that there had been 'ameeting for some years of apeople called puritans [sic], or Jndependants, a seeking people to know the way of truth'. 'Most of those meeters' came to hear the Quaker, and 'many in and about Naylsworth' were convinced. Or again, in Sussex in May 1655, a Quaker evangelist 'came to a seekers meeting held in Southouer, neere Lewis', and convinced three members of the meeting, which thereafter broke up. Another evangelist in Reigate eighteen months later described how 'a dore was opened for me … there were seuerall sekers (soe called) and many of them were Convinced'. A further account actually

---

[12] For example, Barclay, *Inner Life*, 412.

[13] Kate Peters, 'Quakers and the Culture of Print in the 1650s', in Laura Lunger Knoppers, ed., *The Oxford Handbook of Literature and the English Revolution* (Oxford, 2012), 568–90, at 571.

[14] William C. Braithwaite, *The Beginnings of Quakerism* (London, 1923), 83; cf. Richard J. Hoare, 'The Balby Seekers and Richard Farnworth', *Quaker Studies* 8 (2004), 194–207.

written by someone who was 'at a private Meeting ... of those called Seekers' described how when Quakers visited them, he and 'divers also of the same Meeting at the same time' became 'strongly affected' with the new message. A final example: in Bristol in 1654, a group of as many as twenty of those 'which were seeking after the Lord' gathered weekly, spending the day in silent waiting, 'bowed and broken before the Lord, in Humility and Tenderness'. Two Quaker missionaries visited the meeting, and one of meeters was convinced by them, but apparently not many more.[15] So even these accounts – which are, to be clear, the Quakers' own telling of the story – claim merely that 'many', 'most' or 'divers' members of Seeking groups were convinced by Quaker preaching, or even that only a handful did so. If early Quakers had considerable success recruiting from these groups, they plainly did not convert them wholesale. 'It must not be supposed', Braithwaite warned, 'that the Quaker movement, except in certain districts, absorbed the Seekers *en masse*'.[16] Quaker historiography has not exactly disregarded that warning: it is has simply shown no interest in those Seekers who rejected their Quaker destiny, other than assuming that they collapsed into Ranterism. From the perspective of the history of Quakerism, that is perhaps fair enough. If we are trying to understand the Seekers themselves, this perspective is seriously distorting.

In Quaker historiography, then, 'Seeker' has become an openly teleological category, a word meaning 'not-yet-Quaker', and used to describe people who may not have had the label Seeker applied to them at the time. Fox's journal itself never uses the word. On a few occasions he described visiting what he called 'Separate' teachers and congregations, which the principal twentieth-century edition of the journal supplements with an editor's note explaining that he meant Seekers.[17] As we have already seen, some of these near-contemporary accounts describe these people as Independents or

[15] Norman Penney, ed., *The First Publishers of Truth*, 5 vols (London and Philadelphia, PA, 1904), 18–19, 106, 115, 235 (continuously paginated); William Hull, *The Rise of Quakerism in Amsterdam, 1655–1665* (Philadelphia, PA, 1938), 122; John Toldervy, *The foot out of the snare. Or, A restoration of the inhabitants of Zion into their place*, Wing T1767 (London, 1655), 4–7; Charles Marshall, *Sion's Travellers Comforted, And the Disobedient Warned* (London, 1704), sigs d3v–d4r.

[16] Braithwaite, *Beginnings of Quakerism*, 27.

[17] George Fox, *The Journal of George Fox*, ed. Norman Penney (New York, 2007; this edn first publ. 1924), 63, cf. 145, 148.

puritans instead of, or as well as, Seekers. Even Penn speaks of people 'called *Seekers* by some, and the *Family of Love* by others', an alarming conflation of two rather different radical lineages. For Quakers, therefore, 'Seeker' is a theological category rather than a historical one, a label applied retrospectively to almost any religiously discontented person who eventually becomes or might become a Quaker. Thomas Taylor was an ordained parochial minister before his Quaker convincement in 1652, but he was described as having in those days been 'a Seeking Man, having Real Desires to understand the Things of God ... a true Seeker and Inquirer after the best Things'.[18] This is no doubt true, but also takes full advantage of the word's ambiguous range of meaning. If we define Seekers in their own terms, it is clear both that by no means all early Quakers started out as Seekers, and that by no means all Seekers became either Quakers or Ranters.

Non-Quaker sources characterize the Seekers rather differently. A heresiographical broadside from 1647 described them as follows:

All Ordinances, Church and Ministry,
The Seeker that hath lost his beaten way,
Denies: for miracles he now doth waite,
Thus glorious truths reveal'd are out of date.[19]

This is terse, but fair. Baxter's sixfold classification a decade later did little more than spell it out. The first, entry-level variety of Seekers, Baxter said, are '*Seekers* for the true Church and *Ministry*; holding that such a Church and Ministry there is, but they are at a loss to know which is it'. The second sort question whether such a church or ministry exists at all; a third openly deny it; a fourth deny the existence of an invisible, universal church as well as of specific churches. The fifth accept that true churches and ministries exist but 'suppose themselves above them: for they think that these are but the Administrations of Christ to men in the passage to a *higher state*'. The final kind 'think the whole company of believers should now be over-grown the Scripture, Ministry and Ordinances'.[20] The fifth and perhaps the

---

[18] Thomas Taylor, *Truth's innocency and simplicity shining through the conversion, Gospel-ministry, labours, epistles of love, testimonies and warnings ... of ... Thomas Taylor*, Wing T591 (London, 1697), sigs B3r, C2r.

[19] *A catalogue of the severall sects and opinions in England and other nations. With a briefe rehearsall of their false and dangerous tenents*, Wing C1411 ([London], 1647).

[20] Baxter, *A key for Catholicks*, 332–4.

sixth variety stretch the category of Seeker as it was conventionally used: these people appear to have found something, and so are strictly speaking no longer quite Seekers. This, at least, was the view of one such person, the spiritualist preacher John Saltmarsh. Saltmarsh's 1647 book *Sparkles of Glory* – the title is suggestive of the provisionality so typical of this milieu – was warm about the Seekers, whom he saw as measuring the churches of their own day against the ministry and gifts of the apostolic age and finding them so severely wanting that they could not plausibly be seen as churches in the same sense. Therefore,

> ... now in this time of the *Apostacie* of the *Churches*, they finde no such *gifts*, and so dare not meddle with any *outward Administrations*, dare not *preach*, *baptize*, or *teach*, &c. or have any *Church-fellowship*.
> ... They wait ... as the *Apostles* and *Disciples* at *Jerusalem*, till they were endued with power from on *high*.

Saltmarsh respected this attitude, but believed it was mistaken. To him, such Seekers were backward-looking, expecting the old ministry to be restored: 'a discovery of the *Gospel* rather as to *Christ* after the *flesh*, then [*sic*] after the *Spirit*'. He argued that 'to wait in any such way of *Seeking* or expectation, is *Antichristian*'. He particularly disapproved of the Seekers' tendency to subsist in '*secret chambers*, or *single fellowships*' rather than working together and openly for the new era. In other words, his critique was both doctrinal and institutional.[21] And well it might be, because the central tenet of the Seeker position that he, Baxter and many other witnesses describe is a rejection of institutional churches in any form. There is no church, or at least no church one can be confident deserves the name; and the risk of affirming an erroneous ministry is so intolerable that it is better to remain outside, and better to go thirsty than to risk drinking poison. Revealingly, in some of the earliest texts which use the term *Seeker* in this sense, the terms *Waiter* or *Expecter* are given as synonyms.[22] The Seekers, in this sense, were

---

[21] John Saltmarsh, *Sparkles of Glory, Or, Some Beams of the Morning-Star*, Wing S504 (London, 1647), 290–5; cf. idem, *The smoke in the temple. Wherein is a designe for peace and reconciliation of believers*, Wing S498 (London, 1646), sigs c2r–3r.
[22] See, for example, Edwards, *The first and second part of Gangraena*, 13; 'Wellwisher of Truth & Peace', *A relation of severall heresies ... Discovering the originall ring-leaders, and the time when they began to spread*, Wing R807 (London, 1646), 15; Ephraim Pagitt, *Heresiography, or, A discription of the hereticks and sectaries of these latter times*, 2nd edn,

not a sect at all, but an anti-sect: defined by their ironclad commitment to uncertainty.

THE ROOTS OF SEEKERISM

We may trace the origins of this paralysing conviction in two ways. The classic method of historians of ideas, intellectual genealogy, is not too different from the heresiographical approach popular at the time. Edwards's *Gangraena*, which helped to popularize the label 'Seeker' but did not invent it, quite correctly compared the Seekers' principles to those of the self-described 'spiritualist' Sebastian Franck, Luther's contemporary who believed that 'for fourteen hundred years now there has existed no gathered church nor any sacrament'.[23] There is a spiritualist, radically anti-institutional thread, or rather a series of dots which may or may not be connectable, running from Franck to 1640s England.[24] Alongside Franck there is the parallel Schwenckfeldian tradition, which is more openly provisional, denying all current churches but allowing and even expecting that God might act to renew them. There is an isolated but potentially important English precedent in radical circles around the turn of the century, apparently arising from the suspicion that Roman Catholic baptism was invalid, and that true baptism had therefore vanished from the earth and could only be renewed by direct divine initiative. This doctrine, naturally enough, led some individuals to claim to be the new John the Baptist, including the last person to be burned for heresy in England, Edward Wightman in 1612. However, the second-to-last victim of the heresy laws, Bartholomew Legate, who died only weeks before Wightman, took a different tack. Legate,

---

Wing P175 (London, 1645), 141; John Bastwick, *The second part of that book call'd Independency not Gods ordinance*, Wing B1069 (London, 1645), 37.

[23] Thomas Edwards, *The third part of Gangraena*, Wing E237 (London, 1646), 116; Sebastian Franck, 'A Letter to John Campanus', in George Huntston Williams and Angel M. Mergal, eds, *Spiritual and Anabaptist Writers*, Library of Christian Classics 25 (London, 1957), 149. This edition of *Gangraena* includes (at p. 167) a letter from an informant of Edwards's in Lancashire, dated 10 October 1646, which lists 'Seekers' amongst the sectarians troubling the county by that date, implying that by then the term was in use across much of England.

[24] This thread is traced in more detail in Alec Ryrie, *Unbelievers: An Emotional History of Doubt* (Cambridge, MA, 2019), 141–60; but see especially the fuller treatment of it in Jones, *Studies in Mystical Religion*; idem, *Mysticism and Democracy*.

according to the second-hand report we have, taught that 'New Baptism there cannot be, till there come new Apostles. New Apostles there cannot be, who are not endued (from aboue) with miracles'.[25] Yet he did not go on to anoint himself as such an apostle, instead denying all reports of such miracles as 'idle dreams', and so insisting that there is 'no true Baptism in the earth, nor any one true visible Christian'. He supposedly refused to pray with others, on the grounds that Christian fellowship is an impossibility. When a listener begged to join his church, he replied: 'How sillily you speak. I have all this while taught you, that there is no Church.'[26]

It is, therefore, unsurprising we can trace no institutional continuity following Legate's execution: how could there have been? There are at least some parallels in the world of underground London radicalism in the 1620s and 1630s that David Como has reconstructed: the antinomianism of that world was distinct from Legate's anti-ecclesiasticism, but they share a common anti-formalist impulse.[27] Como's antinomians were commonly described as the Family of Love or as Familists, invoking the sixteenth-century mystical Dutch sect of that name: William Penn was not the first to make the connection between the Familists and the Seekers. There does not in fact seem to be any direct link to the original Familists, but other Dutch connections are more plausible and, intriguingly, the Legate family had mercantile connections in the Netherlands. The great vernacular Dutch ethicist of the late sixteenth century, Dirck Volckertsz Coornhert, who was equally ill at ease with Catholicism and with Calvinism, advocated an interim church, which in Schwenkfeldian style he called a *stilstandskerk*, until a proper apostolic refoundation should come.[28] In some Remonstrant circles, the idea that there was no true church was taken in radically Erastian directions, as in

---

[25] Henoch Clapham, *Errour on the right hand*, RSTC 5341 (London, 1608), 29–31; cf. the briefer report from John Etherington, *A discouery of the errors of the English Anabaptists*, RSTC 14520 (London, 1623), 76–7.

[26] Clapham, *Errour on the right hand*, 31–2, 37–8.

[27] David Como, *Blown by the Spirit: Puritanism and the Emergence of an Antinomian Underground in pre-Civil War England* (Stanford, CA, 2004); J. C. Davis, 'Against Formality: One Aspect of the English Revolution', *TRHS* 6th series 3 (1993), 265–88.

[28] Gwyn, *Seekers found*, 61, 63; Andrew C. Fix, *Prophecy and Reason: The Dutch Collegiants in the Early Enlightenment* (Princeton, NJ, 1991), 89; Ruben Buys, *Sparks of Reason: Vernacular Rationalism in the Low Countries 1550–1670* (Hilversum, 2015); Gerrit Voogt, '"Anyone who can read may be a Preacher": Sixteenth-Century Roots of the Collegiants', *DRChH* 85 (2005), 409–24.

the anonymous 1647 tract *Grallator Furens*, attributed to the minister Pieter Lansbergius, which argued that, since no-one could claim authoritatively to be Christ's representative, anyone might preach, but the state ought not to permit such preachers any status or privileges.[29] There is something Hobbesian about this strand of thinking: Thomas Hobbes was no Seeker, but his philosophy does depend on a Seeker-like commitment to radical uncertainty.

As Rufus Jones argued, however, the more significant Dutch strand runs through the Collegiant movement, which emerged in the 1620s where the wilder fringes of defeated Arminianism overlapped with the fissiparous world of the Dutch Mennonites. The Collegiants were enthusiasts for Sebastian Franck, and the openness and provisionality of their meetings anticipated Seeker scruples. The most direct connections cluster around the intriguing figure of Adam Boreel. Boreel had family connections across the Channel: his father had been a part of a Dutch embassy to England in 1613, and had been knighted by King James I. At some point in the 1630s, Boreel himself came to study in England. Almost all we know about this visit is that he was 'noted for zeal to Religious ways', and that, according to the hostile witness who is our only substantial source for this episode, he was arrested for being an enthusiast and prophet. After a few months his English friends secured his release, although he was expelled from the country. What mark he may have made during this period we do not know, but it is at least clear that the experience did not sour his view of England as a whole. When the Civil War of the 1640s brought with it a religious revolution, Boreel became deeply involved with a group of prominent English and Scottish thinkers who were trying to put together a bulletproof rationalist defence of Christianity. These friendships, which Boreel regarded sufficiently seriously that he took the trouble to learn the English language, plugged him into an intellectually adventurous milieu which spanned Protestant orthodoxy and emerging

---

[29] [Pieter Lansbergius]?, *Grallator furens, de novo in scenam productus cum pantomimo suo, Bombomachide ulissingano* (Franeker, 1647). For this book's salience to Anglophone readers, see George Gillespie, *A treatise of miscellany questions wherein many usefull questions and cases of conscience are discussed and resolved*, Wing G761 (Edinburgh, 1649), 1, 7; 'The Correspondence of John Selden (1584–1654)', transcribed by G. J. Toomer, in Cultures of Knowledge Project, *Early Modern Letters Online*, 193–4, at: <http://emlo.bodleian.ox.ac.uk/blog/wp-content/uploads/2015/01/selden-correspondence.pdf>, last accessed 15 January 2021.

radicalisms. His most constant English correspondent, Samuel Hartlib, was a formidable networker, theologian and scientist, who amongst other things collaborated closely with a rising young radical writer named John Milton.[30]

In 1645–6 Boreel would become, in effect, the second founder of the Collegiants. He set up meetings in Middelburg and Amsterdam around which a new movement formed, and published a weird, compelling manifesto. *Ad legum, et ad testimonium* appeared in Latin in 1645, was never published in Dutch, but did appear in English translation in 1648. By now the outline of his argument will be familiar. Boreel begins from the position that the first apostles' preaching was 'wholly, intrinsically, undoubtedly, and merely true', and that their hearers could be 'infallibly assured of the truth of that word', so much so that even a 'doubting examiner, after a due search, might be infallibly assured that no error … was to be found there'. He then asks how Christians in his own time might attain that same level of utterly invincible certainty. After many tortuous pages of exhaustive logical sifting, he reaches the obvious conclusion: they cannot. And since no ministers can be fully certain whether they are preaching in accordance with God's will 'or only as it seemeth good to themselves', their ministry is 'tainted'. Any church built on such a foundation is corrupt and therefore intolerable. Such churches have merely split Christendom into a kaleidoscope of factions, and the very fact that none of them have been able to convince the others of their authority shows that they have none. As such, these pseudo-churches 'ought to have been very shy of preaching in the name of God' or of claiming divine authority for anything they did. Since they have in fact done the very opposite, he concludes, his readers ought 'to separate themselves from such societies … accounting them not longer Churches of God, but malignant societies; whereinto the soule of a man fearing God … ought not to enter'. He has rather less to say about what these scrupulous objectors should do instead.

---

[30] Walther Schneider, *Adam Boreel. Sein Leben und seine Schriften* (Giessen, 1911), 41–2, who bridles at the charge of 'enthusiasm'; Sheffield, University of Sheffield, Hartlib Papers 3/3/32B; cf. ibid. 3/3/60B on Boreel's command of English. On his English links in general, see Rob Iliffe, '"Jesus Nazarenus legislator": Adam Boreel's Defence of Christianity', in Silvia Berti and Francoise Charles-Daubert, eds, *Heterodoxy, Spinozism and Free Thought in Early Eighteenth-Century Europe* (Dordrecht and Boston, MA, 1996), 375–96; Ernestine van der Wall, 'The Dutch Hebraist Adam Boreel and the Mishnah Project', *Lias* 16 (1989), 239–63.

They ought to worship 'privately ... making use of the Scripture as it is', but he struggles to reconcile the plain fact that the Bible requires collective worship with his deduction that no-one can be sure that any form of worship is valid. He concludes tentatively that it may be 'profitable' to join a community which worships tolerantly and 'with an ear always open readily and thankfully to receive better information', in order both to praise God in the unadorned words of Scripture and 'mutually to edify his neighbour in conference'.[31]

The parallels with the English Seekers are unmistakable. Yet actually piecing together the direct connections – if there are any – is not straightforward. By the time Boreel's book was published in English in 1648, English Seekerism was already well established. There may be a link running through the litigious Worcestershire clothier Clement Writer. According to Edwards, Writer dallied with several different heresies before he eventually 'fell to be a Seeker', claiming that 'there is ... no Ministery, nor no Faith, nor can be, unlesse any can shew as immediate a call to the Ministerie as the Apostles had, and can do the same Miracles as they did'. Edwards called Writer an 'arch-Heretique'.[32] He was not, in fact, a Seeker leader – there was no such thing, by definition – but he was one of the boldest and most articulate Seeker voices. He laid out his early position most clearly in his 1646 book *The jus divinum of presbyterie*, a book which is strongly reminiscent of Boreel's 1645 *Ad legum, et ad testimonium*, both in the way its unusual question-and-answer structure sidles crabwise towards its conclusion, and in the argument itself. Writer's book is not a translation of Boreel but is perhaps an imitation of him. Yet we know of no direct contact between them and we know that Writer did not read Latin. And while the arguments are closely parallel, Writer is less cautious and more far-reaching. He rejects the validity of Christian ministry of any kind, including the validity of water baptism, unless such ministry is authorized by 'mighty works which ... none could do, but by the special power of God'.[33]

[31] [Adam Boreel], *To the lavv, and to the testimonie or, A proposall of certain cases of conscience by way of quaere*, Wing T1562 (London, 1648), especially 5, 28, 37–8, 83, 92–3, 96; cf. idem, *Ad legem, et ad testimonium* (n.pl., 1645).

[32] Thomas Edwards, *Gangraena, or, A catalogue and discovery of many of the errours, heresies, blasphemies and pernicious practices of the sectaries of this time*, Wing E228 (London, 1646), sigs M1r–v.

[33] [Clement Writer], *The jus divinum of presbyterie*, Wing W3724 (London, 1646), especially 12, 34.

There are, therefore, all manner of suggestive hints and half-submerged connections which could be woven together into several plausible intellectual genealogies for the Seeker position, but only with the addition of generous amounts of supposition and guesswork. In the 1930s Jones was asking, of the Seekers: 'Did the movement have a founder? If so, who was he? Was it indigenous, or did it originate abroad and migrate to England? If it came from the Continent, when did it originate there and what place was its native habitat?'[34] Almost a century later, we have little more in the way of answers than he did, but we are also coming to suspect that this genealogical mode of explanation – which privileges institution above inspiration – can lead us to ask the wrong questions. It is all very well to ask out where ideas come from, but it is perhaps more important to notice that ideas which had been out there in Protestant Europe's meme pool for a century or more suddenly started to flourish as never before in mid-1640s England. Whatever thread may connect the Seekers to earlier generations of radicals, they may be better understood as the most purely distilled example of the spirit of anti-formalism which gripped the conscience of English Protestant culture more widely during the revolutionary decades.[35] On this view, they were not exotic intrusions but arose from the mainstream. If so, our story is not one of the long descent of a Seeker movement, but the sudden precipitation of a Seeker moment.

Take, for example, what was happening in contemporary New England, a radical Protestant hothouse with its own distinct pressures. It is well known that Roger Williams had, by the mid-1640s, reached a very Seekerish position, to the extent of casting doubt on baptism, although when Cotton Mather describes Williams and his disciples as being of 'that sort of Sect which we term *Seekers*', he makes it plain that Williams did not use that word himself.[36] Nor, apparently, did those who (wittingly or unwittingly) followed him. In the summer of 1651, one John Spurr was disciplined by the First Church of Boston 'for his insolent bearing witnes against Baptisme and singing and the church covenant as noe ordinances

---

[34] Jones, *Mysticism and Democracy*, 72.
[35] Davis, 'Against Formality'.
[36] Cotton Mather, *Magnalia Christi Americana: Or, The Ecclesiastical History of New-England from its First Planting in the Year 1620. unto the Year of our Lord, 1698*, 7 parts (London, 1702), 7: 9; cf. Jones, *Mysticism and Democracy*, 100–3.

of god'. Eventually, and a little farcically, he was excommunicated 'for his with Drawinge communion from the church at the Lords table'. He had 'professed he could hold noe more communion with the church as it stood', and condemned all of the church's practices, sacraments and ordinances as 'humaine Inventions'. Two more church members were excommunicated on the same grounds later that year, and refused even to come to the church to explain themselves.[37] The following spring two men in the neighbouring Plymouth Colony were sentenced to a hefty fine or a whipping for 'vild and deriding speaches against Gods word and ordinances', and two years later one of those two was disciplined, along with two others, for withdrawing from public worship: one of the trio 'aefirmed hee knew noe publicke vizable worship now in the world'.[38] Some at least of them were New Englanders of long standing, not new arrivals from England carrying their sectarian infection with them. The word 'Seeker' was not used, and the churches seem to have been genuinely puzzled by these people's behaviour. And yet there are plainly close parallels between these people and the English Seekers. What are we to make of such parallels? It seems futile to wonder whether or not there were threads of influence, traceable or irrecoverable, linking these New Englanders to Roger Williams, the English Seekers, the Dutch Collegiants or the earlier Spiritualists. The point surely is that whether the seed was imported or home-cultivated, it was finding fertile soil in which to grow. It is quite possible that this was a pristine creation: that the Seekers of Boston and Plymouth were being consumed, not by others' dangerous ideas, but by their own hair-trigger scrupulosity.

For importing intellectual influences was not strictly necessary. To plenty of observers, the Seeker phenomenon did not seem like an alien intrusion, but a logical end point, a *reductio ad absurdum*, of certain widespread tendencies within the world of Protestant radicalism. In 1645, in one of our very earliest uses of the term 'Seeker' in a sectarian sense, Robert Baillie traced it back to the persistent fear that 'no Church anywhere can have any solid foundation': you cannot be sure it is built on rock rather than shifting sands. This was the root of all separatism, he believed, and drove separatists in the end, 'when they

---

[37] Richard D. Pierce, ed., *The Records of the First Church in Boston 1630–1868*, 3 vols, Publications of the Colonial Society of Massachusetts 39–41 (Boston, MA, 1961), 1: 52–4.
[38] Nathaniel B. Shurtleff, ed., *Records of the Colony of New Plymouth in New England. Court Orders*, 3: *1651–1661* (Boston, MA, 1855), 4, 74.

have run about the whole circle of the Sects, at last to break out into the newest way of the *Seekers*, and once for all to leap out of all Churches'.[39] Essentially the same view comes from another very early witness, Edmund Calamy, preaching in January 1646. Very proper Protestant scruples about episcopacy and correct rites of ordination had, he believed, slipped out of control. The Solemn League and Covenant of 1643 had led some worrywarts first to claim that all previously ordained ministers ought to renounce their pretended orders and seek reordination; then to worry that none of the new forms of ordination were sufficiently pure or could be shown from Scripture to be adequate; and thus finally 'to turn *Seekers*, and to wait till *God* send *Apostles* to ordain *Ministers*'.[40]

Most observers, however, agreed that the root of the problem was not ordination, but a still more fundamental rite of initiation and laying on of hands: baptism. William Bartlet, a minister in Wapping, thought the Seeker phenomenon arose out of a Baptist milieu, with scruples over the correct gospel ordinance of baptism metastasizing into a paralysed inability to be sure any actual baptismal practice was uncorrupt. Baptists themselves were alarmed: the baptistic congregationalist Christopher Blackwood warned in 1646 that 'when you have condemned all ministerie & baptisme ... you will hardly finde a way to set up any ministery, re-establish any baptisme, but leave us among the seekers, who deny any Church or ministery at all upon earth'.[41] As early as 1644, the radical prophet Sarah Jones warned that 'some are seekers out of a Baptism, looking for Elijah, as *John* the Baptist, to bring it from heaven, forsaking all fellowship till Christ shall send forth new Apostles to lay on hands'.[42] The word 'seeker' here does not yet have its full sectarian sense, but it is plainly on the way.

---

[39] Robert Baillie, *A dissuasive from the errours of the time: wherein the tenets of the principall sects, especially of the Independents, are drawn together in one map*, Wing B456 (London, 1645), 163.

[40] Edmund Calamy, *The great danger of covenant-refusing, and covenant-breaking*, Wing C254 (London, 1646), 27.

[41] William Bartlet, *Ba`al-shakoz or, Soveraigne balsome, gently applied in a few weighty considerations*, Wing B987 (London, 1649), 4; Christopher Blackwood, *Apostolicall baptisme: or, A sober rejoinder, to a treatise written by Mr. Thomas Blake*, Wing B3096 (London, 1645 [vere 1646]), 76. On the term 'baptistic congregationalist' for those conventionally described as Particular Baptist, see Matthew Bingham, *Orthodox Radicals: Baptist Identity in the English Revolution* (Oxford, 2019).

[42] S[arah]. J[ones]., *To Sions louers, being a golden egge to avoid infection, or, A short step into the doctrine of laying on of hands*, Wing J990 (London, 1644), sig. A2v.

Several Seekers recalled having passed with growing scruples and disillusionment through Baptist groups and out the other side. Laurence Claxton, one of the first to be called a Seeker, wrote that most of them were initially 'fallen from the Baptists'. Mary Springett and her husband were initially drawn to the new baptism, but they 'found it not to answer the cry of our hearts'. 'I sufficiently saw', said the one-time Baptist Stephen Crisp, that 'I ... had grasped but at a Shadow, and catched nothing but Wind, and that my Baptism was short of *John's*'.[43] Luke Howard, a shoemaker's apprentice from Dover, was baptized one February 'when the Ice was in the Water ... with great Joy'. But over the months that followed, observing that neither he nor his brethren were transformed in spirit, he began to worry that it was merely a 'carnal ordinance'. The crux for him came when he was asked to baptize a new convert, and felt he had to refuse. He could not administer baptism to others because 'I was not satisfied in my own'. He told his dismayed fellow-believers that 'I saw myself out (and them also) of the Faith of the Gospel, and that if ever I do come to know it; I shall know it as plain as my Natural Eyes knows that Door. ... And from that time I gave my self up to a seeking state again.'[44] That sounds painfully principled, and no doubt it was, but as Claxton's chequered career reminds us, there could be more worldly motives. So-called 'dippers', practitioners of adult baptism, were still subject to harassment and persecution in the mid-1640s. Claxton spent six months in prison in Bury St Edmunds in 1645 for baptizing converts. He was eventually released, in part because he was able to swear that his study of the Scripture had now convinced him 'that he ought not to Dip any more'. He pledged to refrain, promising he would 'only wait upon God for a further manifestation of his truth'. The committee understandably did not appreciate that he was renouncing baptism altogether. This far more radical position was, for the moment at least, much less likely to attract legal trouble.[45]

---

[43] Laurence Claxton, *The lost sheep found: or, the prodigal returned*, Wing C4580 (London, 1660), 19; David Booy, ed., *Autobiographical Writings by Early Quaker Women* (Aldershot, 2004), 82; Stephen Crisp, *A memorable account of the Christian experiences, Gospel labours, travels, and sufferings of that ancient servant of Christ, Stephen Crisp*, Wing C6921 (London, 1694), 13.

[44] Luke Howard, *Love and Truth in Plainness Manifested* (London, 1704), 8–11.

[45] Edwards, *Gangraena, or, A catalogue and discovery*, sigs K4v–L1r, which triumphantly reveals the implicit deception.

No doubt to begin with some of these people were genuine seekers, in the sense that they were actively searching for something better to replace what they had renounced as inadequate. This is the sense of the word that later Quaker appropriation of the term encouraged. But in fact many Seekers ceased to believe that a true church existed or might exist out there if only they searched for it long and hard enough. If they did search, they deliberately framed the effort in such a way that it could not succeed, measuring it by standards against which the apostles themselves would surely have fallen short. In the meantime, they insisted, as several observers noticed, that 'there is no true Church upon earth'.[46] That is not a provisional admission of ignorance, but a definitive statement of faith. It was becoming a truism by the end of the 1640s that there was a 'sort of Seekers, who neither seek nor find'.[47] Mary Springett, passing discontentedly from sect to sect as a young widow, concluded

> ... that the Lord and his truth was, but that it was made known to none upon the earth. ... There was nothing manifest since the Apostles' days that was true religion, and so would often express that I knew nothing to be so certainly of God, as I could shed my blood in defence of it. ... I ... resolved in my heart I would ... be without a religion until the Lord manifestly taught me one.[48]

That stance has steeliness in it as well as despair. Repeated disillusionment has hardened into a principled conviction that, as this world stands, no church is possible. It is reminiscent of nothing so much as the apostle Thomas's nihilistic blend of faith and doubt, so unwilling to be taken in by comforting lies that he demands to be able to plunge his hands into Christ's wounds; an ultimatum issued to God, in the same deep confidence that he will be able to meet the challenge.

LIVING AS A SEEKER

Living under such austere principles, Seekers could not avoid becoming exemplars of the dialectic between institution and inspiration

---

[46] Richard Allen, *An antidote against heresy: or a preservative for Protestants*, Wing A1045A (London, 1648), 106–7.

[47] *The manner of the election of Philip Herbert late Earle of Pembroke*, Wing M467 ([London], 1649), 3.

[48] Booy, ed., *Autobiographical Writings*, 82–4, 88.

which this volume considers. Since they believed that they lacked the institution, they found themselves virtually compelled to renounce the inspiration.

It is at this point that the Quaker tradition, with its talk of 'groups' of Seekers loosely defined, and even of 'gathered Seeker churches', becomes positively misleading. The more purist Seeker position renounced collective piety of any kind. In 1645, the Presbyterian minister John Brinsley described that 'the new and strange *Generation of seekers*' as people who 'stand alone (like a lost sheep in a desert)'.[49] Robert Baillie described 'the opinion and practice of those whom we call Seekers' as simply that 'they served God single and alone, without the society of any Church'.[50] By this account, anti-institutionalism was not so much a consequence of Seeker doctrines as the heart of what it meant to be a Seeker. Much direct testimony confirms the point. Whatever we make of the communities whom George Fox converted, his description of his own life during his early turmoil in Derbyshire in 1647 is compelling:

> I fasted much, and walked abroad in solitary places many days ... and went and sate in hollow trees and lonesome places till night came on. ... During all this time I was never joined in profession of religion with any, but gave up myself to the Lord, having forsaken all evil company.[51]

Mary Springett 'gave over all manner of exercises of religion in my family, and in private'.[52] When John Gratton's conscience drove him out of an Independent church, 'I left them, and all Churches and People, and continued alone, like one that had no Mate or Companion. ... [I] was now afraid to join with any, lest they should not worship God aright.'[53] When Luke Howard left the Baptists behind, 'I mourned in secret with Tears ... in a waste Howling Wilderness, where I could find no Trodden Path, nor no Man to lead me out'.[54]

---

[49] John Brinsley, *A looking-glasse for good vvomen, held forth by way of counsell and advice*, Wing B4717 (London, 1645), 12.

[50] Robert Baillie, *Anabaptism, the true fountaine of Independency*, Wing B452A (London, 1647), 31.

[51] Fox, *Journal*, ed. Penney, 7–8.

[52] Booy, ed., *Autobiographical Writings*, 83.

[53] John Gratton, *A Journal of the Life of that Ancient Servant of Christ, John Gratton* (London, 1720), 16.

[54] Richard Farnworth, *The heart opened by Christ*, Wing F485 (London, 1654), 12.

What remained of such people's religion? Perhaps prayer and Bible reading alone: but was even that pure, redolent as it was of the hypocritical pious formalities of puritanism? 'When I used all these duties,' a radical named Paul Hobson claimed, 'I had not one jot of God in me.' The seventeen-year-old Edward Burrough tried to steel himself to prayer in 1650, but heard an inner voice reproving him: 'Thou art ignorant of God, thou knowest not where he is, nor what he is; to what purpose is thy Prayer?' This 'broke me off from praying [and] I left off reading in the Scripture', severing the last moorings still tying him to Christian convention.[55] Seekers, one sympathizer wrote, 'are entered into their rest, they cease from their labours ... all external forms ... duties of prayer, etc.'[56] Such Seekers were not, could not be, a sect.[57] They were something more significant: a mood – a diffuse, leaderless, mood which could surface anywhere and which dissolved the bonds which held Christian communities together. Stripping away every remnant of institution, they left no scope for inspiration either. They did not throw out the baby *with* the bathwater. They deliberately threw out the baby so as to ensure that not so much as a drop of bathwater might be left behind.

This is the farthest point out, at which Seekers had to make a decision: would they really live in this holy vacuum? Those who actually did so are a mystery to us. These people – the truest and most authentic Seekers, if they actually existed – vanish from the record by their very nature. We might question how sustainable such a forbiddingly rarefied apophatic spirituality could truly be, but doubting the existence of such people is in the end an argument from silence, and when we are considering people whose principles committed or

---

[55] Edwards, *Gangraena, or, A catalogue and discovery*, sig. N1v; Edward Burrough, *The memorable works of a son of thunder and consolation*, Wing B5980 ([London], 1672), sig. E1v.

[56] Francis Freeman, *Light vanquishing darknesse. Or a vindication of some truths formerly declared*, Wing F2129 (London, 1650), 2.

[57] Compare the parallel and still controversial argument advanced by J. C. Davis in relation to the supposed Ranters: *Fear, Myth and History: The Ranters and the Historians* (Cambridge, 1986); idem, 'Fear, Myth and Furore: Reappraising the "Ranters"', *P&P* 129 (1990), 79–103. Davis had no more patience with 'Seeker' as a category of analysis than with 'Ranter', but his description of the those labelled Ranters as disparate figures whose common antipathy to partisanship led, ironically, to their being formed into a party by hostile contemporaries and by historians also applies, perhaps more convincingly, to the Seekers.

even sentenced them to silence, such an argument is even more dubious than usual. The best we can say is that, since Seekers were human, they may have found it difficult to gaze unblinkingly into the glare of this dazzling darkness. Laurence Claxton's account of his time with communities he called Seekers describes how his former beliefs were peeled away from him like the layers of an onion, until all that was left was appetites, and he was cynically preaching doctrines he no longer believed in order to line his pockets and lure zealous women into his bed.[58] Claxton's account is deeply problematic, and the dangers of falling for the prurient moral panic that surrounded the so-called Ranters are all too well known. Yet with all the institutional guard-rails of conventional piety removed, it is not hard to believe that some Seekers may have turned their attention to searching for less impossibly transcendent goals.

There was of course an alternative, for those who never went quite so far, or who, having looked over the edge into the void, pulled back. Those have concluded that no existing church, worship or ordinance is valid could be forgiven for wanting to discuss that devastating insight with others of like mind; for wanting to gather regularly to do so; perhaps, even, for doing so at the same hour as their spiritually blind neighbours assembled in their false churches. In July 1645, the Welsh Seeker William Erbury preached forcefully against 'gathering Churches' and baptism, and did so to a gathered congregation numbering some forty people. He compared them to the Israelites in the wilderness, who had manna but not yet the full covenant of circumcision. 'So now we may have many sweet things, conference and Prayer, but not a Ministery and Sacraments.'[59] To be an anti-partisan party is certainly an irony, but it is not necessarily a contradiction. In a tract of 1651 which was one of the most thoughtful and balanced defences of the Seeker position, John Jackson insisted that Seekers did not reject *all* ordinances. They believed they were called to 'searching the Testimonies of the Holy Writings of Truth', and 'the same touching Prayer, and distributing to the necessity of those that want'. And while these duties were chiefly solitary, there is also some 'coming together into some place on the First-dayes [Sundays], and at other times, as their hearts are drawn forth, and opportunity is offered'. The purpose of these gatherings was to

---

[58] Claxton, *Lost sheep found*, especially 19–33.
[59] Edwards, *Gangraena, or, A catalogue and discovery*, sig L3v.

... keep alive, and hold out in their measure their witness and testimony against the false, and waite for the manifestation of the true Lord Jesus, in his pure Ordinances of Mi|nistery and Worship ... expressing their deep sence of the want of what they enjoy not, behaving themselves ... as Sheep unfolded, and as Souldiers unrallied, waiting for a time of gathering, and restitution to the knowledge of what as yet they understand not.

That is certainly deeply austere, but there is at least the ghost of an institution: a body is being kept ready so that inspiration might one day fill it.[60]

This is what we may imagine when we read of Claxton joining 'the society of those people called *Seekers*, who worshipped God onely by prayer and preaching',[61] or of John Toldervy attending 'a private Meeting ... of those called Seekers', in which 'two or three ... were making enquiry what should be the meaning of the Spirit of God in two Scriptures, which seemingly did appear to contradict each other'.[62] We may even believe Charles Marshall's account of how, in 1654, of

... many which were seeking after the Lord ... a few of us ... kept one day of the Week in Fasting and Prayer; so that when this day came, we met together early in the Morning, not tasting any thing; and sat down sometimes in silence; and as any found a Concern on their *Spirits*, and Inclination in their *Hearts*, they kneeled down, and sought the Lord; so that sometimes, before the day ended, there might be Twenty of us might pray, Men and Women, and sometimes Children spake a few words.[63]

Or perhaps we do not entirely believe him. For Marshall, like so many of our retrospective witnesses of the Seeker experience, became a Quaker, and all of those accounts are shaped by hindsight. When he describes something that sounds for all the world like a Quaker meeting *avant la lettre*, we are entitled to be suspicious.

And yet, for all that we must recognize the relentless undercurrent in this subject's historiography tugging us towards Quakerism; for all

[60] John Jackson, *A sober word to a serious people: or, A moderate discourse respecting as well the Seekers, (so called) as the present churches*, Wing J78A (London, 1651), 3.
[61] Claxton, *Lost sheep found*, 19.
[62] Toldervy, *The foot out of the snare*, 3–4.
[63] Marshall, *Sion's Travellers Comforted*, sig. d3v.

that we must treat the Seeker experience as a phenomenon in its own right, not simply a Quaker warm-up act, there is no escaping the fact that plenty of Seekers did become Quakers, and that Seekerism dissolved into darkness while Quakerism flourished. The takeover was not complete but it was substantial. And it is supremely a story of inspiration and institution: for the Quakers' achievement, in stark contrast to the Seekers, was eventually to develop a structure and a form of collective life and worship which was faithful to the inspiration that drove them, but which also channelled, disciplined and nurtured it. In particular, where Seekers had nothing aside from their own consciences to keep them from sliding into hypocrisy or depravity, the Quakers quickly acquired that rarest and most invaluable of Christian characteristics: a reputation for fiercely authentic morality. It was that which convinced the former Mary Springett, now Mary Penington, that these wandering nobodies whom she had at first dismissed as fanatics were in fact the real thing.[64] Toldervy, too, was won over by the Quakers' implacable opposition to sin, 'the sincerity of their discourse, with the sobriety of their appearance. ... I concluded, that surely these people were of God, sent forth as witnesses for himself.'[65] When faced with an audience so resolutely sceptical that they denied that a true church was even possible, it turned out that a community who became known for their daunting and unimpeachable moral perfection could make headway.

Even this, however, may have been a symptom of something deeper. The Quakers had, with their doctrine of the light of Christ within, successfully discovered what the Seekers had despaired of finding: a genuinely invincible certainty, a certainty which *felt*, as Boreel would put it, 'wholly, intrinsically, undoubtedly, and merely true', and of which they could be 'infallibly assured'. Take the case of the former Leveller John Lilburne, in Dover in 1655, where he was visited by Luke Howard, the ex-Baptist and Seeker who had by now turned Quaker. Lilburne asked him, 'I pray, sir, of what Opinion are you?' – a weary question which may be curious for novelty, but does not expect enlightenment. Howard gave an unexpected reply: 'None.' Pressed on the subject, he insisted repeatedly that 'really I am of no Opinion', and he also refused to instruct Lilburne on how to act: 'Thou mayest speak what is in thine owne Minde, & after thy

[64] Booy, ed., *Autobiographical Writings*, 89.
[65] Toldervy, *The foot out of the snare*, 3.

owne Manner.' This was the exact opposite of how sectarians usually behaved, and Lilburne was both perplexed and intrigued. Eventually he accompanied Howard to a Quaker meeting. He was unimpressed, feeling that 'his Wisdom was aboue it'. But another Quaker preacher there, George Harrison, told him, 'Friend, thou art too high for Truth', which words, Lilburne claimed, 'gaue him ... "such a Box on ye Eare," that stund him againe'.[66] He would go on to live and die a Quaker. In a world of shifting opinions and dubious claims to wisdom, to meet a group who denied holding any opinions, who were confident that everyone who looked inside themselves would find the same truths, and who met only to share in the secret that there are no secrets, was to find unexpectedly what the Seekers had given up seeking. No wonder if, for many of those who had gone out to the farthest point and discovered the hard way that you cannot have inspiration without some form of institution, it was the form of institutionalized inspiration we call Quakerism that offered something they had despaired of ever finding: a home.

---

[66] Penney, ed., *First Publishers of Truth*, 144–5.

'A Blessed and Glorious Work of God, … Attended with Some Irregularity': Managing Methodist Revivals, c.1740–1800

Clive Murray Norris*

Oxford Brookes University

The Connexion established by John Wesley (1703–91) experienced many outbreaks of local revival in the late eighteenth century. These were examples of the tension between reason and emotion, spontaneity and regularity, which characterized the movement. This article discusses how, amidst concerns from within Methodism and beyond, the leadership sought to manage but not suppress what was perceived to be this work of the Holy Spirit. Its challenge to the connexional polity was especially acute in the 1790s, during the Great Yorkshire Revival. In 1800, a Methodist-inspired publication sought to present good practice on validating and encouraging local revivals while maximizing their effectiveness and minimizing any disruption to the connexional order or wider civil society. However, despite fears that institutional concerns were dampening the Spirit's work, around 1800 Wesley's successors acted to reassert the control of the Preachers' Conference over Methodist practice and premises, and a cautious rationalism came to the fore.

In the later eighteenth century, John Wesley's Methodist Connexion experienced periodic but sudden outbreaks of religious fervour, leading to 'multiplied conversions':[1] what were termed local revivals. Typically, these were spontaneous rather than planned; were led by lay members, often women; involved child conversions; and emphasized the ministry of prayer rather than preaching. As Henry Rack observes, however: 'By the 1830s the professionals had moved in

* 18 Parkfields, London, SW15 6NH. E-mail: cnorris@brookes.ac.uk.
I am most grateful to my anonymous reviewers, and to Bill Gibson, Peter Forsaith and John Lenton, for their comments on earlier versions of this article.
[1] The key characteristic of revival, according to one Victorian manual: Henry C. Fish, *Handbook of Revivals, for the Use of Winners of Souls* (London, 1873), 13. Of course, revivals also occurred in many non-Wesleyan contexts, including Wales and Scotland.

Studies in Church History 57 (2021), 210–232 © The Author(s), 2021. Published by Cambridge University Press on behalf of Ecclesiastical History Society
doi: 10.1017/stc.2021.11

with prescriptions and special techniques which guaranteed a revival if they were followed.'[2]

Other students of revival such as John Kent, David Bebbington and Michael McClymond have also perceived this trend.[3] From its inception as part of the mid-eighteenth-century Evangelical Revival,[4] Wesley's mission had been characterized by what David Hempton has called 'the interior dialectic of Methodist experience – its combination of spiritual freedom and order'.[5] Over time, however, the 'institutional' dimension had grown more powerful than the 'inspirational' one, and 'Methodism was transformed from a renewal movement within Anglicanism into an autonomous organized church.'[6] This article explores this transition through reviewing the debate around 1800 about whether and how continuing outbreaks of local revival could find their place within this new church.

THE CHALLENGE OF LOCAL REVIVALS

For Wesley and many of his Anglican colleagues, while the Spirit worked quietly and routinely through grace in the daily lives of believers, the era of widespread extraordinary action had ended with the primitive church; Wesley argued that once Christianity had become the state religion, under the emperor Constantine, such events ceased 'because the Christians were turned heathens again, and had only a dead form left'.[7] However, he sometimes portrayed Methodism as the rekindling of the flame of Pentecost, and did not exclude the possibility that the Spirit was again at work in an

---

[2] Henry D. Rack, *Reasonable Enthusiast: John Wesley and the Rise of Methodism* (London, 1989), 491–4, at 494.

[3] John Kent, *Holding the Fort: Studies in Victorian Revivalism* (London, 1978); David Bebbington, *Victorian Religious Revivals: Culture and Piety in Local and Global Contexts* (Oxford, 2012); Michael J. McClymond, 'Revival', in Andrew C. Thompson, ed., *The Oxford History of Protestant Dissenting Traditions*, 2: *The Long Eighteenth Century*, c.*1689–c.1828* (Oxford, 2018), 225–42.

[4] The classic account is W. Reginald Ward, *The Protestant Evangelical Awakening* (Cambridge, 1992). My use of the term 'revival' is a matter of convenience, not a judgement on the eighteenth-century Church of England.

[5] David Hempton, *The Religion of the People: Methodism and popular religion, c.1750–1900* (London, 1996), 13.

[6] Phyllis Mack, *Heart Religion in the British Enlightenment: Gender and Emotion in Early Methodism* (Cambridge, 2008), 261.

[7] John Wesley, Sermon 89, 'The More Excellent Way', in A. C. Outler, ed., *Bicentennial Edition of the Works of John Wesley*, 3: *Sermons III* (Nashville, TN, 1986), 262–77, at 264.

extraordinary way.[8] In practice, after the excitement of the 1730s and 1740s had subsided, smaller-scale revivals continued to occur periodically within the Connexion, in a wide range of localities. Indeed, as Wesley had predicted, there was an 'almost rhythmic pattern of generational revivalism'.[9] In Cornwall, local revivals were reported broadly once in every sixteen years.[10] Wesley's preachers eagerly shared news about revivals with him and with each other. In 1754 the Scottish minister John Gillies published his exhaustive collection of narratives of the Evangelical Revival, for which Wesley acted as marketing agent in England.[11] By 1800, twenty articles on revivals within Wesley's Connexion had appeared in its journal, the *Arminian Magazine*, often contemporary accounts. Among them were reports on revivals across the British Isles, including Yorkshire (1747–8, 1778–9, 1782–3, 1792, 1794), Cornwall (1781–2), Norfolk (1781–2), northern Ireland (1767) and Cork (1782).

Some revivals arose in response to preaching, for example by the Irish Wesleyan John Smith (1713–74). In 1767 he wrote of widespread revival in northern Ireland, which he linked to his own preaching visits.[12] John Valton (1740–94) sent Wesley a stream of reports of revivals in response to his preaching, as at Bath in 1782,[13] and Batley, Yorkshire, in 1783.[14] Other preacher-led revivals included those in Manchester (1783) and Kent (1784).[15] In the 1790s, preachers such as Mary Barritt (1772–1851) and William Bramwell (1759–1818) enjoyed sustained success in encouraging a series of local

---

[8] John Wesley, Sermon 4, 'Scriptural Christianity', in A. C. Outler, ed., *Bicentennial Edition of the Works of John Wesley*, 1: *Sermons I* (Nashville, TN, 1984), 159–80, at 160.
[9] David Hempton, *The Religion of the People: Methodism and Popular Religion, c.1750–1900* (London, 1996), 40.
[10] John C. C. Probert, *The Sociology of Cornish Methodism to the Present Day* (Redruth, 1971), 29.
[11] John Gillies, ed., *Historical Collections Relating to Remarkable Periods of the Success of the Gospel and Eminent Instruments Employed in Promoting it* (Glasgow, 1754); John Gillies to John Wesley, 1 September 1757, in *A Collection of Letters on Religious Subjects, from various eminent Ministers, and Others, to the Rev. John Wesley* (London, 1797), 55.
[12] John Smith to Mrs King, 4 November 1767, Letter CCLXVII, *Arminian Magazine* [hereafter: *AM*] 5 (1782), 668–9.
[13] John Valton to John Wesley, 19 December 1778, *AM* 22 (1799), 204–5.
[14] 'Mr. Valton's Account of a Revival of the Work of God', 1 February 1783, *AM* 10 (1787), 98–100.
[15] John Allen, 'A Short Account of the Revival of the Work of God at Manchester', *AM* 9 (1786), 664–5; Zechariah Yewdall, 'The Experience of Mr. Zechariah Yewdall', *AM* 18 (1795), 321.

revivals in northern England;[16] in Yorkshire alone, membership rose by 59 per cent between 1790 and 1797 in what has been called the Great Yorkshire Revival.[17] Women evangelists were often prominent; indeed they dominated this revival.[18]

What excited contemporary Methodists most, however, was when the Holy Spirit seemed to work directly through the Methodist people, women and men, children and adults, or even drew on non-connexional agents. In 1796 the preacher Thomas Taylor (1738–1816) analysed the origins of the 1778–9 revival in Birstal:

The preaching of the word was attended with much energy and life … But our Lord did not confine himself to preaching alone; he let us see that he could carry on his own work without us: Prayer-meetings were singularly useful … But in short, dreams and visions, thunder and lightning; yea, the very chirping of a bird was made successful to the awakening sinners.[19]

Some local revivals drew on extraordinary manifestations of the divine, although the preachers always viewed these with caution. Visions by young girls were a major feature of a revival on the Isle of Man in the late 1770s, but the preacher Thomas Wride (1733–1807) complained, in reporting to Wesley, that he could 'never get regular information' since they prophesied in Manx.[20] And as revival spread across Yorkshire in the mid-1790s, a central role was played by the mystic Ann Cutler, known as 'Praying Nanny', who claimed to be in union with the Holy Trinity, a claim which Wesley acknowledged, but suggested she keep to herself.[21]

---

[16] See John Baxter, 'The Great Yorkshire Revival 1792–6: A Study of Mass Revival among the Methodists', in Michael Hill, ed., *A Sociological Yearbook of Religion in Britain 7* (London, 1974), 46–76; Paul Wesley Chilcote, *She offered them Christ: The Legacy of Women Preachers in Early Methodism* (Eugene, OR, 2001), 111–15; Herbert McGonigle, 'William Bramwell: A Re-appraisal', *PWHS* 54 (2004), 219–36; John H. Lenton, 'Mary Barritt Taft (1772–1851): A Successful Female Revivalist?', *PWHS* 62 (2019), 15–34.

[17] Analysis based on published returns in Baxter, 'Great Yorkshire Revival', Appendix.

[18] See Jennifer Lloyd, *Women and the Shaping of British Methodism: Persistent Preachers, 1807–1907* (Manchester, 2009), for example 47–8; Mack, *Heart Religion*, 290.

[19] Thomas Taylor to the Editor, 6 February 1796, *AM* 19 (1796), 411–14.

[20] Manchester, John Rylands Library, Methodist Archives and Research Centre [hereafter: MARC], MA1977/610/140a, Thomas Wride to John Wesley, 24 May 1777.

[21] William Bramwell, *A Short Account of the Life and Death of Ann Cutler, commonly known by the name of Praying Nanny* (Leeds, 1798). Wesley advised her: 'You may tell all your experience to me at any time: but you will need to be cautious in speaking to

Whilst welcome in many ways as evidence of God's continuing support for Wesley's mission, local revivals were also hugely problematic for the leadership, in four related ways. Firstly, by definition they went beyond the scope of existing national and local plans, and were therefore potentially destabilizing. Of course, Methodists often longed for revival. The 1762 Dales revival was preceded by months of fasting and prayer each Friday;[22] and in early 1782 John Valton told John Wesley that his Manchester members were fasting in the hope of revival.[23] However, revivals typically involved short-term and frequently large-scale increases in attendance at chapels and other meetings, and the local Methodist infrastructure sometimes struggled to cope. During the mid-1780s revival at St Austell, the preacher Adam Clarke (c.1762–1832) reported that on one occasion 'Our chapel, though the largest in the circuit, is so filled, that the people are obliged to stand on the seats to make room … Last Sunday night I preached there, and was obliged to get in at the window in order to get to the pulpit.'[24] Even worse, mass conversions often failed to yield long-term increases in membership. As the leading preacher Alexander Mather (1733–1800) told a colleague in 1796, spiritual after-care was essential to forestall such attrition:

> [You must] 1. … see that they meet with some leader who is a real friend to the Work. 2. You must carefully watch the time when there is a decrease of that exceeding great joy which they first experienced … 3. Prevail upon them likewise to meet in band with one who will prove a nursing father or mother to them.[25]

Secondly, local revivals disturbed the existing connexional order in other ways. In the early stages, confusion was often rife; when revival came to Weardale in 1771, one local leader reported: 'We met again

---

others, for they would not understand what you say': John Wesley to Ann Cutler, 15 April 1790, in John Telford, ed., *The Letters of the Rev. John Wesley, A.M.*, 8 vols (London, 1931), 8: 214–15.

[22] Entry for 7 June 1763, in W. R. Ward and R. P. Heitzenrater, eds, *Bicentennial Edition of the Works of John Wesley*, 21: *Journal and Diaries IV* (Nashville, TN, 1992), 415.

[23] John Valton to John Wesley, 1 January 1782, Letter DXX, *AM* 13 (1790), 105–6; see also Rack, *Reasonable Enthusiast*, 492–4.

[24] Adam Clarke to Eliza Cook, n.d, but between 14 June 1784 and 20 February 1785, in Adam Clarke, *The Miscellaneous Works of Adam Clarke*, 12 vols (London, 1843–4), 12: 421–3, at 422. Circuits were sub-regional groupings of local Methodist societies.

[25] Alexander Mather to George Marsden, 29 January 1796, *AM* 20 (1797), 515.

at two, and abundance of people, came together from various parts, being alarmed by some confused reports'.[26] Across Yorkshire in 1794, Mather found that '[t]here no doubt is, & in the nature of things must be a noise & some degree of confusion.'[27] The rhythm of regular worship and corporate activity was interrupted. Mather suspended weekday preaching in Hull, explaining: 'I have lately adapted to prayer meetings with short exhortations, instead of preaching, wishing to work with God.'[28]

Even where the Holy Spirit seemed to be working within the connexional framework, Methodist preachers, leaders and members could feel threatened. In the early 1760s Mather had encountered opposition from 'some of the old Methodists' when using prayer meetings as a tool for evangelism in Staffordshire, possibly because his wife led some of them; malicious stories circulated 'either against the work, or the instruments employed therein, my Wife in particular; whom indeed God had been pleased to make eminently useful'.[29] As Bramwell observed frankly of Cutler's missionary activities in 1790s Yorkshire:

> Wherever she went there was an amazing power of God attending her prayers. This was a very great trial to many of us: to see the Lord make use of such simple means, and our usefulness comparatively but small. I used every means, in private, to prevent prejudice in the societies; but with many of my good elder brethren it was impracticable.[30]

Thirdly, the extravagant expressions of fervour which characterized revival meetings troubled many, both within and outside Methodism, because of their perceived lack of 'decorum'.[31] Such concerns were of long standing. In his highly influential account of the 1730s New England revival, the Congregationalist preacher Jonathan Edwards

---

[26] Account of a meeting of 8 December 1771: Anthony Steele, *History of Methodism in Barnard Castle and the Principal Places in the Dales Circuit* (London, 1857), 110.

[27] MARC, MA1977/487, Early Preachers' Letters, vol. 2, fol. 258, Alexander Mather to William Marriott, 11 March 1794.

[28] Ibid., fol. 259.

[29] 'An Account of Mr. Alexander Mather: in a Letter to the Rev. Mr. John Wesley', *AM* 3 (1780), 156; see also Andrew F. Goodhead, 'A Crown and a Cross: The Origins, Development, and Decline of the Methodist Class Meeting in 18th century England' (PhD thesis, University of Sheffield, 2007), 265–6.

[30] Bramwell, *Ann Cutler*, 12.

[31] 'Decorum' was associated with gentlemanly behaviour: see the entry in Samuel Johnson, *A Dictionary of the English Language* (Hildesheim, 1968; first publ. 1755).

(1703–58) had noted that 'it is a stumbling to some, that religious affections should be so *violent* (as they express it) in some persons'.[32] Accusations of fanaticism had dogged Methodists. In 1764 one Welsh minister had ridiculed their 'wild Pranks ... singing, capering, bawling, fainting, thumping and a Variety of other Exercises'.[33] At the Methodist Preachers' Conference in 1796, Bramwell led prayers at a love-feast in spectacular fashion. One description echoed the account in Acts 2 of the day of Pentecost:

> Bro. Bramwell went to prayer, & the power of God fell like lightning for quickness & like the rushing wind for effect. Many of the people in the gallery seemed to fall upon the floor & others was [*sic*] so frightened by the noise that they got up from their places & ran downstairs & out of the doors without looking behind them.[34]

For the Yorkshire clergyman Joseph Nelson, however, such comparisons were outrageous. For him, the operations of the Holy Spirit had been almost entirely institutionalized, leaving the Bible, as interpreted by clergy who had been well educated, as the only sure guide.[35]

Fourthly, however, there was a more fundamental issue. In encouraging local revivals, Wesley and his colleagues were taking significant risks. His itinerant preachers were carefully selected, trained (through a combination of on-the-job training and planned reading) and supervised, and were subject to annual performance appraisal. Through imposition of the Connexion's Model Deed, Methodist chapels were open only to preachers following approved doctrine; and within their walls only approved hymns could be sung.[36] Yet

---

[32] Jonathan Edwards, *Thoughts Concerning the Revival of Religion in New-England. Abridged by John Wesley* (London, 1798), 8.

[33] David Lloyd to Posthumus Lloyd, 27 April 1764, in George E. Evans, ed., *Lloyd Letters (1754–1796): Being Extant Letters of David Lloyd, Minister of LLwynrhydowen; Posthumus Lloyd, his Brother; and Charles Lloyd, LL.D., his Son* (Aberystwyth, 1908), 52.

[34] Early Preachers' Letters, vol. 2, Thomas Dixon, autobiography and journal, fols 312–13; cf. 'suddenly there came a sound from heaven as of a rushing mighty wind' (Acts 2: 2).

[35] 'A Clergyman of the Church of England', *A Treatise on Inspiration; in which the Pretence to Extraordinary Inspiration is Considered, and clearly and fully Refuted* (York, 1799), 13–14. Joseph Entwisle, who published a response, identified the author as Revd Joseph Nelson (1764–1817), vicar of Skipwith and curate of Riccall; see Clergy of the Church of England Database, person ID 121583, online at: <https://theclergydatabase.org.uk/jsp/search/index.jsp>, accessed 22 December 2020.

[36] See Frank Baker, 'The People called Methodists – Polity', in Rupert E. Davies and E. Gordon Rupp, eds, *A History of the Methodist Church in Great Britain*, vol. 1 (London, 1965), 213–55.

in many cases, local societies were now falling under the sway of revivals led by lay members of all ages, and focusing on unscripted, extempore prayer sessions, often held in private homes.

In thus casting themselves adrift from the connexional anchor, how could Methodists be sure that what they were experiencing was the work of the Holy Spirit and not of the devil? In Norfolk in 1782, the preacher James Wood (1751–1840) recorded his concerns over some apparent converts, 'whose experience, I strongly suspect; not from their fainting, fits &c. but from an inability to give any clear, rational account of their conviction or conversion'.[37] Joseph Entwisle (1767–1841) responded similarly to an ecstatic meeting at Bell Isle in Yorkshire in 1794: 'All was confusion and uproar. I was struck with amazement and consternation ... What shall I say to these things? I believe God is working very powerfully on the minds of many; but I think Satan, or, at least, the animal nature has a great hand in all this.'[38]

THE PUBLICATION OF *A SELECTION OF LETTERS*

At the end of the eighteenth century, interest in local Methodist revivals, both within the Connexion and beyond, was particularly intense, for three related reasons. First, criticisms of popular demonstrations of religious faith were especially strident during times of economic hardship and of social and political stress. In 1790s Britain, fears of French-inspired unrest led to government repression,[39] and to widespread tensions between supporters of 'Church and King' and those seen as outsiders, which could well include Methodists.[40] This worked both ways. In December 1792, Entwisle feared for his family as rioters paraded around Leeds, praying: 'O Lord, hide me, my dear wife, all my friends, and thy dear people in the secret of thy pavilion till every calamity of life be overpast.'[41]

---

[37] James Wood to John Wesley, 6 June 1782, Letter DXXXVI, *AM* 13 (1790), 388.

[38] Joseph Entwisle, *Memoir of the Rev. Joseph Entwisle, Fifty-Four Years a Wesleyan Minister* (Bristol, 1848), 132, cited in McGonigle, 'William Bramwell', 227.

[39] Such measures included the 1795 Seditious Meetings Act: Lloyd, *Women and the Shaping of British Methodism*, 45–6.

[40] David Hempton, *Methodism and Politics in British Society, 1750–1850* (Stanford, CA, 1984), 55–6; John Walsh, 'Methodism and the Mob in the Eighteenth Century', in G. J. Cuming and Derek Baker, eds, *Popular Belief and Practice*, SCH 8 (Cambridge, 1972), 213–27, at 226–7.

[41] Journal entry for 17 December 1792, in Entwisle, *Memoir*, 110.

For Wesley and his contemporaries, religious and political order were inseparable; Joseph Nelson was lauded in his obituary as 'a firm and zealous supporter of the Protestant Religion, and the British Constitution, as by Law established, in Church and State'.[42] Popular movements were often tainted by association with the excesses of the French Revolution, and Methodists understood these risks. One leading preacher wrote in 1794: 'I would recommend all our Societies at this time, to be much in prayer; the state of the nation & the state of the Church (I mean the Church of Christ) demands it. It is surely an awful time, & such as calls aloud for humiliation.'[43] Mather took action in Sheffield in 1797 on finding that a Methodist-funded teacher 'had become a strong republican in civil & religious things',[44] while Entwisle recognized that lay Methodists were sometimes over-enthusiastic in revival work: 'Many who are exceedingly active in this way are truly pious: if their zeal and fervour were under the direction of wisdom and prudence, they might be very useful.'[45]

Second, Wesley's movement was experiencing sustained and wide-ranging tensions as it struggled to find a new way to define and govern itself following the death of its ever-dominant founder in 1791,[46] which led to the mass secession of Alexander Kilham's Methodist New Connexion in 1797.[47] There were numerous linked power struggles: between local societies and the connexional centre, between Wesley's surviving itinerants and a new generation of preachers, between chapel trustees and society leaders, and between champions of what was often seen as lay democracy as distinct from clerical oligarchy. For the leading Bristol Methodist layman William Pine, disorder in the Connexion and in chapel revival meetings were two sides of the same coin. He told one preacher in 1796: 'The Spirit

---

[42] *Gentleman's Magazine* 87 (1817), 182.

[43] MARC, MA1977/485, Early Preachers' Letters, vol. 1, fol. 27, Joseph Benson to George Merryweather, 22 December 1794.

[44] Early Preachers' Letters, vol. 2, fol. 252, Alexander Mather to William Marriott, 30 September 1797.

[45] Joseph Entwisle to Frances Pawson, 19 March 1800, in Entwisle, *Memoir*, 211–12. Her husband was the leading preacher John Pawson (1737–1806); she was therefore his aunt by marriage.

[46] John Walsh, 'Methodism at the End of the Eighteenth Century', in Davies and Rupp, eds, *History*, vol. 1, 275–315.

[47] Edward A. Rose, 'The Methodist New Connexion 1797–1907', *PWHS* 47 (1990), 241–53. Five thousand members left Wesley's Connexion.

of Disloyalty and Innovation go Hand in Hand, and will most certainly spread if it be not firmly opposed by those who have Piety and Respectability in the Connection ... Decency and Decorum should be preserved in all Places of public Worship, for God is not the Author of Confusion.'[48]

Third, however, some Methodists hoped that the Great Yorkshire Revival might presage another national 'Great Awakening', if not the Second Coming of Jesus Christ. John Moon (1751–1801) wrote excitedly from Sheffield that the phenomenon 'must surely be a prelude to that glorious conquest of Grace, which we are prophetically assured, shall take place in the last days; and hence, is eminently preparing the way for the *grand Millennial Reign* of our *Redeeming God*'.[49]

This tension between fear of disorder and expectation of a new order runs throughout *A Selection of Letters, &c., upon the late Extraordinary Revival of the Work of God*. The publisher was William Shelmerdine, who was based in Manchester.[50] He clearly had some links with Methodism and wider Evangelical religion, having published a collection of pastoral letters by the Evangelical clergyman William Romaine (1714–95) in 1798[51] and a work by the Methodist writer Joseph Nightingale (1775–1824) in 1799,[52] while subscribers to his collection of improving verse included the leading Wesleyan Thomas Coke (1747–1814).[53] The firm had a varied portfolio: it published *Robinson Crusoe* (which also had moral and religious content) around 1800, and various tradesmen's practical guides, but it was probably best known for its broadsheet ballads

---

[48] William Pine to Joseph Benson, 14 January 1796, in Jonathan Barry and Kenneth Morgan, eds, *Reformation and Revival in Eighteenth-Century Bristol* (Bristol, 1994), 163.

[49] John Moon to Thomas Coke, 22 August 1794, in Anon., *A Selection of Letters, &c., upon the late Extraordinary Revival of the Work of God; chiefly collected from the Arminian Magazines* (Manchester, 1800), 24–5.

[50] The company appears as 'letter-press printers' at 3 Deansgate: G. Bancks, *Banck's Manchester and Salford Directory* (Manchester, 1800), 155. He may have been related to the Manchester-born Wesleyan preacher William Shelmerdine (1759–1849), although the name was not uncommon in the area.

[51] *A Collection of Letters on Serious Subjects* (Manchester, 1798).

[52] Joseph Nightingale, *Elegiac Thoughts occasioned by the Death of the Rev. D. Simpson, M. A.* (Manchester, 1799). Simpson (1745–99) was an evangelical clergyman and a friend of John Wesley.

[53] *Miscellaneous Poems* (Manchester, 1800?). The publisher was 'W. Shelmerdine and Co., No. 5, Hanging-Ditch'; presumably the firm's previous premises.

and cheap editions of short stories: the Bodleian Library collection of broadside ballads has some thirty items with a Shelmerdine imprint between 1800 and 1849.[54]

Most of the slim volume of sixty-six pages comprised accounts of eight recent local revivals; there was also a brief spiritual biography of James Chimley, who had been converted before dying in 1795, in his fourteenth year; and a ten-page essay entitled *Thoughts on the Revival of Religion in the Prayer-Meetings* by an anonymous 'Well-Wisher to Zion'. All the material had already appeared in the *Arminian Magazine*, and (apart from the report on Hull) the sequence was unchanged.

At this period the *Methodist Magazine* (as the *Arminian Magazine* was titled from 1798) had a print run of many thousands, so these accounts were already familiar to many Methodists.[55] There is every reason to think that Shelmerdine intended the publication to be helpful to Methodism; perhaps it arose from discussions at or around the Preachers' Conference of 1799, held in Manchester. The layout of the pamphlet (including its lack of a contents page, preface or introduction, or index) suggests that it was produced at pace; but what precisely was its purpose?

A clue can be found in the choice of material. The *Selection of Letters* drew from *Magazines* between June 1791 and January 1800, but accounts of seven other revivals published during this period were excluded. Most of these related to events which were relatively distant in time (such as the 1778–9 Birstal revival in Yorkshire) or place (for example, the 1797–8 revival in St Bartholomew, West Indies). But the omission of the report by Zechariah Yewdall (1751–1830) on the revival at Otley, Yorkshire, in 1792–3 is surprising. It seems to reflect the unorthodox, indeed unique, origins of that revival. In 1792 Elizabeth Dickerson, aged around nineteen, with no Methodist connections, began itinerating north of Leeds, following two ecstatic trances in which she had visions of heaven and hell. Thousands heard her speak, sometimes also hearing 'the sweetest music', and while two of Wesley's preachers, Yewdall and Thomas Dixon (1745–1820), both recorded doubts about her authenticity, they accepted that

---

[54] See <http://ballads.bodleian.ox.ac.uk/>, accessed 18 August 2020.
[55] The Connexion's book steward, Robert Lomas, reported to the Conference of 1804: 'we print 21,500': MARC, MS 691, Book Committee minutes.

Table 1. Sources of material in Anon., *A Selection of Letters*

Item	Selection of Letters ref.	Arminian Magazine ref.
Account of revival at Blidworth, near Nottingham (1790)	3–6	Vol. 14 (1791), 307–9
Account of revival at Newry (1790–1)	7–10	Vol. 14 (1791), 413–16
Account of revival at Hull (1793–4)	11–19, 57–66	Vol. 17 (1794), 603–7, 649–54
Account of revival at Sheffield (1793–4)	19–25	Vol. 18 (1795), 415–18
Account of revival at Wakefield (1793–4)	25–8	Vol. 18 (1795), 519–20
Account of revival at Halifax (1793–4)	28–30	Vol. 18 (1795), 520–1
James Chimley biography	30–5	Vol. 19 (1796), 137–40
'Thoughts on the Revival of Religion'	35–44	Vol. 21 (1798), 240–5
Accounts of revival at Penzance (1797–9)	44–8, 49–51	Vol. 22 (1799), 409–11, 412–13
Account of revival at Redruth (1798–9)	51–6	Vol. 23 (1800), 44–7

revival followed shortly afterwards.[56] So in essence the *Selection of Letters* was addressing the questions: what was going on in Yorkshire and elsewhere? Was it truly the work of the Holy Spirit? If so, could it be replicated?

The narrative accounts were clearly intended as exemplary; indeed they shared many common features and used consistent terminology.[57] They explored six key themes. First, and in striking contrast to events at Otley, these local revivals were all presented as led by Wesleyan preachers. At Blidworth, revival followed prayer meetings held after preaching services in the chapel, and was sustained through the efforts of both (full-time) itinerant and (part-time, volunteer) local preachers;[58] and the reports on events at Newry, Hull and Halifax were equally explicit that itinerant preachers had initiated

---

[56] Early Preachers' Letters, vol. 2, Thomas Dixon, autobiography and journal, fols 302–5; Yewdall, 'Experience', 473–4.

[57] Many followed narrative conventions on lines similar to those found in contemporary accounts of individual conversions: see D. Bruce Hindmarsh, *The Evangelical Conversion Narrative: Spiritual Autobiography in Early Modern England* (Oxford, 2005), 322.

[58] Anon., *Selection of Letters*, 3–4.

and then presided over the revival.[59] At Redruth, the spark of revival was lit at a service conducted by John Hodgson, an itinerant preacher.[60]

Second, and again unlike the Otley case, these revivals were portrayed as developing from within the ecclesiastical structures of mainstream Wesleyan Methodism. Some accounts emphasize the importance of Quarterly Meetings in spreading revival. On such occasions, a circuit's preachers and lay officials would come together to review its spiritual and financial health, plan preaching for the coming quarter and enjoy Christian fellowship. At Sheffield and Wakefield, revival began during the Quarterly Meeting; at St Ives, that was when it was at its height.[61] Other revivals were linked to highlights of the church year: in Penzance it was 'at our Love feast, on the Christmas quarter-day, the Lord began to breathe on the dry bones';[62] at Redruth the first stirrings came during the New Year's Eve service, and were echoed a week later at the annual Covenant Service (with which Methodists mark the new year) at Truro.[63] At Riverbridge, near Hull, revival burst out on Easter Sunday.[64]

A third feature shared by all these accounts was the central importance accorded to prayer meetings in generating and maintaining the momentum of the Holy Spirit's work. At Newry, for example, such meetings were held after the preaching services, and often lasted four hours.[65] Frequent, often lengthy and large-scale, prayer meetings were a core feature of revival in every area.[66] Chimley himself had been converted at one such meeting.[67] As Mather told the prominent Methodist layman William Marriott (1753–1815) in 1794, as revival spread across Yorkshire: 'The means it pleases God to own most are prayer meetings. These continue from 7 to 9, 10, 12 o'clock at night, yea till 2, 4 & 6 in the morning. In some of them 5, 7, 12, 20 & at

[59] Ibid. 6–7, 12–13, 28.
[60] Ibid. 52.
[61] Ibid. 19, 26, 47.
[62] Ibid. 46.
[63] Ibid. 52.
[64] Ibid. 60–4.
[65] Ibid. 7.
[66] Ibid. 3–4, 12–16, 19, 24, 25–6, 29, 50–1, 54–5.
[67] Ibid. 30.

one time more than 30 have professed to be awakened & converted.'[68]

Fourthly, as so often in Methodist revivals, these reports revealed the prominent role played by children and young people as active participants in, and exemplars of, the work of grace. Chimley's biography of course highlighted this phenomenon, and asserted that '[t]he holy life, and happy death of James Chimley is one proof' that these revivals were 'a blessed and glorious work of God', albeit 'attended with some irregularity'.[69] Many of the accounts describe significant numbers of conversions amongst the young. At Blidworth, a fifteen-year-old was an early convert;[70] at Sheffield, Moon recorded, '[i]t was marvellous to behold boys and girls of ten or twelve years of age, so violently agitated, and so earnestly engaged to obtain mercy ... Even little boys and girls now have prayer-meetings among themselves'.[71] From Riverbridge, Hull, Mather offered a detailed report of his successful struggle to save a group of young men from the evils of football.[72] Nearby, two boys aged eight and twelve were converted: 'Next day they each of them wrote a letter to their relations, describing the work which the Lord had wrought upon their souls, and the consolations they experienced, interspersed with pertinent remarks and observations, that would not have discredited persons who have been long acquainted with the things of God.'[73] There were also striking events at Redruth, where one father brought two small children into the pulpit to testify to their conversion, 'and tho' they could scarcely be seen, they lifted up their hands to heaven, and with tears of humble praise, calmly told the congregation what the Lord had done for their souls'.[74]

Fifth, these published accounts emphasized the transformative impact of revival. Quantitatively, the numbers of conversions were impressive: at Hull, Mather reported adding 'upwards of one hundred and fifty' members in a week in April 1794, with conversions averaging twenty to thirty at each meeting;[75] while a report from Redruth

---

[68] Early Preachers' Letters, vol. 2, fol. 258, Mather to Marriott, 11 March 1794.
[69] Anon., *Selection of Letters*, 34.
[70] Ibid. 4.
[71] Ibid. 22, 24.
[72] Ibid. 50, 53, 60–4.
[73] Ibid. 60.
[74] Ibid. 55.
[75] Ibid. 16.

claimed in June 1799 that more than two and a half thousand new members had been recruited since Christmas.[76] The accounts also emphasized the immediate and positive impact of revival on the daily lives of new converts. Chimley was one exemplar; Charles Atmore (1759–1826) was convinced that the Holy Spirit was active amongst the people of Halifax in 1793–4 because '[s]ome have now evidenced the reality of the change upon their hearts, for twelve months, by a holy life.'[77] Similarly, Mather reported that across Yorkshire new converts 'shew it to be <u>real</u> work by their lives & conversations'.[78]

One final theme runs through all these reports, and that is the authors' concern to address the charge that such revivals generated 'confusion' or 'wildness'. The picture set out in the *Selection of Letters* was nuanced. The authors accepted that the 'cries of the distressed' during revival meetings could be noisy and disturbing. But the evidence was clear that the Holy Spirit was at work. In Hull, '[t]here were [*sic*] nothing irrational or unscriptural in these meetings', wrote Mather; while Moon reported from Sheffield that '[i]t could not but appear to an idle spectator, all confusion, but to those who were engaged therein, it was a glorious regularity.'[79] Linked with this was an attempt to overcome the class prejudice sometimes found amongst leading Methodists; Wesley's close associate Elizabeth Ritchie had been contemptuous on this score of the Sheffield revival.[80] However, Owen Davies claimed that the Penzance revival was the height of respectability: 'I was called upon some time past to pray with a gentleman, an officer in the army, and other respectable men, together with some of the most dressy women of the place.'[81]

That said, this was clearly not connexional 'business as usual'; at one Cornish service, Hodgson found it impossible to deliver a sermon because of the noise, while at a Sheffield love-feast, the 'customary collection for the poor' was disrupted.[82] It was a challenge for the preachers: during the Yorkshire revivals of the 1790s, Mather feared

---

[76] Ibid. 52.
[77] Ibid. 29.
[78] Early Preachers' Letters, vol. 2, fol. 258, Mather to Marriott, 11 March 1794.
[79] Anon., *Selection of Letters*, 14, 21.
[80] Mack, *Heart Religion*, 291–2.
[81] Anon., *Selection of Letters*, 50.
[82] Ibid. 55, 21.

initially that they would be inhibited by 'a too anxious attachment to decorum and order'; but in due course even he felt obliged to introduce 'some regulations, in the most gentle way' to manage the lengthy prayer meetings being held locally, after reports that they were 'offensive to the magistrates'.[83] Large-scale meetings of men and women, with no set procedure and probably no clergy or gentry present, held at night and behind closed doors, were of obvious concern to the authorities.

Of course, there had never been a simple binary choice between 'inspiration' and 'institution'. Even the mystic Cutler worked alongside Wesley's preachers within the circuit system, and her mentor Bramwell was not only a passionate prayer leader but adopted a systematic approach to evangelism. While clearly inspirational, he did not act alone, but 'employed the talents of the local preachers, leaders, and other individuals, in prayer';[84] his techniques included 5 a.m. prayer meetings, intensive house-to-house visiting and pastoral care for new converts, comprising one-on-one advice sessions and supervised reading programmes.[85]

Managing Revival: A Code of Good Practice

The essay on good practice, *Thoughts on the Revival of Religion in the Prayer-Meetings*,[86] set out a clear strategy for generating and sustaining local revivals. It was to maintain the systematic organization developed by Bramwell and others, to reassert connexional control, to reduce dependence on charismatic individuals (whether prophets or preachers) and to lower the emotional temperature. First it compared recent events with the London 'revival' of 1761. This had been led by the maverick millenarian Methodist preacher George Bell (d. 1807) and driven by his personal revelation through dreams and visions, but collapsed in ridicule and embarrassment. In contrast, the essay adopted a primarily institutional perspective, although its author, in proposing detailed 'regulations' for the management of revivals, added: 'Sometimes when the power of God is uncommonly present in a meeting, attending too minutely to any

---

[83] Ibid. 11, 57.
[84] Sigston, *Bramwell*, 76.
[85] Ibid. 47, 54, 56, 71.
[86] Previously published in *AM* 21 (1798), 240–5; Anon., *Selection of Letters*, 35–44.

particular plan, might do much harm: God alone can direct at such blessed seasons.'[87]

The essay argued that the work of God was best advanced through a local team effort, managed by trained and experienced preachers, supported by active members of local Methodist societies, and grounded firmly in the connexional mainstream: 'The case at present is widely different [from that of George Bell]; the active persons in the Prayer-Meetings, in general, are remarkable for an affectionate attachment to their preachers, they constantly attend all the means of grace: they ardently love their Bibles; and they steadily adhere to the Methodist doctrines and discipline.'[88]

Once it had been ascertained that the Holy Spirit was at work, the Methodist society should establish a cadre of members under the guidance of a full-time preacher, to manage the anticipated upsurge in interest. They should organize a series of prayer meetings, and deliberately use a variety of prayer leaders: 'Our friends who preside in the Prayer-meetings, ought to be exceeding careful that those who exercise in prayer, are exemplary in their lives and conduct ... It is likewise necessary ... to take care not to depend too much on any particular persons ... lest our dependance [sic] be more in man than in God.'[89]

A detailed format for such meetings was suggested. Though revival meetings often attracted public interest, entry to chapels was to be strictly controlled. In Newry in 1790, for example, '[m]any of the careless and profane gathered about the house, but were not admitted'.[90] Teams of prayer leaders, counsellors and administrative support staff were to be deployed, under the management of a preacher or senior member. The meeting's president was to supervise a programme of 'short and lively' prayers, interspersed with hymns.[91]

If individuals showed signs of experiencing the pain of awareness of their sins or the joy of salvation, they were assigned a counsellor to encourage and support them; apparent manifestations of God's grace might in fact be due to sickness or fantasy, or even demonic in origin. But when these personal crises ended in conversion, the counsellor

---

[87] Anon., *Selection of Letters*, 40.
[88] Ibid. 36.
[89] Ibid. 41.
[90] Ibid. 7.
[91] Ibid. 40.

would brief the president, who would inform the congregation and lead general thanksgiving. Meanwhile an administrator would record the convert's contact details, and assign them to a class in the local society. This was accepted good practice; Bramwell followed it, as did Entwisle during the Leeds revival of 1794: 'I proposed to the young converts, who wished for it, that they should give in their names, and our friends would meet them once a week in little companies ... One hundred and twenty persons gave in their names.'[92]

Finally, a calm and orderly atmosphere should prevail as far as possible, and when the meeting ended the participants should disperse immediately, without annoying the neighbours: 'Much good has been lost, and much evil arisen, from several persons collecting together at the door, or in the street, and in a trifling manner conversing about what has been done.'[93]

In short, whilst celebrating evidence that the Holy Spirit was so obviously at work, and offering practical suggestions on how such success could be replicated, both the essay on good practice and the accompanying accounts of local events stressed the measures needed to keep revivals under moral and political control. If one purpose was to attract new members, including their weekly penny subscriptions, it was vital also not to scare the authorities, nor indeed the respectable middle-class supporters of Methodism, whose large but discretionary financial contributions were increasingly important.[94]

The managerial approach set out in *Thoughts on the Revival of Religion in the Prayer-Meetings* was however not only about organizational survival and development, nor was it just a response to external and internal pressures. It reflected core Wesleyan theological positions. One, as we have seen, was the firm view that both God and Satan were active in contemporary Britain, and that distinguishing between their work was a significant challenge requiring both discipline and discernment. Another was that sinners were called not only to a momentary act of repentance but to a life of sacrificial love for

---

[92] Entwisle, *Memoir*, 131.
[93] Anon., *Selection of Letters*, 42–3.
[94] Clive Murray Norris, *The Financing of John Wesley's Methodism c.1740–1800* (Oxford, 2017), 232.

God and humankind. Yet another was the Wesleyan morphology of spiritual development, in which the sinner was first 'awakened' or 'convicted' of sin, next 'converted' or 'justified', and then (at least as an aspiration) achieved 'sanctification' or 'perfection', complete release from the power of sin. The phase of 'conviction' prior to 'conversion' was traumatic, especially if prolonged;[95] while 'sanctification' was often found only at the end of life, if at all. Furthermore, individual spiritual development might be nonlinear: there could be troughs as well as peaks. As Rack and Bebbington note, conversion was therefore only one of many possible positive results of the Spirit's work.[96]

John Allen (1737–1810) observed during the Manchester revival of 1783: 'We have still hardly a meeting but one or another finds peace with God, or has his backslidings healed, or else is renewed in love.'[97] During the Great Yorkshire Revival, Mather also reported varying outcomes: 'Many are awakened, converted, & profess to be sanctified ... In some of the above circuits there is a very agreeable recovery amongst many of the old members.'[98] Throughout this hazardous journey, the sinner needed emotional, spiritual and practical support, and that required human, physical and indeed financial resources to be marshalled and deployed. As Fredrick Dreyer has noted, Wesley's Methodism was '[a] mixed association whose ranks included members in all states of spiritual development'.[99]

There was also a theological perspective on the fluctuations in membership often seen in revivals. The 1800 Conference took place against the immediate background of revival in Cornwall, where some of the inflow of recruits proved temporary.

The essay on good practice offered an explanation: as news of revivals spread beyond local Methodist societies, it drew in the unchurched, whose immediate emotional response was not grounded

---

[95] However, in Sheffield in 1794, 'some were both convinced and justified in an hour's time': Anon., *Selection of Letters*, 23.
[96] Rack, *Reasonable Enthusiast*, 494; Bebbington, *Victorian Religious Revivals*, 9–11.
[97] Allen, 'Work of God at Manchester', 664–5.
[98] Early Preachers' Letters, vol. 2, fols 258–9, Mather to Marriott, 11 March 1794.
[99] Frederick Dreyer, 'A "Religious Society under Heaven": John Wesley and the Identity of Methodism', *JBS* 25 (1986), 62–83; Robert A. Schofield, 'Methodist Spiritual Condition in Georgian Northern England', *JEH* 65 (2014), 780–802.

Table 2. Membership in selected Cornish circuits, 1798–1800

Circuit	1798	1799	1800
Redruth	2,519	4,866	4,050
Penzance	2,118	4,118	3,440

Sources: *Minutes of the Methodist Conferences,* vol. I (London, 1862), 424; *Minutes of the Methodist Conferences,* vol. II (London, 1813), 16, 54.[100]

in any spiritual preparation and might therefore not last.[101] As John Pawson commented in 1796: 'After any extraordinary revival of the work of God in any place there has been what has been frequently called a sifting time, and the gold has been separated from the dross and there has been a falling away.'[102]

CONCLUSION

The *Selection of Letters* documents what Rack has called 'a transitional phase from the old spontaneous revivalism to the planned revivalism of the nineteenth century'.[103] From its inception, Wesley's movement had sought to respond to the promptings of the Holy Spirit within the context of limited organizational capacity and wariness of over-enthusiasm. In Mack's phrase, it always exhibited a 'creative tension between spirit and discipline, creativity and regulation, expansion and consolidation';[104] for Hempton, 'revivalism and connectional managerialism were always unhappy bedfellows'.[105] In many ways it struck an effective balance: between 1770 and 1810, membership in the British Isles (as published in the annual Conference *Minutes*) more than quadrupled, from some 30,000 in 1770 to approaching 140,000 in 1810. Indeed, for the next century,

---

[100] Data for 1800 reflect the restructuring of Cornish circuits to accommodate membership growth: thus Redruth includes the new circuit of Truro, and Penzance includes Helston.

[101] Anon., *Selection of Letters,* 39.

[102] John Pawson to George Marsden, 4 June 1790, in John C. Bowmer and John A. Vickers, eds, *The Letters of John Pawson, Methodist Itinerant, 1762–1806,* 3 vols (Peterborough, 1995), 2: 84–5, at 84.

[103] Rack, *Reasonable Enthusiast,* 494.

[104] Mack, *Heart Religion,* 262.

[105] David Hempton, *Methodism: Empire of the Spirit* (New Haven, CT, and London, 2005), 27.

the Connexion continued both to grow in membership and to avoid financial disaster.[106] The growth trajectory was far from smooth, however.

In the later 1700s, many Methodists eagerly devoured a succession of exciting reports of local revival, including the Spirit-led work of teenage boys and the prophetic witness of teenage girls and women, looking towards nationwide revival or even the Second Coming. Meanwhile, within the Connexion and beyond, there was growing concern at this apparent breakdown of ecclesiological, social and potentially political order, and a new generation of preachers, exemplified by Clarke, was delivering the gospel through reasoned argument and biblical exegesis.[107] By 1800, it was evident that a choice was to be made; and implicitly, the Connexion decided to contain and channel local fervour: 'inspiration' was forced back inside an 'institutional' carapace. But a heavy price was paid.

In a letter of 1785, published in 1800, Mather had warned of the growing preponderance of 'reason' over 'enthusiasm':

> Has not the attempt to avoid what has been called Enthusiasm, or the appearance of it, … been one grand cause of every revival of religion not continuing in its prosperity? And are we now in no danger from the same quarter? And have not many of our preachers and people, suffered much from it already? I greatly fear they have.[108]

In 1791, a hostile pamphlet presented Methodism as a conspiracy against the vulnerable and gullible: 'However enthusiastic, the Followers may be, the Leaders seem perfectly cool, and collected. There is a Semblance of Enthusiasm, but wary prudence regulates every step.'[109]

In a series of moves in the early 1800s, the Conference sought to impose control by the preachers, and greater regularity of Methodist

---

[106] Henry D. Rack, 'Wesleyan Methodism 1849–1902', in Rupert E. Davies, A. R. George and E. Gordon Rupp, eds, *A History of the Methodist Church in Great Britain*, vol. 3 (London, 1983), 128–32. David Bebbington describes the Victorian Methodist approach to revival as 'an effective formula for church growth': *Victorian Religious Revivals*, 10.

[107] Mack, *Heart Religion*, especially 261–301, 'Methodism and Modernity'.

[108] Alexander Mather to John Pawson, 30 September 1785, *Methodist Magazine* 23 (1800), 191–2.

[109] Anon., *A Review of the Policy, Doctrines and Morals of the Methodists* (London, 1791), 51. The point had of course been made before: see, for example, Anon., *A Fine Picture of Enthusiasm, chiefly drawn by Dr. John Scott* (London, 1744).

practice. In 1800 it moved to downplay emotional responses to religion, through this resolution:

Q.13. Do we sufficiently explain and enforce practical religion, and attend to the preservation of order and regularity in our meetings for prayer, and other acts of Divine worship?

A. Perhaps not. We fear there has sometimes been irregularity in some of the meetings. And we think that some of our hearers are in danger of mistaking EMOTIONS OF THE AFFECTIONS for experimental and practical godliness. To remedy or prevent, as far as possible, these errors, let Mr. Wesley's Extract of Mr. Edwards's pamphlet on Religious Affections be printed without delay, and circulated among our people.[110]

In 1802 Conference addressed a number of 'evils' including standing or sitting at prayer: 'We strongly recommend it to all our people to kneel at prayer; and we desire that all our pews may, as far as possible, be so formed as to admit of this in the easiest manner.'[111] (It was not until 1820 that Conference adopted regulations for 'public prayer meetings', and then only 'when prudently conducted by persons of established piety and competent gifts, and duly superintended by the Preachers, and by the Leaders' Meetings'.[112]) In 1803 strict limits were imposed on women preaching,[113] while a series of regulations in 1805 reasserted preachers' rights over music in chapel: 'Let no Preacher suffer any thing to be done in the chapel where he officiates but what is according to the established usages [*sic*] of Methodism', insisted the Conference.[114]

In 1800 the *Methodist Magazine* printed a depressing manifesto for the movement's increasingly pervasive rationalism:

---

[110] *Minutes* II, 56–7. The 'pamphlet' was John Wesley's publication *An Extract from a Treatise concerning Religious Affections* (Bristol, 1773); the Conference Office published a new edition, as requested, in 1801: see Christopher M. B. Allison, 'The Methodist Edwards: John Wesley's Abridgement of the Selected Works of Jonathan Edwards', *Methodist History* 50 (2012), 144–60.

[111] *Minutes* II, 141–2.

[112] *Minutes of the Methodist Conferences,* vol. V (London, 1825), 149. From 1820, references to such prayer meetings 'multiply': William W. Dean, 'The Methodist Class Meeting: The Significance of its Decline', *PWHS* 43 (1981), 41–8, at 45. Missionary prayer meetings had been established some years earlier.

[113] *Minutes* II, 188–9.

[114] Ibid. 291.

A CAUTION
Regard the world with cautious eye;
Nor raise your expectation high;
See that the ballanc'd scale be such,
You neither hope nor fear too much.
For disappointment's not the thing; –
'Tis pride and passion point the sting.
Life is a sea, where storms must rise;
'Tis folly talks of cloudless skies:
He who contracts his swelling sail,
Eludes the fury of the gale.[115]

But while the men of the Methodist leadership implemented a cautious strategy of managed growth, careful resource management and social respectability (notably under Jabez Bunting), some members continued to prioritize the spontaneous promptings of the Holy Spirit, as found throughout the whole community of saints. For them, and for women preachers driven from the Wesleyan mainstream, new opportunities to advance the kingdom of God were emerging in an increasingly fissiparous Methodism, notably in Primitive Methodism.[116]

---

[115] *Methodist Magazine* 23 (1800), 100. Writing in 1905, the American psychologist F. M. Davenport saw this as an inevitable and welcome progression: 'Religious experience is an evolution. We go on from the rudimentary and the primitive to the rational and spiritual': *Primitive Traits in Religious Revivals: A Study in Mental and Social Evolution* (New York, 1905), 323.

[116] See John Lenton, Clive Murray Norris and Linda A. Ryan, eds, *Women, Preachers, Methodists* (Oxford, 2020).

Continuing Revelation and Institutionalization: Joseph Smith, Ralph Waldo Emerson and Charismatic Leadership in Antebellum America

Claudia Jetter*

Ruprecht-Karls Universität, Heidelberg

Nineteenth-century North American religious history is filled with divinely inspired people who received and recorded new revelations. This article presents Joseph Smith Jr and Ralph Waldo Emerson as charismatic prophets who promoted the idea of continuing revelation. Drawing on Max Weber's concept of charismatic authority, it will contrast their forms of new sacred writing with one another to show how both had experienced encounters with the divine. The second part will then explore how different conceptualizations of revelation led to opposing concepts of religious authority, with consequences for the possibility of institution-building processes. While Smith would reify revelation in hierarchy, Emerson eventually promoted extreme spiritual individualization by rejecting the idea of an exclusive institution as the centre of revelatory authority.

On 22 March 1839, while being held at Liberty Jail in Clay County, Missouri, Joseph Smith Jr (1805–44), founder of the Mormon church, dictated a response letter to Isaac Galland, a non-Mormon land broker from Iowa.[1] In the letter, Smith elucidated the core belief of the Mormon faith:

* Heidelberg Center for American Studies (HCA), Curt und Heidemarie Engelhorn Palais, Hauptstraße 120, D-69117 Heidelberg, Germany. E-mail: cjetter@hca.uni-heidelberg.de.

[1] Joseph Smith Jr founded the Church of Jesus Christ of Latter-Day Saints in 1830. He translated the *Book of Mormon* and was prophet and the highest member of the church for the rest of his life. He was assassinated in 1844 by a violent mob while imprisoned in Carthage, Illinois. For an in-depth biography of Smith, see Richard L. Bushman, *Joseph Smith: Rough Stone Rolling* (New York, 2007).

Studies in Church History 57 (2021), 233–253 © The Author(s), 2021. Published by Cambridge University Press on behalf of Ecclesiastical History Society. This is an Open Access article, distributed under the terms of the Creative Commons Attribution-NonCommercial-ShareAlike licence (http://creativecommons.org/licenses/by-nc-sa/4.0/), which permits non-commercial re-use, distribution, and reproduction in any medium, provided the same Creative Commons licence is included and the original work is properly cited. The written permission of Cambridge University Press must be obtained for commercial re-use.
doi: 10.1017/stc.2021.12

... the first and fundamental principle of our holy religion is that we believe that we have a right to embrace all, and every item of truth, without limitation or without being circumscribed or prohibited by the creeds or superstitious notions of men, or by the dominations [*sic*] of one another, when that truth is clearly demonstrated to our minds, and we have the highest degree of evidence of the same ... We believe that we have a right to revelations, visions, and dreams from God, our heavenly Father.[2]

In this short paragraph, it becomes evident what distinguished the Mormon faith from most contemporary religious movements: belief in an ever-communicating and self-revealing deity. For Smith and his followers, dreams and visions had not been confined to the apostolic age but were actual manifestations of divine truth in the present and therefore superior to human knowledge, traditional practices and ecclesiastical creeds. God was still communicating his will, and his divine orders needed to be defended and followed even in the face of severe opposition.

Only eight months earlier, on 15 July 1838, in Cambridge, Massachusetts, the former Unitarian minister Ralph Waldo Emerson (1803–82) had given his radical critique of historical Christianity, the infamous 'Divinity School Address', in front of the Unitarian elite.[3] He lamented: 'The stationariness of religion; the assumption that the age of inspiration is past, that the Bible is closed ... indicate with sufficient clearness the falsehood of our theology. It is the office of a true teacher to show us that God is, not was; that He speaketh, not spake.'[4]

At first glance, these two men seemed to have shared the same belief, namely that God was still communicating with people, and that people had simply turned away from their immediate relation

[2] Joseph Smith Jr, 'To Isaac Galland: 22 March 1839', in *The Personal Writings of Joseph Smith*, rev. edn (Salt Lake City, UT, 2002), 454–62, at 458–9.

[3] Ralph Waldo Emerson was a Unitarian minister before becoming an influential essayist, lecturer and philosopher. Today he is canonized in American literature as one of the major writers of the American Renaissance and dubbed the 'Sage of Concord'. For a comprehensive biography, see Robert D. Richardson, *Emerson: The Mind on Fire: A Biography* (Berkeley, CA, 1996).

[4] Ralph W. Emerson, 'An Address: Delivered before the Senior Class in Divinity College, Cambridge, Sunday Evening, 15 July, 1838', in Ralph W. Emerson, *The Collected Works of Ralph Waldo Emerson*, 1: *Nature, Addresses and Lectures*, ed. Alfred R. Ferguson (Cambridge, MA, 1971), 76–93, at 89.

to him, had stopped listening to divine truth and had turned towards hollow creeds that rejected new revelation as heretical. Yet Emerson would have regarded any self-declared prophet with suspicion, especially if that prophet demanded exclusive authority over others, warning his readers: 'Beware of the man who says, "I am on the eve of a revelation."'[5] Emerson's suspicion was grounded in the belief that revelation was not tied to a divine mission and channelled through one chosen vessel but a continuing process of nature revealing itself to humanity, through which every individual could experience the divine.[6]

It cannot be denied, however, that both men rejected a supposedly corrupted Christianity in favour of belief in continuing revelation as the only true source of religious authority.[7] While their records of divine revelation seem different, they are structurally related attempts to restore what sociologist Max Weber called charismatic authority. Although the two men were separated by deep differences in social and cultural position, they responded similarly to a perceived crisis of religious authority in a competitive religious sphere that followed an intense period of revivalism and the disestablishment of churches after the Revolution. For Smith, a poorly educated farmer from the 'burned-over district' of New York state, as well as for Emerson, the Harvard-trained genteel Bostonian, locating religious authority in immediate communication with the divine emerged as a possible alternative to traditional carriers of authority in a highly fragmented religious realm. Smith and Emerson were not the only people who hungered for new revelation. Rather, they had been part of a broader

---

[5] Ralph W. Emerson, *The Collected Works of Ralph Waldo Emerson*, 6: *The Conduct of Life*, ed. Barbara L. Packer, Joseph Slater and Douglas E. Wilson (Cambridge, MA, 2003), 70–1.

[6] Emerson's concept of 'Nature' would correspond with a naturalized and spiritualized form of God who pervaded nature and history. He would also give this concept labels such as 'Supreme Being' and 'Over-Soul'. Emerson believed the Divine Spirit would reveal itself through Nature, which he would define as 'all that is separate from us, all which Philosophy distinguishes as the NOT ME, that is, both nature, and art, all other men and my own body': Emerson, 'Nature', in *Collected Works* 1, ed. Ferguson, 7–45, at 8.

[7] I follow sociologist Rodney Stark's definition of supernatural communication as an individual's 'capacity to perceive revelations, whether this be an openness or sensitivity to real communications or consists of unusual creativity enabling them to create profound revelations and then to externalize the source of this new culture': Rodney Stark, 'A Theory of Revelations', *Journal for the Scientific Study of Religion* 38 (1999), 287–308, at 295.

public discourse that would embrace divine communication and the production of new sacred writings as a way to restore true religion.[8]

Although Smith and Emerson were born only two years apart, and extensive scholarship exists on both, scholars have usually regarded them as iconic figures from completely different worlds. While literary scholars concentrate on Emerson when investigating themes such as prophetic authority or revelation, the same themes in Smith's life and work have tended to be reserved for religious historians and sociologists.[9] Only a handful of studies discuss Smith and Emerson as contemporaries. Two major studies stand out here. One is David Holland's *Sacred Borders*, in which Smith and Emerson figure among a variety of people who challenged scriptural authority with new sacred writing. The other is Paul Conkin's *American Varieties*, which presents both as part of a larger discourse community acting out of a restorationist impulse to recover an uncorrupted Christianity.[10] Apart from a few articles that explicitly compare the two as scholars, typical examples of Romanticism or advocates of

---

[8] I use the term 'new sacred writing' for a broad range of recorded divine experiences and inspirations. This includes Joseph Smith's translation of the *Book of Mormon*, and his recorded visions and inspired translations, as much as Ralph Waldo Emerson's poetic descriptions of his visionary encounters with the divine. David F. Holland argues that Shakers, Mormons and Adventists grappled with the canonical boundaries of the Christian Scriptures just as much as Deists, Hicksite Quakers or others, 'and in that sense they rightly belong to the same community of discourse': *Sacred Borders: Continuing Revelation and Canonical Restraint in Early America* (New York, 2011), 10.

[9] For Smith and revelation, see Terryl Givens, *By the Hand of Mormon: The American Scripture that Launched a New World Religion* (New York, 2002). On Smith and prophetic charisma, see Lawrence Foster, 'The Psychology of Prophetic Charisma: New Approaches to understanding Joseph Smith and the Development of Charismatic Leadership', *Dialogue: A Journal of Mormon Thought* 36/4 (2003), 1–14. For Smith's beginnings as a visionary, see Richard Lyman Bushman, *Joseph Smith and the Beginnings of Mormonism* (Urbana, IL, 1984). On Emerson and revelation, see Alan D. Hodder, *Emerson's Rhetoric of Revelation: Nature, the Reader, and the Apocalypse within* (University Park, PA, 1989); Evelyn Barish, *Emerson: The Roots of Prophecy* (Princeton, NJ, 1989). On Emerson's use of biblical imagery, see B. L. Packer, *Emerson's Fall: A New Interpretation of the Major Essays* (New York, NY, 1982). For Emerson as a secular prophet, see David Robinson, *Apostle of Culture: Emerson as Preacher and Lecturer* (Philadelphia, PA, 1982). On Transcendentalism and Romantic scripture-writing, see Lawrence Buell, *New England Literary Culture: From Revolution through Renaissance* (repr. Cambridge, MA, 1993).

[10] See Holland, *Sacred Borders*; Paul Keith Conkin, *American Originals: Homemade Varieties of Christianity* (Chapel Hill, NC, 1997); Catherine L. Albanese, *A Republic of Mind and Spirit: A Cultural History of American Metaphysical Religion* (New Haven, CT, 2008).

autonomy, only the historian Richard Brodhead discusses them as prophets, but without regard to institution-building.[11] This article therefore examines them specifically as inspired leaders and investigates their shared openness to new divine communication, while differentiating their concepts of legitimate religious authority.

Drawing on Max Weber's concept of charisma, this article considers Joseph Smith Jr and Ralph Waldo Emerson as charismatic prophets who contested existing ecclesiastical institutions with their belief in continuing revelation, offering such a perspective to more general scholarly discussion on religious authority and agency in mid-nineteenth-century America. While many historians, including Nathan Hatch in his seminal study *The Democratization of American Christianity* (1989), have framed the erosion of traditional forms of religious authority, the rise of populist religious leaders and the rapid pluralization of the American religious landscape as a process of liberation that added to a more general growth of democratic culture, a number of recent studies have emphasized the widely felt anxiety of many Americans amidst the upheavals of the Second Great Awakening that followed the disestablishment of the churches.[12] By applying the concept of charisma to these two historical examples, the article provides deeper insights into different forms of leadership and institutionalization processes in the historical context of antebellum America, thereby demonstrating how historians can benefit from the deployment of such theories. The theoretical background regarding charismatic authority will help uncover shared commonalities among Smith and Emerson, who are usually seen as contemporaries from culturally opposing worlds, without obscuring their crucial differences. This article argues that both Smith and Emerson advocated

---

[11] Richard H. Brodhead, 'Prophets in America circa 1830: Ralph Waldo Emerson, Nat Turner, Joseph Smith', in Reid L. Neilson and Terryl L. Givens, eds, *Joseph Smith, Jr: Reappraisals after Two Centuries* (Oxford, 2009), 13–31. For other themes, see Evan Carton, 'American Scholars: Ralph Waldo Emerson, Joseph Smith, John Brown, and the Springs of Intellectual Schism', *New England Quarterly* 85 (2012), 5–37; Benjamin Park, '"Build therefore, your own world": Ralph Waldo Emerson, Joseph Smith, and American Antebellum Thought', *Journal of Mormon History* 36 (2010), 41–72; Ryan W. Davis, 'Frontier Kantianism: Autonomy and Authority in Ralph Waldo Emerson and Joseph Smith', *Journal of Religious Ethics* 46 (2018), 332–59.

[12] See James D. Bratt, 'Religious Anti-Revivalism in Antebellum America', *Journal of the Early Republic* 24 (2004), 65–106; Amanda Porterfield, *Conceived in Doubt* (Chicago, IL, 2012). For Hatch's democratization thesis, see Nathan O. Hatch, *The Democratization of American Christianity* (New Haven, CT, 1989).

continuing revelation and developed charisma based on visionary experiences. By contrasting their different forms of new sacred writing, it demonstrates how they began by democratizing charismatic authority through 'spiritual self-authorization' and the promotion of revelation as something available to all.[13] The second part of the article will show, however, that they held differing concepts of revelation and opposing ideas on the degree to which believers were expected to submit to new divine communication. These would lead in Emerson's case to extreme spiritual individualization that precluded any form of established religion, and in Smith's case to the establishment of a fixed religious community with a canon of sacred texts and hierarchical institution-building.

THE RELATION BETWEEN REVELATIONS, CHARISMATIC AUTHORITY AND BELIEVERS

First, it is necessary to establish a theoretical framework to understand why the personal spiritual distress of Smith and Emerson led them away from established religious institutions and doctrines and towards a belief in an active and communicative God who would reveal himself to them. Weber believed that charismatic authority emerged in times of political or spiritual crisis as an absolute and extraordinary form of authority that could affect the religious as well as the secular realm. He defined charisma as

> … a certain quality of an individual personality by virtue of which he is set apart from ordinary men and treated as endowed with supernatural, superhuman, or at least specifically exceptional powers or qualities. These are such as are not accessible to the ordinary person, but are regarded as of divine origin or as exemplary, and on the basis of them the individual concerned is treated as a leader.[14]

Charismatic authority is legitimized by its extraordinariness. In regard to religious authority, charisma finds its purest expression in the

---

[13] By 'spiritual self-authorization', I mean the turn away from mediating authorities such as ministers and denominational hierarchies towards an immediate and ultimate source of religious authority. By democratization, I mean the possibility of establishing a charismatic authority which in theory is open to everyone, to the extent of their spiritual giftedness.
[14] Max Weber, *On Charisma and Institution Building: Selected Papers*, ed. S. N. Aiznštadt (repr. Chicago, IL, 1992), 48.

prophet who establishes authority based on his claim to immediate access to an ultimate, divine source, mostly through visions and revelations.[15] Weber argues that charisma, as a pure type, is disruptive as it usually entails a complete reorientation of the prevailing value system and the rejection of all forms of traditional authority. This exceptionality, however, is difficult to maintain for long. Therefore Weber believed charisma necessarily transformed itself into a more sustainable form of authority over time. Weber called this 'a routinization of charisma': the integration of charisma into everyday life to make it practicable.[16] Over time, charisma would transform into traditional authority, with established rituals that would help to legitimize the transfer of authority to another person or group, or even an office. The process of routinization, however, only becomes relevant once a coherent group is formed in which the leader wishes to maintain a leadership position.

Although various aspects have been criticized throughout the twentieth century, many sociologists made use of, and further developed, Weber's category, which was also transformed in the late twentieth century into a popularized form of mystical appeal on the part of influential public figures.[17] These figures were for Weber exclusively male: his failure to acknowledge and include female charismatic leaders has figured amongst the most prominent points of critique in recent years.[18] Among sociologists who looked into a broader conceptualization of charisma was Edward Shils, who critiqued 'the "segregation" of charisma in the course of institutional establishment through its concentration into specific action, roles, or occasions, while it evaporated from the rest of the system',[19] and argued for the possibility of charisma existing in a dispersed or more attenuated form in secular institutions where it would function as a disruptive force but could also maintain social order.[20] Challenging Weber's leader-centredness, Charles

---

[15] Ibid. 51–2.

[16] Ibid. 54.

[17] For the trajectory of the word 'charisma', from its Pauline conception through Weber's re-invention to its appropriation by twentieth-century media, see John Potts, *A History of Charisma* (Basingstoke, 2009).

[18] On the trajectory of the charisma and gender discussion and why the concept still carries value if critically applied, see Paul Joosse and Robin Willey, 'Gender and Charismatic Power', *Theory and Society* 49 (2020), 533–61.

[19] Edward Shils, 'Charisma, Order, and Status', *American Sociological Review* 30 (1965), 199–213, at 202.

[20] Ibid. 200.

Camic investigated the preconditions for charisma and their implications for different phenomena associated with it. Highlighting followers' 'differing extraordinary needs' which need to be fulfilled by a prophet, Camic emphasized the agency of the disciples 'who impute the specialness' to the charismatic figure.[21] Sociologists in the 1990s then continued this trajectory of charisma as a dynamic and non-essential category which is ascribed to somebody, with Rodney Stark pointing out the reciprocal ascription processes between a charismatic figure and 'holy families', that is, a prophet's earliest and closest disciples,[22] in what sociologist Paul Joosse has most recently called 'the charismatic aristocracy'.[23] Scholars from other fields have also drawn attention to a set of character traits apparently shared among many charismatic leaders.[24]

Weber believed 'charismatic inspiration'[25] to be the foundation of authority but he was generally more interested in its legitimizing function than in the actual nature of the inspiration. Whether a prophet was truly inspired or a fraud did not matter to Weber as long as people recognized a prophet's inspiration as authentic and thus followed him (or his example). Thus, Weber's list of 'classical' examples of charismatic figures would not only include religious prophets with visions or Native American shamans, but also secular figures such as war heroes or demagogues. In a specific treatment of prophets in his *Sociology of Religion* (1920), however, Weber focused on the *religious* charismatic figure, thereby highlighting prophets who transmit revealed knowledge and distinguishing them from gurus with acquired knowledge or reformers who lack 'that vital emotional preaching which is distinctive of prophecy, regardless of whether this is disseminated by the spoken word, the pamphlet, or any other type

---

[21] Charles Camic, 'Charisma: Its Varieties, Preconditions, and Consequences', *Sociological Inquiry* 50 (1980), 5–23, at 16.

[22] Stark, 'Theory of Revelations', 305.

[23] Paul Joosse, 'Max Weber's Disciples: Theorizing the Charismatic Aristocracy', *Sociological Theory* 35 (2017), 334–58, at 337.

[24] Religious studies scholar Catherine Wessinger suggests energetic leadership, exemplary behaviour and willingness to personal sacrifice are among them: 'Charismatic Leaders in New Religions', in Olav Hammer and Mikael Rothstein, eds, *The Cambridge Companion to New Religious Movements* (Cambridge, 2012), 80–96, at 90–1. Psychologist Len Oakes sees narcissism as the defining trait of charismatic leaders: *Prophetic Charisma: The Psychology of Revolutionary Religious Personalities* (Syracuse, NY, 2011).

[25] Weber, *On Charisma and Institution Building*, 51–2.

of literary composition'.[26] What Weber described as the 'vital emotional preaching' is the key aspect when it comes to the dynamic relation between prophet and disciple. On the one hand, there is the prophet who feels called to communicate spiritual experience through preaching or writing; on the other hand, a receptive audience who believe in the prophet's ability to access 'an unseen source of authority'[27] is just as essential. Charisma is thus ascribed to a prophet and effectively co-created by both prophet and believers.[28]

While it could be argued that adopting a concept from the twentieth century and applying it to nineteenth-century figures may risk de-historicizing them, it should also be noted that there are inherent as well as historical connections between Weber's concept of charisma and these prophets that justify the application of the concept. In a footnote, Weber himself mentions Smith as a recent example of a charismatic prophet of the modern world.[29] With this example in mind, it is not surprising that Smith as a prophet is in perfect accordance with Weber's subcategory of the 'ethical prophet'. This kind of prophet serves as 'an instrument for the proclamation of a god and his will, be this a concrete command or an abstract norm. Preaching as one who has received a commission from God, he demands obedience as an ethical duty'.[30] Yet there are less obvious examples of charismatic prophets, including Emerson. Although Emerson rejected religious institutions and discouraged discipleship, he nevertheless enchanted his audience in lectures, addresses and essays with his poetically framed experiences of the divine, inviting them to follow his path to spiritual self-reliance. While this does not resemble the 'ethical prophet', Emerson often praised history's exceptionally gifted

---

[26] Ibid. 261. Charles Camic discusses the problem of discontinuity in Weber's charisma concept. He believes Weber's increasing focus on the dualism of charisma and institution to be responsible for the subtle changes: 'Charisma', 8.

[27] Wessinger, 'Charismatic Leaders', 80–1.

[28] Oakes suggests that followers are not simply swept away but follow because it helps their own 'spiritual quest': *Prophetic Charisma*, 126–7. He thus follows Benton Johnson's approach to charismatic leadership with his focus on personal and relational factors that characterize charismatic leadership: see Benton Johnson, 'On Founders and Followers: Some Factors in the Development of New Religious Movements', *Sociological Analysis* 53 (1992), 1–13; cf. Weber, *On Charisma and Institution Building*, 254.

[29] Max Weber et al., eds, *Wirtschaft und Gesellschaft. Soziologie. Unvollendet 1919–1920*, Gesamtausgabe Schriften und Reden 23 (Tübingen, 2013), 491–2.

[30] Weber, *On Charisma and Institution Building*, 263.

men and in his writings of the late 1830s he regularly assumed a pseudo-prophetic persona that strongly resembled the figure of the inspired genius. The same Romantic discourse that informed Emerson's idea of the 'holy bard', and thus his own performance, similarly informed Weber's category of charismatic authority, and more specifically his sub-category of the 'exemplary man', whose preaching 'says nothing about a divine mission or an ethical duty of obedience, but rather directs itself to the self-interest of those who crave salvation, recommending to them the same path as he himself traversed'.[31] These two different types of charismatic prophets and their notions of inspiration and authority play a decisive role in determining the possibility of the community of followers taking institutional shape.

RECEIVING REVELATIONS

Although he was a young, uneducated farmer, Joseph Smith assumed the powerful leadership position in one of the fastest growing new religious movements of the 1840s, based simply on his claims to be God's chosen mouthpiece. Like Emerson, Smith believed that the heavens had not been closed; God was still willing to reveal himself to his people. According to his personal account, Smith had been unable to settle with any congregation, as the revivalist spirit of most congregations had soon dissolved into sectarian strife and competition:

> [It] was seen that the seemingly good feelings of both the Priests and the Converts were more pretended than real, for a scene of great confusion and bad feeling ensued; Priest contending against priest, and convert against convert so that all their good feelings one for another (if they ever had any) were entirely lost in a strife of words and a contest about opinions.[32]

Frustrated by this corruption of pure religious enthusiasm, Smith reports how he randomly opened the Bible at James 1: 5: 'If any of

---

[31] Ibid. Several sociologists have pointed out the similarities between Weber's concept of the charismatic leader and the Romantic concept of the artistic genius, as presented in Thomas Carlyle's *On Heroes*: see Hans H. Gerth and C. W. Mills, 'Introduction', in eidem, eds, *From Max Weber: Essays in Sociology* (New York, 1958), 3–76, at 53. John Potts also suggests a similarity between Weber's charismatic leader and Nietzsche's 'Übermensch', a concept partially inspired by Emerson, as Nietzsche himself was an avid Emerson reader: *History of Charisma*, 112.

[32] Joseph Smith Jr, 'History (1838)', in *Personal Writings*, 226–40, at 228–9.

you lack wisdom, let him ask of God, that giveth to all men liberally, and upbraideth not; and it shall be given him', and took these words to heart. He circumvented ministerial guidance and turned to God instead to find out which church to join. In his 1838 account he remembered the vision of 1820 as follows:

> After I had retired into the place where I had previously designed to go, having looked around me and finding myself alone, I kneeled down and began to offer up the desires of my heart to God, ... I saw a pillar of light exactly over my head above the brightness of the sun, which descended gradually untill [*sic*] it fell upon me. When the light rested upon me I saw two personages (whose brightness and glory defy all description) standing above me in the air. One of them spake unto me calling me by my name and said (pointing to the other) 'This is my beloved Son, Hear him.' My object in going to enquire of the Lord was to know which of all the sects was right, that I might know which to join. ... I was answered that I must join none of them, for they were all wrong, and the Personage who addressed me said that all their creeds were an abomination in his sight ...[33]

Although this vision did not yet include a specific mission, it is still striking that, for Smith, communicating with God did not seem extraordinary. He was surprised by the intensity of the visitation by God and Jesus Christ, but he never doubted the reality of the vision. The content was special, not the communication itself. Smith's visions and the visionary encounters of people within *the Book of Mormon* were not 'shadowy spiritual intimations'[34] but what Terryl Givens calls 'Dialogic Revelation'.[35] Smith accepted revelation as a supernatural event and as the appropriate way in which God would communicate with people. Revelation had become an act of spiritual self-authorization, a practice that was available to all, regardless of their social position. By randomly opening his Bible at James 1: 5 and following God's word instead of a minister's advice, the farmer Smith had developed spiritual authority. In this initial moment of the movement, Smith democratized revelation.

By the time Emerson gave his rebellious 'Divinity School Address', he had already left the Unitarian ministry, had become a member of

---

[33] Ibid. 230–1.
[34] Givens, *By the Hand of Mormon*, 219.
[35] Ibid. 218.

the notorious Transcendentalists, and had begun to establish his second career as a lecturer and writer.[36] By leaving behind the ministerial office, he was able to overcome his spiritual crisis caused by a church which he diagnosed as marked by empty formalism and second-hand inspiration. It was obvious to him that tradition and institutionalization had slowly killed religious sentiment. He thus proposed to the young graduates, many of whom were about to enter the ministry, that they should become 'newborn Bards of the Holy Spirit',[37] and reveal their own experience of divine truth to their future congregations.

Emerson did not wait until he had left the ministry to begin developing his concept of an eternally revealing divine spirit. Indeed, the first traces of his spiritualized idea of present-day prophecy, in the form of preaching and writing, could already be found in his sermons of the early 1830s.[38] Even as a minister at Boston's Second Church, Emerson had occasionally warned against restricting divine inspiration: 'do not confine it to one season or one gift. ... [A]ll is spiritual influence, and its omnipresence excludes every superstitious distinction.'[39] In the first sermon after ordination in 1829, he blamed Christianity's corruption on Christians being 'much addicted to a few words' and holding on 'to phrases when the lapse of time has changed their meaning'.[40] Restricting religious sentiment to one

[36] The 'Transcendentalists' were a network of progressive writers, reformers and (former) Unitarian ministers who actively shaped and influenced antebellum intellectual life. Among their most prominent members were social activists and writers, including Margaret Fuller, Theodore Parker and Henry David Thoreau. For a helpful introduction to Transcendentalism and its roots, see Barbara L. Packer, *The Transcendentalists* (Athens, GA, 2007).

[37] Emerson, 'An Address', in *Nature, Addresses and Lectures*, 90.

[38] My analysis of Emerson's concept of revelation is based on selected sermons and his early post-ministerial writing, thus focusing on the period 1830–41. During this time, he was preoccupied with themes that are relevant for the discussion here, including questions of moral self–culture, revelation through history and nature, and the relation between the divine soul and man. After 1841, there is a perceptible decline in Emerson's Romantic millennial enthusiasm and in the attention given to divine revelation, while ethical considerations expressed in social and political activism become more central to his thought amid rising tensions about slavery in the United States.

[39] Ralph W. Emerson, Sermon 110, in *The Complete Sermons of Ralph Waldo Emerson*, vol. 3, ed. Albert J. von Frank (Columbia, MO, 1991), 118–25, at 124 (emphasis mine). Emerson preached this sermon five times between 1831 and 1837.

[40] Ralph W. Emerson, Sermon 28, in *Complete Sermons*, vol. 1, ed. Albert J. von Frank (Columbia, MO, 1989), 231–7, at 234–5.

completed text was wrong when God would continue to reveal himself. Therefore, Emerson affirmed: 'If to me were given that starlike vision which could see and make report how they all bear evidence to it, I cheerfully would. ... It would be silly to shut myself voluntarily within a yet narrower circle, and only use a part of my pittance of truth.'[41] The egalitarian tendency of receiving divine knowledge is already visible in this passage, but what Hodder called the 'democratization of the sacred'[42] becomes even more apparent when Emerson proclaimed explicitly two years later: 'Probably all men have the same capacity of prophecy and miracle. What is prophecy but more knowledge? What is miracle but more dominion of the soul over matter than is now evinced?'[43] This egalitarian tendency, however, needs to be regarded critically. Although Emerson did not explicitly exclude women or men with an ethnic minority background, his lists of ideal historical examples of inspired leaders were made up almost exclusively of white men.[44]

Like Smith, Emerson believed that humankind had separated itself from an ever-revealing God. People had stopped listening to their own soul, through which they could connect to the divine, and had turned towards worldly distractions, empty ritual and doctrines instead: 'The reason why the world lacks unity, and lies broken and in heaps, is, because man is disunited with himself.'[45] A distorted perception of nature had misled mankind to a distorted concept of religion. For Emerson, Jesus had been one of the few examples of exceptionally inspired prophet-poets. But most people had mistaken him for an ultimate authority and had become obsessed with the biographical Jesus, while what had been truly divine about Jesus – his immediate relation to God – had been forgotten.[46]

For Emerson, it was incomprehensible that people believed divine inspiration to have ended. He felt 'that the need was never greater

---

[41] Ibid. 235.

[42] Hodder, *Emerson's Rhetoric of Revelation*, 10–11.

[43] Emerson, Sermon 110, 122.

[44] One exception is the occasional remark about the exceptional religiosity of his aunt Mary or the inspired writing of the French mystic Jeanne Guyon. These occurred primarily in his personal writings. See, for example, Ralph W. Emerson, *The Journals and Miscellaneous Notebooks of Ralph Waldo Emerson*, 5: *1835–1838*, ed. Merton M. Sealts (Cambridge, MA, 1965), 5, 323–4.

[45] Emerson, 'Nature', 43.

[46] Cf. Emerson, 'An Address', 81.

of new revelation than now [as] ... [t]he Church seems to totter to its fall, almost all life extinct'.[47] New inspiration was needed and therefore Emerson asked rebelliously: 'Why should not we also enjoy an original relation to the universe?'[48] Revelations were not commandments received by one person for others to obey, but transforming spiritual experiences that anyone could have. Prophets were exceptional because they had perfected their perception of the divine further than most ordinary people, but they were not essentially different. Therefore, Emerson asked

> ... whether prophecy is not a state of mind more sagacious than that of other men only as that mind is more fully surrendered to God. Every day's experience shows us the different degrees of reception of wisdom by the same mind at different times. ... The prophet in an exalted state of holiness therefore sees more truth than other men, but under the same conditions.[49]

Rather than locating divine truth in something external that could be measured empirically or grasped rationally, people could use their imagination to access divine truth within the soul. Revelation, for Emerson, came to be an encounter with the sublime, a fusion of the Universal Mind with the individual mind.[50] He believed these mystical experiences to be natural rather than supernatural. These experiences demanded an emptying out of the historical, personal self and a silencing of all the worldly noise that would constantly distract. His most cited revelation, the 'transparent eye-ball' passage, describes the dissolution of his body and the union of his mind with nature, when he becomes pure perception:

> Crossing a bare common, in snow puddles, at twilight, under a clouded sky, without having in my thoughts any occurrence of special good fortune, I have enjoyed a perfect exhilaration. Almost I fear to think how glad I am. ... Standing on the bare ground, – my head bathed by the blithe air, and uplifted into infinite space, – all mean egotism vanishes. I become a transparent eye-ball. I am nothing. I see all. The currents of

---

[47] Ibid. 84.
[48] Emerson, 'Nature', 7.
[49] Emerson, Sermon 110, 122–3.
[50] Cf. Ralph W. Emerson, 'The Over-Soul', in *The Collected Works of Ralph Waldo Emerson*, 2: *Essays: First Series*, ed. Alfred R. Ferguson and Joseph Slater (Cambridge, MA, 1979), 159–75, at 166.

the Universal Being circulate through me; I am part and particle of God.[51]

This passage was the climax of a highly individualized experience. If a person left tradition and external guidance behind, it was possible to reconnect to the divine. Rather than being the exceptional gift of only one prophet, revelation had been opened as an experience for all. Over time, Emerson developed his concept of revelation even further into a mode of perceiving the divine, which could and should be cultivated by everyone. In the end, the purpose of opening the soul for revelations was to help man to recover his divine potential. After all, 'man is a god in ruins'.[52]

The Consequences of different Conceptions of Revelation for possible Institution Building

Both Smith and Emerson believed divine inspiration to be as real and intense as it had been at Pentecost. They even shared the idea that people (albeit 'people' generally implied white men) were gifted with charisma to different degrees. Despite these shared ideas, however, one crucial difference would ultimately separate them and determine the possibility of institution building within a coherent movement of believers. For Smith, the restitution of charismatic gifts, on which the (re-)establishment of the one saving church rested, entailed a sacred hierarchy. While some of Smith's closer associates, such as his wife Emma, Oliver Cowdery or David Whitmer, occasionally received authoritative revelations themselves (mostly in the company of Smith), Smith occupied an exceptional position from the very beginning of the movement.[53] He was not one visionary coexisting among many. Instead, he was the divine vessel, chosen by God and not elected by fellow believers, to preside over the new church.

---

[51] Emerson, 'Nature', 10.

[52] Ibid. 42.

[53] In July 1830, Smith's wife Emma received a divine order through her husband, today recorded as *Doctrine & Covenants* [hereafter: *D&C*] 25. *D&C* 6 and 7 were given to Smith and Oliver Cowdery, when Cowdery began recording as a scribe Smith's translation of the *Book of Mormon*. *D&C* 18 was a revelation to Smith, Cowdery and David Whitmer, given at Fayette, NY, in June 1829: see *The Doctrine and Covenants of the Church of Jesus Christ of Latter-day Saints: Containing Revelations given to Joseph Smith, the Prophet with some Additions by his Successors in the Presidency of the Church* (Salt Lake City, UT, 2013).

As a result, revelations articulated by Smith correlate with the divine commandments of Weber's 'ethical prophet'. The doctrines Smith received were meant to lead believers into the one redeeming church. Unlike Emerson's individualized practice of spiritual seeking, Smith's concept of revelation included a God who was sending specific orders to reinstate God's only true church. Once that true church had been established, authoritative revelations were relocated within that sacred order. In the revelation given to Smith at the formation of the church, on 6 April 1830, God did not send a divine message of equality but first and foremost revealed Smith's divinely sanctioned superior position within the new institution. Smith was to be 'a seer, a translator, a prophet, an apostle of Jesus Christ, an elder of the church through the will of God the Father'.[54] By divine commandment, Smith immediately occupied the highest position in order to lead humanity towards salvation although, at least theoretically, the same Spirit could speak through all members. God had sanctioned Smith's revelatory superiority and ordered all believers to 'give heed unto all his words and commandments which he shall give unto you as he receiveth them, walking in all holiness before me; For his word ye shall receive, as if from mine own mouth'.[55] Revelation was reified as a hierarchy.

Smith established his position as the charismatic leader of a new church, but his ability to do so was not based simply on the visions he had received.[56] The essential foundation for the new church was his new sacred writing, the *Book of Mormon*. For Smith, everything related to the production of this additional Bible – including recovering and hiding the gold plates and translation instruments, translating the text, enduring persecution and ridicule by neighbours, and suffering chastisement by God when he failed – served to establish his charismatic authority because it related the production to a specific mission. To recover this text and publish it was the first step towards an ecclesiastical institution for what previously had been a visionary movement. In the early years of the movement, the *Book*

---

[54] *D&C* 21: 1.
[55] Ibid.
[56] Richard Bushman has argued that Smith played down his visionary experiences in the early years of the movement: 'The Visionary World of Joseph Smith', *Brigham Young University Studies* 37 (1997–8), 183–204.

of Mormon thus acted as a '*signifier*',[57] as Givens has argued. It became the key identification marker for the early converts and separated believers from unbelievers. Thus Smith's prophetic persona was intricately linked to this new sacred writing.

Yet successful institutionalization did not only rest on additional revelation of scripture. Instead, what we find is a dynamic interplay between new revelations and the ordering of structures on the institutional level, which helped sustain charismatic gifts as a vital source in Mormonism without threatening the survival of the church. These ordering structures often developed from further revelations and they helped secure Smith's own authority as first prophet of the church. A case in point would be the revelation, now recorded as *D&C* 28, given through Smith to his close associate Cowdery in September 1830 in response to the confrontation with Hiram Page, who challenged Smith's exclusive revelatory authority when claiming to have received new revelations with the help of seer stones.[58]

Even before the formation of the church, Smith began to reinstate ancient priesthoods through baptismal rites that helped institutionalize the movement. Over the years, more sacred rites would be added, transforming the church into a complex system of various priesthoods and offices. But while on an organizational level Smith would distribute executive power into different offices, councils and conferences, additional divine instructions eventually transformed him into the 'Prophet, Priest & King' of a quasi-theocracy in Nauvoo on 11 April 1844.[59] By then, only high-ranking church officials could reveal divine communications with authority binding on others. Several historians have therefore argued that from 1830 onwards, when the *Book of Mormon* was published and the church officially organized, we can no longer speak of Mormonism as an anti-clerical, democratized movement, because Smith had already begun to implement complex

---

[57] Givens, *By the Hand of Mormon*, 63–4. More recently, scholars have indicated that the *Book of Mormon* was more than just a signifier, as historical evidence suggests its devotional and liturgical use by early Mormon converts: Janiece Johnson, 'Becoming a People of the Books: Toward an Understanding of Early Mormon Converts and the New Word of the Lord', *Journal of Book of Mormon Studies* 27 (2018), 1–43.

[58] See also Bushman, *Joseph Smith*, 119–22.

[59] Ronald K. Esplin, Matthew J. Grow and Matthew C. Godfrey, *The Joseph Smith Papers*, 1: *Administrative Records* (Salt Lake City, UT, 2016), 94–5.

power structures.[60] Michael MacKay's proposed term 'hierarchical democracy' most fittingly describes the tension between Smith's leadership as a 'type of theological king' and an ecclesiastical system in which power was diffused among chosen church leaders.[61]

In Weberian terms, charisma had been routinized with the effect that it

> ... may be transmitted by ritual means from one bearer to another or may be created in a new person. It involves a dissociation of charisma from a particular individual, making it an objective, transferable entity. In particular, it may become the charisma of office. In this case, the belief in legitimacy is no longer directed to the individual, but to the acquired qualities and to the effectiveness of the ritual acts.[62]

True democratization of charisma was therefore only present in the initial moment of movement building in Mormonism when an uneducated farmer claimed to have received divine commands to restore an ancient sacred order. Once the process of church organization had begun, revelation with comprehensive authority over all believers could only come from within the ecclesiastical order, which, from the mid-1800s until 1978, was reserved for white men.[63]

In contrast, Emerson would have abhorred the idea of locating the gift of revelation within a new church. He asked: 'What shall we do? I confess, all attempts to project and establish a new Cultus with new rites and forms, seem to me in vain.'[64] For him, the mistake was to establish religion in any kind of institutional form, as all institutions would eventually restrain an individual's spiritual practice. To capture the religious sentiment within a church would always kill the divine element. To establish something as authoritative was to fix it, but the

---

[60] Among them is Kathleen Flake, arguing for a system of 'shifting status relationships' instead: 'Ordering Antinomy: An Analysis of Early Mormonism's Priestly Offices, Councils, and Kinship', *Religion and American Culture* 26 (2016), 139–83.

[61] Michael Hubbard MacKay, *Prophetic Authority: Democratic Hierarchy and the Mormon Priesthood* (Urbana, IL, 2020), 2.

[62] Weber, *On Charisma and Institution Building*, 57.

[63] *D&C*, Official Declaration 2 refers to 'a few black male members of the Church' being ordained to the priesthood during Smith's life, but the practice was stopped after his death. In 1978, the First Presidency and the Quorum of the Twelve Apostles received a revelation that allowed 'all worthy male members of the Church [to] be ordained to the priesthood without regard for race or color'. See Joseph Smith Jr, 'Official Declaration 2', in *Doctrine and Covenants*.

[64] Emerson, 'An Address', 92.

divine Spirit could not be fixed. However divinely inspired a prophet or text may be, they could never claim exclusive possession of all sacred knowledge, as divine truth would continue to be revealed and therefore could not be fully presented in one book by one church. New revelation would appear constantly, making the whole concept of authoritative sacred writing obsolete. Only the act of recording divine communication, or, in Emerson's poetic view, the act of 'scripturalizing' could be regarded as sacred. A new scripture could never be completed. Therefore Emerson neither advocated the fixing of new divine revelation in a new Bible nor encouraged the foundation of a new 'Emersonian' church.

Still, a prophetic element remains in Emerson's writings of the 1830s. He shared his experiences of the divine with a perceptive audience through his published writing. Although he presented his experiences only as examples of a way towards spiritual truth and not as a dictation of religious practice, he nevertheless assumed a pseudo-prophetic tone at times to lament the brokenness of the human soul and seemed to encourage others to follow his example of spiritual reversal. Recalling charisma's attributive nature, a group of disciples ascribed 'post-life charisma'[65] to their spiritual teacher Emerson. While some enthusiastic followers attempted to establish Emerson as a Western prophet at interreligious gatherings, the 'Poughkeepsie Seer' Andrew Jackson Davis actively tried to sacralize the wisdom of Emerson, 'one of the inspired Scripturalists of this century',[66] in his 'Gospel of St Ralph'.[67]

Emerson, however, never explicitly declared himself to be a prophet. Instead, he pointed towards history's more spiritually gifted people, who could act as inspiring teachers to show humanity how to reconnect with the divine, and he prophesied that many more would follow. These past and future prophet-poets acted as 'liberating gods'.[68] Yet the only way to divine revelation was through the

---

[65] Wessinger, 'Charismatic Leaders', 86–7.

[66] Andrew Jackson Davis, *A Sacred Book Containing Old and New Gospels: Derived and Translated from the Inspirations of Original Saints* (Boston, MA, 1873), 32–3, 44.

[67] On F. B. Sanborn and George Malloy, the 'Emersonians' at the turn of the century, see Leigh Eric Schmidt, *Restless Souls: The Making of American Spirituality*, 2nd edn (Berkeley, CA, 2012) 193–200.

[68] Ralph W. Emerson, 'The Poet', in *The Collected Works of Ralph Waldo Emerson*, 3: *Essays: Second Series*, ed. Joseph Slater and Alfred R. Ferguson (Cambridge, MA, 1983), 3–24, at 18–19.

cultivation of the individual soul through first-hand experiences of the divine rather than subjection to past genius.

CONCLUSION

This article has shown how sociological theories can provide a deeper understanding of the dynamic relationship between revelation and institutionalization processes in the actual historical context of antebellum America, and thereby demonstrated how historians can benefit from the use of such theories. The concept of charismatic authority provided a theoretical background that helped to uncover both Smith and Emerson as charismatic prophets who challenged existing ecclesiastical institutions by their belief in continuing revelation. While they are usually presented as contemporaries from culturally opposed worlds, the concept of charisma highlights a shared belief in continuing revelation without blurring their fundamental differences. As the case of Emerson as the 'exemplary man' has shown, the category of charisma provides a theoretical framework that enables us to present inconspicuous prophets alongside more obvious examples. It thus invites further analysis of previously under-represented charismatic women and men alongside well-known examples, thereby demonstrating the existence of a socially and culturally diverse speech community that grappled with the idea of new revelation and reached from intellectual Boston to the uncouth frontier of nineteenth-century America.

Both Smith and Emerson effectively communicated their personal experiences with the divine and established charisma. However, it was their diverging understandings of the concept of revelation that ultimately determined whether institution-building was possible (or necessary). While Smith retained revelation as a vital element, it became reified in hierarchy as all revelation with authority for the community became tied to the highest ecclesiastical offices after the foundation of the church. Smith tied revelation to a sustainable structure that would guarantee the church's survival as a united body of believers. Thus he succeeded in balancing inspiration and institution-building by incorporating the disruptive charisma in a tight concept of ecclesiastical hierarchy.

This contrasted strongly with Emerson's individualistic concept of revelation which did not require charisma to routinize within an institutional form, as there was no church to speak of. While Emerson elevated some exceptionally gifted poets and prophets in history, in general charismatic authority had been relocated within every single soul. The experience of divine communication had become naturalized and internalized and was an end in itself. Revelations were the vehicles that gave short glimpses into human divine potentiality and they had become so highly individualized that they could never be binding on others. Emerson could thus be regarded as the more consistent advocate of democratized charisma, given his commitment to individual spiritual authority and revelation as a universalized act of moral self-cultivation. While Smith demanded loyal support for his radical revelation of the 'new and everlasting covenant',[69] Emerson's recommendation for the future Unitarian ministers at Harvard was quite different: 'to go alone; to refuse the good models, even those most sacred in the imagination of men, and dare to love God without mediator or veil'.[70]

---

[69] *D&C* 132. This revelation would give rise to the controversial doctrine concerning polygamy.
[70] Emerson, 'An Address', 90.

Visions and Realities in Hong Kong Anglican Mission Schools, 1849–1941

Tim Yung*

University of Hong Kong

This article explores the tension between missionary hopes for mass conversion through Christian education and the reality of operating mission schools in one colonial context: Hong Kong. Riding on the wave of British imperial expansion, George Smith, the first bishop of the diocese of Victoria, had a vision for mission schooling in colonial Hong Kong. In 1851, Smith established St Paul's College as an Anglo-Chinese missionary institution to educate, equip and send out Chinese young people who would subsequently participate in mission work before evangelizing the whole of China. However, Smith's vision failed to take institutional form as the college encountered operational difficulties and graduates opted for more lucrative employment instead of church work. Moreover, the colonial government moved from a laissez-faire to a more hands-on approach in supervising schools. The bishops of Victoria were compelled to reshape their schools towards more sustainable institutional forms while making compromises regarding their vision for Christian education.

Dana Robert's edited volume, *Converting Colonialism: Visions and Realities in Mission History*, explores the way in which local and socio-political conditions shaped mission practices so that indigenous churches under European colonialism often did not become the institutions that missionaries envisaged.[1] Historical reality deviated from missionary vision. For instance, one case study explores shifting ideals regarding the constitution of indigenous churches after contentious encounters in the dioceses of Colombo and on the Niger. Although

* Department of History, 10.63, 10/F Run Run Shaw Tower, Centennial Campus, University of Hong Kong, Hong Kong SAR. E-mail: timyung@connect.hku.hk.

[1] Dana L. Robert, ed., *Converting Colonialism: Visions and Realities in Mission History, 1706–1914*, SHCM (Grand Rapids, MI, 2008), 5–6. On indigenous churches being shaped through mission and empire, see Donald M. Lewis, ed., *Christianity Reborn: The Global Expansion of Evangelicalism in the Twentieth Century*, SHCM (Grand Rapids, MI, 2004); Kevin Ward and Brian Stanley, eds, *The Church Mission Society and World Christianity, 1799–1999*, SHCM (Grand Rapids, MI, 2000).

Studies in Church History 57 (2021), 254–276 © The Author(s), 2021. Published by Cambridge University Press on behalf of Ecclesiastical History Society.
doi: 10.1017/stc.2021.13

the original intention was to achieve the consecration of indigenous bishops at all costs, conflicts relating to episcopal authority and missionary control resulted in more cautious approaches towards indigenous church organization.[2] In the broader study of the history of Christianity, this historical method reflects how non-Western Christianity is no longer treated merely as a derivative of missionary activity, but as a complicated entanglement of cross-cultural contexts, colonial government, Christian essentialism and both missionary and indigenous agency.[3]

The following article extends this approach to Anglican mission schools in Hong Kong from 1849 to 1941, which are exemplars of how inspired visions took institutional shape differently from the form initially planned, owing to the nineteenth- and twentieth-century imperial context.[4] This case study builds upon extensive historiography tracing the worldwide development of Protestant mission schools in the nineteenth and twentieth centuries.[5] Although

---

[2] C. Peter Williams, 'The Church Missionary Society and the Indigenous Church in the Second Half of the Nineteenth Century: The Defense and Destruction of the Venn Ideals', in Robert, ed., *Converting Colonialism*, 86–111.

[3] Joel Cabrita and David Maxwell, 'Introduction', to eidem and Emma Wild-Wood, eds, *Relocating World Christianity: Interdisciplinary Studies in Universal and Local Expressions of the Christian Faith*, Theology and Mission in World Christianity 7 (Leiden, 2017), 1–9.

[4] The trend depicted in this article also applies to other mainline Protestant denominations, who likewise established mission schools with a view to growing indigenous churches but encountered similar challenges. However, the scope here is limited to Anglican schools in Hong Kong. For other mission schools in Hong Kong, see Anthony Sweeting, *Education in Hong Kong, Pre-1841 to 1941: Fact and Opinion. Materials for a History of Education in Hong Kong* (Hong Kong, 1990); Patricia P.-K. Chiu, *A History of the Grant Schools Council: Mission, Vision and Transformation* (Hong Kong, 2013). For an overview of schools in China, which followed an alternative trajectory since they were under different government, see Jessie G. Lutz, *Chinese Politics and Christian Missions: The Anti-Christian Movements of 1920–28* (Notre Dame, IN, 1988), 27–54; Thomas D. Curran, *Educational Reform in Republican China: The Failure of Educators to Create a Modern Nation*, Chinese Studies 40 (Lewiston, NY, 2005).

[5] See, for instance, Derek R. Peterson, *Creative Writing: Translation, Bookkeeping, and the Work of Imagination in Colonial Kenya*, Social History of Africa Series (Portsmouth, NH, 2004); also David Maxwell, 'The Creation of Lubaland: Missionary Science and Christian Literacy in the making of the Luba Katanga in Belgian Congo', *Journal of Eastern African Studies* 10 (2016), 367–92, on mission schooling and ethnic formation. For examples in China, see T'ien Ju-K'ang, *Peaks of Faith: Protestant Mission in Revolutionary China* (Leiden, 1993), on mission schooling resulting in the introduction of an economic lifestyle and the removal of alcoholism; Ryan Dunch, *Fuzhou Protestants and the Making of a Modern China 1857–1927* (New Haven, CT, 2001), 112–77, on mission schooling and social mobility. See Brian Stanley, *Christianity in the Twentieth Century: A World History*

missionaries aimed to enable indigenous converts to encounter the Bible through English education, they were often confronted by the realities of government restrictions on school operations as well as graduates deploying their literacy differently from how the missionaries imagined.

The first Anglican mission school in Hong Kong was founded as a by-product of burgeoning missionary expansion worldwide during the 1840s. Eugene Stock observes that the growth of Church Missionary Society (CMS) activity in this decade stemmed from unprecedented voluntary subscriptions in England as well as British imperial conquests in China and India, which led ultimately to the establishment of new bishoprics around the world.[6] The Revd Vincent Stanton was accordingly dispatched as colonial chaplain to Hong Kong after it was ceded by China's Qing Empire in 1842 following the First Opium War.[7] Stanton's ultimate aim was to reach China, an endeavour which in his mind would begin with an Anglo-Chinese college and a cathedral church in Hong Kong.[8] Stanton's hope was eventually realized by Bishop George Smith, the first bishop of the newly-constituted diocese of Victoria (Hong Kong). In a memorandum to Earl Grey, Secretary of State for War and the Colonies, Smith expressed his hope that the diocese would diffuse 'the blessings of liberty of civilization and of Christianity', in line with imperial and missionary activity across the British Empire.[9] His ideal was to enable Hong Kong to become 'a scene of educational measures of a high order and on a large scale … as the most eligible locality for a central base of indirect missionary operations in China'.[10] To this end, Smith advocated the formation of St Paul's College (SPC) as an Anglo-Chinese college to train indigenous evangelists who would propagate both Christianity and civilization:

(Princeton, NJ, 2018), 57–78, for appropriations of the faith unintended by missionaries in Congo and Melanesia.

[6] Eugene Stock, *The History of the Church Missionary Society: Its Environment, its Men and its Work*, vol. 1 (London, 1899), 367, 406–9.

[7] Rowan Strong, ed., *Oxford History of Anglicanism, 3: Partisan Anglicanism and its Global Expansion, 1829–c.1914* (Oxford, 2017), 323–4.

[8] George B. Endacott and Dorothy E. She, *The Diocese of Victoria, Hong Kong: A Hundred Years of Church History, 1849–1949* (Hong Kong, 1949), 10–13.

[9] London, CERC, OBF/5/2/7/3/9, Bishop Smith to Earl Grey, 16 January 1847.

[10] CERC, OBF/5/2/7/3/16, 'Prospectus of Missionary Plans for the Benefit of the Chinese', June 1849, 1.

A proficiency in the more elementary branches of education, conveyed to [Chinese youths] through the medium of books composed by missionaries … will in due time point out proper subjects for receiving the more solid advantages which a thorough education in the science and theology of the West … will confer on native youths in their endeavours to diffuse the gospel among their fellow-countrymen.[11]

In effect, Smith foresaw graduates of the school being so moved by their encounter with Western Christian education that they would passionately spread Christianity throughout the rest of China. This was consistent with wider expectations and assumptions at the time about the superiority of Western civilization vis-à-vis Chinese culture. For example, the Revd S. R. Brown, headmaster of the nearby Morrison Education Society School, which sent its students to SPC after closing down, thought poorly of the 'passive inanity' of indigenous students and of the 'unfit instruments of education' in Chinese literature, but was hopeful for their enlightenment through Christianity and Western learning.[12]

The beginnings of SPC showed promise. A permanent site was obtained after the colonial government granted Inland Lot 76 to the archbishop of Canterbury for 999 years 'for the object of training a body of native clergy and Christian teachers for the propagation of the gospel of China'.[13] After two years' operation, some thirty-three male students aged between twelve and eighteen had enrolled in the college. Staying on school premises, they took part in daily morning and evening services and also took classes in English, Chinese, Geography, Astronomy, Divinity and History.[14] In 1858, the Diocesan Native Female Training School (which became the Victoria Home and Orphanage in 1869, when it opened to boys as well, and then the Diocesan Boys' School in 1902) was founded by Bishop Smith's wife with a similar aim in mind. By simultaneously evangelizing and civilizing colonial subjects, Lydia Smith sought 'to

---

[11] Ibid. 2.

[12] S. R. Brown, 'Report of the Morrison Education Society, 1844', *Chinese Repository* 13 (1844), 632–4, cited in Sweeting, *Education in Hong Kong*, 20–2. The Morrison Education Society School was established as an Anglo-Chinese mission school in Malacca in 1820, moving to Hong Kong in 1843.

[13] London, LPL, Fisher Papers, vol. 46, fol. 40, St Paul's College Old Boys Union to Fisher, 3 December 1947.

[14] Vincent H. Y. Fung, ed., *From Devotion to Plurality: A full History of St Paul's College 1851–2001* (Hong Kong, 2001), 31.

introduce among a somewhat superior class of native females the blessings of Christianity and of religious training'; her hope was that graduates would become the wives of SPC graduates.[15]

It is, however, important to note that Bishop Smith's articulation of the benefits of mission education was published in a prospectus addressed to potential subscribers. From the outset, the college was dependent on an annual grant of 1,200 Hong Kong silver dollars (HK$; approximately £255) from the Foreign Office, which had been transferred from the recently closed Morrison Education Society school.[16] Furthermore, the college never received the anticipated support from the endowment fund of the diocese. Of the £8,000 endowment donated by 'a brother and a sister' in England, Bishop Smith used only £643 to repay a loan advanced by Stanton for the college before allocating the remainder to other diocesan expenses and investment in Dent & Co., a trading company in the colony.[17] Stanton lamented the fact that during the succeeding years, in which SPC expanded, he never received any further support from the endowment fund. Instead, Stanton was compelled to make his own personal donation of £1,000, supplemented by gifts from family and friends.[18]

In addition, the colonial government was reluctant to increase the grant awarded to the college. Henry Pottinger, the first governor of Hong Kong, wrote to the Secretary of State for the Colonies in 1843 expressing his opinion that funding two schools in Hong Kong would be 'totally superfluous' since Chinese residents in the colony were largely uninterested in English education, as suggested by the fact that very few families were willing to pay high school fees to attend mission schools.[19] This was because English education

---

[15] Patricia P.-K. Chiu, '"A Position of Usefulness": Gendering History of Girls' Education in Colonial Hong Kong (1850s–1890s)', *History of Education* 37 (2008), 789–805, at 791; Fung Yee Wang and Moira Chan-Yeung Mo Wah, *To Serve and to Lead: A History of the Diocesan Boys' School Hong Kong* (Hong Kong, 2009), 10.

[16] Hong Kong Public Records Office [hereafter: HKPRO], HKMS94/1/1/9, Stanton to Alford, 21 March 1867; *Hong Kong Blue Book for the Year 1871* (Hong Kong, 1872), 130. A Hong Kong silver dollar (issued by the Royal Mint) was then worth about 4s 3d: *Hong Kong Blue Book for the Year 1871* (Hong Kong, 1872), 130. For further information on currency and exchange in Hong Kong, see the annual Hong Kong Government Reports.

[17] HKPRO, HKMS94/1/1/5–6, 'St Paul's College: Early History', n.d.

[18] HKPRO, HKMS94/1/1/9, Stanton to Alford, 21 March 1867.

[19] Kew, TNA, CO129/2/251, Pottinger to Stanley, 23 August 1843, in Sweeting, *Education in Hong Kong*, 167–8; *Dates and Events connected with the History of Education in Hong Kong* (Hong Kong, 1877), 19.

was closely associated with degradation. This attitude was exemplified when, in 1864, Mary Winefred Eaton, the first headmistress of the Diocesan Native Female Training School, was assaulted by a mob while riding in a sedan chair.[20] Her school had to be repurposed in 1869 to cater for orphans since the school's original purpose of training 'native females' had resulted in financial difficulty.[21] Smith's successor, Bishop Charles Alford, wrote to Archbishop Charles Longley that SPC had entered bankruptcy by 1867.[22] The Foreign Office had withdrawn their annual grant of HK$1,200; the properties owned by the college, which had in the past yielded £500 per annum, had failed in recent years; and the investments in Dent & Co. had vanished when the entire company folded in 1867 following the 1866 global financial crisis.[23] In effect, the grand vision of establishing mission schools that would impart Christianity and civilization struggled to take off as a result of wavering finances: the initial grants had run dry and the anticipated income and interest never materialized.

In addition, graduates did not go where missionaries intended. Scandalously it was revealed in 1865 that with a few notable exceptions, most girls from the Diocesan Native Female Training School were sold by their parents as mistresses to Europeans in the colony, who valued their English proficiency and the 'refinement in their countenances'.[24] As for the male graduates of SPC, Bishop Smith complained that they never pursued full-time church work once they discovered more lucrative options within the mercantile community of Hong Kong, for their proficiency in English proved to be indispensable in trade, commerce and local government.[25] A polemicist of the period noted that SPC produced 'the best instructed Chinese, who ... [held] the highest positions among their countrymen'.[26] This trend was amplified by the paucity of schooling in pre-colonial Hong Kong, which had mostly consisted of informal education in homes and the fluctuating presence of academies

---

[20] Sweeting, *Education in Hong Kong*, 152–3.
[21] Fung and Chan-Yeung, *To Serve and to Lead*, 11–12.
[22] CERC, OBF/5/2/7/3/55, Bishop Alford to Archbishop Charles Longley, 6 December 1867, 1.
[23] Ibid. 1.
[24] TNA, CO129/342, 80, Eitel to Stewart, 5 July 1889, in Chiu, '"A Position of Usefulness"', 795–6.
[25] Endacott and She, *Diocese of Victoria*, 20.
[26] *Dates and Events*, 4.

preparing youths for the Qing civil service examination.[27] In addition, from the 1860s the colonial government shifted to indirect rule through indigenous leaders. Studies by Carroll and Munn highlight the increasingly prominent role of self-conscious English-speaking Chinese elites from mission schools in public life.[28]

Wu Ting-fang, who graduated from SPC in 1861, was the first Chinese to be called to the bar, the first Chinese member of Hong Kong's Legislative Council, Qing ambassador to the US, and ultimately Minister of Foreign Affairs for the Republic of China.[29] Another prominent early graduate was Tong Mow-chee (also known as Tang Ting-gui), who graduated from SPC in 1851. Tong pursued a career in business in California before returning to China in 1857, where he worked as the chief translator for Shanghai Imperial Customs, and subsequently as the head of Jardine, Matheson & Co.'s Shanghai office from 1873 until his death in 1897.[30] English education was valued highly and could be redeployed beyond Anglican missions in both colonial Hong Kong and Chinese treaty ports. This dilemma persisted even fifty years later: the fifth bishop of Victoria, Gerard Heath Lander, made the same complaint, lamenting that most SPC graduates preferred to become clerks or schoolmasters, earning double the salary of catechists and more than ordained ministers.[31]

Nevertheless, SPC and the Victoria Home and Orphanage discovered a new identity in the 1870s during Bishop John Shaw Burdon's episcopate, when Burdon switched the emphasis of schools away from curricular content and towards the boarding experience. The

---

[27] Sweeting, *Education in Hong Kong*, 89–90, 138.

[28] John M. Carroll, *Edge of Empires: Chinese Elites and British Colonials in Hong Kong* (Cambridge, MA, 2005), 13–15; Christopher Munn, *Anglo-China: Chinese People and British Rule in Hong Kong 1841–1880* (Richmond, 2001), 367–73. Munn explains the incorporation of Chinese gentry into the colonial polity as a turning point in colonial government, which previously struggled to manage crime and punishment among the Chinese population.

[29] Fung, ed., *Devotion to Plurality*, 32. For a detailed study of Wu's public service and political activity, see Linda Pomerantz-Zhang, *Wu Tingfang (1842–1922): Reform and Modernization in Modern Chinese Society* (Hong Kong, 1992).

[30] 聖保羅書院同學會 [Shengbaoluoshuyuan Tongxuehui; St Paul's College Alumni Association], 中國・香港・聖保羅：165 年的人與時代 [*Zhongguo, Xianggang, Shengbaolo: 165 Nian de Renyushidai; China, Hong Kong, St Paul's: 165 Years of People and Times*] (Hong Kong, 2016), 47.

[31] 'Hongkong's Diocesan Conference: Striking Address by Bishop Lander', *South China Morning Post*, 15 September 1910, 10.

Revd M. J. Ost, a missionary educator in Hong Kong, gratefully recalled the impact of Christian schoolmasters on boarders. For the Victoria Home and Orphanage, the Revd Kwong Yat-sau (Kuang Ri-xiu) and his wife were able to establish good relations with the girls while residing with them, helping many in their faith, leading to six baptisms on Christmas Day 1889. The spiritual experience of the girls was also strengthened by the presence of two Chinese Bible teachers, as well as by the fact that over half the students were from the second generation of Chinese Christian families in South China.[32] Between 1881 and 1892, Mok Shau-tsang (Mo Shou-zeng), who in 1935 would become assistant bishop of the Chung Hua Sheng Kung Hui (the Chinese Anglican Church) and Hong Kong's first Chinese bishop, studied at SPC after a moving encounter with a distant relative who quit opium and gambling dramatically after becoming a Christian. Although most of Mok's contemporaries pursued professional careers after graduating, Mok chose to enrol in SPC's theological training programme after formative encounters with his missionary teachers.[33] The Revd William Hipwell, who was temporarily in charge of SPC in 1905, commented on the importance of school instructors having 'high Christian character', for he understood this to be the key in influencing students.[34] The converse could also be true, with the lack of boarding facilities limiting the influence of mission schools. For example, in 1874, two boys were withdrawn from the Victoria Home and Orphanage by their mother because she adamantly refused to allow them to be baptized.[35] The shift in outlook was described in 1899 by a letter addressed to the bishop which argued: 'A day school, however Christian in its management, bears but scanty fruit ... The children go home to their heathen parents ... and are led to a sort of compromise.'[36]

---

[32] HKPRO, HKMS94/1/5/73, 'The Victoria Home or Orphanage: Reminiscences by M. J. Ost', *c.*1889.

[33] 鍾仁立 [John Y. L. Chung], 莫壽增會督傳 [*Moshouzeng Huidu Zhuan*; *The Life of Bishop Mok Shau Tsang*] (Hong Kong, 1972), 3–4. Only a handful of students opted to pursue theological training at St Paul's College after secondary schooling. Even some of those dropped out, preferring the financial stability of a professional career over the pastorate.

[34] 'Conference', *From Month to Month* 61 (November 1905), 2.

[35] W. T. Featherstone, *The Diocesan Boys School and Orphanage Hongkong: The History and Records, 1869 to 1929* ([Hong Kong], 1930), 101.

[36] HKPRO, HKMS94/1/5/41, Extract from letter of Edward Davis, 10 May 1899.

Another important shift in the 1870s concerned access to alternative funding. Renewed support for schools arrived in wake of the 1870 Forster Education Act passed in England, which enacted the provision of universal elementary education, but with conditions such as secular education and a timetable conscience clause enabling parents to withdraw their children from religious instruction.[37] This approach filtered down to colonial policy in Hong Kong, which saw the introduction of a grant-in-aid scheme in 1873 to provide schools with up to HK$300 (around £105) per annum, but with similar conditions, such as a daily minimum of four hours' secular instruction or grants being given according to school examination results.[38] The supervisory body ensuring proper observance of funding conditions was Hong Kong's Department of Government Schools (later known as the Education Department), which had been established in 1865 after the removal of a more informal system that depended mostly on the voluntarism of mission agencies.[39] Subsequently, Anglican mission schools which wished to qualify for the government subsidy were compelled to conform to the regulations and to provide a more balanced education not solely oriented around proselytism. In 1875, Bishop Burdon provided SPC with a modified set of statutes which stated that tutor stipends could thenceforth be taken from the colonial government or any other public society, rather than only from missionary and diocesan funds.[40] This enabled the college to join the grant-in-aid scheme the following year, but also meant that students would have to study a broader curriculum as well as take government examinations.[41] Similarly, the Victoria Home and Orphanage was given a new constitution in 1878 so that it could receive grant-in-aid funding, but was also obliged to adjust its teaching curriculum and to incorporate government examinations.[42]

At the same time, mission schools turned to the philanthropy of foreign merchants and trading firms in Hong Kong, but again this

---

[37] Sweeting, *Education in Hong Kong*, 209.

[38] Ibid. 209–11; Fung and Chan-Yeung, *To Serve and to Lead*, 25. The 1873 *Hong Kong Blue Book* indicates that HK$1 was now equivalent to around 4s 2d.

[39] Sweeting, *Education in Hong Kong*, 153.

[40] LPL, Frederick Temple Papers, vol. 50, fols 375–6, 'Statutes of St Paul's College, Hongkong', 26 July 1875.

[41] Fung, ed., *Devotion to Plurality*, 41.

[42] Featherstone, *Diocesan Boys School*, 1; Fung and Chan-Yeung, *To Serve and to Lead*, 19–25.

was not without strings attached. For example, the Victoria Home and Orphanage received sizeable subscriptions throughout the 1870s from Jardine, Matheson & Co. and even had their accounts audited by the company free of charge. However, in 1878, the company's director, William Keswick, opposed Bishop Burdon's proposal to place the school under the care of the Female Education Society, which would have stopped the school from admitting boys.[43] Keswick reasoned that such a move ran counter to the intentions of the subscribers, who understood the role of the Victoria Home and Orphanage in two inseparable ways. First, the school ought to serve as wide a demographic as possible, boys and girls alike, of Chinese, Eurasian and European origin. Second, the school was providing male graduates to take up much-needed positions in Hong Kong's economic context, especially in the civil service, at the docks, in stores and in lawyers' and merchants' offices.[44] To hand over the school to the Female Education Society would essentially sever this supply of incoming staff. Eventually, the school was given a revised constitution in the 1880s, mandating it to provide 'a wide and liberal education well fitting for professional, commercial, and clerical classes'.[45]

It was not until the episcopate of Burdon's successor, Joseph Charles Hoare, that the original missionary purpose of the Anglican mission schools was rediscovered. Shortly before his arrival in 1899, Hoare wrestled with the question of how to further the vision of training Chinese Christian church workers while meeting government demands relating to educational standards and also creating a financially viable system. He wrote: 'Nothing would please me more to see SPC fulfilling the object for which it was founded ... that object being the training of Chinese catechists and clergy.'[46] His subordinate, the Revd William Banister, had expressed the same sentiment the previous year in a memorandum for the CMS, pointing out that many catechists in the diocese were in fact 'ransacked' from neighbouring dioceses since the diocese lacked its own training

---

[43] Featherstone, *Diocesan Boys School*, 25, 34–5, 102.
[44] Fung and Chan-Yeung, *To Serve and to Lead*, 22; Featherstone, *Diocesan Boys School*, 25.
[45] Featherstone, *Diocesan Boys School*, 2.
[46] HKPRO, HKMS94/1/5/65, Hoare to Sharpe, 25 September 1898.

institution following the reconfiguration of SPC.[47] Hoare was particularly disturbed by the fact that the college had strayed so far from its original purpose that it was being occupied by a Chinese school providing English lessons without the slightest hint of Christianity.[48] *From Month to Month*, a regular publication set up by Hoare to provide updates on Anglican mission work in South China, re-emphasized the envisaged purpose of Anglican mission schools to train indigenous evangelists and to provide graduates of 'high Christian character'.[49] With reference to the fear of mission schools losing their essence by becoming distracted with secular content and the quest for funding, the article concluded with the reflection: 'Christianity would sacrifice its divinity if it abandoned its missionary character and became a mere educational institution.'[50]

Consequently, Hoare restructured Anglican schools so that their evangelistic purpose could be reinstated. SPC was re-established in 1900 with a renewed focus on evangelism. Hoare implemented a scheme in which the CMS would take responsibility for training indigenous clergy and covering the college's working expenses, while the bishop would support the college with an annual grant of HK$900 (approximately £320) and oversee building maintenance.[51] The aim was to free the college from dependence on state funding and the need to conform to secular schooling requirements. In 1903, the Revd G. A. Bunbury, the new principal of the college, celebrated the three-year-old identity of the new SPC as 'the training college of the CMS South China Mission', highlighting the twelve students who were receiving training in church history, gospel outlines and sermon composition.[52] Bunbury praised the fact that 'habits of truthfulness and industry have been formed or strengthened, and several of the elder lads are ... true servants of the Lord Jesus Christ ... the future Native Church of China'.[53] A famous graduate of this period

---

[47] HKPRO, HKMS94/1/5/66, W. Banister, 'Memorandum on the Hong Kong and Kwangtung Mission', 12 August 1898, 16.

[48] LPL, Frederick Temple Papers, vol. 50, fols 373–4, Hoare to Temple, 5 December 1900.

[49] 'Conference', 2.

[50] Ibid. 4.

[51] LPL, Frederick Temple Papers, vol. 50, fols 377–8, Agreement between Hoare and CMS regarding St Paul's College, 1900.

[52] 'St Paul's College, Hongkong', *From Month to Month* 36 (May 1903), 2–4.

[53] Ibid. 4.

was Wang Jimin, who in 1930 would become the head doctor of Zhejiang Postal Service. Keeping his Christian faith to the end, he helped to form the True Jesus Church in the 1920s and represented China at the 1938 Madras Conference of the International Missionary Council.[54] Hoare would dedicate himself wholeheartedly to training indigenous clergy, to the extent that he would take students on preaching tours and eventually die in the process. On 18 September 1906, while returning from Ping Shan with four students, his boat sailed through a typhoon and encountered 'a tremendous gale ... with high seas and blinding rain', which resulted in the vessel capsizing. It was thought that Hoare tried to save the students, but in so doing was unable to save himself.[55]

At the same time as his re-visioning of SPC, Hoare had satisfied the growing demand for secular education through other mission schools. In effect, theological training and English education in Hong Kong were to become distinctly separate but simultaneous endeavours. Fairlea School, an offshoot of the Victoria Home and Orphanage, was rebranded during Hoare's episcopate as an institution providing Chinese girls with a Christian education, thereby empowering them to pursue careers as teachers or 'to become wives of young Christian Chinamen'. Most of all, they would leave the school with 'moral and spiritual results ... witnessing themselves humble and faithful followers of the Lord Jesus'.[56] It also had an emphasis on the quality of education which was a distinct departure from earlier decades. Another pertinent illustration is St Stephen's College (SSC), which was founded in 1903 for Chinese elites as an institution modelled after British state schools.[57] The constitution emphasized 'offering to the Chinese an English education with Western Knowledge, upon Christian lines'.[58] This was followed by the founding of St Stephen's Girls' College (SSGC) in 1905, which was also driven by Chinese elites who sought to provide high-quality English instruction

---

[54] 聖保羅書院同學會 [Shengbaoluoshuyuan Tongxuehui; St Paul's College Alumni Association], 165 年的人與時代 [*165 Nian de Renyushidai*; *165 Years of People and Times*], 120–1.

[55] Mrs Hoare to J. E. Hoare, 21 September 1906, online at: <http://www.spc.edu.hk/upload_files/na/103_assembly0918.pdf>, accessed 21 January 2019.

[56] 'CMS Baxter Mission', *From Month to Month* 54 (January 1905), 5–6.

[57] Endacott and She, *Diocese of Victoria*, 158.

[58] 'St Stephen's College, Hongkong Constitution', *From Month to Month* 35 (April 1903), 2.

for their children. Chinese Christian elites conveyed that on the one hand, they wished their children to share in 'newly awakened' Western learning, but on the other hand, they sought an education that met the pupils' spiritual needs as well as their intellectual and physical needs.[59] As revealed by statistical tables published by the Chinese Anglican Church in 1915 and 1918, this development took place simultaneously in the foreign concessions of Shanghai and Hankow. In these cities, Chinese elites donated generously to Anglican schools in order to provide high-quality English education, sometimes up to ten times the per capita rate of contributions in rural provinces.[60]

Although the CMS Local Governing Body was aware of the potential pitfalls of schools becoming 'mere educational institutions', it was believed that having missionaries as teachers in these schools would nevertheless enable students to come under the influence of Christian character.[61] Missionaries came to terms with the reality of having to refashion their schools so that they could become eligible for government support, as well as broaden their appeal to the shifting demands of Chinese families. By the turn of the century, Smith's ideal of a single path from literacy to ordination was no more. In 1905, the revised outlook of Christian education was depicted at length by W. S. Pakenham Walsh, a missionary at Foochow Trinity College. Pakenham Walsh imagined mission schools shaping children in their formative years, after which they might take a career as a teacher at a Christian day-school while assisting their local church through outdoor preaching or by reading the lesson. It was widely accepted that graduates might take on jobs outside the ministry but ideally remain active in church as laypeople. However, the hope was that some graduates would choose to attend theological college before being ordained out of a 'great desire to see the gospel transform and enrich [their] fellow-countrymen'.[62] Essentially, the financial

[59] Birmingham, CRL, CMS/G/AZ/4/172, 'Memorandum regarding St Stephen's College, Hong Kong', 1910.
[60] New Haven, CT, Yale Divinity Library Special Collections, HR114, General Statistics of the Chung Hua Sheng Kung Hui, 1915, Table 5, 'Educational Work'; General Statistics of the Chung Hua Sheng Kung Hui, 1918, Table 5, 'Educational Work'.
[61] Kathleen E. Barker, *Change and Continuity: A History of St Stephen's Girls' College, Hong Kong, 1906–1996* (Hong Kong, 1996), 12–13.
[62] W. S. Pakenham Walsh, 'The Native Ministry', *From Month to Month* 56 (March 1905), 1–3.

situation of the diocese in the late nineteenth century, as well as a more refined understanding of the Chinese cultural context, forced Anglican mission schools to compromise in their manner of schooling. As the number of schools expanded, only SPC was maintained purely for theological training, while other institutions had to balance the demand for secular education with the dissemination of the Christian faith in order to secure sufficient funding and interest.

During the early twentieth century, however, Anglican mission schools were confronted with increasing government control. In Hong Kong, the colonial government implemented stricter regulations in the wake of the 1911 Xinhai Revolution, which overthrew the Qing dynasty. In an attempt to reduce politicization and 'unlawful propaganda' in schools that might destabilize the colony, the 1913 Education Ordinance demanded that all schools register with the government in order to be considered lawful.[63] School inspectors would be empowered to regulate administrative records, discipline, hygiene and (above all) teaching materials, since education was regarded as a means of social control.[64] Government control over education in Hong Kong expanded in the 1920s in parallel with growing anti-colonial sentiment, which stemmed from the perceived injustice of the 1919 Paris Peace Conference in which Qingdao was ceded to Japan and the 1925 May Thirtieth Incident when a violent public demonstration was met with gunfire from British police.[65] In response, the Colonial Office instructed the Hong Kong government to increase their monitoring of schools in regard to anti-British propaganda.[66] By 1929, the Advisory Committee on Education in Colonies had issued a circular indicating their intention to regulate textbooks in all colonies. In practice, this meant all mission schools having to submit their existing textbooks and assessments of each volume, in addition to extensive information on the constitution, functions and proceedings of publication committees. No stone was left unturned, as even the price and quality of paper and print were scrutinized.[67]

---

[63] Sweeting, *Education in Hong Kong*, 343.
[64] 'An Ordinance to Provide for the Registration and Supervision of Certain Schools', Ordinance no. 26 of 1913, *Hongkong Government Gazette*, 8 August 1913, 344–8.
[65] John M. Carroll, *A Concise History of Hong Kong* (Hong Kong, 2007), 96–105.
[66] TNA, CO129/489, 179, Colonial Office minute, J. Paskin, 16 September 1925, in Sweeting, *Education in Hong Kong*, 398.
[67] CRL, CMS/G1/CH1/L5/189-91, Thornton to Blanchett, 8 May 1929.

To complicate matters further, during the 1910s paradigms of education were shifting. Between 1912 and 1922, the republican government in China introduced regulations which required all schools to offer Western curricular content through academic subjects and lessons in handicrafts, singing and physical education, while adopting the simpler vernacular Chinese over the classical literary form.[68] The 1922 School Reform Decree from the Peking Ministry of Education went so far as to place all schools under the national administration and called for the secularization of all teaching content.[69] While educational reform in Hong Kong was not as drastic, there were similar trends in the secularization of education. E. A. Irving, director of education and a former civil servant in the Straits Settlements, called for English education to adopt a vocational emphasis, for he viewed education 'not as a moral obligation but as a commercial necessity'.[70]

The impact of closer government supervision in Hong Kong as well as in other mission fields was not viewed lightly by the CMS in London. As early as 1916, the CMS decided to form an educational committee to provide expert advice on pedagogy, to regulate the quality of mission workers who could satisfy both the professional and spiritual requirements of the job, and to monitor the increasingly tight budget.[71] It was set up to correspond with missionaries about educational work and to keep them informed about related work around the world.[72] The entire situation is best summed up by J. H. Oldham, organizer of the 1910 World Missionary Conference and secretary of the International Missionary Council, who depicted the perceived crisis in Christian education in the

---

[68] Curran, *Educational Reform in Republican China*, 236–40.

[69] Lutz, *Chinese Politics and Christian Missions*, 110. For the impact of Chinese republican nationalism on Christian schools, see Jennifer Bond, '"The One for the Many': Zeng Baosun, Louise Barnes and the Yifang School for Girls at Changsha, 1893–1927', in Morwenna Ludlow, Charlotte Methuen and Andrew Spicer, eds, *Churches and Education*, SCH 55 (Cambridge, 2019), 441–62; Marina Xiaojing Wang, 'Western Establishment or Chinese Sovereignty? The Tientsin Anglo-Chinese College during the Restore Educational Rights Movement, 1924–7', ibid. 577–92. On the way political changes in the 1910s and 1920s influenced the Chung Hua Sheng Kung Hui, see Tim Yung, 'Keeping up with the Chinese: Constituting and Reconstituting the Anglican Church in South China, 1897–1951', in Rosamond McKitterick, Charlotte Methuen and Andrew Spicer, eds, *The Church and the Law*, SCH 56 (Cambridge, 2020), 383–400.

[70] E. A. Irving, *The Educational System of Hong Kong* (Hong Kong, 1914), 8–13, in Sweeting, *Education in Hong Kong*, 361–7.

[71] CRL, CMS/G/R/1, 'Memorandum on Educational Committee', 1916.

[72] Ibid., 'Memorandum on Education Policy Committee', 2 February 1921.

mission field in a 1921 paper. To Oldham, mission schools now existed in 'an entirely different kind of world', in which governments were assuming greater responsibility for education and mission schools were becoming outnumbered by public schools.[73] Consequently, mission schools would have to meet the higher standards required by civil authorities and missionaries would require professional training.[74] Gone were the days of the missionary monopoly on vernacular schooling across European empires. The alternative ideal in the first decades of the twentieth century was to provide a distinct type of education that balanced the Christian worldview with the requirements laid out by civil authorities.[75]

In Hong Kong, mission schools were adjusted to meet the demands of the 1913 Education Ordinance. In 1909, SPC relocated its clergy training to Canton, before merging in 1914 with the newly formed Canton Union Theological College, a joint venture between seven missionary organizations in South China, who all agreed that theological education had to be separated from other educational institutions.[76] This led to less missionary involvement in Anglican mission schools as the CMS switched their attention to the new seminaries.[77] In the same year, Archdeacon Barnett wrote to Fred Baylis of the CMS Far East Committee, explaining the new scope of SPC and SSC. For SPC, although its goal was still to prepare students for potential further theological study, the school now turned to the broader ideal of 'education as is necessary for the Christians at Hong Kong'.[78] This emphasis on a broad education was accentuated by SPC's admitting non-Christians from 1909 as well as rejoining the grant-in-aid scheme from 1919.[79] SSC endeavoured to 'offer a first class education on Western lines ... primarily towards preparing students to enter the University of Hong Kong'; the only way to

---

[73] CRL, CMS/G/R/1, J. H. Oldham, 'The Crisis in Christian Education in the Mission Field: Papers on Educational Problems in Mission Fields', November 1921, 50–1.

[74] Ibid. 52–3.

[75] Ibid. 62–3.

[76] Hong Kong, Hong Kong Sheng Kung Hui Archive [hereafter: HKSKH], 1234, 'St Paul's College Scheme of Management', 1925; John Stewart Kunkle, 'History of the Canton Union Theological College 1914–1924', in *Canton Union Theological College: The First Ten Years 1914–1924* (Hong Kong, 1924), 15–38.

[77] LPL, Fisher Papers, vol. 46, fols 40–2, McLeod Campbell to Eley, 19 January 1948.

[78] CRL, CMS/G1/CH/1/L3/153, Baylis to Barnett, 11 December 1914.

[79] Fung, ed., *Devotion to Plurality*, 59–61.

maintain spiritual influence was to provide a boarding house in order to make 'a strong Christian impression' on students.[80]

In effect, growing intervention from the colonial government and greater emphasis on standardized education steadily encroached on the spiritual work of Anglican schools. This transition is captured through a comparison of the 1903 deed of foundation for SSC with a 1921 memorandum to the government concerning the college. The original deed underlined the aim of providing Western education built upon Christian principles as professed by the Church of England, whereas the 1921 memorandum portrayed the college's purpose 'solely in the interests of education', with examinations, university admissions and modern facilities.[81] Unlike the deed of foundation, the memorandum made no mention whatsoever of 'Christian principles', offering only a statement of intention 'to bring the school into line … with the theory and practice of English public schools'.[82] During the 1920s and 1930s, religious instruction and biblical knowledge were stripped of their elevated status and were taught as classroom subjects like any other.[83] Another telling sign of the times was revealed in the weekly cycle of prayers issued by Bishop C. R. Duppuy for supporters of the diocese. On Tuesdays, prayers were offered for 'educational work', which were conspicuously separate from Thursday prayers for evangelistic work:

> For St Stephen's College, exerting Christian influence among the wealthy families in South China … for the Diocesan Boys' School and Girls' School, aiming especially to reach the Eurasian families in Hong Kong and Kowloon … for St Stephen's Girls' College, attracting children from the best families in Hong Kong and offering many opportunities of bringing those families in touch with Christianity … for CMS Girls' School ('Fairlea') giving a first rate vernacular education at a comparatively low [fee] … for Victoria Home and Orphanage, mainly for the daughters of poor Chinese, supported by Government grant and

---

[80] CRL, CMS/G1/CH/1/L3/153, Baylis to Barnett, 11 December 1914. The University of Hong Kong was established in 1911 as 'a beacon of Western modernity' for China: see Peter Cunich, 'Making Space for Higher Education in Colonial Hong Kong, 1887–1913', in Laura A. Victoir and Victor Zatsepine, eds, *Harbin to Hanoi: The Colonial Built Environment in Asia, 1840 to 1940* (Hong Kong, 2013), 181–206.

[81] HKSKH, 1339, 'Deed of Foundation of St Stephen's College in Hongkong', 1912; 'St Stephen's College: Appeal to Government for Site', 1921.

[82] Ibid.

[83] Fung and Chan-Yeung, *To Serve and to Lead*, 252–5, 337.

donations from friends … for vernacular schools, with low fees assisted by government grants.[84]

In sum, religious education in Anglican schools was marginalized as general education became more specialized. On the whole, the emphasis of educational institutions had become more secular. W. T. Featherstone, the newly appointed headmaster of the Diocesan Boys' School (DBS) from 1918, called in his inaugural speech for better buildings, playing fields, scholarships and new endowments, for he understood that the school's existence depended on its performance according to government standards as opposed to its spiritual nurturing.[85] Nevertheless, as an Anglican mission school, spiritual teaching was to be provided through classes on Holy Scripture and catechisms, but freedom of conscience had to be maintained in accordance with government regulations.[86] The next best thing was for senior boys to be encouraged to read books on religion, ethics and social reform.[87] As for SPC, although theological training had been relocated after 1909, teaching content in the 1910s was still supervised by a CMS appointee, who would have prioritized spiritual content.[88] In contrast, by 1925, school operations were delegated to the council of SPC, whose primary purpose was to superintend the school with respect to its facilities, daily operations and financial sustainability.[89] SPC religious activity in the 1920s was sidelined, comprising Scripture Union meetings, Sunday school classes and an evangelistic band of teachers and senior boys going one evening a week to a preaching hall in the city.[90] Edna Atkins, headmistress of SSGC, depicted the examination results of the school at length in her 1927 annual letter before explaining that students engaged with their faith through voluntary Bible study circles and weekly prayer meetings after school on Saturdays, as opposed to other institutionalized forms.[91] In a separate article which reflected the extent of

---

[84] HKPRO, HKMS94/1/7/1921/1, 'Prayer for Diocese', 1921.

[85] Featherstone, *Diocesan Boys School*, 52–3.

[86] Ibid. 58.

[87] HKPRO, HKMS94/1/7/1923/29, Bishop's Prize-Giving Day speech at Diocesan Boys' School, 1923.

[88] CRL, CMS/G1/CH1/L3/115, Baylis to Lander, 16 July 1914.

[89] HKSKH, 1234, 'St Paul's College Scheme of Management', 1925.

[90] HKPRO, HKMS94/1/7/1923/33, Bishop's Prize-Giving Day speech at St Paul's College, 1923.

[91] CRL, CMS/G1/AL/A–BA, Edna Atkins, Annual Letter, August 1927.

secularization, Atkins highlighted that graduates were 'taking their place more and more in public life' by becoming doctors, teachers, or embarking on other professional careers.[92]

The pattern of missionary schooling becoming secularized was expedited by the thinning supply of qualified missionary educators, exacerbated by dwindling CMS finances.[93] In 1921, although a suitable and willing missionary teacher to assist in Hong Kong schools was located in Australia, the CMS Far East Committee was unable to provide the required funding.[94] Instead, the CMS could only sponsor candidates of the highest calibre, such as Miss J. L. Vincent, who was ultimately accepted as a teacher for SSC in view of her BA from London with honours in History and her teaching diploma.[95] For the most part, the CMS agreed only to provide the salaries of the school principals.[96] With fewer missionaries, religious instruction simply could not be administered. In 1923, Edna Atkins expressed a strong desire to do more beyond educational work, such as visiting the homes of the students or addressing the children at local churches. However, she conceded that this would be impossible until there were more workers at the school.[97] Since the pressure of their other duties meant that missionary teachers lacked the time to engage in evangelism, the remaining compulsory religious activity without contextualization proved to be ineffective in bringing students to faith. For instance, Chan Ting-fong, a 1908 DBS graduate, recalled how he understood morning prayers at assembly as nothing more than part of the strict disciplinary system that characterized his school experience.[98] Similarly, William J. Howard, a 1919 DBS graduate, referred to the many church services as 'puritanical', with Sunday communion at 6.50 a.m. and with boys having to learn the collect of the day and a section of the gospel by heart on Sunday afternoons.[99] In effect, although prayers and services remained, their

---

[92] E. S. Atkins, 'New Developments in the CMS Associated Schools', *Outpost* 21 (January 1930), 15–16.
[93] CRL, CMS/G1/CH/1/L3/11, Baylis to Lander, 3 September 1913; CMS/G1/CH/1/L3/31, Baylis to Barnett, 19 December 1913.
[94] CRL, CMS/G1/CH/1/L4/125, Saywell to Barnett, 15 December 1921.
[95] CRL, CMS/G1/CH/1/L4/211, Manley to Barnett, 6 July 1923.
[96] HKSKH, 2138/63, E. J. Barnett, 'Diocese of Victoria Hong Kong', 1925, 3.
[97] CRL, CMS/G1/AL/A-BA, Edna Atkins, Annual Letter, 14 November 1923.
[98] Fung and Chan-Yeung, *To Serve and to Lead*, 216.
[99] Ibid. 217.

spiritual effects were limited by the surrounding ecology of predominantly secular education. A master at SSC, the Revd Ernest Martin, questioned the efficacy of compulsory religious education, observing that despite morning prayers and a Scripture lesson at the start of each school day, a morning service on Sundays, and voluntary Christian Union meetings during Tuesday tiffin, most boys did not identify with Christianity since they came from non-Christian homes and no missionaries or clergy were available to follow up the school's religious activities.[100]

The trend of government regulation and tighter mission budgets was not unique to Hong Kong. By the 1930s, Anglican bishops around the world had become rattled by the changing religious education scene. A report to the 1930 Lambeth Conference observed that in British colonies, the grants-in-aid system required aided schools to reach 'the required standard of educational efficiency', a standard which was continually rising due to heightened competition from non-missionary public schools, which were also growing in number.[101] Moreover, a survey of Anglican mission schools domestically and worldwide revealed that teaching religion as a subject often yielded weak results. The teachers themselves frequently lacked the necessary religious experience to convey the message while the students encountered 'conflicting claims' in the 'bewildering complexities of modern life'.[102] The proposed solution was to have religious lessons administered only by teachers with 'a spiritual experience and a spiritual outlook' and for Christianity to be practised through school activities, such as 'in fellowship of work and play ... [and] in fellowship of corporate worship'. The report concluded that there was no room for missions to express Christianity fully in what had now become public institutions: 'Christian missions in non-Christian lands might urge the religious leaders of those lands to seek similar ways of bringing religious influences to bear upon the State systems while ... providing and maintaining *private institutions* in which they may be able to give unhampered expression to their ideals.'[103]

---

[100] CRL, CMS/1917–1934/G1/AL/MA–MD, E. W. L. Martin, Annual Letter, 11 August 1927.
[101] LPL, LC168, no. 10, 'Governments and Religious Education', 6–7.
[102] Ibid. 10.
[103] Ibid. 12 (emphasis added).

The Lambeth Conference report proved to be an accurate diagnosis of the situation in Hong Kong. For the few students who sought to become Christians after their time in mission schools, the most significant aspect of their encounter with Christianity tended to be their affection towards missionary teachers and Christian social service, rather than their experience of religious education.[104] Mary Baxter, a teacher at SSGC, discovered that informal discussions after dinner provided a warm, conducive atmosphere for reflecting on religion with the boarders, whereas her colleague found that discussion circles achieved the same aim.[105] Li Luk-wa, a graduate of SSGC who in 1935 went on to open Hong Kong's first school for deaf children, developed her faith through a strong rapport with her teacher, Beatrice Pope. Li became so attached to Pope that she accompanied her almost as a daughter to London following Pope's retirement in 1963, on occasion even speaking on her behalf at CMS events due to Pope's tiredness in old age. Li remained with Pope for over a decade until she died in Hove, after which Li returned to Hong Kong.[106]

In addition, the students of SSGC readily supported missionaries in their social service. For instance, individual girls would take turns accompanying Edna Atkins on her weekly visits to the women's wards of the Government Hospital.[107] A number of girls also joined the regular visits to Victoria Gaol, helping to teach and preach to the women inmates.[108] Other students volunteered to teach at a free school for poor children, while graduates helped to facilitate a school for the illiterate housekeepers.[109] Even after graduation, Chan Shuk-ching, former head girl at SSGC, voluntarily taught Hakka fishermen in a makeshift boat school. After storing possessions from the boat in a neighbouring vessel to make room for the class, a blackboard

---

[104] CRL, CMS/G1/CH1/1/File 9, CMS Day Schools Report for 1940. Out of over a thousand students, only ten were preparing for baptism and confirmation.
[105] CRL, CMS/1917–1934/G1/AL/A–BA, Mary Baxter, Annual Letter, 23 August 1930.
[106] 'The Annual Reunion', *Outpost* (October 1974), 11–12; CRL, CMS/ACC821/F3, 'Li Luk Wa', n.d. The available CMS sources do not indicate the year of Beatrice Pope's death, but it occurred in September 1977. See Free BMD Entry Information, online at: <https://www.freebmd.org.uk/cgi/information.pl?cite=VlaZNMXsDIBAVx5mNjRc6Q& scan=1>, accessed 4 February 2021.
[107] CRL, CMS/1917–1934/G1/AL/A–BA, Edna Atkins, Annual Letter, 17 November 1925.
[108] Ibid., 24 July 1929.
[109] Ibid., August 1927.

would be secured to the floor to withstand the wind and waves as the lesson took place.[110] It is apparent, therefore, that the inability to maintain religious education in mainstream curricula by the 1930s did not necessarily equate to the absence of evangelism. If anything, this leads to questions about the alternative ways in which Chinese Christian students developed their faith if not through curricular content, although such an inquiry lies beyond the scope of this study.

By the late 1930s, religious activity in schools had become completely subject to the conditions of grant-in-aid support and ordinances concerning education. This was heightened in Hong Kong, where a 1935 government report determined that schools ought to be shaped to meet the exceptionally high demand for clerks with proficiency in English to work in the city's many merchant firms, shipping offices, warehouses and banks.[111] Four years later, Bible knowledge was officially removed from public examinations of the School Certificate and University Matriculation in Hong Kong. Edna Atkins lamented the shrinking 'freedom and initiative with regard to the running of schools'.[112] By the time of the Japanese occupation in 1941, only a few traces of Smith's vision for missionary education remained in the operations of Anglican mission schools, as economic limitations and steadily growing government controls had all but pushed Christian instruction into a corner. After the war, the SPC Old Boys' Association identified itself more as an educational establishment than a missionary vehicle, as revealed by its petition to Archbishop Fisher to restart SPC as 'the well-known and public-spirited institution ... in the educational field of Hong Kong'.[113]

For Hong Kong Anglican mission schools, the bishops of Victoria struggled to come to terms with the colonial context of education. Repeated attempts to maintain the evangelistic aspect of mission schooling were overcome by unforeseen financial constraints. Projected income did not materialize and the inherent instability of mission finances meant that schools were compelled to turn to the colonial government and private funding for support. In so doing,

---

[110] CRL, CMS/ACC821/F4, 'Chan Shuk Ching & Family', n.d.

[111] Sweeting, *Education in Hong Kong*, 344, 405–6.

[112] CRL, CMS/G1/CH/1e7, 'Memorandum on Hong Kong Education', 25 July 1939.

[113] LPL, Fisher Papers, vol. 46, fols 33–5, St Paul's College Old Boys Union to Fisher, 3 December 1947.

mission schools in Hong Kong (and across all European empires) became subject to government regulation and external interests. With the trend towards secular schooling and the professionalization of teaching during the early twentieth century, religious education in mission schools was relegated to being a subsidiary feature rather than the main aspect. Theological training was completely relocated to seminaries. Moreover, graduates generally did not pursue church work, for they were presented with a myriad of employment options in the bustling mercantile community of Hong Kong. Despite Bishop Smith's original vision, only traces of religious education remained in Anglican schools by the mid-twentieth century, whilst the number of missionary educators dwindled in parallel with declining mission finances. A handful of students were inspired by their encounter with Christianity during their school years; however, these encounters did not usually occur through the institutions envisaged by Smith, but mostly through relationships with individual missionaries.[114]

---

[114] The arguments presented in this article constitute part of my forthcoming PhD thesis on Chinese Anglican identity in the South China Diocese, c.1850–1950.

Led by the Spirit and the Church: Finland's Licensed Lutheran Lay Preachers, c.1870–1923

Matleena Sopanen*

Tampere University

This article examines the interplay between religious agency and institutional control. The Church Law of 1869 gave members of the Lutheran Church of Finland the right to apply to chapters for permission to preach. Men who passed the examinations became licensed lay preachers, who could take part in teaching Christianity and give sermons in church buildings. Applicants had varying backgrounds, skills and motivations. In order to avoid any disruption in church life, they had to be screened carefully and kept under clerical supervision. However, licensed lay preachers could also be of great help to the church. In a rapidly changing modern society with a growing population and a recurring lack of pastors, the church could not afford to disregard lay aid. The article shows how the Lutheran Church both encouraged and constrained the agency of the licensed lay preachers.

In its Church Law of 1869, the Lutheran Church of Finland[1] gave laymen the right to apply for official permission to preach. Men who passed the required examinations before a diocesan chapter and met all the other necessary criteria became licensed lay preachers. They could take part in teaching Christianity and give sermons in church buildings. During the five decades that followed, more than three hundred men submitted applications. The applicants had different backgrounds, skills, and motivations, and it was up to the diocesan chapters to decide who was best suited for public preaching and teaching under the church's guidance and surveillance.

This article seeks to describe lay agency at the intersection of inspiration and institution. Lay preachers had, of course, been common in Finland long before the 'permission to preach system'

* Pinni B3028, PO Box 300, Kanslerinrinne 1, 33014 Tampere University, Finland. E-mail: matleena.sopanen@gmail.com.

[1] Officially known as the Evangelical Lutheran Church of Finland; 'Evangelical' does not imply that the church was revivalist in its spirit.

Studies in Church History 57 (2021), 277–299 © The Author(s), 2021. Published by Cambridge University Press on behalf of Ecclesiastical History Society.
doi: 10.1017/stc.2021.14

was introduced. From the Lutheran Church's perspective, lay preachers were a double-edged sword. If not properly supervised, they could harm the church by unorthodox teaching and cause disturbance in congregations. On the other hand, among these preachers were plenty of men who wanted to spread the gospel in a way that did not compromise the Lutheran Church's position. With the system of granting permission to preach, the church was trying to set standards for lay preachers and harness the skills of the most promising ones to the building of modern, Lutheran Finland. However, members of the clergy and men seeking to become licensed preachers had various, often contradictory, ideas about what kind of tools this building required and, perhaps most importantly, who should be in charge of using them. This discussion around licensed lay preachers reflects the hopes and fears of the rising civil society, in which old power relations had to be renegotiated.

Finnish lay preachers have been widely studied, especially in the context of revival movements. Lauri Koskenniemi has provided multiple studies of the Lutheran Evangelical Association and its travelling preachers, of whom many also applied for the church's permission to preach.[2] Erkki Kansanaho has discussed licensed lay preachers as a part of the Finnish home mission.[3] There are also plenty of biographies and memoirs of individual preachers, including those who had obtained permission to preach from the church, or at least applied for it.[4] However, we are only starting to discover the different motives and expectations brought to the surface by the system of granting permission to preach.[5] This article offers a general account of the

[2] Lauri Koskenniemi, *Suomen Evankelinen liike 1870–1895* [*The Finnish Evangelical Movement 1870–1895*] (Helsinki, 1967); idem, *Suomen Evankelinen liike 1896–1916* [*The Finnish Evangelical Movement 1896–1916*] (Helsinki, 1984); idem, *Maallikkosaarna: Evankelisen liikkeen voima* [*The Lay Sermon: The Power of the Evangelical Movement*] (Helsinki, 2008).

[3] Erkki Kansanaho, *Sisälähetys ja diakonia Suomen kirkossa 1800-luvulla* [*Home Mission and Diaconia in the Church of Finland in the Nineteenth Century*] (Helsinki, 1960); idem, *Suomen kirkon sisälähetysseuran historia: Sortavalan aika 1905–1944* [*History of the Finnish Home Mission Society: The Sortavala Era 1905–1944*] (Helsinki, 1964).

[4] For example, Pentti Laasonen, *Kristuksen asevelvollinen, K. J. Rahikainen* (Helsinki, 1953); K. A. Wrede, *Minnen från mitt arbete för Herren* (Helsinki, 1940); Aapeli Saarisalo and Erkki Talasniemi, *Aku Räty – körttisaarnaaja* (Porvoo, 1975).

[5] See Matleena Sopanen, 'Kirkon hajottaja vai rakentaja? Suomen evankelisluterilaisen kirkon saarnaluvan anojat ja maallikkosaarnaajan kriteerit 1870–1923' ['Builders or Destroyers of the Church? Applicants for Permission to Preach in the Evangelical Lutheran Church of Finland and Criteria for Lay Preachers 1870–1923'], *Lähde:*

heterogeneous group of applicants, the licensed lay preachers' field of work and the different means of control used by the church. The period covered reaches from the Church Law of 1869 to 1923, the year the Freedom of Religion Act, which gave Finns the right to leave the Lutheran Church without having to join another religious community, was ratified.[6]

Two key sources used in this study are the applications for permission to preach and minutes of chapter meetings in which applications were evaluated. The application process began with the candidate sending a letter to the chapter of his home diocese. During the period studied here, Finland was divided into four dioceses. The archdiocese of Turku and the diocese of Porvoo covered the most populous western and southern parts of the country; the diocese of Kuopio was located in the north, and the diocese of Savonlinna in the east.[7] Chapter archives also hold annual reports about the whereabouts and actions of licensed lay preachers. In addition to these sources, the article draws on minutes of the General Synod and of bishops' and synod meetings, where lay preachers were frequently discussed.

THE LUTHERAN CHURCH AMID MODERNIZATION

The new Church Law was enacted at a time when the Lutheran Church was trying to find its feet in modern Finnish society. Under Swedish rule, Lutheranism had been the state religion since the end of the sixteenth century.[8] Amid modernization, the

---

Historiatieteellinen aikakauskirja 15 (2018), 39–59; eadem, 'Maallikkosaarnaajan paikka: Suomen evankelisluterilaisen kirkon saarnaluvan saaneiden maallikoiden työala 1870–1923' ['The Lay Preacher's Place: The Work of Licensed Lay Preachers in the Evangelical Lutheran Church of Finland 1870–1923'], *Suomen kirkkohistoriallisen seuran vuosikirja* 108 (2018), 116–40. Hannu Mustakallio has studied the applicants of the diocese of Kuopio: Hannu Mustakallio, 'Saarnalupatutkinnon suorittaminen Kuopion hiippakunnassa 1878–1910' ['Obtaining Permission to Preach in the Diocese of Kuopio 1878–1910'], in Timo Kapanen and Nico Lamminparras, eds, *Aatteiden ja herätysten virrassa: Jouko Talosen juhlakirja* (Helsinki, 2019), 25–37.

[6] See Juha Seppo, 'The Freedom of Religion and Conscience in Finland', *Journal of Church and State* 40 (1998), 847–72, at 855.

[7] In 1923 the diocese of Kuopio became the diocese of Oulu, and in 1925 the diocese of Savonlinna became the diocese of Viipuri.

[8] Both the Church of Sweden and the Lutheran Church of Finland accept the *Book of Concord* as their doctrinal standard: Kauko Pirinen, 'Luterilaisen kirkon tunnustuskirjat', in *Luterilaisen kirkon tunnustuskirjat* (Helsinki, 2003), 15–27.

old uniform Lutheran culture started to shatter. Urbanization, industrialization, migration and different religious and secular worldviews challenged the church's position and forced it to reconsider its established ways of working. As in many other parts of Europe, declining church attendance was linked to secularizing trends in society.[9] Religion was still important, but it 'ceased to provide a common language', as Hugh McLeod puts it.[10] In 1809, Sweden ceded Finland, until then its eastern province, to the Russian empire. Tsar Alexander I, an Orthodox Christian, promised to uphold the Lutheran faith of his new province, which was officially known as the autonomous Grand Duchy of Finland until its independence in 1917.[11] The Church Law of 1869 strengthened the Lutheran Church's position by formally separating church and state: the new law applied only to members of the Lutheran Church, not to all the country's inhabitants. The Tsar and the estates still had the right to approve or discard any modifications made to ecclesiastical law, but only the General Synod, the highest legislative organ of the church, could propose amendments to its content. The Church Law of 1869 tore down some of the old power hierarchies. In 1854, Frans Ludvig Schauman, a professor of theology and bishop of Porvoo from 1865 to 1877, was put in charge of preparing the new law. For Schauman, the Lutheran Church was both an important national institution and a community of believers, so parishioners needed to have some control in matters that concerned them. Laymen were given decision-making power at all levels of administration, and in the General Synod they had the majority of seats.[12]

---

[9] See Eino Murtorinne, *Suomen kirkon historia*, 3: *Autonomian kausi 1809–1899* [*History of the Church of Finland*, 3: *The Era of Autonomy 1809–1899*] (Porvoo, 1992), 288–90, 297–311, 336–51, 354–6; Eino Murtorinne, *Suomen kirkon historia*, 4: *Sortovuosista nykypäiviin 1900–1990* [*History of the Church of Finland*, 4: *From the Years of Oppression to the Modern Era 1900–1990*] (Porvoo, 1995), 32–46, 56–9, 88–90; Mikko Juva, *Valtiokirkosta kansankirkoksi: Suomen kirkon vastaus kahdeksankymmentäluvun haasteeseen* (Helsinki, 1960).

[10] Hugh McLeod, *Secularisation in Western Europe, 1848–1914* (New York, 2000), 50.

[11] Jyrki Knuutila, 'Lutheran Culture as an Ideological Revolution in Finland from the 16th Century up to the 21st Century: A Perspective on Ecclesiological Perspective', in Kaius Sinnemäki et al., eds, *The Legacy of Lutheranism in Finland: Societal Perspectives* (Helsinki, 2019), 175–92.

[12] Kauko Pirinen, *Schaumanin kirkkolain synty* (Helsinki, 1985), 104–9, 111–12, 124, 127–8, 132–40, 157–9; Eino Murtorinne, *The History of Finnish Theology 1828–1918* (Helsinki, 1988), 79–93; Mikko Juva, *Kirkon parlamentti: Suomen kirkolliskokousten historia 1876–1976* (Helsinki, 1976), 13–17.

Strengthening the position of the lay sermon was a part of this larger democratization process in the Lutheran Church. Domestic revival movements also had an impact on the new law. The four big revival movements in Finland – the Laestadians, the Prayer movement, the Awakened, and the evangelicals[13] – had all established their position with the help of lay preachers. These movements have their origins in the late eighteenth and early nineteenth centuries.[14] By creating a system in which permission to preach could be granted to laymen, the Lutheran Church gave institutional acknowledgement to lay preaching. The basic idea of permission to preach (*venia concionandi*) had already appeared in the previous legislation, which dated from 1686. According to Hans Cnattingius, it was used mainly to prepare theology students for the ministry by letting them assist pastors.[15] The Church Law of 1869 continued this practice, but these future pastors lie beyond the scope of this article.

APPLICANTS FOR PERMISSION TO PREACH: ALLIES OR ENEMIES?

Between 1870 and 1923, 313 men applied for permission to preach. In the populous dioceses of Turku and Porvoo, the number of applicants was significantly higher than in the country's eastern and northern regions. During the decades examined here, the chapter of Porvoo evaluated 136 applicants and Turku 110; in the diocese of Kuopio, which was the largest of all the dioceses but sparsely populated, the number of applicants was 42. The diocese of Savonlinna was formed in 1897 from the eastern congregations of the older Porvoo diocese.[16] By 1923, it had had 36 applicants.[17]

---

[13] The Finnish evangelicals are not to be confused with the evangelicals of the Anglo-Saxon world. The Finnish evangelical movement was born in the 1840s when minister F. G. Hedberg experienced a powerful awakening after reading Luther's postils: Lauri Koskenniemi, 'Fredrik Gabriel Hedberg', Matti Klinge et al., eds, *Suomen kansallisbiografia*, 3: *Forsblom-Hirn* [*National Biography of Finland*] (Helsinki, 2004), 626–7.

[14] Murtorinne, *Suomen kirkon historia* 3: 110–17, 127–35, 154–63, 178–86, 199–200; Kansanaho, *Sisälähetys ja diakonia*, 66–7, 228–9.

[15] Hans Cnattingius, *Diakonat och venia concionandi i Sverige intill 1800-talets mitt* (Stockholm, 1952).

[16] The decision to form a fourth diocese was made in 1895: Murtorinne, *Suomen kirkon historia* 3: 319.

[17] Some aspiring preachers applied more than once before either succeeding or giving up; many sent several applications to the same chapter, and nine men approached two different

The law provided only loose guidelines regarding the qualifications required: 'For reputable and Christian-minded spirits, the bishop and the chapter may, after testing them, give permission to preach and take part in teaching Christianity in the congregation.'[18] Nothing is said about gender, but all the applicants between 1870 and 1923 were men.[19] Considering how critical the Lutheran Church in this period was of female preachers, this is no surprise. Public teaching and preaching were seen as the domain of men, while women's God-given calling lay in the private sphere of the home.[20] This attitude was also reflected at an administrative level. It was not until 1933 that the General Synod allowed women to take part in its meetings as delegates.[21] There had, however, been famous female preachers in domestic revival movements. Women tended to have a more visible role in the early phases of revivals, but as the movements became more stable and organized, men usually took charge.[22] The permission to preach system strengthened the idea that men and women had different religious vocations.

---

dioceses. One man obtained permission to preach from the dioceses of Turku, Porvoo and Kuopio. The figures given here represent the number of applicants, not applications.

[18] Church Law of 1869, §106, in Markus Lång, ed., *Kirkkolaki evankelis-luterilaiselle seurakunnalle Suomen suuriruhtinaanmaassa 1869–1908: Alkuperäiset säädökset Suomen asetuskokoelmasta* (Helsinki, 2015), 39.

[19] The earliest female applicants I have found so far were in the 1970s.

[20] From the nineteenth century onwards, women also became active in Christian charitable and social care. According to Pirjo Markkola, women both upheld and redefined the idea of gender difference, which formed the base for the Christian conception of the world: Pirjo Markkola, 'The Calling of Women. Gender, Religion and Social Reform in Finland', in eadem, ed., *Gender and Vocation: Women, Religion and Social Change in the Nordic Countries, 1830–1940* (Helsinki, 2000), 113–45.

[21] The first female theologian graduated from the university in 1913, but it was not until 1988 that the first women pastors were ordained: Pirkko Lehtiö, *Nainen ja kutsumus: Naisteologien tie kirkon virkaan 1800-luvun lopulta vuoteen 1963* (Helsinki, 2004), 32–4, 218, 260; Pirkko Lehtiö, 'Naisten pitkä tie kirkon virkoihin', in Minna Ahola, Marjo-Riitta Antikainen and Päivi Salmesvuori, eds, *Eevan tie alttarille: Nainen kirkon historiassa* (Helsinki, 2002), 196–209.

[22] This is a common phenomenon globally: see, for example, Irma Sulkunen, *Liisa Eerikintytär ja hurmosliikkeet 1700–1800-luvulla* (Helsinki, 1999); Hanne Sanders, *Bondeväckelse og sekularisering. En protestantisk folkelig kultur i Danmark og Sverige 1820–1850* (Stockholm, 1995); Janice Holmes, 'Women Preachers and the New Orders – A: Women Preachers in the Protestant Churches', in Sheridan Gilley and Brian Stanley, eds, *The Cambridge History of Christianity, 8: World Christianities c.1815–1914* (Cambridge, 2006), 84–93.

Applicants for permission to preach were generally devout men who longed to take part in God's work. In 1882, ambulatory school teacher Johan Lehtonen explained to the Turku chapter that the reason for his humble plea was 'a heartfelt desire and love for spreading God's word in a non-sectarian way'.[23] Some applicants believed that they had been called directly by God to become preachers. In 1910, teacher Juho Rajavaara wrote to the chapter of Savonlinna that 'God wants to use me as his meagre instrument'.[24] Since licensed lay preachers were officially acknowledged by the Lutheran Church, it was important to make sure they were not only Christian but church-minded as well. The Baptists and Methodists were the first dissenting movements to arrive in Finland in the 1850s, and the Salvation Army and the Adventists soon followed; Pentecostals arrived in the country at the beginning of the twentieth century.[25] The system of granting permission to preach could not stop the new groups from spreading, but it did offer the church another means of control. Pastors could refuse to let unlicensed preachers speak in churches, which were the heart of traditional, clerically-led religious life. Strong dissenting sympathies would hopefully be revealed in the application process. For example, Nikolai Smorodin's application in 1912 was denied when the chapter of Savonlinna found out he was not only a leading figure in the Russian Pentecostal movement but also 'apparently not a member of the Lutheran Church of Finland'.[26]

The domestic revival movements had also challenged and reshaped the church from within. Since the second half of the nineteenth century, these movements had, for the most part, managed to co-exist peaceably with the church, but confrontations could not be completely avoided. Many pastors, including the long-standing archbishop, Gustaf Johansson (in office from 1899 to 1930), were

[23] Turku, National Archives [hereafter: NAT], Turku Archdiocesan Chapter [hereafter: TAC], Applications for Permission to Preach, F I j: 1, 1882.
[24] Mikkeli, National Archives [hereafter: NAM], Viipuri [formerly Savonlinna] Diocesan Chapter [hereafter: VDC], Letters Received, Ea: 23, no: 169/1910.
[25] Kimmo Ketola and Jouni Virtanen, 'Protestanttiset kirkot ja yhteisöt', in Kimmo Ketola, ed., *Uskonnot Suomessa 2008* (Tampere, 2008), 95–126; Murtorinne, *Suomen kirkon historia 3*, 307–11.
[26] NAM, VDC, Chapter meeting minutes, Ca: 16, 15 May 1912, §20; 23 May 1912, §36. For more about Smorodin and the Russian Pentecostals, see David A. Reed, 'Then and Now: The Many Faces of Global Oneness Pentecostalism', in Cecil M. Robeck and Amos Yong, eds, *The Cambridge Companion to Pentecostalism* (Cambridge, 2014), 52–70.

strongly opposed to the Laestadians and considered them a sect which did not respect the Lutheran Church's authority.[27] Due to the tense relationship between the church and the movement, only a handful of Laestadian preachers applied for permission to preach.[28] Another group to cause disagreement among the clergy were the evangelicals. Men with evangelical backgrounds were frequently seen amongst the applicants. This was due mainly to the Lutheran Evangelical Association of Finland, founded in 1873, with its travelling booksellers and lay preachers. The association proclaimed that it wanted to support the Lutheran Church, but critics complained that some of the evangelical preachers were only keen to talk about salvation, not about bettering one's ways. They were also accused of openly challenging the authority of local pastors.[29]

MEANS OF CONTROL

The diocesan chapters were responsible for the practicalities of the application process. Aspiring preachers were carefully screened by a bishop, a dean and two pastor assessors. The full application comprised a freely composed application letter, letters of recommendation (sometimes missing) from employers or other individuals of standing and a certificate of character provided by the pastor of the applicant's home congregation.[30] Applicants were required also to provide information about the level of their education. The chapter would test the applicants' theological knowledge and practical skills in preaching and teaching. (According to the Church Law of 1869, only licensed lay

[27] Murtorinne, *Suomen kirkon historia 3*, 99–117, 127–35, 142–50, 154–63, 186–8; Gustaf Johansson, *Laestadiolaisuus* (Kuopio, 1892); *Kuopion pappeinkokouksen pöytäkirjat* [*Kuopio Synod Meeting Minutes*; hereafter: *KSM*] *1896* (Kuopio, 1896), 21–2, 238–9.
[28] Applications for permission to preach do not always offer clear information about applicants' religious affiliation, so identifying them as members of a particular revival movement can be quite difficult. One known Laestadian preacher is Aatu Heiskanen, who obtained permission to preach in 1910 in the diocese of Porvoo: Hämeenlinna, National Archives [hereafter: NAH], Porvoo Diocesan Chapter [hereafter: PDC], Ca: 217, 10 March 1910, §72.
[29] Koskenniemi, *Suomen Evankelinen liike 1870–1895*, 36–47, 50–4, 118–29, 182–7.
[30] In the Porvoo Diocesan Chapter archives, only applications submitted before 1902 have survived, but the minutes of chapter meetings also offer information about applicants. In Savonlinna and Kuopio dioceses, applications are scattered among other documents. For applications, see NAT, TAC, Applications for Permission to Preach, F I j; NAH, PDC, Applications for Permission to Preach, Ej 1:1; Oulu, National Archives [hereafter: NAO], Oulu [formerly Kuopio] Diocesan Chapter [hereafter: ODC]; NAM, VDC, Ea.

preachers could preach in church buildings and take part in teaching Christianity in congregations, but many applicants already had some preaching experience, especially those active in revival movements.) In 1892, the bishops' meeting proposed to the chapters that henceforth they should require applicants to write an essay on an exegetical, pastoral or theological topic chosen by the chapter.[31] The four chapters had slightly different practices, and there were several attempts to standardize these examinations. In 1912, the bishops' meeting proposed that all applicants be tested in practical Bible knowledge, dogmatics, ecclesiastical history, catechesis and church law.[32] However, these requirements were not officially codified until 1932.[33]

The approval rates of the different dioceses varied. In the diocese of Kuopio, approximately half the applicants passed the examinations. The northern chapter was the only one to demand a statement about the applicant's skills, character and reputation, provided by the pastor of his home congregation. In the archdiocese of Turku and the diocese of Porvoo, the pass rates were around 54 per cent and 68 per cent respectively. In the diocese of Savonlinna, nearly 70 per cent of the applicants passed. In addition, many applications were not completed. To take the required examinations, applicants had to travel to the administrative centre of their diocese and present themselves before the chapter. This required time and money, which for some applicants were in short supply. Lack of money, time or interest are probably the main reasons why only a fraction of Finland's lay preachers applied for permission to preach. For the average preacher, the chapter's approval was more a feather in their cap than an absolute necessity.

Licensed lay preachers were expected to work under clerical guidance, and the less they moved, the easier it was to keep an eye on them. The Church Law stated that their field of work lay 'in the congregation', but it remained unclear whether the scope was a particular local congregation or the whole of Finland. When the topic was discussed in the General Synod meeting of 1893, the delegates eventually agreed that it was up to the chapters to decide how much leeway

---

[31] E. Haahtela, ed., *Piispainkokousten pöytäkirjat ajalta 17.5.1891–5.2.1909* (Sortavala, 1936), 16.
[32] *Suomen kirkon julkisia sanomia* no. 1 (1912), 18–19.
[33] *Maallikoiden saarnakoulutus ja-tutkinto: Suomen evankelis-luterilaisen kirkon piispainkokouksen 14.9.1999 asettaman työryhmän mietintö* (Helsinki, 2001), 4.

preachers could have.[34] For example, in the dioceses of Kuopio and Savonlinna, permission to preach was usually valid for only one pre-determined congregation.[35] In 1912, the bishops' meeting recommended that permission to preach should only be granted when the applicant had been called to serve a specific congregation or a reputable Christian association. Annual reports were another form of surveillance. In 1907, the archdiocese of Turku asked parish ministers to give an account of the number of licensed lay preachers living or working in their congregation and describe the impact their work had had on local religious life. Five years later, the bishops' meeting advised the other chapters to follow the archdiocese's example.[36]

In addition to licensed lay preachers, the clergy also tried to keep all unlicensed preachers under supervision. Among them were both domestic and foreign preachers, men and women from various denominational backgrounds. However, the church had little control over these (often itinerant) preachers. The Church Law of 1869 had abolished the Conventicle Act of 1726, which had forbidden public religious meetings outside the church. According to the new law, vestries could prohibit preaching in public, but only if the preacher in question taught against Lutheran doctrine or caused a general disturbance. Pastors were also encouraged to visit religious gatherings as often as they could.[37] However, for large and remote congregations, local religious authorities might not hear about visiting preachers until they were long gone.[38]

Lay preachers, both licensed and unlicensed, were frequently discussed by church institutions.[39] The General Synod met every five

---

[34] *Kirkolliskokouksen pöytäkirjat* [*General Synod Meeting Minutes*; hereafter: *GSM*] *1893* (Turku, 1893), 940–54, Annex 19, Church Law Commission report.
[35] There were exceptions to this rule. For example, the Vyborg Bible Society's preacher Antti Ahvonen was granted a permission that was valid in all the congregations where the society operated: NAM, VDC, Ca: 14, 20 December 1910, §50.
[36] *Suomen kirkon julkisia sanomia* no. 1 (1912), 18–19.
[37] Church Law of 1869, §33, in Lång, ed., *Kirkkolaki evankelis-luterilaiselle seurakunnalle*, 19.
[38] *Turun pappeinkokouksen pöytäkirjat* [*Turku Synod Meeting Minutes*; hereafter: *TSM*] *1875* (Turku, 1876), 76; *Porvoon pappeinkokouksen pöytäkirjat* [*Porvoo Synod Meeting Minutes*; hereafter: *PSM*] *1892* (Porvoo, 1893), 82; *GSM 1886* (Turku, 1886), 602, 606.
[39] For example, *TSM 1875*, 74–88, 198–201, Annex 1; *TSM 1880* (Turku, 1881), 74–84, 203, 205–17; *PSM 1880* (Porvoo, 1881), 43–52; *PSM 1890* (Helsinki, 1891), 196–208; *PSM 1892*, 80–93; *GSM 1876* (Turku, 1876), 290–306; *GSM 1886*, 212–24, 581–607; *GSM 1893*, 940–54. For a summary of General Synod discussions about lay preachers, see Kansanaho, *Sisälähetys ja diakonia*, 242–57.

years and considered propositions initiated by synod meetings, dioceses and individual delegates.[40] It was suggested, for example, that preachers who wished to preach outside their own parish should always meet with the local pastor or vestry before organizing any meetings. Some wanted their skills to be tested in a similar way to licensed lay preachers.[41] In the General Synod meeting of 1886, lay delegate Sandbacka suggested that only ordained pastors or men with permission to preach should be allowed to preach in public.[42] Changing church law was not easy, since a proposal to do so needed to gain a three-quarters majority in a General Synod vote.[43] Finding common ground in regard to lay preachers proved to be especially challenging.

In the Protestant tradition, lay preaching is often justified by the principle of the priesthood of all believers. According to Martin Luther, bishops, priests and laypeople are all servants of God's word and are, in principle, equals. Based on their faith and baptism, all believers are spiritual priests. Luther's words have often been interpreted as arguing that all believers are entitled to preach, which makes an ordained ministry redundant. According to many scholars, though, this was never his intention.[44] The concept of the priesthood of all believers was a starting point for several debates in Finnish Synod and General Synod meetings as well. Many pastors and lay delegates insisted that restrictions on lay sermons were against the principle of the priesthood of all believers and the spirit of the new Church Law. Restraining lay sermons would signify a return to the era of the Conventicle Act. In modern Protestant society, there was simply no room for a purely clergy-led church. Some delegates were reminded that lay preachers had had an important role in the early Christian church, and even the apostles had been laymen. Restrictions could also harm the church if reputable, church-minded

---

[40] Before 1893, the General Synod only met once a decade: Juva, *Kirkon parlamentti*, 18–19.
[41] For example, *TSM 1875*, 85–7; *GSM 1876*, 293–4, 299, 304–6; *PSM 1892*, 79–80; *GSM 1893*, Annex 19.
[42] *GSM 1886*, Annex 18, 53–4.
[43] Church Law of 1869, §456, in Lång, ed., *Kirkkolaki evankelis-luterilaiselle seurakunnalle*, 161.
[44] Timothy J. Wengert, *Priesthood, Pastors, Bishops. Public Ministry for the Reformation & Today*, (Minneapolis, MN, 2008), 4–16, 19–21, 27–30; Eduardus Van der Borght, *Theology of Ministry: A Reformed Contribution to an Ecumenical Dialogue* (Leiden, 2007), 7–12.

preachers became too cautious and ceased spreading God's word. Naturally, heresy should be fought, but only with spiritual weapons.[45]

Pastors and lay delegates who were in favour of restricting the lay sermon argued that the principle of the priesthood of all believers had been gravely misunderstood. Every member of the Lutheran Church had the right – even the obligation – to spread the gospel, but not in public. All believers were equal, but only some were called upon to become preachers. In addition to an inner God-given calling, aspiring preachers needed the approval of other believers. In the very first General Synod meeting in 1876, minister Bergh reminded that Luther himself was strongly opposed to self-ordained 'corner priests'.[46] Many critics emphasized that they had nothing against lay agency per se, but it was necessary to make sure that only preachers with good reputations, Christian lifestyles and acceptable views were allowed to speak to the flock. True friends of the church would be only too happy to obey stricter rules. Some claimed that it was the clergy's responsibility to protect parishes from disarray and false prophets, since the parishioners themselves tended to be both easily pleased and too often led astray by their curiosity.[47]

Of course, these concerns were by no means new or unique. For instance, the Church of Sweden had been balancing the calls of different domestic and foreign religious associations and their lay preachers since the early nineteenth century. In 1856, some sort of middle ground was found when the Evangelical Homeland Foundation (Evangeliska Fosterlandsstiftelsen) was established to organize domestic mission. Lay preacher Carl Olof Rosenius became the leading figure in this new agency. The foundation received both praise and criticism from Swedish clergy; while based on the same Lutheran confession as the Church of Sweden, it was still an independent agency challenging traditional church order.[48] The Finnish pastors followed Sweden's religious development closely, sometimes with concern. In the 1890 Turku synod meeting, Pastor Troberg claimed that because Swedish lay preachers had been given too much power,

[45] *TSM 1875*, 74, 76, 78–9; *GSM 1876*, 292, 295–8, 300–1; *GSM 1886*, 584–6, 598, 600–1; *PSM 1890*, 203–4; *GSM 1893*, 943–4.

[46] *GSM 1876*, 295.

[47] *TSM 1875*, 76–86; *GSM 1876*, 294–5, 299, 301, 303–6; *GSM 1886*, 212–16, 221–2, 592–9, 602–5; *TSM 1890* (Turku, 1891), 15, 77–8; *PSM 1892*, 81–93.

[48] Kansanaho, *Sisälähetys ja diakonia*, 21–8.

they had started to envy clergymen and wished to become pastors themselves.[49]

The debates over lay preachers were caused in part by the different theological schools the pastors represented. By the 1890s, most leading Finnish theologians had become supporters of Beckianism, a biblically oriented theology originating from the Tübingen academic Johann Tobias Beck (1804–78). The evangelical movement also had supporters among the clergy. Doctrinal differences caused friction between the Beckians and the evangelicals, and the travelling preachers of the Lutheran Evangelical Association were often at the centre of arguments. For Beckians, the Bible was the only guiding star congregations needed; associations caused unnecessary trouble. Many evangelical pastors supported the Lutheran Evangelical Association's work and hence took a positive stance towards the free lay sermon (i.e. not restricted under the 1869 legislation).[50] Some evangelicals, however, thought that more severe restrictions were in order.[51] The Lutheran Evangelical Association itself dismissed several preachers for their undisciplined behaviour. At the end of the nineteenth century, the association divided over doctrinal matters.[52]

Even though the General Synod found it hard to agree on anything related to lay preachers, it did manage to make one alteration to the law. In 1893, delegates decided that permission to preach could be withdrawn if needed.[53] The idea was first initiated in the General Synod meeting of 1886 when Dean Lindelöf expressed his concern that licensed lay preachers were out of reach of proper disciplinary action. Since the preachers did not hold permanent office in the church, they could not be expelled like pastors. Furthermore, the vestries' control over visiting preachers was not exerted over visiting pastors or licensed lay preachers.[54] The change was ratified in

---

[49] *TSM 1890*, 49.

[50] Koskenniemi, *Suomen Evankelinen liike 1870–1895*, 64–8, 115–17, 190–205, 240–5; Murtorinne, *Suomen kirkon historia 3*, 167–74.

[51] See, for example, Dean Rosengren's speech in the General Synod meeting of 1886; Rosengren was one of the founding members of the Lutheran Evangelical Association: *GSM 1886*, 588–90.

[52] Koskenniemi, *Suomen Evankelinen liike 1870–1895*, 99–108, 248–73; Koskenniemi, *Suomen evankelinen liike 1896–1916*, especially 17–30, 36–40, 48–56.

[53] *GSM 1893*, 940–54.

[54] *GSM 1886*, 581–3, 607; Church Law of 1869, §33, in Lång, ed., *Kirkkolaki evankelis-luterilaiselle seurakunnalle*, 19.

1895,[55] but the first preacher had lost his licence five years earlier. Constantin Boije (1854–1934), a former missionary student and a member of an old noble family, had obtained permission to preach in 1875 in the diocese of Porvoo. He soon became known for his connections to the free churches, but it was not until Boije became head of the Finnish Salvation Army in 1890 that the Lutheran Church decided to cut ties with him.[56] Taking away a licensed lay preacher's right to speak in churches was the ultimate disciplinary sanction. By 1923, only seven preachers had had their permission revoked. However, the decision was not always irreversible. In 1912, the chapter of Kuopio removed permission to preach from the carpenter Joel Halonen because of his connection with the Jehovah's Witnesses. In 1921, Halonen approached the chapter again and asked to have his permission restored. He had now become the head of a boys' workshop in the city of Kuopio, which was run by a local home mission association. The chapter was not unanimous in its decision, but it finally decided to restore Halonen's permission to preach.[57] Halonen had managed to prove that he was, after all, loyal to the Lutheran Church, and he had found a way to be useful in Christian work.

LICENSED LAY PREACHERS AT WORK

In addition to the ideals expressed by the Church Law, there was also good practical reason for the church to be interested in lay preachers. Finland had suffered from a recurrent lack of theology students since the beginning of the nineteenth century. The first big drop came in the 1860s, the second at the beginning of the twentieth century and the third in the 1920s. According to the church historian Eino Murtorinne, the ministry became less appealing as modernization of society proceeded. Young upper-class men now had more potential

---

[55] Church Law of 1869, §106, in Lång, ed., *Kirkkolaki evankelis-luterilaiselle seurakunnalle*, 39.

[56] NAH, PDC, Chapter meeting minutes, Ca: 182, 30 November 1875, §3; Ca: 197, 10 January 1890, §32; 27 February 1890, §40; 3 April 1890, §18; 10 April 1890, §32; 8 May 1890, §39; 5 July 1890, §18; Elsa Könönen, *Hengen miekka, auttava käsi: Pelastusarmeijan vaiheet Suomessa* [*Spirit's Sword, Helping Hand: The Salvation Army in Finland*] (Porvoo, 1964), 26, 33–5, 72.

[57] NAO, ODC, Chapter meeting minutes, Ca: 62, 21 November 1912, §24; Ca: 71, 3 February 1921, §25; NAO, ODC, Ea: 259, no: 22/1921.

career options. There was also a financial aspect, since only a limited number of well-paid pastoral offices existed.[58] In a land with a growing population, the low number of pastors became a major challenge for the church. In 1912, it was estimated that there were about 3,639 parishioners per pastor, and in the metropolitan region of Helsinki some pastors had congregations of more than ten thousand people.[59] This was not uncommon in the wider European context. Anthony Steinhoff, who has studied urban religious culture in Germany, notes that in Hamburg and Berlin, for example, there were about eight thousand people per pastor at the beginning of the twentieth century.[60] In Finland, the under-developed road network posed another problem. Especially in large and remote parishes, pastors struggled to fulfil their duties; one factor in this was the tendency of pastors to stay in office until they were very old or died. Some congregations were even left without a permanent pastor. Especially in the northern diocese, finding clergy to serve long-term was often difficult.[61] The lack of pastors is evident in the numerous applications for permission to preach. Applicants mentioned the situation when describing their motives, and pastors asked for lay assistance in their recommendation letters. In 1894, Chaplain Lilius and Pastor Kiljander tried to persuade the chapter of Porvoo to give teacher Albin Suhonen permission to preach: 'In Räihäranta village, which is located on the crossroads of Antrea, Räisälä, Muola and Valkjärvi parishes, a talented preacher would be necessary, and since we are already elderly men, it would be good for us as well to have some help at hand, if needed.'[62]

The annual reports written by local pastors differ in detail, but when those from all the dioceses are combined, they give a good general idea of what the work of a licensed lay preacher entailed.[63] Local circumstances and personal relationships with pastors

[58] Murtorinne, *Suomen kirkon historia 3*, 233–4.

[59] Eero Hyvärinen, ed., *Kertomus Suomen evankelis-luterilaisen kirkon tilasta vuosilta 1908–1912* (Kuopio, 1913), 18.

[60] Anthony Steinhoff, 'Religion as Urban Culture: A View from Strasbourg, 1870–1914', *Journal of Urban History* 30 (2004), 152–88.

[61] On the diocese of Kuopio, see Hannu Mustakallio, *Pohjoinen hiippakunta: Kuopion-Oulun hiippakunnan historia 1850–1939* (Helsinki, 2009), 485–91; *KSM 1922* (Oulu, 1923), 62–73.

[62] NAH, PDC, Applications for Permission to Preach, Ej 1:1, 1894.

[63] Besides the Porvoo diocesan chapter, the reports are scattered among other incoming letters: NAH, PDC, Ed: 7:1; NAT, TAC, E VII; NAO, ODC, Ea; NAM, VDC, Ea, Eb.

determined how much responsibility and freedom the individual preacher had. According to the reports, licensed lay preachers would most often organize prayer meetings and catechism and Bible classes, conduct Sunday schools, assist at confirmations and help with the teaching in ambulatory schools.[64] Some offered pastoral care to the sick and helped pastors with administration. The recommendation letters reveal that many applicants were already familiar with such tasks.

Interestingly, some pastors had even allowed lay men to preach occasionally and to lead non-sacramental services in church, although the Church Law of 1869 permitted only pastors and licensed lay preachers to officiate.[65] Shortage of clerical personnel seems to have been the main reason behind such decisions. For instance, according to Pastor Skogström's recommendation letter, teacher David Hämäläinen had held services in the chapel of Konginkangas because the chapel did not have its own pastor. Hämäläinen worked in Konginkangas from 1870 to 1871 but did not apply for permission to preach until 1873.[66]

The case of David Hämäläinen is not unique. In some remote chapelries like Konginkangas, it was common for teachers to officiate at services in the local church.[67] These so-called teacher-preachers often became long-lasting substitutes for pastors. One prerequisite for obtaining a post like this was to become a licensed lay preacher. Some applicants were open about their motives and their wish to become qualified as teacher-preachers.[68] Since the application process could take months or even years, some men worked as teacher-

---

[64] Ambulatory schools were schools without a permanent school building. Teachers would travel between villages and teach in different locations, such as vicarages. These schools were introduced in Finland by the Lutheran Church, and had provided primary education for young children since the early eighteenth century. During the twentieth century, they were gradually replaced by folk schools.

[65] The law does not specifically say that licensed lay preachers can conduct services, but according to the annual reports, this was a common interpretation. If needed, a trusted parishioner, for example the sexton or a member of the vestry, could also lead a simplified service: Church Law of 1869, §§27, 29, 106, in Lång, ed., *Kirkkolaki evankelis-luterilaiselle seurakunnalle*, 17, 39.

[66] NAT, TAC, Applications for Permission to Preach, F I j: 1, 1873.

[67] Sofia Kotilainen, 'From Religious Instruction to School Education: Elementary Education and the Significance of Ambulatory Schools in Rural Finland at the end of the 19th Century', in Mette Buchardt, Pirjo Markkola and Heli Valtonen, eds, *Education, State and Citizenship* (Helsinki, 2013), 114–37.

[68] For example, the application of Manasse Ojanen: NAT, TAC, Applications for Permission to Preach, F I j: 2, 1909.

preachers for a long time before securing official recognition.[69] Licensed lay preachers from other occupational groups also held services, but not, to my knowledge, before passing the preachers' examinations. During the period studied here, calls for better clerical surveillance of lay preachers continued. Nevertheless, at the end of the nineteenth century the emphasis shifted: instead of finding ways to restrict lay preachers, there were now more attempts to organize lay agency and to harness it as part of the church's regular activity. One reason for this change of heart was the Act regarding Dissenters, which in 1889 allowed people to leave the Lutheran Church and join another Protestant community. The Act clarified the dissenters' position, but it did not completely alleviate the tensions between them and the church.[70] The church also began to focus increasingly on home missionary work aimed at awakening people. Before the Freedom of Religion Act in 1923, all Finns had to belong to a religious community. For the great majority, this was the Lutheran Church. The Orthodox community was the largest religious minority, comprising just 1.7 per cent of the population in 1900.[71] However, the Lutheran Church was well aware that a growing number of its members were only nominal Christians.

The church was especially concerned about the working classes. The labour movement's cause had some support and understanding among the clergy, but the fear of socialism was nourished by the statements of leading socialists.[72] Lay agency was needed more than ever in the battle against secularization. In the General Synod meeting of 1908, Dean Bergroth supported a proposition which aimed at strengthening home mission through association work. Bergroth

---

[69] Kaarle Wesala, *Muistiinpanoja* (n.pl., 1935), 94, 98, online edn 2010, at: <https://drive.google.com/file/d/0B-rY7FCaK4ttc1lWVXlLVEZzdmM/edit>, accessed 5 June 2020.

[70] Kansanaho, *Sisälähetys ja diakonia*, 253–5; Juva, *Valtiokirkosta kansankirkoksi*, 168–83; Murtorinne, *Suomen kirkon historia 3*, 347–51.

[71] 'Statistics Finland: Population Structure', online at: <http://www.stat.fi/tup/suoluk/suoluk_vaesto_en.html>, accessed 7 June 2020.

[72] There are plenty of studies that discuss the church's position in regard to the working classes, the general strike of 1905 and the Finnish Civil War in 1918: for example, Murtorinne, *Suomen kirkon historia 4*, 19–22, 32–4; Esko Hartikainen, 'Kansa vai kaikkivaltias?', in Pertti Haapala, ed., *Kansa kaikkivaltias: Suurlakko Suomessa 1905* (Helsinki, 2008), 137–62; Ilkka Huhta, *Papit sisällissodassa 1918* (Helsinki, 2010); Ilkka Huhta, ed., *Sisällissota 1918 ja kirkko* (Helsinki, 2009).

stated that the clergy needed 'the help of laymen, who have been enlightened by God's word, especially during these times, when God-deniers, the apostles of unbelief so diligently roam around countries and continents, spreading their destructive ideas'.[73] The spirit of the era had also encouraged some applicants to take action. In his application letter to the Turku chapter, written in 1913, teacher Olavi Mäkinen expressed his willingness to fight 'the atheist and materialistic worldviews that are trying to plant their seeds in our beloved church's spiritual field'.[74]

Home mission also includes charitable care, in which the emphasis is on caring for people's material and social needs. Before the end of the nineteenth century, Finnish home missions were largely organized by the voluntary sector.[75] The early twentieth century saw a rise in the number of Christian associations.[76] An increasing number of applicants for permission to preach found work in Christian associations instead of local congregations. Men working for the Finnish Missionary Society, the Finnish Seamen's Mission, the Finnish Sunday School Association and a myriad of regional home mission associations submitted applications. The largest individual group among these applicants were the preachers of the Lutheran Evangelical Association. By demanding, or at least encouraging, their employees to apply for official permission to preach, associations could show their support for, and loyalty to, the Lutheran Church. Many of these associations employed pastors or were otherwise closely connected to the church, but they were nonetheless independent organizations. Becoming a licensed lay preacher could also be beneficial to one's career. For example, when Juho Alarik Varski approached the Turku chapter in 1923, he was working as a temporary travelling preacher for the Finnish Mission Society. The terms of Varski's permanent employment required him to apply for permission to preach.[77]

---

[73] *GSM 1908* (Helsinki, 1908), 291.

[74] NAT, TAC, Applications for Permission to Preach, F I j: 2, 1913.

[75] This was due partly to shifts in the balance of power between the church and secular authorities. Poor relief had come under municipal control after the Local Government Acts of 1865 and 1873, which differentiated between municipal and parochial administrations: Murtorinne, *Suomen kirkon historia 3*, 206–9.

[76] Markku Heikkilä, *Kirkollisen yhdistysaktiivisuuden leviäminen Suomessa: Virallisen jäsenorganisaation kehitys 1900-luvun alusta toiseen maailmansotaan* (Helsinki, 1979), especially 93–7, 117, 153; Murtorinne, *Suomen kirkon historia 4*, 70, 74–9, 98–9.

[77] NAT, TAC, Applications for Permission to Preach, F I j: 3, 1923.

Licensed lay preachers could never replace the pastors completely. The Church Law of 1869 stated that laymen could only administer the sacraments (baptism and holy communion) in an emergency.[78] However, in 1907 the Turku synod meeting discussed the possibility that selected licensed lay preachers be given the temporary right to baptize children, 'bless' (i.e. bury) the dead and conduct communion services. The idea came from the archdiocese's chapter. Assessor Björklund emphasized that such a proposition would never have been made in 'regular circumstances', but the prolonged lack of pastors had forced the chapter to venture into uncharted waters.[79] In fact, there was already a precedent where the boundaries between laity and clergy had been stretched. Teacher Pietari Toikka had received his permission to preach in 1906, in the archdiocese of Turku. A year later, the congregation of Ikaalinen chose him to work as an additional pastor for a fixed term of five years. The parishioners and the local clergy had been asking the Turku diocesan chapter to provide them with another pastor, but due to the lack of clergy, it was unable to fulfil their needs. Toikka was allowed to baptize children and occasionally to administer holy communion to the sick, but he did not fulfil other ministerial duties.[80]

After a long debate, the Turku synod decided to send a proposal to the General Synod meeting of 1908, requesting that selected licensed lay preachers be allowed, in some circumstances, to administer the sacraments and bury the dead. Many delegates found the proposition unfair to ordained pastors, who had spent years at university to achieve their current positions. They also felt that blurring the boundaries between laity and clergy might confuse people and weaken the church from within. Others countered that the proposition's purpose was to help pastors and to lessen their workload, not to question the authority of the clergy or the church. Eventually, the General Synod decided to reject the proposal, but the same basic request was presented in slightly different forms in the General Synod meetings of 1913, 1918 and 1923. Finally, delegates agreed that teachers who had permission to preach and who were working on some of the more remote islands in the Gulf of Finland could

---

[78] Church Law of 1869, §§39, 63, in Lång, ed., *Kirkkolaki evankelis-luterilaiselle seurakunnalle*, 20, 28.
[79] TSM 1907 (Turku, 1908), 92–113.
[80] Sopanen, 'Maallikkosaarnaajan paikka', 131–4.

administer the sacraments.[81] As in Toikka's case, the decision was reached because of local needs and circumstances.

WHO IS AN ACCEPTABLE PREACHER?

Men from all layers of society submitted their applications in the hope of becoming licensed lay preachers. The biggest professional group, comprising approximately 40 per cent of all the applicants, were teachers. There were also several ambulatory school teachers, who offered basic education for small children and were usually paid by the congregation. Sextons, cantors and organists were also common applicants. Applications were made by numerous men who earned a living from manual labour: farmers, carpenters, shoemakers, tanners, tailors, factory workers and mechanics, to name but a few, approached their local chapters. All in all, nearly sixty different professions are represented in the applications for permission to preach.

Even though chapters might have preferred some applicants over others, permission was granted to all kinds of men. Only the Savonlinna chapter decided to establish any professional or education-related criteria for aspiring preachers. In 1900, the eastern chapter decided that all men applying for permission to preach had to present a graduation certificate from an upper secondary school, teacher seminar, deacon institute or missionary school.[82] A number of pastors expressed doubts about letting uneducated men speak in church. Preaching at a public prayer meeting was thought to be completely different from preaching from a pulpit, which symbolized the church's authority. Again, not all clergymen shared this view. Some pastors claimed that parishioners might find lay preachers more approachable than pastors, since they could relate to the simple and straightforward language lay preachers usually used.[83] There might have been some truth in this notion. From the first half of the nineteenth century, the Church of England had also used lay agents in its work in urban congregations. Bible women and Scripture readers visited the sick, dispensed charity and persuaded

---

[81] *GSM 1908*, 371, 395–6, 1137–42; *GSM 1913* (Helsinki, 1913), 1406–22; *GSM 1918* (Helsinki, 1918), 389–400, 563–4; *GSM 1923* (Helsinki, 1923), 481–5, 531–43.

[82] NAM, VDC, Chapter meeting minutes, Ca: 4, 29 August 1900, §40.

[83] See, for example, *TSM 1875*, 77–8; *TSM 1890*, 44; *PSM 1875* (Porvoo, 1876), 41–2; *GSM 1876*, 297.

people to attend church. According to Hugh McLeod, such work often proved more fruitful than the interaction between the clergy and their working-class parishioners.[84]

By the turn of the century, even the most hesitant clergymen openly acknowledged that the Lutheran Church needed the assistance of active laypeople. It was widely agreed that laypeople were well suited to social and educational work with children and young people. Youth work was much needed, because after finishing confirmation school around the age of fifteen, there were no firm ties between young people and the church.[85] They were rarely eager to attend service, and the church could not provide as much for them as could Christian youth associations. Laity could also support God's work in the domestic sphere. When it came to public preaching, however, opinions varied. At the end of the nineteenth century, the debate about lay preachers' education and the church's home missionary ambitions led to the idea of special schools for lay preachers. The idea that one could study to become a professional lay preacher and hold a long-term post in the institutional church was met with both enthusiasm and suspicion. Some shunned the idea that a lay preacher could hold office like a pastor, even if it was temporary. It was also feared that lay preacher schools might attract people who were more interested in making a living than serving God.[86]

A leading contributor to the debate about schools for lay preachers was Dean Otto Aarnisalo. The efforts of Aarnisalo and like-minded pastors bore fruit in 1901, when the Missionary Society started training preachers exclusively for the home missionary field. Aarnisalo was also the head of the Finnish Home Mission Society, which ran the country's only training institution for deacons, also founded in 1901.[87] Aarnisalo wanted to start preparing two kinds of deacons: some would focus on Christian social work, while others would become professional lay preachers, who could also substitute temporarily for pastors. In 1910, the diaconal institute started to offer courses for lay preachers. Both the home mission students of the

---

[84] McLeod, *Religion and Society in England*, 16–19, 26, 113.

[85] *TSM 1917* (Turku, 1917), 125–31.

[86] *TSM 1871* (Turku, 1876), 206–7; *TSM 1890*, 43–5, 48, 56; *KSM 1907* (Oulu, 1908), 91; *TSM 1912* (Turku, 1912), 111, 114.

[87] At first, the deacons' institute was run by the Evangelical Society of Sortavala, but the newly established Finnish Home Mission Society took it over in 1905: Kansanaho, *Suomen kirkon sisälähetysseuran historia*, 28.

missionary school and those following the diaconal institute's courses for preachers had to apply for the church's permission to preach at the end of their studies. Despite high hopes, the schools' results were modest. Between 1901 and 1911, only ten home missionaries graduated from the Missionary Society's school, and the majority of them remained in the society's service. Due to financial difficulties, the diaconal institute had to wind up the preachers' courses after just five years.[88]

Licensed lay preachers had constantly to balance being innovative and submissive. When reading the annual reports about them, it soon becomes clear what kind of qualities pastors appreciated in their lay assistants. The ideal preacher was hard-working, humble, obedient and not seeking personal glory. Applicants for permission to preach seemed to understand the kind of personality traits favoured by the chapters. 'I would humbly like to assure you that I have not made my plea out of any personal ambition', sexton Juho Ristreimari wrote to the Savonlinna chapter in 1910.[89] Teacher Jaakko Kolanen explained to the Turku chapter in 1872 that he did not lightly seek permission to preach. Should they decide to grant it, Kolanen understood that he would be accountable not only to the chapter but 'to God's righteous judgement on the last day'.[90]

CONCLUSION

Licensed lay preachers of the Lutheran Church of Finland operated in a liminal space, located somewhere between laity and clergy but not quite belonging to either of these categories. Many applicants for permission to preach sought institutional affirmation of their inner call to extend God's kingdom, either because they wanted to show their support for the Lutheran Church or to avoid conflicts with pastors. Some applicants also hoped to enhance their career prospects. In a best-case scenario, applicants' motives were compatible with the needs of local congregations or dioceses. Due to a recurrent lack of

---

[88] Toivo Saarilahti, *Lähetystyön läpimurto: Suomen lähetysseuran toiminta kotimaassa 1895–1913* (Helsinki, 1989), 153–61; Kansanaho, *Suomen kirkon sisälähetysseuran historia*, 27, 77–80, 82–3.
[89] NAM, VDC, Ea: 29, no: 425/1910. Ristreimari's application is mistakenly archived with letters from 1913.
[90] NAT, TAC, Applications for Permission to Preach, F I j: 1, 1872.

pastors, home missionary goals and the overall spirit of society, the Lutheran Church could not overlook the issue of lay preachers. They were a common starting point for arguments among the clergy, whose opinions were influenced by different theological schools, local circumstances in dioceses and congregations, and previous encounters with lay preachers. At a legislative level, the system of granting permission to preach remained practically unchanged during the five decades examined here. In the parishes, however, the official guidelines of the Church Law were often interpreted in a way that best fulfilled the community's needs. Future research at a regional level might tell us more about how licensed lay preachers managed to tread the thin line between institution and inspiration.

The Early Years of the Christian Endeavour Movement: Innovation and Consolidation at a Local Level, 1881–1914

Roger Ottewill*

Southampton

From its American roots in the early 1880s, within twenty years the Young People's Society of Christian Endeavour (YPSCE) had become a worldwide phenomenon. This article focuses on how the YPSCE developed at a local level, specifically within the English county of Hampshire. Here, as elsewhere, it touched a 'spiritual nerve'. With its motto, 'For Christ and the Church', it quickly became established in the various denominations that constituted evangelical Nonconformity. Consideration is given to the spiritual, social and service attributes of the YPSCE, which inspired young people to become involved, together with the attendant institutional imperatives in the form of committees, combinations and conventions. Attention is also drawn to the challenges the YPSCE faced in seeking to consolidate its position as a central feature of church life. In so doing, the article contributes to the historiography of Christian youth movements in general, and of the YPSCE, which has attracted relatively little attention from historians, in particular.

In the summer of 1900 a Young People's Society of Christian Endeavour (YPSCE) convention, attracting up to thirty thousand delegates from around the world, was held at Alexandra Palace in London. This received considerable coverage in the press, with *The Times* reporting that there were now about seven thousand societies in the United Kingdom. It quoted the Revd F. B. Meyer, the renowned Baptist minister, evangelist and President of the British National Christian Endeavour Union, as saying 'that in travelling from end to end of … [the] country he found Christian Endeavour everywhere the hope and inspiration of the churches'.[1] A part of the country where this was particularly true was the county of Hampshire, the geographical focus of this article.

* 15 Atherley Court, Southampton, SO15 7NG. E-mail: rogerottewill@btinternet.com.
[1] *The Times*, 19 July 1900, 12.

Studies in Church History 57 (2021), 300–317 © The Author(s), 2021. Published by Cambridge University Press on behalf of Ecclesiastical History Society.
doi: 10.1017/stc.2021.15

Although the YPSCE had only been founded in 1881 by the Revd Francis Edward Clark, minister of Williston Congregational Church in the American state of Maine, it was clearly a timely innovation since it spread rapidly. Within a few years it had been adopted in many countries. In his comments on the Alexandra Palace convention, the editor of the *Hampshire Advertiser* observed that '[a] movement that can ... increase a membership of fifty persons to three millions and a half in less than twenty years must have some remarkable features'.[2] It is with these features that this article is primarily concerned. A number relate to the inspirational attributes that contributed to the early success of the YPSCE, and others to its institutional characteristics. Consideration is also given to some of the challenges that it faced in the years leading up to the First World War. As examples drawn from Hampshire will illustrate, the YPSCE with its motto 'For Christ and the Church' undoubtedly touched a 'spiritual nerve'. Consequently, it put down roots quickly, especially within those Congregational, Baptist, Primitive Methodist[3] and Bible Christian churches that retained their evangelical fervour.[4] These churches were also becoming more ecumenically minded, recognizing that what united them was greater than what divided them. Indeed, the YPSCE was part of a general trend towards closer collaboration and warmer relations across denominational boundaries as evidenced by the establishment of free church councils at the local level and, in 1896, the National Council of Evangelical Free Churches at the national level.[5] Within Hampshire, its influence was felt in every part of the county from the large urban centres (Southampton, Portsmouth and Bournemouth) to market towns and many villages. Developments in Hampshire mirrored those elsewhere. By 1910, when Clark's article on the YPSCE appeared in the *Encyclopaedia of Religion and Ethics*, there were 'seventy-three

---

[2] *Hampshire Advertiser* [hereafter: *HA*], 21 July 1900, 5.

[3] From 1898 the Primitive Methodists required each circuit to complete a pro-forma giving details of their Christian Endeavour [hereafter: CE] societies. This was prompted by the establishment that year of a CE Department, which had a full-time secretary, and a secretary in each district of the connexion to oversee the work.

[4] The Wesleyan Methodists established their own version of CE, the Wesley Guild, in 1896.

[5] See E. K. H. Jordan, *Free Church Unity: History of the Free Church Council Movement 1896–1941* (London, 1956).

thousand Societies ... in every part of the world, with more than ten thousand being in Great Britain'.[6]

Notwithstanding the fact that the YPSCE quickly became a worldwide phenomenon and as such had a profound influence on Nonconformist youth ministry during the late nineteenth and early twentieth centuries, it has received relatively little attention from historians.[7] David Bebbington, for example, in his major study of evangelicalism, refers to the YPSCE only in passing,[8] and it is not mentioned at all in Clyde Binfield's seminal work on English Nonconformity.[9] Tudor Jones in his history of Congregationalism provides some background information but does not go far beyond identifying a number of Congregational enthusiasts.[10] Two historians who provide more detail are Michael Watts and Peter Yalden. Watts does so by linking the YPSCE to the concept of the 'institutional church'.[11] It was one of the plethora of organizations which churches sponsored as they sought to engage more effectively with different sections of the population. Yalden sees it as an example of the associational principle which contributed to the internal secularization of Nonconformist churches.[12] Although both discussions are of considerable relevance and value, neither provides a comprehensive analysis.

What follows will build upon the foundations laid by Watts and Yalden, thereby making a contribution to the historiography of Christian youth movements. Much of the empirical material has

---

[6] Francis E. Clark, 'Christian Endeavour', in James Hastings, ed., *Encyclopaedia of Religion and Ethics*, 13 vols (Edinburgh, 1908–26), 3: 573.

[7] There are a number of documents on the internet that provide historical information about CE. See, for example, Francis E. Clark, *World Wide Endeavour: The Story of the Young People's Society of Christian Endeavor from the Beginning and in All Lands* (Philadelphia, PA, 1895), online at: <https://archive.org/details/worldwideendeavo00clar>, accessed 27 December 2020; idem, *Christian Endeavor in all Lands: A Record of Twenty-Five Years of Progress* (n. pl., 1906), online at <https://archive.org/details/christianendeavo00clar>, accessed 27 December 2020. However, these tend to be somewhat triumphalist in tone and lack academic rigour.

[8] David Bebbington, *Evangelicalism in Modern Britain: A History from the 1730s to 1980s* (London, 1989), 129, 226.

[9] Clyde Binfield, *So down to Prayers: Studies in English Nonconformity, 1780–1920* (London, 1977).

[10] Robert Tudur Jones, *Congregationalism in England 1662–1962* (London, 1962), 315–16.

[11] Michael Watts, *The Dissenters*, 3: *The Crisis and Conscience of Nonconformity* (Oxford, 2015), especially 168–80.

[12] Peter Yalden, 'Association, Community and the Origins of Secularisation: English and Welsh Nonconformity, c.1850–1930', *JEH* 55 (2004), 293–324.

been derived from local newspapers, since in Hampshire very few society records from the early years have survived or, if they have, they are not in the public domain. Although newspaper reports need to be treated with a degree of caution, the fact that the YPSCE attracted a considerable amount of attention from the press is itself testament to its initial impact. The reports also lend a sense of immediacy to the events reported and provide insights into how they were experienced at the time. Moreover, while the influence of the YPSCE was felt in many parts of the world, it began life as a local initiative and consequently it is at this level that its inspirational attributes and institutional imperatives are most in evidence.

INSPIRATIONAL ATTRIBUTES

As spelt out in its founding constitution, the key objectives of the YPSCE were '[t]o promote an earnest Christian life among its members, to increase their mutual acquaintance, and to make them more useful in the service of God'.[13] These aims undoubtedly resonated with many ministers who were seeking ways of harnessing the idealism and enthusiasm of the young and of bridging the gap between Sunday schools and full church membership. Although Sunday schools were still thriving, ministers and lay leaders frequently lamented the fact that relatively few scholars became full church members. For example, addressing the annual meeting of Andover's Congregational Sunday School in 1903, the Revd Hugh Ross Williamson, Romsey's Congregational minister, suggested that one of the great problems facing the church 'was how to keep those they had and how to retain them so that they should be brought into the fellowship of the Christian church'.[14] Similarly, in his report to the 1908 annual meeting of the London Street Congregational Sunday School in Basingstoke, the secretary referred to the question of 'how are we to retain our scholars when they arrive at the ages of 14 and 15'. He went on to mention, with more than a hint of frustration, 'the astonishing fact that a very great proportion of those who are outside our Churches were once scholars in our Sunday Schools'.[15] Likewise, the mayor of Bournemouth, at the anniversary of East

---

[13] Clark, *World Wide Endeavour*, 92.
[14] *Andover Advertiser*, 20 November 1903, unpaginated.
[15] *Hants and Berks Gazette* [hereafter: *HBG*], 11 April 1908, 5.

Cliff Congregational Church in 1910, referring to young people aged about fifteen or sixteen, many of whom were working, commented:

> ... there was something lacking in their work if they could not keep boys and girls of that age in their schools. If they could not do this could they not get them into classes, which they could make interesting? They knew that on Sunday there were hundreds of boys and girls with nowhere to go when they ought to be in some church or chapel.[16]

Both Watts and Yalden acknowledge that the rapid expansion and extensive uptake of the YPSCE was testimony to the growing awareness in many churches of the need for a means by which they could inspire, enthuse and hence retain young people when they outgrew Sunday school. Moreover, they needed to do so in a way that appealed to the religious sensibilities of adolescents, rather than simply their recreational, or even intellectual, interests. As Watts observes, 'Nonconformists who believed that the gap between Sunday school and church should be bridged by something more Evangelical, supported the Christian Endeavour movement.'[17] Although there is some doubt as to how effective the YPSCE was in this respect, for those concerned about the loss of young people from church life the movement was seen as 'providential'. By blending the spiritual, social and service aspects of the Christian life, it offered church leaders the prospect of additional assistance in undertaking the various ministries with which their churches were involved, such as Sunday school teaching and providing support for the elderly. Moreover, it was testament to the developing solidarity within evangelical Nonconformity at this time, as churches from different denominations who faced similar challenges shared ideas, experiences and resources. There was a feeling afoot that the opportunities the YPSCE presented would assist in motivating and energizing those in their teens as well as encouraging them to remain loyal to the faith into which they had been socialized through attendance at Sunday school. As Jones affirms, the YPSCE was a 'creative' movement, intended to inspire.[18]

At the movement's heart was the notion of discipleship, with members being encouraged to consider how Jesus would behave in

---

[16] *Bournemouth Guardian* [hereafter: *BG*], 17 December 1910, 6.
[17] Watts, *Dissenters*, 3: 175; see also Yalden, 'Origins', 309.
[18] Jones, *Congregationalism*, 315.

situations they encountered and act accordingly. Particularly influential in this respect was Charles Sheldon's book *In his Steps: What would Jesus do?*, which was first published in 1896.[19] This imperative and how it was to be put into practice was reflected in the Christian Endeavour pledge:

> Trusting in the Lord Jesus Christ for strength, I promise Him that I will strive to do whatever He would like to have me do; that I will make it the rule of my life to pray and to read the Bible every day, and to support the work and worship of my own church in every way possible, and that just as far as I know how, throughout my whole life, I will endeavour to lead a Christian life.

> As an active member I promise to be true to all my duties, to be present at and to take some part, aside from singing, in every Christian Endeavour meeting, unless hindered by some reason which I can conscientiously give to my Lord and Master, Jesus Christ. If obliged to be absent from the monthly consecration meeting of the society, I will, if possible, send at least a verse of Scripture to be read in response to my name at the roll call.[20]

As evidenced by the pledge, the YPSCE was in many ways primarily a 'spiritual movement'. Indeed, when speaking at a gathering of Christian Endeavourers in Portsmouth in October 1908, the founder observed that 'people were most susceptible to spiritual influences between the ages of 14 and 19, and therefore boys and girls between those limits of age should receive great consideration from such a society as that of Christian Endeavour'. Such comments were made in the context of 'The "increase" campaign'. This involved Christian Endeavourers being encouraged 'to more strenuous efforts by telling them that he expected to see the number of societies in a given district increased by a certain percentage in a given time'. In responding to this challenge, he claimed that such enterprise 'generally proved marvellously fruitful', an example of what was described as 'prophetic optimism'.[21]

It was recognized, however, that there also needed to be opportunities for social intercourse, provided this did not undermine the

---

[19] Tens of millions of copies of this religious novel have been sold.

[20] World's Christian Endeavor Union, 'The Christian Endeavor Pledge', online at: <http://www.worldsceunion.org/files/the_christian_endeavor_pledge.pdf>, accessed 15 December 2020.

[21] *Hampshire Telegraph* [hereafter: *HT*], 24 October 1908, 2.

activities of a spiritual nature. To this end, Christian Endeavourers frequently organized entertainments which some would have regarded as more 'worldly' or social expressions of supportive fellowship. A typical example was arranged in February 1903 by the YPSCE attached to Basingstoke's London Street Congregational Church, at which there was a 'large attendance'.[22] On this occasion, 'the programme was of a very varied character', consisting of live music, recitations and gramophone selections. These were 'attentively listened to and much appreciated by the audience'.[23] Judging from the reports of similar gatherings, they proved immensely popular. Thus, when members and friends of Forton Baptist YPSCE in Gosport gathered for an 'At Home' in March 1914, the proceedings, which consisted of dialogues, musical items and refreshments, were deemed to be 'most successful'.[24]

The spiritual and social wellbeing of Christian Endeavourers, however, were not intended to be ends in themselves. Rather they were seen as underpinning 'good works' or practical Christianity, with a leading objective of the YPSCE being 'to apply practically to the actualities of everyday life the principles on which Christianity rests'.[25] At a meeting of the Portsmouth and District CE Union in 1903, the president 'laid stress on the consecration of the intellect, the power of prayer, and the cultivation of the memory, imagination and will, with the object of *benefiting others*'.[26] Similarly, in a paper on the 'Proper Sphere of Christian Endeavour' presented at a gathering of Hampshire Christian Endeavourers in 1912, the Revd Schofield Thomson, minister of Immanuel Church in Basingstoke, emphasized 'the importance of the training of young Christians in the principles of Christian living, which carried with it the duty of personal service'. Indeed, he argued that 'every Endeavourer must be a social reformer'.[27] At the same meeting, Professor D. L. Ritchie stressed that the YPSCE 'must not merely be a school of introspective

---

[22] Although the YPSCE was primarily an organization for younger people in their midteens to early twenties, events of this kind attracted people of all ages.

[23] The proceeds were devoted to the Pleasant Sunday Afternoon fund: *HBG*, 21 February 1903, 5. In March 1904 the same society organised a concert: *HBG*, 26 March 1904, 6.

[24] *Portsmouth Evening News* [hereafter: *PEN*], 26 March 1914, 3; about 80 attended.

[25] *HA*, 21 July 1900, 5.

[26] *HT*, 24 January 1903, 6 (emphasis mine).

[27] *HT*, 12 April 1912, 2. The Revd Schofield Thomson was the minister of Immanuel Church (Countess of Huntingdon's Connexion) in Basingstoke from 1907 to 1915.

piety'.[28] Instead its underlying aim was 'to train young people for active service in the life of a church', although there was also an emphasis on 'efficient evangelism'.[29]

Such service was manifested in a variety of ways. For example, in the early 1890s YPSCE members from Lake Road Baptist Church in Portsmouth 'conducted open-air services during the summer months, and held religious meetings in a room on church premises during the winter. They also paid visits to the sick and sought to relieve the wants of the poor by distributing gifts of tea, coal, etc'.[30] Likewise, it was reported that at the 1904 annual rally of Portsmouth Endeavourers, the keynote speaker, the Revd J. W. Ewing of London, had been gratified 'to know what they were doing for the poor and sick around them, while they had not forgotten Dr Barnardo's work in the great city'. He went on to praise them for contributing to 'the fund for the new "C. E." steamer on the Congo River, carrying on missionary work'.[31] Meals and entertainments were also provided for particular groups, especially the elderly. Thus, in 1906, in 'a new departure', Christian Endeavourers from Basingstoke's Immanuel Church arranged 'a pleasant evening for a number of old folk'. Members served their guests with a 'meat tea' and entertained them with songs and recitations. The pastor's wife 'gave one of her quiet simple talks', the theme being 'the road of life'. In addition, 'parcels of good things were subsequently distributed' to those unable to attend.[32] In an editorial comment from 1905, the *Bournemouth Guardian* observed that '[s]ome of the work achieved by the societies ... is of such vital importance to the community, as it directly seeks to carry into private and public life the spirit of religion.'[33] This was very evident in 1912 when, at the annual tea of the Boscombe Congregational Church YPSCE, reference was made to the society doing 'a lot of good work including visiting and ... distribut[ing] food and toys at Christmas'. Coal was 'given to the poor, and garments made for the Ragged School children'.[34]

---

[28] Ibid. The Revd David Lakie Ritchie was a prominent Congregational academic and between 1904 and 1919 was principal of Nottingham Congregational Institute.
[29] Yalden, 'Origins', 312.
[30] *HT*, 30 January 1892, 2.
[31] *HT*, 6 February 1904, 2.
[32] *HBG*, 17 February 1906, 5.
[33] *BG*, 17 June 1905, 5.
[34] *Bournemouth Graphic*, 1 March 1912, 14.

Unsurprisingly perhaps, given that two major seaports, Portsmouth and Southampton, were in Hampshire, a number of YPSCE societies focused some of their attention on meeting the needs of seamen. Known as 'Floating Endeavourers', they contributed to this ministry by writing letters to crew members; donating magazines, newspapers and New Testaments; making and distributing needle cases and book bags; and fund raising.[35]

Thus there could be little doubt that societies made an impact well beyond the confines of the churches to which they were attached, with members seeking to be 'good neighbours' to those in need. Moreover, the Revd David Barron, minister of Lake Road Baptist Church, at his farewell gathering in 1909, stated that 'the CE Movement had greatly helped him in Portsmouth'. He reflected that 'the highlands of Christian Endeavour ideals had been an inspiration to him, and the friendship, cheering help and optimism of the young people had been gifts which he greatly valued'.[36] It is probable that many other ministers and lay people would have echoed these sentiments.

Demonstrating concern for the spiritual, social and service aspects of the Christian life, however, was not a guarantee of success for societies. Attention also needed to be given to various organizational requirements. In other words, if the inspiration underpinning the YPSCE was to be given full expression, it required a robust institutional framework to sustain it. Indeed, Yalden argues that Christian Endeavour societies were 'intensely associational'. That said, 'with the possible exception of the bible class and the Sunday school ... [they] were also the least secular of all the subsidiary associations' within churches.[37] In this respect, they continued to be sustained by the spiritual impulse which had originally inspired Clark.

INSTITUTIONAL IMPERATIVES

Three institutional features of YPSCE societies, namely committees, combinations and conventions, played an important part in

---

[35] Between February and October 1912, YPSCEs in the Bournemouth area sent '250 hand written letters, 500 magazines, 290 papers, 50 New Testaments, 90 needle cases, 50 book bags, and £2 9s 6d in money': *BG*, 22 February 1913, 9.
[36] *HT*, 29 May 1909, 2.
[37] Yalden, 'Origins', 312.

consolidating their progress. They indicate that ministers and others concerned with the future prospects for the YPSCE were aware that, from a human perspective, structures had a crucial role to play. Underlying these was a very strong emphasis on the obligations of membership. As Yalden explains, there were three categories of member: active, associate and honorary. Active members were bound by the pledge to be conscientious attenders at prayer meetings and 'the regular monthly consecration meeting at which they recounted their recent experiences as Christians'.[38] Associates were those who might become active members at some point in the future. Honorary members were older folk who wanted to retain their links with the YPSCE and offer their support and encouragement.

Central to the organization of each society was a complex committee structure, making them 'remarkably bureaucratic'.[39] Here the comments of Miss Annetta Tull from Overton are particularly insightful. At the ninth annual convention of the Hants [*sic*] County Christian Endeavour Union, held in Bournemouth in June 1905, she spoke on 'The Importance and Value of Committee Work'. Central to her argument was the belief that, although committee work might 'become prosaic and uninteresting', it was essential if YPSCE societies were to remain true to their constitution. This, she reminded her audience, 'provided not only that … [members] should live a Christian life but also that they should … [be] reaching out to others'. Moreover, by engaging in committee work members were able 'to develop unused talents' and pursue latent interests. In her view, 'the well-being and usefulness' of societies depended upon the attention given to their committees by the active members.[40] This could be seen as an apprenticeship enabling young people to acquire the practical skills they needed to serve their church in later life. Henry Macfarland alluded to this aspect in a very positive review of the early years of the YPSCE and the character and fervour of its founder, written at the beginning of the twentieth century, asserting that committee membership afforded an 'extensive training in applied Christianity'.[41]

---

[38] Ibid. 313.
[39] Ibid. 314.
[40] *BG*, 17 June 1905, 6.
[41] Henry MacFarland, 'The Christian Endeavor Movement', *North American Review* 182 (1906), 194–203, at 199.

Societies were in many respects defined by their committees, which reflected the various preoccupations of Christian Endeavourers. An idea of what this meant in practice can be gained from a report of the quarterly business meeting held in March 1902 of the YPSCE attached to Winchester's Primitive Methodist Church. This had no fewer than eleven committees, some with very evocative names, such as the Look-out Committee, which had a very useful role 'in welcoming strangers to the Sunday services and giving invitations to the Sunday afternoon Bible Class and the weekly Christian Endeavour meeting'. The Sunshine Committee was responsible for arranging visits to the sick, a task 'made all the more cheery by the flowers which had been provided them by the Flower Committee for that purpose'. The members of the Tract Committee 'were highly gratified at the very kind way they were being received at the homes of the people' when delivering Christian literature to them. In addition, 'their visits had already resulted in children attending the Sunday School, who had not regularly attended anywhere previously'. The Temperance Committee reported 'that nearly every member of the society was a total abstainer and they hoped that all would be shortly'.[42] Reference was also made to the Social, Music, Prayer Meeting, Church Membership and Junior Committees.

From a relatively early stage, YPSCE societies also demonstrated a desire to combine with each other in order to encourage, motivate and share ideas. This led to relations between neighbouring societies being formalized through the establishment of unions. In Yalden's words, 'the institutional character of the Christian Endeavour movement was further highlighted by the formation of local, regional and national unions of societies before the end of the nineteenth century'.[43] By 1905, there were seven local or district unions in Hampshire, centred on Andover, Basingstoke, Bournemouth, Gosport, Portsmouth, Southampton and Winchester, and comprising 102 senior societies, 29 junior and one intermediate. A notable feature of union gatherings was the roll call of affiliated societies, with representatives announcing their presence by singing a verse of a hymn, reading a portion of Scripture or highlighting matters for prayer.[44]

[42] *Hampshire Chronicle* [hereafter: *HC*], 22 March 1902, 5.
[43] Yalden, 'Origins', 314.
[44] *BG*, 17 June 1905, 6.

At a regional level, in 1895 the decision was taken to form 'The Hampshire Christian Endeavour Union', its object being 'to stimulate interest and personal fellowship and relationship amongst the different sections of the society in the county'. At its foundation conference, held at various churches in Winchester, one of the speakers, the Revd Knight-Chaplin, reminded the delegates that while 'the Christian Endeavour Society had its social and literary features ... first and paramount it was a spiritual movement, and they must always remember their hearts were temples of the Holy Ghost'. Another speaker, the Revd J. T. Jones-Miller, rallied the delegates by claiming that 'at no time in the history of the Church had the spirit of God come down with such power and proportion on the young men [*sic*] as at the present day'.[45] He went on to argue that through their actions Christian Endeavourers could benefit wider society:

> Their work, after first pledging themselves to the service of their King, was to go forth in His name and pick up those who were fallen, to go into the world and try to bind up the broken hearted. Their work was a preventative work, and they were gradually learning as a nation that the greatest service was to prevent evil. For the young women especially there was a great sphere of labour in this Society, for they had great influence, and if they only used it in God's cause they could do a great amount of good, and he trusted that a large number would join them [applause].[46]

The specific reference to young women is a reminder that, unlike some organizations for young people, such as the Girls' Life Brigade, which were open to only one sex, the YPSCE provided opportunities for both sexes to pursue their Christian vocations jointly with each other.

Amongst other things, the union, along with the district unions, held annual conventions in various towns, at which visiting speakers addressed issues associated with different aspects of the YPSCE, such as the committee work mentioned previously. Other weightier topics included 'Christ's Call to Service',[47] 'In Praise of Seriousness',[48]

---

[45] *HC*, 22 June 1895, 3.
[46] Ibid.
[47] Address by Sister Mary of the West London Mission at a convention of the Bournemouth and District CE Union: *BG*, 2 October 1897, 6.
[48] A 'very stirring address' by the Revd J. D. Jones at the annual meetings of the Bournemouth and District CE Union: *BG*, 16 February 1901, 6.

Roger Ottewill

'Christian Endeavour and Religious Education'[49] and 'Christian Endeavour and Social Work'.[50] Conventions also provided Christian Endeavourers with opportunities for making themselves known to the wider community through their presence in substantial numbers at particular locations. This attracted press coverage. For example, in 1904 the *Hampshire Chronicle* printed an extensive report of the eighth annual convention of the Hampshire Christian Endeavour Union held at Easter in Winchester:

> It is seldom there is anything like so large a demonstration of the forces of Nonconformity in the city, and the union is to be congratulated on having made so big a success of their convention ... The last event of ... [Easter Sunday] was a gathering of Endeavourers at the Westgate at eight o'clock where a procession of between three and four hundred persons was formed, which proceeded down the High-street, singing hymns, to the Primitive Methodist church where an evangelistic service was held.[51]

Such publicity would have helped to raise further the profile of the YPSCE amongst the inhabitants of Winchester.

During the last decade of the nineteenth century and in the years leading up to the First World War, yearly conventions of the district unions and the county-wide union played an important part in the annual cycle of YPSCE activities. They appear to have been well supported and offered delegates opportunities to share their experiences and encourage each other. Moreover, such unions and conventions were another manifestation of the increased willingness of churches of different traditions within the sphere of evangelical Nonconformity to co-operate with each other.

CHALLENGES

In the three decades following its establishment, the YPSCE undoubtedly made a positive contribution to the life of many churches and communities. Almost inevitably, however, the rapid growth of this innovation brought with it challenges to be faced.

[49] Discussed at the annual meetings of the Portsmouth and District CE Union: *HT*, 14 January 1903, 6.
[50] A paper delivered by A. C. Bunch of Winchester at the ninth annual convention of the Hants CE Union, in Winchester: *BG*, 17 June 1905, 6.
[51] *HC*, 16 April 1904, 9.

To succeed, societies required a committed leadership and a highly motivated core membership, creative ways of synthesizing the spiritual with the practical aspects of Christianity, and a willingness to adopt a 'brotherly spirit'. At the same time, various criticisms and concerns surfaced which needed to be addressed. A number of these were articulated by the Revd Reginald Thompson, minister of London Street Congregational Church in Basingstoke and an Endeavourer of fourteen years' experience. In an article entitled 'The Christian Endeavour Outlook', published in the July 1908 edition of his church's magazine, he began by observing that 'in many parts of the country [there was] a general feeling of dissatisfaction with the present state of Christian Endeavour. Some societies ... [had] turned into guilds, others ... [had] watered down the pledge, others ... [were] listless and decaying'. His concerns included the fact that young people did not participate freely; there was little opportunity to discuss 'subjects more closely allied to ... modern social and theological problems'; and societies achieved 'no great tangible results'. Thompson responded by reminding his readers that the YPSCE was essentially a bridge for 'young people on the way from [Sunday] School to Church who ... [were] willing to train themselves for more serious work for the Church'. He did not have a remedy for these criticisms of the YPSCE but was convinced of the movement's value, since progress depended upon 'the energy and enthusiasm that should mark youthful work'.[52] Moreover, the YPSCE was essentially a training ground for Christian service and members should not be judged by standards applied to more mature Christians.

Although not specifically mentioned by Thompson, a particular challenge was securing an appropriate balance between the spiritual, social and service aspects of the YPSCE to avoid one aspect being emphasized at the expense of the others. For example, an overemphasis on the spiritual could lead to opportunities for service being missed. Similarly, a preoccupation with social and recreational pursuits could result in the diminution of the spiritual. As Yalden argues, 'even the fundamentally devotional character of the Christian Endeavour movement was compromised by the fact that it operated in an intensely associational manner through its bureaucratic promotion of efficient evangelism'.[53]

---

[52] *Basingstoke Congregational Magazine* 1/7 (1908), 2–4.
[53] Yalden, 'Origins', 323.

As with any voluntary organisation, another challenge faced by the YPSCE was that of ensuring good and constructive relations amongst its members. From time to time, resignations occurred which suggested a lack of rapport. As an example, the minute book of Andover's Wesleyan Methodist YPSCE records that three leading members left in the autumn of 1901. On this occasion, the chairman remarked that 'unless the members could all work together as one body they were best apart'.[54] It is unlikely that this society was alone in experiencing such discord; personality clashes and differing priorities were doubtless evident elsewhere.

There were also signs that by 1914 the growth experienced in the early years was not being sustained, perhaps in line with church membership more generally. At the eighteenth convention of the Hampshire CE Union, held in Gosport, the secretary reported that the total membership in the county was 4,099, a decrease of 288 from the previous year.[55] However, in seeking to put a positive gloss on the statistics, 'he did not think it represented a falling off of energy and enthusiasm'.[56] Barry Doyle, however, in his study of Congregationalism in Norwich, quotes from the magazine of the Old Meeting Congregational Church to the effect that while the addresses and papers 'at weekly YPSCE meetings were excellent', they were 'worthy of better audiences'.[57]

In reviewing these challenges, a key question remains. Did the YPSCE succeed in meeting what Watts describes as 'the widely acknowledged need to staunch the haemorrhaging of young people from the Sunday schools and churches'?[58] Here the evidence is mixed and not that precise. Not surprisingly, perhaps, in their annual reports societies were keen to accentuate the positive. For example, at Romsey Baptist YPSCE's eighth anniversary meeting in 1901, it was reported that although the number of active members had fallen from

[54] Winchester, Hampshire RO, 96M72/NMS/B6, Andover Bridge Street Society (Wesleyan), Young Peoples' Christian Endeavour Society minute book, 1898–1901.

[55] Of the six districts which now constituted the union, three recorded increases: Andover (44), Basingstoke (15) and Gosport (69). Three recorded decreases: Bournemouth (221), Portsmouth (51) and Southampton (144): *PEN*, 14 April 1914, 3.

[56] *HT*, 17 April 1914, 7.

[57] Barry Doyle, 'Gender, Class and Congregational Culture in Early Twentieth-Century Norwich', *Journal of the United Reformed Church Historical Society* 5 (1992–7), 317–35, at 325.

[58] Watts, *Dissenters*, 3: 175.

29 to 24 'owing to removals ... four members had joined the church ... and three had become teachers in the Sunday school'. Moreover, 'the relations between the Society and the Sunday School were very happy': out of thirteen teachers, ten were Christian Endeavourers.[59] By way of contrast, a somewhat pessimistic assessment of the situation is presented by Stephen Yeo. In support of his thesis that religion and voluntary organizations in Reading were facing a crisis in the early years of the twentieth century, he reports that, out of a total membership of 1,468 Christian Endeavourers in societies affiliated to the local union, 'only 163 became church members'.[60] The basis of the latter statistic, however, is not provided and others may have joined their churches as full members in later years. A detailed quantitative analysis of societies in Hampshire is not possible, since comprehensive data are unavailable. Furthermore, by emphasizing statistical evidence other considerations, such as the deepening of the spiritual life of members, may be undervalued.

In seeking to offer a summary of the position of the YPSCE in Hampshire in 1914, it can be said that the rapid growth of the early years had come to a halt and numerically some societies were in decline. To a degree, however, this was offset by the tenacity and loyalty displayed by those active members for whom the YPSCE had become an indispensable and essential ingredient of their way of life.

CONCLUSION

Notwithstanding the challenges and setbacks it faced, the evidence from Hampshire confirms that the YPSCE was one of the most inspired innovations of late Victorian and Edwardian Christianity. It offered congregations and their ministers, particularly those with strong evangelical convictions, a means of channelling the energies and fervour of young people and in so doing enabled them to give practical expression to their blossoming Christian faith. By this means it assisted in bolstering the loyalty of some young people, who might have otherwise been lost, to the churches in which they had taken their first steps of faith as Sunday school scholars. Although the YPSCE was by no means the complete answer, it can be seen as

---

[59] *HT*, 19 October 1901, 11.
[60] Stephen Yeo, *Religion and Voluntary Organisations in Crisis* (London, 1976), 165.

making a vital contribution to the efforts being made to ensure that churches were able to continue to engage young people when they reached adolescence, started work and thereby became more susceptible to wider societal influences. In addition, it appealed to those who were suspicious of the alternatives, such as uniformed organizations, about which some were apprehensive because of their militaristic features, and guilds, which were primarily recreational. That the YPSCE quickly became a global movement also served to inspire and sustain local societies. MacFarland claimed that 'no philosopher who sees life as a whole, as it is today, can ignore the immense significance of such an organisation'.[61] Its weekly publication, *The Golden Rule*, subsequently renamed *The Christian Endeavor World*, and the annual conferences attracting delegates from across the globe, including Australia and the Pacific and parts of Asia and Africa, confirmed the YPSCE's 'world-wide form and influence'.[62] These also helped the YPSCE to remain focused on its key mission of invigorating youth ministry and providing outlets for the altruism and creativity of the young.

The institutional structures required to consolidate and sustain the YPSCE, however, ran the risk of stifling the initial vision. With the complex committee structures, unions and conventions there was an ongoing danger that members would devote their energies to meeting organizational demands instead of cultivating their personal spiritual growth and engaging in good works. Thus, vigilance was required to ensure that institutionalization did not undermine the inspiration that encouraged young people to become members of the YPSCE. This problem was addressed in a paper entitled "The Christian Endeavour Movement as a Spiritual Force" which was delivered at the 1904 Convention of the Hampshire CE Union by the Revd H. T. Dibben, pastor of Branksome Baptist Chapel. He asserted that although 'their organisation might be perfect, and their committees numerous and in good-going order ... unless there ... were enthusiasm for love as a spiritual force they would not capture the careless and sceptical fellows and maidens around them'.[63] In a similar vein, at the equivalent convention in 1914, the Revd D. Walters argued that although 'organisation was necessary and important ...

---

[61] MacFarland, 'Christian Endeavor', 195.
[62] Ibid. 194.
[63] *HC*, 16 April 1904, 9.

individuality in the ranks was also essential'.[64] By individuality he presumably meant the need for personal commitment and enterprise to be displayed by every active member.

Such aspirations, and the associated tensions between inspiration and institutionalization, were a factor in many Nonconformist churches, where the YPSCE remained a key ingredient of youth ministry in the years leading up to the First World War. The movement continued to flourish during the inter-war years and served as a model for the development of youth fellowships and similar organizations that were not predominantly recreational, but sought to provide young people with a solid grounding in the Christian faith and opportunities for applying their faith through undertaking good works.[65] Christian Endeavour, albeit a pale shadow of its former self, continues to train and equip 'today's young people to be tomorrow's Church Leaders'.[66] Thus something of the original inspiration for the YPSCE survives alongside recognition of the need for a robust institutional framework to sustain the work.

[64] *PEN,* 14 April 1914, 3.
[65] For example, Crusaders and Soul Survivor. Here, too, conferences and publications are used to further these ends.
[66] 'CE Online', at: <http://www.ce-online.org/>, accessed 28 May 2019.

Inspiration and Institution in 1960s Anglican Radicalism: The Cases of Nick Stacey and John Robinson

Sam Brewitt-Taylor*

Witney

This article explores how Nick Stacey and John Robinson, two central figures in Anglican radicalism, navigated the tensions between their institutional embeddedness and their radical theological inspiration during the 'religious crisis' of the 1960s. These tensions operated on the level of strategy, as radicals calculated the opportunities and costs of leaving Anglican institutions, but also on the level of emotion, as radicals weighed institutional loyalties that went deep inside themselves. In the mid-1960s, Anglican radicals attempted to resolve these tensions by campaigning to transform the Church of England. By the early 1970s, however, the failure of these attempts had led to the movement's disintegration, leaving individuals to address the emotional tensions between inspiration and institution in their own particular ways. Thus Anglican radicals failed to evade the central paradox of their movement, namely that their brief moment of prominence in the early 1960s owed much to the prestige of the institution they were critiquing so influentially.

As this volume of Studies in Church History has considered the theme of 'Inspiration and Institution', some of its case studies have concerned insiders, operating within institutions of size and longevity, whilst others have concerned radicals, who succeeded or failed in creating institutions from scratch. The Anglican radicals of the 1960s provide an interesting variation because they were insiders and radicals simultaneously.[1] On the one hand, their leaders were bishops and deans in the post-war Church of England, offices which in the

---

* E-mail: samuel.brewitttaylor@protonmail.com.

[1] The most common contemporary term was 'Christian radicals': this article uses 'Anglican radicals' to denote Christian radicals in the Church of England. For more on definition, see Sam Brewitt-Taylor, *Christian Radicalism in the Church of England and the Invention of the British Sixties, 1957–1970: The Hope of a World Transformed* (Oxford, 2018), 32–6. For other recent treatments, see Hugh McLeod, *The Religious Crisis of the 1960s* (Oxford, 2007), 83–90; Keith Robbins, 'Contextualizing a "New

Studies in Church History 57 (2021), 318–340 © The Author(s), 2021. Published by Cambridge University Press on behalf of Ecclesiastical History Society.
doi: 10.1017/stc.2021.16

declaredly Christian culture of early Cold War Britain conferred specific cultural authority to pronounce on moral and 'religious' matters in the national media.[2] On the other hand, Anglican radicals issued drastic and highly public critiques of the Christian churches, conventional morality and British society, thereby participating authentically in the cultural revolution of the 1960s.[3] From the mid-1960s, as the metanarrative of irreversible 'secularization' began to reshape Britain's public sphere, these Anglican critiques were rapidly overtaken in prominence by rationalist and humanist interventions, not least because Anglican radicalism had itself done much to normalize secular moral perspectives.[4] Nonetheless, for a brief but decisive moment in the early 1960s, as two rival ideologies of modernity fought for dominance over British moral culture, Anglican radicals were in the strategically important position of belonging simultaneously to both camps, as ordained representatives of the established Christian moral culture, who critiqued that culture powerfully from an avowedly 'secular' perspective.[5]

This article argues that this simultaneity allowed Anglican radicalism briefly to achieve cultural influence greatly in excess of its numerical size, but at the cost of entrapping it within two painful dilemmas. The first of these dilemmas was strategic: whilst Anglican radicals made dramatic critiques of the Church of England, and often

---

Reformation"': John A. T. Robinson and the Church of England in the Early Sixties', *Kirchliche Zeitgeschichte* 23 (2010), 428–46.

[2] Dianne Kirby, 'Ecclesiastical McCarthyism: Cold War Repression in the Church of England', *Contemporary British History* 19 (2005), 187–203; Matthew Grimley, 'Law, Morality and Secularization: The Church of England and the Wolfenden Report, 1954–1967', *JEH* 60 (2009), 725–41, at 726; Callum G. Brown, *The Battle for Christian Britain: Sex, Humanists, and Secularization, 1945–1980* (Cambridge, 2019), 116–27.

[3] Brewitt-Taylor, *Christian Radicalism*, 129–223.

[4] Sam Brewitt-Taylor, 'The Invention of a "Secular Society"? Christianity and the Sudden Appearance of Secularization Discourses in the British National Media, 1961–4', *Twentieth Century British History* 24 (2013), 327–50. For humanists, see Brown, *Battle for Christian Britain*, 216–55.

[5] This article consistently uses 'Anglican' as a shorthand for 'of the Church of England'. A central contention of Anglican radicalism was that people could be Christian and secular at the same time: see John Robinson, *Honest to God* (London, 1963), 8. For these two rival visions of modernity, see further Sam Brewitt-Taylor, '"Christian Civilization", "Modern Secularization", and the Revolutionary Re-Imagination of British Modernity, 1954–1965', *Contemporary British History* 34 (2020), 603–28.

resented the institutional limitations it imposed, they also derived much of their unity and cultural authority from it, which meant that leaving and remaining within church employment each entailed distinct disadvantages. The second of these dilemmas was emotional: whilst Anglican radicals were, almost by definition, deeply frustrated with the Church of England, many of them also loved it and desired its approval, and this meant that decisions about whether to challenge or to leave its institutional structures were fraught with personal ambivalence. In the mid-1960s, Anglican radicals attempted to dispel these tensions by fighting to transform the Church of England, an endeavour which they hoped would bring their inspiration and their institution back into alignment. By the late 1960s, however, the failure of this endeavour caused both dilemmas to return with redoubled force. The result was the disintegration of Anglican radicalism in 1970, as the movement split between those who left Church of England employment and those who stayed.[6] This disintegration left Anglican radicals to address the emotional tensions between inspiration and institution in their own individual ways, a task which some accomplished more satisfactorily than others. Yet, despite these difficulties, Anglican radicalism had achieved a brief but highly significant moment of cultural impact in the early 1960s. By using their institutional credentials to redefine Britain as a 'secular society', they had played an important role in unleashing the 1960s 'secular revolution', which others then took further than they did.[7]

This article explores the creation and consequences of these dilemmas by focusing on two central figures within Anglican radicalism: John Robinson, bishop of Woolwich from 1959 to 1969, and Nick Stacey, rector of Woolwich from 1960 to 1968. In the 1960s Woolwich was a relatively deprived area of south-east London, dominated by council estates constructed after the Second World War; it

---

[6] Brewitt-Taylor, *Christian Radicalism*, 224–9.

[7] Brewitt-Taylor, 'Invention of a "Secular Society"?', 340–6. The term 'secular revolution' was coined in Callum G. Brown, *Religion and the Demographic Revolution: Women and Secularisation in Canada, Ireland, UK and USA since the 1960s* (Woodbridge, 2012), 252. Simon Green is incorrect to argue that the bond between faith and people 'finally broke … sometime in the 1950s'; 93% of Britons still defined themselves as Christians in 1963, and the Cold War strengthened the association between Christianity and British national identity throughout the 1950s: Clive Field, *Britain's Last Religious Revival? Quantifying Belonging, Behaving, and Believing in the Long 1950s* (Basingstoke, 2015), 19, table 2.2; *pace* Simon Green, *The Passing of Protestant England: Secularization and Social Change, c.1920–1960* (Cambridge, 2011), 87.

was Woolwich's location south of the river Thames that gave rise to the media moniker 'South Bank Religion'.[8] Woolwich Arsenal, a major local employer, closed down in 1967 after a long period of contraction, and in 1974 Woolwich became the first British town to boast a McDonald's. Robinson was an internationally famous academic theologian who spent much of his career at Cambridge: he first came to British attention when appearing in the *Lady Chatterley's Lover* trial of 1960, and his global bestseller *Honest to God* was published in 1963. Since he was an intellectual who spent much of his time writing and speaking, he leans towards the 'inspiration' side of this volume's theme. Stacey, by contrast, was amongst the most organizationally gifted of the Anglican radicals: through ingenious fund-raising and ambitious management practices, he transformed the ministry of his parish radically, and so he leans towards the 'institution' side of this volume's theme.[9] As Stacey later commented on his activities in Woolwich, 'what [Robinson] was to the theological, we were trying to be to the parochial'.[10] By tracing the trajectories of these two figures before, during and after the 'religious crisis' of the 1960s, this article examines the strategic and emotional paradoxes of possessing radical inspiration within the post-war Church of England.[11]

INSTITUTION AND INSPIRATION IN THE MAKING OF ANGLICAN RADICALISM, 1919–60

The first horn of Anglican radicalism's emotional dilemma arose from the fact that most of its leadership were upper middle-class British men, who had been shaped by elite British institutions from childhood and were sincerely attached to the Church of England.[12] A particularly pure example is John Robinson, who could count seven Anglican clergymen in his immediate family, and who was

---

[8] Nicolas Stacey, *Who Cares* (London, 1971), 81. See, for example, 'Anglicans: South Bank Religion', *Time*, 26 July 1963, 42.

[9] Don Brand, *Nick Stacey and Kent Social Services: A Study in Leadership* (Faversham, 2008), 12, 14.

[10] London, LPL, MS 4370, Robinson correspondence and papers, fol. 32, Nicolas Stacey to Eric James, 1 November 1985.

[11] For this context, see McLeod, *Religious Crisis*.

[12] Notable exceptions include E. R. Wickham, Sheffield Diocesan Missioner to Industry 1944–59, and Eric James, Director of Parish and People 1964–9.

born in 1919 in the precincts of Canterbury Cathedral, where his age-ing father was a canon residentiary.[13] Robinson was baptized, his father proudly recorded, 'in the presence of a large crowd, including 1 Bishop, 1 Dean, 2 Archdeacons, and 2 other Canons'.[14] This eccle-siastical background ensured, as his biographer notes, that Robinson 'could not remember a time when it did not seem right for him to follow in his father's, and so many of his uncles', footsteps' by becom-ing ordained in the Church of England.[15] As was typical for boys of his class, Robinson's childhood was highly institutionalized: the Robinsons employed a nanny, and John was sent to boarding school at the age of nine.[16] From thirteen he boarded at Marlborough College in Wiltshire; from nineteen was resident at Jesus College, Cambridge, where he read theology; and from twenty-one at Westcott House, Cambridge, where he completed his ordination training. In 1943 he won the Burney Studentship to Trinity College, Cambridge, where he undertook doctoral research until the beginning of his curacy in 1945.[17] In 1947 he married Ruth Grace, a linguist from Liverpool and Newnham College, Cambridge, whom he had met at a Student Christian Movement meeting.[18] If elite educational institutions count as a third parent, providing housing, meals and a sense of identity – a poignant obser-vation in Robinson's case, since his father died when he was nine, shortly after his departure for prep school – then Robinson was chiefly parented by institutions from the ages of nine to twenty-six, and from earlier if one counts the nanny. Perhaps unsurprisingly, therefore, Robinson's early career was relatively conventional for an intellectually minded Anglican clergyman. After a curacy at St Matthew Moorfields, Bristol, he became chaplain to Wells Theological College in Somerset, and then dean of Clare College, Cambridge. He was appointed suffragan bishop of Woolwich at the young age of forty because he was chosen specially by Mervyn Stockwood, the recently consecrated diocesan bishop of Southwark,

[13] Eric James, *A Life of Bishop John A. T. Robinson: Scholar, Pastor, Prophet* (London, 1987), 7.

[14] Ibid. 3.

[15] Ibid. 11.

[16] Ibid. 4.

[17] Eric James, 'Robinson, John Arthur Thomas (1919–1983)', *ODNB*, online edn (2011), at: <https://doi.org/10.1093/ref:odnb/31619>, accessed 21 December 2020.

[18] James, *Life of Robinson*, 17–18, 30–1.

under whom he had served his curacy at Bristol, and who, like Robinson, had spent the late 1950s in Cambridge.[19] Although Geoffrey Fisher, archbishop of Canterbury, wrote to Stockwood on two occasions warning that Robinson should attain more age and experience before becoming a bishop, the Church of England's institutional conventions gave precedence to the diocesan bishop's choice, and Robinson was duly consecrated in 1959.[20] His early elevation to the episcopacy, in other words, was chiefly due to the conventional institutional factor that he had a senior patron who knew him personally and valued his abilities.

Nick Stacey's background was less ecclesiastical, but he too was stamped by the imprint of British institutions. He was born in 1927 into a 'comparatively privileged' family (his father had a successful career as a City stockbroker); he had a 'deeply religious' nanny and from the age of seven or eight he boarded at prep school.[21] His parents intended him for Eton, but he insisted instead on attending the Royal Naval College at Dartmouth, the naval equivalent of Sandhurst, which he joined aged thirteen, and from which he graduated at seventeen to serve on the battleship HMS *Anson*. While at sea he felt God's call to ordination, and he abandoned his promising naval career when he was twenty, having spent seven formative years in the Royal Navy.[22] He re-entered civilian life by reading history at St Edmund Hall, Oxford. While in the navy and at Oxford he also had a career as a sprinter, representing Great Britain in the 1950 Empire Games and the 1952 Olympic Games. After graduation Stacey prepared for ordination at Cuddesdon Theological College in Oxfordshire, where he received a spiritual training which he deeply appreciated. As he later wrote, he found 'the daily two hours of compulsory prayer, meditation and worship a great help. I rebelled against the details of it ... but it gave me an opportunity of laying what I hope were spiritual foundations.'[23] In 1955 he married the Hon. Anne Bridgeman, daughter of the second Viscount Bridgeman, then Lord Lieutenant of Shropshire.[24] After a curacy at Portsea, Hampshire, and a spell as chaplain to the bishop of Birmingham,

---

[19] Ibid. 58.
[20] Ibid. 59–67.
[21] Stacey, *Who Cares*, 7–8.
[22] Ibid. 19.
[23] Ibid. 37.
[24] Ibid. 47.

during which he founded the sensationalist newspaper, the *Birmingham Christian News*, Stacey was chosen as rector of Woolwich at the young age of thirty-two, having also caught the eye of Mervyn Stockwood.[25] Like Robinson, therefore, Stacey enjoyed early promotion through the established forms of Anglican patronage.

There was often a sparkle about Stacey's rebelliousness, such as his practice at Cuddesdon of maintaining an illicit bottle of sherry in his bedroom, whereas Robinson's tended to be much more earnest, as when he read a sermon by the existentialist theologian Paul Tillich in place of his own compline address while chaplain at Wells.[26] Despite these rebellious streaks, however, both men clearly relished the approval of institutions. Robinson was particularly proud of having won Cambridge's Burney Prize for 1942, 'exactly fifty years after his uncle Forbes had won it'.[27] Stacey had been Chief Cadet Captain at Dartmouth, and winner of the King's Telescope, the naval equivalent of Sandhurst's Sword of Honour, and he included both pieces of information in his autobiography.[28] He always regretted the fact that he had not achieved a First at Oxford, and as rector of Woolwich deliberately ensured that five of his ministry team had Firsts; when I interviewed him in 2011, he waited only a few minutes before asking if I had one.[29] Consequently, when both men came to accept secular theology's critique of Anglican institutions, it caused them no little amount of soul-searching: they were rebelling partly against their upbringing, and partly against themselves.[30]

Whilst both Robinson and Stacey had long desired the reform of the Church of England, it was not until the very late 1950s and early 1960s that they embraced secular theology, and in both cases disillusionment with the institution they served was the central factor in their conversion. John Robinson had wished for the eschatological renewal of church and society since at least 1946, and he had been familiar with Dietrich Bonhoeffer's metanarrative of irreversible secularization since the translation into English of the latter's *Letters and*

[25] Ibid. 60.
[26] Ibid. 35; James, *Life of Robinson*, 36–7.
[27] Ibid. 14.
[28] Stacey, *Who Cares*, 17.
[29] Ibid. 23–4, 156; personal recollection of interview with Nick Stacey, 6 July 2011.
[30] Secular theology is the belief that God wishes all Christian beliefs and institutions to be reorientated towards the goal of improving 'the secular world', that is, human society.

Papers from Prison in 1953, but he nonetheless remained confident throughout the 1950s that the Church of England could prosper in its current form.[31] In 1959, during his first weeks as bishop of Woolwich, he told his first cohort of confirmation candidates, 'I believe that in England we may be at a turning of the tide.'[32] Consequently, it seems right to accept Robinson's statement in 1962 that the 'changed convictions' contained in *Honest to God* were 'almost entirely borne in upon me by my experience since I left [Cambridge] University'.[33] Stacey told the story rather more bluntly: in his account, he visited the Robinsons at Woolwich in 1959, and found them 'almost as depressed as I was; they were wondering whether they had not made a ghastly mistake by leaving Cambridge'.[34] Particular concerns included the rising numbers of burnt-out clergymen and the apparent alienation of Southwark's working class from the Church of England.[35] Although Robinson had been developing his critique of conventional Christianity since the late 1940s, it was not until his disappointing experiences in Woolwich that he began to demand a radical restructuring of Britain's churches.[36]

Stacey, similarly, began his path to theological radicalism as a result of his frustrating experiences as chaplain to the bishop of Birmingham. On his own account, published in the *Birmingham Mail* in 1959, 'I came to Birmingham a callow conformist from the South. I leave next week for South London a roaring nonconformist and unrepentant rebel.'[37] As he noted in his autobiography, he was particularly incensed by the Birmingham churches' apparent inability to rationalize their resources, and by the consequent necessity for overstretched incumbents to spend much of their energies fund-raising.[38] Given these difficulties, he argued in his farewell sermon in 1960, it was necessary to create a 'new-look Church', which

---

[31] For 1946, see John Robinson, 'The Social Content of Salvation', in idem, *On Being the Church in the World* (Harmondsworth, 1969; first publ. 1960), 20–38; Dietrich Bonhoeffer, *Letters and Papers from Prison*, trans. R. H. Fuller (London, 1953).

[32] James, *Life of Robinson*, 111.

[33] John Robinson, 'Dons and Parishes', *Church Times*, 7 December 1962, 14.

[34] Stacey, *Who Cares*, 74.

[35] James, *Life of Robinson*, 111.

[36] Brewitt-Taylor, *Christian Radicalism*, 143.

[37] Stacey, *Who Cares*, 61.

[38] Ibid. 57–9.

would reform both its theology and its institutional structures.[39] 'Only a knave or a nitwit', he concluded, 'would fail to agree that an agonizing appraisal of the way the Gospel is presented, and the organization and the strategy of the Church, is urgently and desperately necessary.'[40] For both men, therefore, disappointment with the Church of England had caused their inspiration and their institution to fall out of alignment. Their dilemma was how they were going to reshape the institution that had so profoundly shaped them.

INSTITUTION AND INSPIRATION IN 'EARLY' ANGLICAN RADICALISM, 1960–5

Whilst both men felt that their institutional experience implied a need for change, it was their inspiration that told them what this change should look like. In *Honest to God*, and the widely-read *Observer* article that accompanied it, Robinson drew on Bonhoeffer's *Letters and Papers from Prison* to articulate a fully-fledged 'secular' critique of the Church of England.[41] Prior to the 1960s, British conventional wisdom had typically insisted that all societies need a collective 'religion', and that societies rejecting Christianity would eventually succumb to murderous political 'religions' such as Nazism and Stalinism.[42] Consequently, Robinson's intervention was extremely radical: he argued that God was abolishing humanity's need for 'religion' altogether, such that the decline of the churches was evidence, not of Britain's increasing vulnerability to totalitarianism, but of the irreversible rise of a new 'secular' humanity.[43] The coming of permanent 'secularization', Robinson insisted, was God's way of telling Christians to abandon supernaturalism and reorient themselves towards radical social justice, so that they could join

---

[39] Ibid. 61.

[40] Nicolas Stacey, 'The Church Must be Given a New Look', *Birmingham Post*, 22 February 1960.

[41] Robinson also drew on Bultmann and Tillich, but Bonhoeffer was the guiding influence, as Robinson's *Observer* article makes clear: 'Our Image of God Must Go', *The Observer*, 17 March 1963, 21.

[42] For this context, see Sam Brewitt-Taylor, 'Notes Toward a Postsecular History of Modern British Secularization', *JBS*, forthcoming.

[43] Robinson, 'Our Image of God Must Go'; cf. idem, 'The Debate Continues', in David Edwards, ed., *The Honest to God Debate* (London, 1963), 232–75, at 248. Robinson's gendered language is retained here from the original.

'modern secular man' in creating a glorious new heavenly society.[44] In the field of doctrine, Robinson argued that this reorientation meant abandoning the classical theist doctrine of God in favour of a panentheist alternative: it was this dimension of his argument, often critiqued as atheist, which provoked most of the immediate media controversy.[45] Yet Robinson also spelt out the implications of his secular agenda for Britain's churches, insisting that through 'secularization' God was confronting every denomination with a stark choice between pursuing social justice immediately or suffering catastrophic decline.[46] In the new 'secular world', Robinson argued, quoting Bonhoeffer,

> ... the Church is her true self only when she exists for humanity ... she should give away all her endowments to the poor and needy. The clergy should live solely on the free-will offerings of their congregations, or possibly engage in some secular calling. She must take her part in the social life of the world, not lording it over men, but helping and serving them.[47]

Whilst some Christians might experience emotional tension regarding this reimagination of God and the churches, he conceded – 'inevitably it feels like being orphaned' – it remained the case that all these adaptations were ultimately unavoidable, because rapid and irreversible 'secularization' was God's will.[48] Robinson's intervention was a radical and highly public critique of the established institutional forms of British Christianity.

The irony, however, was that Robinson's ability to project the metanarrative of irreversible 'secularization' into the national media was closely related to his status as a bishop in the Church of England, which during the 1950s, as Dianne Kirby notes, was 'reputedly the national conscience' and 'a significant opinion-former'.[49]

---

[44] For the eschatological dimension, see Brewitt-Taylor, *Christian Radicalism*, 46–9.
[45] See the reviews collected in Edwards, ed., *Honest to God Debate*, 82–186.
[46] Robinson, *Honest to God*, 7.
[47] Ibid. 135.
[48] Ibid. 18, 85, 106; Robinson, 'Our Image of God Must Go'.
[49] Kirby, 'Ecclesiastical McCarthyism', 188. For a wider assessment of the political influence of the 1950s Church of England, see Matthew Grimley and Philip Williamson, 'Introduction: The Church of England, the British State and British Politics during the Twentieth Century', in Tom Rodger, Philip Williamson and Matthew Grimley, eds, *The Church of England and British Politics since 1900* (Woodbridge, 2020), 1–35, at 30–1.

Robinson already enjoyed national name-recognition as the Anglican bishop who had defended D. H. Lawrence's novel *Lady Chatterley's Lover* in the *Regina* v. *Penguin Books* obscenity trial of 1960.[50] In the predominantly Christian culture of early 1960s Britain, it was both newsworthy and controversial for a bishop to attack classical theism, and consequently Robinson's episcopal status was a central focus of the ensuing media furore.[51] Public interest in *Honest to God* was such that by December 1963 it had sold 350,000 copies, and sales of the English-language edition eventually reached over a million; it was also translated into seventeen other languages.[52] Robinson demonstrated an acute awareness of his episcopal office while writing *Honest to God*, mentioning it twice in the preface's first two sentences, and signing the preface 'John Woolwich', the institutional form of his name with which he signed all his episcopal correspondence.[53] The front cover of *The New Reformation?* (1965), the follow-up to *Honest to God*, includes a large black-and-white photograph of Robinson wearing a modern suit, clerical collar, pectoral cross and episcopal ring, an image that simultaneously emphasizes Robinson's modernity and his institutional credentials.[54] In the uproar that followed *Honest to God*, Robinson's institutional status also protected him from the many demands for his resignation or defrocking; as Michael Ramsey, archbishop of Canterbury, was keenly aware, the Church of England's institutional procedures ensured that sacking an Anglican bishop was extremely difficult, and Ramsey was in any case keen to avoid anything smacking of what he referred to as a 'heresy hunt'.[55] Despite the fact that Robinson was radically critiquing the established church, therefore, his very status within that church amplified his message and shielded him from professional repercussions.

As in Robinson's case, the institutional procedures of the Church of England facilitated Stacey's activism in the early 1960s. Once

---

[50] Mark Roodhouse, 'Lady Chatterley and the Monk: Anglican Radicals and the Lady Chatterley Trial of 1960', *JEH* 59 (2008), 475–500, at 490, 492.

[51] Robin Gill, *Society shaped by Theology* (Farnham, 2013), 49.

[52] Green, *Passing of Protestant England*, 291; James, 'Robinson, John Arthur Thomas'.

[53] Gill, *Society shaped by Theology*, 49; Robinson, *Honest to God*, 7, 10.

[54] John Robinson, *The New Reformation?* (London, 1965), front cover.

[55] LPL, Ramsey papers, vol. 50, fol. 137, Ramsey to all English diocesan bishops, 26 April 1963 (on *Honest to God*), cited in Peter Webster, *Archbishop Ramsey: The Shape of the Church* (Farnham, 2015), 158.

Stacey had been appointed rector of Woolwich by Bishop Stockwood, he was able to use the established right of the parson's freehold to reform Woolwich's parish ministry without outside interference. Acting on his own initiative, Stacey raised extra funds through networking and tabloid journalism, and was able to employ at his own expense five curates, at a time when most parishes would have been fortunate to have employed two. Like Robinson, Stacey was enthused by secular theology's vision of God calling the church to transform the world. He converted one of the galleries of St Mary's, Woolwich, into a coffee-bar and lunchtime café, in the hope that ordinary Londoners would use it during the week: this was officially opened by Princess Margaret in 1961. He made available the crypt of St Mary's to a local branch of the Samaritans, the suicide helpline charity founded by another Anglican clergyman, Chad Varah, in 1953; and he organized a highly successful bingo club, which gave him valuable opportunities to meet local people.[56] He also orchestrated a number of publicity coups, one of which involved him pulling the English Cheese Maiden for 1960 around Beresford Market in a pushcart. The point of all these activities, he explained, was to transform Woolwich by enabling the church to serve the world. 'One of the tragedies of the situation to-day', he noted, 'is the way that Christianity has been separated from real life instead of permeating every aspect of it. Having the parish church in constant use will, I hope, make it the power house of the whole place. It can really become the great centre for everybody in Woolwich who really cares.'[57] Stacey's hopes of creating an institutional 'power house' were so high that he privately set himself the target of increasing his congregation six- or eight-fold within five years.[58] Thus Stacey resolved the tensions between his institution and his inspiration temporarily by anticipating their resolution in the immediate future.

Similarly, Robinson spent the months following *Honest to God* campaigning for the Church of England to transform itself. 'Any image [of God] can become an idol', he wrote in his *Observer* article of 1963. 'I believe that Christians must go through the agonizing process in this generation of detaching themselves' from the 'idol'

---

[56] Stacey, *Who Cares*, 85.
[57] 'Church to have Coffee Bar and Creche', *Kentish Independent*, 29 July 1960.
[58] Stacey, *Who Cares*, 71–3, 77–8.

of classical theism.[59] After two frenetic years of speaking engagements, Robinson published *The New Reformation?* as an ecclesiological follow-up to *Honest to God*; its headline argument was that 'only a radically reshaped church ... can match the rapid secularization of the world'.[60] In Robinson's view, local churches should be so invested in social activism that they should spend 95 per cent of their time working in the community, and meet as a gathered church for only two weekends and one continuous fortnight each year.[61] As in 1963, Robinson predicted a new and liberating era for his institution if his inspiration were to be put into practice. 'I believe', he concluded, 'in a new Reformation as an exciting and divine possibility'.[62] Like Stacey, consequently, Robinson eased the tensions between inspiration and institution in his own mind temporarily by anticipating the imminent transformation of the Church of England.

INSPIRATION AND INSTITUTION IN 'LATE' ANGLICAN RADICALISM, 1965–70

The problem with this strategy, however, was that most of the 1960s Church of England did not want to be reformed in the manner suggested by the Anglican radicals, and by the mid-1960s this reality was beginning to become unavoidable.[63] By 1967, the radical journal *New Christian* could freely concede that 'the great majority in all the churches form part of a huge inert mass which is complacent and highly resistant to change. Reformers represent only a small minority and realism demands that this should be recognised.'[64] Since this realization destroyed Anglican radicals' existing method of reconciling institution and inspiration, it forced them to seek new ways of coping with this tension.

In Stacey's case, despair at transforming the Church of England had set in by late 1964, and in December he wrote a widely read article for *The Observer*'s colour supplement, entitled 'A Mission's

---

[59] Robinson, 'Our Image of God Must Go'.
[60] Summary of Robinson's arguments on the back cover of Robinson, *New Reformation?*
[61] Ibid. 98.
[62] Ibid. 99.
[63] Brewitt-Taylor, *Christian Radicalism*, 149.
[64] 'Local Enterprise', *New Christian* no. 35 (26 January 1967), 3.

Failure: The Story of One Church in Pagan Britain'.[65] Although Stacey had doubled the size of his congregation within five years, his inspiration had led him to expect a six- or eight-fold increase, and it was for this reason that he concluded that 'we have quite obviously failed'.[66] His response, outlined in a further *Observer* article published in May 1965, was to double down on his existing strategy, insisting that Britain's churches should immerse themselves yet further in the world. The churches, he argued, needed to undergo a 'dramatic dismantling' if they were to adapt to the demands of 'secularization'. There should be a 'greatly reduced number of church buildings', and ninety per cent of clergymen 'should be encouraged to take secular work'. This further integration of the church into the world, Stacey believed, would cause the church to 'lose its life in order to save it': the institution could survive, but only by killing itself and becoming a 'resurrected Church'.[67] Even in this example, however, the irony remained that Stacey's status as an Anglican clergyman was undoubtedly helpful in enabling him to publish so frequently on religious matters in the national press.

In the mid-1960s, Stacey put this new strategy into practice, reorienting his parish ministry away from ecclesiastical duties and towards secular social activism. Whilst one of the curates stayed on as sub-rector to manage the parish, the rest of the Woolwich team took secular jobs, which in most cases, including Stacey's, meant ceasing to draw a salary from the Church of England.[68] The Methodist minister, Ray Billington, who had joined Stacey's team in 1964, started work as a lecturer in Liberal Studies at a local college of further education.[69] Another curate went to teach religious studies at a local comprehensive, and another became a full-time youth worker. Stacey himself focused on social activism, especially as chief executive of Quadrant Housing Association, a start-up charity which bought old houses and converted them into flats for underprivileged families. In December 1965, largely due to Stacey's personal initiative, Quadrant became the first housing scheme to enter a partnership with Greater London Council, which enabled it to expand at the

---

[65] Nicolas Stacey, 'A Mission's Failure: The Story of One Church in Pagan Britain', *Observer Colour Magazine*, 6 December 1964, 30–40.
[66] Ibid. 33.
[67] Nicolas Stacey, 'How the Church could Survive', *The Observer*, 23 May 1965, 21.
[68] Ibid.
[69] Stacey, *Who Cares*, 239.

rate of between 200 and 400 flats each year.[70] Ironically, this achievement required the patient handling of complex secular institutions: as Stacey later recalled, 'there were miles of red tape to disentangle ... I cannot believe that [the GLC's] feathers had ever been stroked so lovingly, or its officials smiled at so sweetly, as they were by me.'[71] Stacey also made further attempts to merge his parish church with the outside world, such as by putting a Citizens' Advice Bureau in a side aisle and a disco in the crypt, which was officially opened by the Duchess of Kent, and by sponsoring a Family Planning Association clinic in a nearby homeless hostel.[72] As *The Times* reported in January 1967, the disco was run by Paul Jobson, a twenty-seven-year old curate, who had a 'tearaway hairstyle', but who always wore his cassock: 'for Mr Stacey, the opening of the discothèque is only one more stage in the long journey towards the final integration of church and society'.[73] By pursuing his existing strategy with increased rigour, Stacey restored his own hope that his inspiration and his institution might one day be realigned. 'I am deeply convinced', he wrote to *The Times* in February 1967, 'that with imaginative and courageous leadership and by wholesale rationalization ... the life of the church could *still* be transformed.'[74]

Since Robinson did not have a parish freehold, he was not able to reorient his local institutional structures in the same fashion as Stacey, but he nonetheless made two important modifications to his public ministry. First, as he sensed the unwillingness of the Church of England to transform itself, he increased the urgency and severity of his prophecies of the Church of England's collapse. 'It seems to me clear', he declared in the radical Anglican journal *Prism* in September 1965, moving beyond even his recently published *The New Reformation?*, 'that we have very much less time than I would have reckoned even six months ago ... I believe the pattern is more and more likely to be one of death and resurrection.'[75] In 1966, similarly, he wrote to Archbishop Ramsey warning that 'the

---

[70] Ibid. 261–2.

[71] Ibid. 262.

[72] 'Switched-On Church opens Discothèque in Crypt', *The Times*, 24 January 1967, 10; Stacey, *Who Cares*, 268–72, 275.

[73] 'Discothèque in Crypt', *The Times*, 24 January 1967, 10.

[74] Nicholas Stacey, 'Transforming the Church', *The Times*, 10 February 1967, 10; italics original.

[75] Robinson, 'And What Next?', *Prism* 101 (September 1965), 9–17, at 17, 15.

straws in the wind point to the near collapse of our traditional structures in considerable areas over the next ten years ... we are approaching, if we have not passed, the point of no return.'[76] 'The next five or ten years, I suspect,' he told a Princeton audience in 1968, 'will tell which way the Church must die.'[77] 'Certainly', he concluded in 1969, looking back on his episcopal ministry, 'I would now freely speak of the death and resurrection of the Church, rather than simply of its resurrection and renewal, in a way that I regarded as irresponsible when I first became a bishop in 1959.'[78] As in Stacey's case, this language of institutional 'death and resurrection' allowed Robinson to keep his faith in the eventual reconvergence of his inspiration and his institution, thus enabling him to bear the disappointment of the Church of England's ongoing resistance to his ideas.

Alongside these heightened prophecies of Anglican collapse, Robinson also spent the late 1960s asking the Church of England to release him from its institutional constraints, so that he could have more time for research, writing and public speaking. In August 1964 he wrote to his diocesan bishop, Mervyn Stockwood, to ask if the diocese could appoint another suffragan bishop to cover most of his pastoral duties.[79] 'I don't in the least want to pull out of Southwark,' he wrote, but 'I feel I very badly need a spell in which I can take stock, think things through, and try and take further many of the things that have been left unclarified.' If this were not possible, he asked whether he could be a part-time bishop, or take a leave of absence without pay, or at least be granted a decent sabbatical.[80] 'There is a part of me which views with horror the prospect of spending the rest of my life as the maintenance-man or manager of a religious club', he wrote in a further letter to Stockwood in March 1966, in a passage that clearly reveals Robinson wrestling with the emotional and strategic dilemmas of combining radical inspiration with an Anglican institution. 'The other half recognizes that we have got to go from where we are to where we want to be by changes in the structures, and that there is no escaping taking responsibility for it.' Yet 'the demands of the organization are so consuming that

---

[76] LPL, MS 4357, Robinson correspondence and papers, fols 43–4, John Robinson to Michael Ramsey, 23 February 1966.
[77] John Robinson, *Christian Freedom in a Permissive Society* (London, 1970), 150.
[78] Ibid. 238.
[79] Cited in James, *Life of Robinson*, 139–44.
[80] Ibid. 140–1.

it is all one can do not to get sucked down by them ... I am guiltily aware that I spend a very limited amount of my (seven day) week being Bishop of Woolwich.'[81]

A contributing factor to these requests was Robinson's back pain, which first flared up in the early 1960s, but which rendered him essentially housebound for the last two months of 1965, and for the last six weeks of 1966, following the surgical removal of two discs from his back.[82] 'An obvious course would be resign', he reflected in a letter to Archbishop Ramsey in February 1966, but 'I am deeply attached to my work in Southwark,' and leaving the episcopacy 'would also remove the platform which has come to give me most of my other opportunities ... I see nothing creative in simply being in the ecclesiastical wilderness.'[83] And so he petitioned Ramsey, in the event unsuccessfully, to stay on as bishop of Woolwich but to be spared most of his pastoral duties.[84] In 1969, realizing that the Church of England could provide the occasional sabbatical but nothing more, Robinson attempted to fulfil his quest for institutional freedom by resigning to take up the post of dean of Trinity College, Cambridge.

In 1968, Stacey also began searching for a new post because he felt that the parish of Woolwich's ecclesiastical structures were preventing him from undertaking further radical innovation.[85] 'The frustration and sadness of the Christian radicals', he wrote in a *Sunday Times* article in 1969, 'is not caused by the hardness of secular man's heart but by the tragic failure of the Church to break out of the strait-jacket of an outmoded tradition.'[86] As Stacey and his curates moved on to other roles, most of his pastoral innovations at Woolwich folded.[87] Having been advised by Stockwood that he was unlikely to obtain another ecclesiastical post, Stacey considered a range of options, including working for BBC Television; he speculatively applied to become deputy director of Oxfam, having spotted the advertisement in a rubbish bin, and was genuinely surprised to be the successful

---

[81] Quoted ibid. 145.
[82] Ibid. 153.
[83] Quoted ibid. 154.
[84] Ibid.
[85] Stacey, *Who Cares*, 282.
[86] Nicolas Stacey, 'The End of Honest-to-God', *Sunday Times*, 28 September 1969, 12.
[87] Malcolm Torry, *Mediating Institutions: Creating Relationships between Religion and an Urban World* (London, 2016), 126.

candidate.[88] In a pattern that echoed his experiences at Woolwich, Stacey tried and failed to persuade Oxfam's board to reorient its activities towards overt political campaigning for social justice, and resigned in 1970: in this respect, at least, the Church of England's institutional structures had given Stacey more freedom than Oxfam's had done.[89] The departures of Robinson and Stacey from Woolwich prefaced the wider disintegration of Anglican radicalism in the early 1970s, as large sections of the movement despaired of transforming the Church of England.[90] *New Christian* wound itself up in 1970, as did 'Parish and People'. By 1973, according to one survey, twelve per cent of Anglican clergymen ordained between 1951 and 1965 had either taken secular occupations, resigned holy orders, or both.[91] The ideas of Robinson and Stacey did have some impact on the wider Church of England: the evangelical Keele Congress of 1967 discussed its own version of Christian 'radicalism', and many radical Anglican ideas, such as house-churches, church-cafés and women's ordination, were taken up and eventually implemented by other groups.[92] Nonetheless, once the possibility of transforming the Church of England seemed lost, Anglican radicals would always find it difficult to reconcile their inspiration and their institution.

Aftermath, 1970–85

Whilst the disintegration of 1960s Anglican radicalism obviated the movement's strategic dilemmas, the emotional dilemmas of individual radicals still remained. In the early 1970s the Church of England still filled posts mostly through taps on the shoulder, but neither Stacey nor Robinson were offered further appointments; the institution had silently closed ranks against them.[93] Writing in 1971, Stacey expressed his disappointment not to have been offered another ecclesiastical post. He had not left the Church of England, he insisted;

---

[88] Stacey, *Who Cares*, 283–5.
[89] Ibid. 294–6.
[90] Brewitt-Taylor, *Christian Radicalism*, 225–6.
[91] McLeod, *Religious Crisis*, 194.
[92] Andrew Atherstone, 'The Keele Congress of 1967: A Paradigm Shift in Anglican Evangelical Attitudes', *Journal of Anglican Studies* 9 (2011), 175–97, at 188.
[93] Stacey, *Who Cares*, 283.

it had left him.[94] 'The Church may reject me,' he commented, 'but I cannot reject it … My love of and my commitment to the Church remain unshaken because of my belief in God'.[95] Neither Stacey nor Robinson were ever sufficiently disenchanted with the Church of England to resign their orders.

In the event, Stacey launched a successful career in social service management, becoming director first of Ealing Borough Social Services in 1971 and then of Kent County Council Social Services in 1974, acquiring oversight of a large secular institution rather than a small Christian one. As his colleague and chronicler Don Brand notes, Stacey found that 'his job as Director of Social Services gave him opportunities to "build the kingdom of heaven on earth" which the church had denied him', and it was for this reason that Stacey's critiques of 'religious' institutions did not always apply to their secular counterparts.[96] Another consideration was that the public sector's access to state funding allowed Stacey to pursue social activism on a much greater scale: as director of Kent Social Services, he was responsible for 6,000 staff and 50,000 clients in a catchment area of 1.5 million people.[97] Under Stacey's leadership, Kent Social Services earned a reputation for innovative reform, especially by pioneering professional fostering schemes, and community care for the elderly, schemes which in both cases removed clients from the direct care of institutions.[98] At the same time, Stacey's irregular respect for institutional procedures sometimes caused trouble, and questions have been raised subsequently about his handling of child abuse allegations.[99] Stacey himself seems to have found this position one of the most congenial of his life: he remained in post for eleven years until resigning in 1985 aged fifty-eight, partly due to frustration with the County Council's insistence on cost-cutting

---

[94] Ibid.

[95] Ibid. 303, 299.

[96] Brand, *Stacey and Kent Social Services*, 14.

[97] Ibid. 12, 14.

[98] London, BL, Sound Archive Transcript, 'National Life Stories: Nicolas Stacey', 92, online at <https://sounds.bl.uk/related-content/TRANSCRIPTS/021T-C1155X0007XX-0000A1.pdf>, accessed 13 January 2020.

[99] Tim Wyatt, 'Archive Interview with Pioneering Priest and Social Worker sheds Light on Kendall House Abuse', *Church Times*, 14 July 2017, online at: <https://www.church-times.co.uk/articles/2017/14-july/news/uk/archive-interview-sheds-light-on-abuse>, accessed 13 January 2020.

and increasing central control.[100] Perhaps surprisingly for someone with his leadership pedigree, he never held another appointment of comparable seniority; instead, he split his time amongst various part-time roles, undertaking social services consultancy, being a Six Preacher at Canterbury Cathedral, chairing the East Thames Housing group and serving as chaplain to sex offenders in Maidstone Prison.[101] Throughout these years, Stacey remained both frustrated and expectant about the Church of England. Even in 2012, in a letter to *The Times*, he reiterated the language of ecclesiastical death and resurrection, prophesying that whilst Anglicans and English Catholics were both facing 'unstoppable terminal decline', 'out of their churches' death an inclusive Church will rise, uncluttered with much of the baggage of the past'.[102]

By contrast, as the radical Anglican moment faded into memory, John Robinson found the interaction of inspiration and institution increasingly difficult: his time at Trinity College, Cambridge was not a happy one.[103] A first disappointment was the loss of the platform that he had enjoyed as a bishop: 'not until he left South London', his biographer notes, 'did he realise ... how much he had grown used to being consulted by the media'.[104] A second disappointment was the realization that Trinity, although not a religious institution, still placed considerable demands upon his time. These demands complicated his family life, such that from the early 1970s Ruth Robinson lived full-time at their house in Reigate, Surrey, where John joined her during vacations.[105] In an opposite trajectory to Stacey, Robinson deliberately remained at the periphery of his institution: he refused to be a tutor, rarely lunched or dined with the fellows, 'studiously avoided College administration and politics', and refused to serve on the College Council, a powerful committee that oversaw much of the day-to-day business of the college.[106]

---

[100] Brand, *Stacey and Kent Social Services*, 59–60.
[101] Ibid., inside front cover.
[102] Nicolas Stacey, 'Church Leadership in a Time of Change', *The Times*, 28 September 2012, 35.
[103] As his biographer unmistakably implies: James, *Life of Robinson*, 190–1.
[104] Ibid. 191.
[105] Ibid. 195.
[106] Ibid. 227.

Given these tensions, it is significant that Robinson did not simply abandon institutions and resign from his post, which his royalties from *Honest to God* would presumably have made possible.[107] Instead, from the early 1970s he began searching for a prestigious institutional appointment outside Trinity, but was unsuccessful, being in the unfortunate position of having interrupted his studies too frequently for the academics, and having disturbed the peace too frequently for the clergymen.[108] In 1974 he was disappointed not to be offered Cambridge's Lady Margaret Professorship of Divinity. In 1975 he cautiously put out feelers to become bishop of Bristol, which would eventually have brought with it membership of the House of Lords.[109] Late that year he expressed interest in becoming dean of Canterbury.[110] In February 1978 he applied for Cambridge's Regius Professorship of Divinity, but was not appointed, the post going to Henry Chadwick; in 1980 he asked Mervyn Stockwood to make enquiries about any full-time job in the Church of England.[111] Perhaps to relieve these disappointments, Robinson also spent more time during the 1970s reflecting on his spiritual heritage. In 1980 he published an autobiographical essay entitled 'The Roots of a Radical', in which he meditated on his ecclesiastical origins.[112] At his final home at Arncliffe, Yorkshire, he kept a substantial collection of Robinson family papers, photographs and memorabilia in his cellar.[113] Robinson's life was cut short by cancer in December 1983 when he was sixty-four; an establishment man to the last, he arranged for his papers to be deposited in Lambeth Palace Library.[114] Whilst Stacey enjoyed some success in resolving his personal tensions between inspiration and institution, Robinson's deep rootedness in his ecclesiastical pedigree seems to have made these dilemmas emotionally more difficult.

[107] Green, *Passing of Protestant England*, 291.
[108] For Robinson's academic reputation, see James, *Life of Robinson*, 242–3.
[109] Ibid. 233–4.
[110] Ibid. 234–5.
[111] Ibid. 242, 316.
[112] John Robinson, 'The Roots of a Radical', in idem, *The Roots of a Radical* (London, 1980), 10–58, at 10.
[113] James, *Life of Robinson*, 254.
[114] Ibid. 314, 319.

CONCLUSION

This article has suggested that examining 1960s Anglican radicalism through the lens of 'inspiration and institution' helps to clarify important aspects of the movement's constant self-transformation during the 'secular revolution' of the 1960s. Anglican radicalism's peculiarly tense dynamic between inspiration and institution arose from the fact that most of its leaders embraced secular theology in the middle of their careers, when they held senior posts in an established institution that had already shaped them deeply. In the early 1960s, this dynamic worked in the movement's favour, allowing it to exploit the institutional structures and privileges of the Church of England successfully, in order publicly to redefine Britain as a 'secular society'.[115] Yet this level of public prominence was inherently unsustainable, because the very act of redefining Britain as an irreversibly 'secular society' marginalized Christian radicalisms in favour of secularist and humanist radicalisms.[116] When Anglican radicals turned to apply their inspiration to their institution, they found ultimately that the deep tensions between secular theology and the Church of England as it existed in the 1960s made their movement inherently unstable. Once their mid-1960s campaign to transform the Church of England had proved unsuccessful, it was always likely that their movement would split between those who stayed in the employment of the Church of England and those who left for other fields. Yet since Anglican radicals often felt unable to reject their church or their faith altogether, the resulting emotional tensions often lasted for decades afterwards.[117]

When viewed in wider perspective, this episode suggests three general hypotheses about the interaction of radical inspiration and established institutions in Christian history. First and foremost, it suggests that radical inspirations can achieve public influence more quickly and more effectively by penetrating established institutions than by creating institutions of their own. In particular, Bishop Stockwood's role in appointing radical Anglicans to his diocese suggests that institutional decisions about whether or not to promote radicals within the established hierarchies can often have very

---

[115] Brewitt-Taylor, 'Invention of a "Secular Society"?', 340–6.
[116] Brewitt-Taylor, *Christian Radicalism*, 26. For humanist voices, see Brown, *Battle for Christian Britain*.
[117] For a fuller discussion, see ibid. 226–7.

significant cultural consequences.[118] Second, this episode suggests that some inspirations have much more radical implications for institutions than insiders initially appreciate. Neither Stacey nor Robinson foresaw the full difficulties of reconciling secular theology with the Church of England when they first embraced it, but throughout the 1960s both found themselves jettisoning more and more of Anglican institutional culture in their quest for the eschatological transformation of modern society.[119] Finally, this episode suggests that radical inspirations, if they achieve sufficient cultural influence, can successfully escape the institutions that promoted them and circulate widely. In the 1960s, the dogma of irreversible 'secularization' successfully detached itself from its ecclesiastical origins and became an accepted idea independent of any one institution.[120] Whilst inspirations may often be dependent on institutions, therefore, the mark of a truly victorious inspiration is that it conceals this dependence successfully, appearing instead as simple inevitable fact.[121]

---

[118] See Mervyn Stockwood, 'South Bank Religion: What I'm trying to do', in idem, *Bishop's Journal* (London, 1964), 65–8.

[119] This argument is developed in Brewitt-Taylor, *Christian Radicalism*, 81–104.

[120] Despite earlier usages and meanings of the term 'secularization', Jan Bremmer has argued, 'the rise of the term in the English world is clearly related to the theological debates of the early 1960s': Jan Bremmer, 'Secularization: Notes towards a Genealogy', in Hent de Vries, ed., *Religion: Beyond a Concept* (New York, 2008), 432–7, at 436.

[121] For the dominance of the secularization paradigm in late twentieth-century scholarship, see J. C. D. Clark, 'Secularization and Modernization: The Failure of a "Grand Narrative"', *HistJ* 55 (2012), 161–94, at 161–2.

'Old-Time Religion in a New-Fashioned Way': The Ministry of 'Billy' Richards, 1943–74

Grant Masom*

University of Oxford

In 1943 a twenty-six-year-old Pentecostal pastor arrived in Slough, a fast-growing industrial town that many church leaders found spiritually tough. Over the next thirty years Billy Richards built a thriving church with six hundred adult members and a thousand children attending groups across the town. His ministry extended beyond Slough through books, radio broadcasts, correspondence courses and international speaking tours. His methods embraced modern media, new forms of worship, conservative theology and a focus on the active work of the Holy Spirit. One local newspaper characterized it as 'Old-Time Religion in a New-Fashioned Way'. This article explores the inspirational aspects of Richards's ministry, how these took institutional expression in his lifetime, and why that institution continues to be influential today. His ministry provides one example of how local churches could adapt successfully to the changing social and cultural landscape of late twentieth-century Britain. This has implications for the understanding of urban mission and the contribution made by the agency of organized religious institutions to twentieth-century secularization.

On 7 September 1974, Pastor W. T. H. Richards, universally known as 'Billy', was taken ill after a normal day's work at his church, the Gospel Tabernacle in Slough, Berkshire, and died later that evening from a massive heart attack. Previously a miner in Wales, Richards was fifty-seven years old, and had spent the previous thirty years founding and building the church, establishing a flourishing and growing ministry not only in the town but in many countries worldwide.

At his funeral, attended by over a thousand people, the great Nonconformist leader Dr Martyn Lloyd-Jones said: 'This man was a spiritual statesman. I have rarely known a man who had a larger and clearer world view of the present situation of the Christian

* E-mail: grantmasom@conted.ox.ac.uk.

Studies in Church History 57 (2021), 341–363 © The Author(s), 2021. Published by Cambridge University Press on behalf of Ecclesiastical History Society.
doi: 10.1017/stc.2021.17

Church and of what we all should be doing.'[1] Lloyd-Jones later hosted a thanksgiving service at Westminster Chapel, attended by 1,600 people.[2] A commemorative magazine contained thirty-eight pages of testimonials from Christian leaders across the world, many from Richards's own Pentecostal denomination, but also from the wider Christian community.[3]

One might question whether an objective view of Richards's work can be found in sentiments expressed so soon after his untimely death. However, the well-known Baptist pastor and author David Pawson rated Richards even more highly, comparing his work to that of the apostle Paul.[4] Commenting on the opening verses of 1 Thessalonians 2, in which the apostle defends his track record in establishing the church in Thessalonica, Pawson wrote:

> There was a man of God called Billy Richards, a Pentecostal pastor in Slough. Many years ago he started a work of God in a chicken hut with a leaking roof. They had six buckets on the floor to catch the rain that first service. Six or seven men gathered in that little hut. But by the time he was taken to glory, in that church in Slough, you would find seven or eight hundred people there worshipping God. They had sixteen daughter groups scattered around Slough and its environment. They had a correspondence course for some enquirers, and some 2000 people learning how to be Christians. They had 40 missionaries working overseas. This is not the work of a bungler, it is the work of a man who knows what he is doing, a man who is effective.[5]

Longevity, outliving the initial work of an inspiring leader, was the key test. The apostle Paul could say 'I've left behind me a strong church full of faith, hope and love' in Thessalonica: and in Slough, the same test showed the enduring value, or institutionalization, of Richards' work forty years after his death.[6]

By the time of his death, then, Billy Richards was widely accepted by the Nonconformist Christian 'establishment'. His influence

---

[1] *Dedication Magazine* [hereafter: *Dedication*], November–December 1974, 21.
[2] 'Pastor Richards: "A Man of Vision and Inspiration"', *Slough Express* [hereafter: *SE*], 20 September 1974; 'Joyous Farewell to Pastor Billy', *Slough Observer* [hereafter: *SO*], 8 November 1974.
[3] *Dedication*, November–December 1974.
[4] David Pawson, *A Commentary on 1 & 2 Thessalonians* (Ashford, 2015), 27–32.
[5] Ibid. 31–2.
[6] Ibid. 31.

extended beyond Slough, both nationally and internationally; and it continues, as can be seen in Pawson's commendation, in the lives of thousands reached by his correspondence courses, radio broadcasts, publications, conferences and speaking tours, and in the ongoing work of the church he founded. This was achieved in what was widely acknowledged as a demanding mission context. This article examines the role of inspiration in establishing, building and maintaining this work, and how that work was institutionalized so that it outgrew and outlasted an individual charismatic personality. It also considers what lessons can be drawn for assessing church ministry in late twentieth-century urban Britain, and the agency of religious institutions in twentieth-century secularization.

The historiography of secularization and urban church ministry in the late twentieth century is a relatively neglected area. Two articles by Jeremy Morris, in part responding to Callum Brown's influential *The Death of Christian Britain*, provide a good overview of the historiography and its perceived weaknesses.[7] Morris characterized secularization under three headings – institutional marginalization, institutional attenuation and cultural attenuation – and identified a tendency by historians to focus on external factors. He commented that 'a refreshingly different reading of British religious history might come into view' through a focus on 'the adaptive strategies of churches in the modern period, as they sought to 'modernize' their ministries, liturgies, missionary, and educational methods and bureaucracies to cope with the challenges of rapid social change'.[8] This article presents one such example of how the actions of religious organizations could affect their own fortunes, and shows how such an analysis might lead to a wider understanding of secularization.

The prevalence of local studies reflects the reality that most people's experience of organized religion was through local contact, with a minister, a congregation or individual church members. However, most local studies have focused on established urban centres in the nineteenth and early twentieth centuries, and coverage

---

[7] Jeremy Morris, 'The Strange Death of Christian Britain: Another Look at the Secularization Debate', *HistJ* 46 (2003), 963–76; idem, 'Secularization and Religious Experience: Arguments in the Historiography of Modern British Religion', *HistJ* 55 (2012), 195–219; Callum G. Brown, *The Death of Christian Britain: Understanding Secularisation 1800–2000* (London, 2001).

[8] Morris, 'Secularization and Religious Experience', 197,219.

of the later twentieth century is notably lacking.[9] Recent exceptions are Ian Jones's study of post-war Birmingham, and a collection of essays on late twentieth-century London.[10] Jones identified the challenges churches faced in dealing with multiple generations, particularly within declining congregations, and this theme is also important to understanding Billy Richards's ministry. The compilation edited by Goodhew and Cooper raises many themes which are pertinent to this article. This study complements that volume by covering the post-war period and considering urban church ministry outside London.

A major theme in the literature is the trajectory of secularization, and whether this is best seen as a steady decline in adherence to organized religion from the late nineteenth century onwards, or whether the progress of decline has been disrupted by the cultural upheavals of the 1960s.[11] Written from a statistical perspective, Peter Brierley's work offers general support for a gradualist explanation, but identifies a fragmentation in adherence after the Second World War, whereby losses in the historic mainstream denominations were offset to an extent by growth in smaller and newer groupings, including Pentecostal and charismatic churches.[12] The historiography is notably weak in considering these movements.

Billy Richards was a member of one such movement, the Assemblies of God denomination. He grew up in a Welsh assembly, attended Bible college in north London, and later spent five years working with the denomination's Evangelistic Society and three London assemblies.[13] At the time of his death, he was playing a key role in planning the Pentecostal World Conference.[14] While

---

[9] See, for example, Jeffrey Cox, *The English Churches in a Secular Society: Lambeth, 1870–1930* (New York, 1982); S. J. D. Green, *Religion in the Age of Decline: Organisation and Experience in Industrial Yorkshire, 1870–1920* (Cambridge, 1996); Sarah Williams, *Religious Belief and Popular Culture in Southwark, c.1880–1939* (Oxford, 1999).

[10] Ian Jones, *The Local Church and Generational Change in Birmingham, 1945–2000* (London, 2012); David Goodhew and Anthony-Paul Cooper, eds, *The Desecularisation of the City: London's Churches, 1980 to the Present* (London, 2018).

[11] For example, Brown, *Death of Christian Britain*; Hugh McLeod, *The Religious Crisis of the 1960s* (Oxford, 2007); S. J. D. Green, *The Passing of Protestant England: Secularisation and Social Change, c.1920–1960* (Cambridge, 2012).

[12] For example, Peter Brierley, 'Religion', in A. H. Halsey and Josephine Webb, eds, *Twentieth-Century British Social Trends*, 3rd edn (New York, 2000), 650–74, especially 654–5.

[13] William Kay, 'A History of British Assemblies of God' (PhD thesis, University of Nottingham, 1989), 198–200; *Dedication*, November–December 1974, 13.

[14] *Dedication*, September–October 1974, 16.

Stephen Hunt's history of the world-wide charismatic movement is too general to focus on more than a few individuals, William Kay's study of the British Assemblies of God contains more local and individual detail, and identifies Richards's Gospel Tabernacle as one of two key ministries in the post-1945 period which acted as institutional 'bridges' between an older group of inspirational 'Pentecostal veterans' and a newer generation of young leaders.[15] Kay does not, however, explore any longer-term influence that Richards had, either within the denomination or more widely.

This article therefore offers local study support to the analysis of secularization in the latter half of the twentieth century, focusing on the agency of religious institutions in secularization, and extending the analysis into the newer urban areas arising from industrialization and suburbanization in south-east England.

Context: The Challenges of Urban Mission

Build my Church, which appeared in 1964, is one of many books and pamphlets published by Richards on matters of belief and ministry. It serves both as a history of the foundation of the church, and a summary of his views on church planting. In it, he recounted how he came to Slough in 1943 in response to 'a call', heard during an air-raid while ministering in London, to 'a town I had heard about only a few times, and in which I had not the slightest interest ... [and where] I did not know one single person'.[16] He had a total of £12 in his pocket. On arrival, he found:

> Here was a respectable, materialistic, and self-satisfied cosmopolitan group of people who needed a change of heart as much as the heathen in the farthest corners of the uncivilised world. It is sometimes more difficult to be a missionary to civilised people than to those who have never known or heard about the Christian faith ... Even some Christians were quick to tell me that I would do no good, the place was 'too hard' ... ministers of other denominations had also agreed that the town was the hardest they had ever ministered in.[17]

---

[15] Stephen Hunt, *A History of the Charismatic Movement in Britain and the United States of America* (Lewiston, NY, 2009); Kay, 'Assemblies of God', 198.
[16] W. T. H. Richards, *'Build my Church': A fascinating Story about the Pioneering & Establishing of a Church through Personal Evangelism* (Slough, 1964), 10.
[17] Ibid. 16–17.

In a book which describes Richards's success in establishing a thriving ministry in unpromising circumstances, this might seem self-serving. But there is much evidence to substantiate the challenging environment which Slough, and towns like it, presented to church leaders. Famously singled out by John Betjeman to characterize all that he disliked about mid-twentieth-century industrial life, Slough was prosperous, and had grown rapidly as new industries relocated around the periphery of London, providing thousands of jobs for workers migrating from depressed areas in the north and west of the British Isles.[18] But this had come at a cost; one local survey noted 'the characteristic that strikes the outsider almost at once ... here is a town with very little civic consciousness, with no centre to the life of the people and with no long tradition in which all have shared'. Too many arriving too quickly had resulted in a lack of cohesion: 'the people themselves have come from all over the country ... large groups of Welsh, Irish and Northcountrymen ... have almost submerged the original inhabitants'.[19]

Slough was not unusual in these respects. Rapid industrialization in the south-east and accompanying economic migration and urban development (particularly in and around London) posed significant challenges for all institutions.[20] The churches were no exception. Speaking to the Church of England Assembly in 1935, Archbishop Lang warned:

> This problem of making spiritual provision for the populations of the new districts which were being formed in many parts of the country was the greatest that had been presented to the Church in our generation. It might almost be said to be one of the greatest ever presented to the Church of England in the course of its long history. ... Some dioceses, notably London and Chelmsford, were almost breaking down under the magnitude of the problem.[21]

His words could have applied to any of the major established Protestant denominations.

---

[18] Grant Masom, *Local Churches in New Urban Britain, 1890–1975: 'The Greatest Challenge'* (Basingstoke, 2020), 63. For Betjeman's sentiments, see 'Slough', in *John Betjeman's Collected Poems* (London, 1958), 21–3.
[19] *Slough, its Present and its Future: 'The Basis for Reconstruction'* (Slough, 1943), 3–4.
[20] A. D. K. Owen, 'The Social Consequences of Industrial Transference', *Sociological Review* 29 (1937), 331–54.
[21] 'Church Assembly: Problems of the New Areas', *The Times*, 19 June 1935.

Table 1 shows the membership of the major non-Catholic Christian groupings in Slough in the period 1940–70, covering the period of Billy Richards's ministry at the Gospel Tabernacle, and Table 2 presents these figures relative to population.[22] The electoral rolls of all six Anglican parishes within which Slough was located suffered both an absolute and a proportional decline. The combined membership of the four major Nonconformist denominations (Baptist, Congregational, Methodist and Presbyterian) remained constant, albeit at low levels relative to the population, before declining in the 1960s. The combined membership of some smaller Nonconformist congregations (two Brethren assemblies, a Quaker meeting and the Salvation Army) was smaller still, but constant relative to population. Only two groups showed strong growth both in absolute and relative terms: the Gospel Tabernacle and groups generally considered to be outside mainstream Christianity, such as Jehovah's Witnesses, Latter-Day Saints and Seventh-Day Adventists.[23]

Table 1 shows that the Anglicans – the largest group – suffered an absolute decline of 20 per cent over the thirty-year period. However, relative to the adult population in a growing town, the decline was far more significant: a 60 per cent decrease, from 7.5 to 3 per cent. For the United Kingdom as a whole over the same period, Brierley has calculated that Anglican electoral rolls reduced from 11 to 7 per cent of the adult population.[24] The significant difference in levels of adherence between the country as a whole and a new urban area such as Slough was evidence both of the challenges highlighted by Archbishop Lang and of the Church of England's failure to address them. The parish system was chronically slow to adapt to the new urban landscape, and this was compounded by increasing pressures on the Church of England's central funding, which limited the scope for building and staffing (or 'planting') churches in new areas. In Slough, for example, the population of one parish expanded

---

[22] For how to characterize membership across different denominations, each of which have different understandings of the term, see Brierley, 'Religion', 652–6.

[23] The Roman Catholic Church is not included in this discussion, as Richards's ministry focused primarily on other sectors of the community. However, Catholicism was another exception to any general story of institutional marginalization and attenuation. For an analysis, see Masom, *Local Churches*, 96–8, 212–15.

[24] Brierley, 'Religion', 654–5; Masom, *Local Churches*, 78–9.

Table 1. Membership of major Christian groupings, excluding Roman Catholic: Slough 1940–70

	Church of England	Major Free Churches	Smaller Free Churches	Gospel Tabernacle	Other Christian groups	Population <15 years	Population 15+ years
1940	3,271	1,171	120	0	70	13,693	43,857
1950	2,794	1,297	160	100	90	15,474	50,997
1960	2,992	1,531	230	350	320	19,714	61,067
1970	2,687	1,435	270	550	600	21,619	80,308

Sources: Anglican electoral rolls from the *Oxford Diocesan Handbook*; Baptist, Congregational, Methodist membership from a variety of published sources; Presbyterian and smaller Free Churches (including Brethren, Quakers and the Salvation Army) and other groups (including Jehovah's Witnesses, Latter-Day Saints and Seventh-Day Adventists) from *SO* sources: see Masom, *Local Churches*, 74–9.

Table 2. Church Membership relative to Adult Population, Slough 1940–70

	Church of England	Major Free Churches	Smaller Free Churches	Gospel Tabernacle	Other Christian groups	Population 15+ years
1940	7.5%	2.7%	0.3%	0%	0.2%	43,857
1950	5.5%	2.5%	0.3%	0.2%	0.2%	50,997
1960	4.9%	2.5%	0.4%	0.6%	0.5%	61,067
1970	3.3%	1.8%	0.3%	0.7%	0.7%	80,308

from 1,500 to 30,000 residents in twenty years, but it was served only by two small church buildings, one incumbent and a curate.[25]

While the Church of England was hampered by institutional factors in its ministry to the new urban areas, mainstream Nonconformist denominations perhaps had greater freedom to respond. With varying levels of success, Baptists, Congregationalists and Methodists all sought to establish congregations in the new areas of the town after the First World War. During the Second World War, a Presbyterian church was formed, catering primarily to the growing Scottish community. These initiatives meant that, as Tables 1 and 2 show, absolute membership across the four denominations grew after the Second World War in line with population growth, before falling by over 25 per cent in the 1960s. However, for the United Kingdom over the same period, Brierley calculated that membership of these denominations declined from 10 per cent to 7 per cent of the adult population. Like the Anglicans, then, these denominations struggled to achieve the levels of adherence in newer urban areas which were seen in more established communities.[26]

There were various reasons for this, some of which also affected the Anglicans. Church planting was expensive and Nonconformist churches had to fund such initiatives largely with money raised locally. Moreover, to a greater or lesser extent, all Nonconformist denominations suffered increasingly from an inability to recruit new members, either from within, through transferring their children into adult membership, or from without, through attracting incomers to the town, to replace those moving away or simply lost through death.[27] While this failure to recruit was partly due to a lack of church extension (now known as church planting), as Richards outlined in *Build my Church*, the environment seemed particularly difficult for church work.[28] In the mid-1950s, one departing Methodist minister, who had previously worked in the north of England and in Wales, declared: 'of all the places I have worked … I believe Slough is one of the worst for lack of spiritual life. I have found the further south I

---

[25] Grant Masom, 'Parishes under Pressure: The Church of England in South Buckinghamshire 1913–1939', *Journal of Religious History* 42 (2018), 317–42.

[26] Brierley, 'Religion', 654–5.

[27] For a fuller discussion, see Masom, *Local Churches*, 81–108, 171–80.

[28] Church extension was the term commonly used by denominations for the setting up of new churches and congregations, including the provision of buildings, clergy and Sunday Schools, as well as external support and finance.

go people are less enthusiastic about spiritual living'.[29] This, however, seems an unlikely explanation, since many Slough residents were migrants from the north and Wales. More plausibly, he felt that 'Slough was difficult because it was such a new town'. Addressing Slough Baptist Church in 1941, the president of the Baptist Union spoke of attendances declining because new housing estates were too far away for children to walk to church, and of wireless services giving the less committed an alternative to Sunday worship.[30] Such dynamics could also affect the internal vitality of congregations. Some years later, Slough's Baptist minister wrote:

> When our church was built, it was in the middle of a neighbourhood area – all walked to church, time was plentiful, everyone knew everyone else intimately and after worship opportunity was taken for conversation in which friendship in the Lord was deepened and strengthened. Now all has changed. Traffic and commerce is all about us, worshippers travel by bus and are more concerned about the bus queue after the service. Attendance in the week is rare, and they scarcely know each other.[31]

Methodist leaders struggled with similar issues. As membership declined (albeit slowly) in the post war period, it became more elderly; commitment declined, reflected in lower attendances; and congregations became scattered across the town and less committed to fellowship meetings outside Sundays. This had a double effect on newcomers: existing congregation members used Sundays as their opportunity for fellowship with friends, and so were less likely to look out for, or even recognize, newcomers; and there were fewer fellowship opportunities for those newcomers in any case.[32]

The minister at the well-funded Methodist Central Hall, the Revd Francis Burns, challenged his congregation regularly about what he saw as their lack of commitment: 'if all of us regarded our Church membership as lightly as some people do, there would be no Church left for us to go to on those few occasions when we decide

---

[29] 'The Church in Slough' *SO*, 24 August 1956.
[30] 'Ald Bowyer at Baptist Church', *SO*, 3 October 1941.
[31] Victor Chudley, *The People of Windsor Road: The History of Slough Baptist Church, 1894–1994* (Slough, 1994), 115–16.
[32] Reading, Berkshire RO, DMS69/2A/1, Methodist Central Hall, Slough, Minutes of Leaders Meetings 1949–72, 1 March 1972.

to be present'.[33] Indifference to Christianity in wider society was directly related: 'I believe that the answer to the apathy of this generation is to be found in the missionary enterprise of all Christian people, and not simply in the zeal of ministers of religion, though that does count enormously'.[34] And in this church at least, he felt it was seriously lacking:

> ... why is it that in these latter days we leave such personal evangelism to cranks and fanatics, to people whose Gospel, we are convinced, is a perversion of the genuine thing. We may laugh at their beliefs, but ... are we Methodists showing one tenth of the zeal of the Jehovah's Witnesses who go from door to door?[35]

Moreover, as noted above, all the main denominations also suffered from an increasing inability to recruit from within by educating children in the faith and transferring them into adult membership. This trend has been commented on widely, others noting the significant role played by Sunday schools and tracing their proportional decline during the twentieth century.[36] Two factors can be noted here: firstly, churches needed to be attractive to families, whether all attending together or parents simply sending their children to Sunday school; secondly, Sunday schools were labour intensive, requiring a committed body of teachers and other helpers. This latter factor could be related to the commitment of church members; at least one previously healthy and growing Sunday school in Slough closed because of lack of helpers.[37]

Table 3 shows the total number of Sunday School scholars across the Baptist and Congregational churches in the town, with the Gospel Tabernacle for comparison. Reliable figures for the Methodists and Anglicans are not available. Baptist numbers grew in line with growth in the population of under-fifteen-year-olds, mainly due to new church plants, before falling back in the 1960s.

---

[33] Berkshire RO, DMS69/8/20/13, Methodist Central Hall Pastoral Newsletters 1957–8, no. 13.

[34] Ibid. 17.

[35] Ibid.

[36] For example, Robert Currie, Alan Gilbert and Lee Horsley, *Churches and Churchgoers: Patterns of Church Growth in the British Isles since 1700* (Oxford, 1977); Doreen Rosman, 'Sunday Schools and Social Change in the Twentieth Century', in Stephen Orchard and John Briggs, eds, *The Sunday School Movement: Studies in the Growth and Decline of Sunday Schools* (Milton Keynes, 2007), 149–60; Jones, *Local Church*.

[37] Masom, *Local Churches*, 227–8; 'The Church in Slough', *SO*, 18 June 1954. This Sunday School had attracted around two hundred children in the pre-war years.

Numbers at Congregational Sunday schools not only failed to keep pace with population growth, but fell steadily in absolute terms.

This, then, was the context in which Billy Richards sought to establish his new church. Immediately after the Second World War, the mainstream denominations maintained their existing memberships, but eventually these declined gradually in absolute terms through death or by people moving from the district. There was some success in establishing new congregations on the expanding housing estates, but overall church adherence lagged well behind the UK averages. The town was seen by experienced church leaders as spiritually apathetic and therefore a hard place in which to work. The congregations of existing churches became less tightly knit as members lived further from the church, and there was some perceived loss of commitment. Sunday schools began to decline relative to population, with the consequence that churches increasingly struggled to replenish their memberships 'from below', and congregations became more elderly.

The Gospel Tabernacle

Beginning from no established base in 1943, over the next thirty years Billy Richards would show that while church planting was certainly challenging, it was not impossible. By the time of his death in 1974, the Gospel Tabernacle had grown to over 600 members, meeting in a 450-seat building that had been extended several times over the years, with all funding raised from the congregation. Over a thousand children per week attended the twenty-eight children's and youth clubs across the town; and several thousand people subscribed to correspondence courses on evangelism, in a ministry that extended well beyond Slough.[38] As Tables 1–3 show, within twenty-five years of its establishment, the Tabernacle had become the largest Free Church group in the town, with the largest children's and young people's work. The remainder of this article will explore the inspirational and institutional roots behind this growth story.

Richards was clear as to the reasons why other churches had struggled. In 1954, he wrote:

[38] 'That Old Fashioned Religion in a New-Fashioned Way', *SO*, 13 September 1974; 'Around Slough Churches', *SE*, 8 November 1974.

Table 3. Major Nonconformist Sunday Schools, Slough 1940–70

	Baptist	Congregational	Gospel Tabernacle	Population <15 years
1940	433	361	0	13,693
1950	590	274	250	15,474
1960	785	210	850	19,714
1970	518	229	1,000	21,619

Source: Masom, *Local Churches*, 229–37.

The church is to be blamed for this shocking state of affairs. For more than a generation the church has been self-centred. She has been 'neither cold nor hot' and her 'couldn't care less' attitude toward the masses outside the fold has produced a situation that is almost irremediable. The leaders of the church have lacked passion and vision, they have pandered to the 'elite' … The gospel they have preached has lacked conviction and has only served to tickle the ears of the listeners. They have not preached Heaven and Hell-Fire, sin and holiness, judgement and reward – the result, there has been a falling away from the church, many have lost faith, the world is unconvinced … The church must repent … throw off the false dignity, needless ceremony and cold ritualism and humble herself to the level of boy and girl, youth and maiden and man in the street and in all sincerity offer the help that alone can be given [by] the living God.[39]

While this did have implications for the content of the church's message, as further discussed below, what this meant was that to appeal to the unchurched, or even to maintain the commitment of those currently within their congregations, churches needed to be spiritually authentic, offer a message relevant to everyday life and build a sense of community. In the same year, the church began to regularly advertise '12 reasons why you should attend the Gospel Tabernacle':

1 You will find real friendship
2 You will find that the Services will appeal to both old and young
3 You will be uplifted and strengthened to do your week's task
4 You will meet hundreds of happy people whose lives and homes have been transformed

[39] 'Aim no Stones at Ald. Manning, but Blame Churches', *SO*, 19 February 1954.

5 You will find healing for body as well as soul
6 You will find a Church that gives priority to your children
7 You will find a Minister and Members whose chief concern is to help you
8 You will find the burdens and cares of life can be lifted
9 You will find Services arranged for all age groups
10 You will find a Gospel that works
11 You will find the Services are 'alive' and enjoyable
12 You will find out the secret that brings over 650 adults, young people and children to the Services, Club and Schools of the Gospel Tabernacle each week.[40]

This formula certainly appealed to some members of the mainstream denominations, who 'wanted something more' than was being offered there, and consequently some of the Tabernacle's growth was through membership transference. For example, one eighty-four-year-old ex-Baptist and Congregationalist, who had at various times been a deacon, Sunday School teacher and lay preacher, moved to the Tabernacle in 1950 because the mainstream churches 'lacked real life and gusto'.[41] However, for other recruits, there was no sign of any pre-existing church connection, and the appeal could be to the young as well as the old. One fourteen-year-old girl was taken to the church by a friend, and six years later was involved in several children's and youth activities and the choir. It appears that, consistent with its '12 reasons', the church created the strong sense of community and commitment that other Nonconformist churches were struggling to maintain. A twenty-year-old reported being in church on four weekday evenings and both Saturday and Sunday, alongside her full-time job as a typist at a local engineering firm.[42] In describing the 'Success Story of a Church' in 1963, the local newspaper referred to it as 'Religion with a Smile'.[43]

The Tabernacle sought not only to be relevant and friendly but to take advantage of contemporary means of communication. Richards broadcast regularly on Radio Caroline, and the BBC's Morning Service came from the church in May 1965.[44] The two local

[40] 'The Church in Slough', SO, 5 November 1954; 'The Church in Slough', SO, 21 February 1958.
[41] 'The Church in Slough', SO, 1 January 1954.
[42] 'The Church in Slough', SO, 30 April 1954.
[43] 'Success Story of a Church', SO, 22 November 1963.
[44] 'Preaching through the Pops', SE, 28 May 1965.

newspapers were generally empathetic and gave helpful publicity. At various times, the *Slough Observer* printed a monthly 'sermonette' from Richards, and its letter pages often contained his views on contemporary culture and morals.[45] In what now looks like a throw-forward to a later age, Richards introduced modern music into services, and was comfortable with a high media profile that made him a local 'celebrity'.[46] It was, as the *Slough Observer* was to put it later, 'that old-fashioned religion in a new-fashioned way'.[47]

But the claim was that this was not just a matter of slick marketing and a friendly congregation, for the Tabernacle was a place where supernatural things happened. A *Slough Observer* reporter attended a healing service in 1952 and published five profiles of named Slough residents who claimed to have been healed of deafness, blindness, diabetes, a stiff neck and severe back pain respectively.[48] Richards said: 'we do believe that God can heal [people] today as he did in the past'. More widely, testimonies of personal spiritual encounter given by ordinary congregation members were a regular feature of services. After one service with testimonies by a butler, a manager, a salesman and a plumber, Richards explained: 'the idea is to show people Christ can satisfy people whatever their occupation'.[49]

The mainstream denominations' recruitment struggles have been noted. Two major foci for the Gospel Tabernacle from its establishment were the young and evangelism. As the general secretary of the Assemblies of God said of Richards later: 'Early in his ministry he discovered the secret of inspiring others to win the lost for Christ. He realised the importance of children's and youth work and forged ahead with this until his work gained almost universal recognition and admiration.'[50] By 1962, the focus on young people had resulted in seventeen Sunday Schools and youth clubs being established around Slough, with 850 children a week attending, while, as

[45] For example, 'One Minute Sermon', *SO*, 23 March 1956; 'Monthly Message', *SO*, 14 January 1972.
[46] 'Sixteen good Reasons for Services to go with a Swing', *SO*, 11 December 1959; 'The Church that began with One Man and a Leaky Hut', *SO*, 26 June 1964.
[47] 'Old Fashioned Religion'.
[48] 'The "Observer" investigates "The Place of Miracles"', *SO*, 13 June 1952.
[49] 'Faith – and Four Men and a Girl', *SO*, 11 September 1953; 'Church in Slough', *SO*, 1 April 1960.
[50] *Dedication*, November–December 1974, 12.

shown in Table 3, Sunday schools in other churches were declining. Many of these schools were on new estates where the traditional churches had struggled to attract unchurched incomers.[51] The groups employed a contemporary and appealing approach to attract children: as Richards said in 1969, 'we believe in a lively and picturesque presentation of the gospel which will appeal to young people'.[52] This 'lively' approach included the use of conjurors, puppet shows and child-friendly songs, in addition to the long-standing highlights of any Sunday school, the family outings and the annual trip to the seaside.[53] While some put the lack of commitment in other churches down to boredom, there was 'no room for gloom at this Sunday School'.[54] But the lively approach was not to devalue the message: '[Richards] set his face against merely entertaining youth ... his object was always to challenge them with the demands of discipleship'.[55] He led from the front ('gospel salesman packs in the kiddies'), but also mustered a large team of teachers and helpers: 'the church relies for its momentum on the fervour of its members'.[56] In 1962, there were sixty teachers in the seventeen Sunday Schools; and the helpers included young people themselves; the worship services were supported by a twenty-two piece 'swing band', and the puppeteers were two sixteen-year-olds.[57]

The focus on the need for personal evangelism was equally explicit; the subtitle of *Build my Church* was *A Fascinating Story about the Pioneering & Establishing of a Church through Personal Evangelism*.[58] Despite the Tabernacle's growth, this focus continued to the end. In the last edition of *Dedication* to which he contributed before his death, Richards devoted two pages to 'The Importance of Door-to-Door Work', declaring 'it is the most productive kind of evangelism and more important by far than any form of mass evangelism'.[59]

[51] 'Britwell: Sunshine Corner attracts 70 Pupils', *SO*, 26 July 1963.
[52] 'Church in Slough', *SO*, 11 July 1969.
[53] 'Puppets lead Children in Gospel Songs', *SO*, 28 January 1955; 'Britwell: Sunshine Corner'; 'The Pied Piper Sunday School of Britwell', *SO*, 10 February 1967; 'Gospel Express takes Slough's biggest Sunday School Outing', *SO*, 23 June 1972.
[54] Guy Daniel, *The Enemy is Boredom* (London, 1964); 'No Room for Gloom at this Sunday School', *SO*, 25 September 1953.
[55] *Dedication*, November–December 1974, 12.
[56] 'No Room for Gloom'; 'Success Story'.
[57] 'Success Story'; 'Puppets lead Children'.
[58] Richards, *Build my Church*.
[59] *Dedication*, September–October 1974, 8–9.

Elsewhere he quoted C. H. Spurgeon, D. L. Moody and Billy Graham (amongst others) in support of this approach.[60] While 'personal evangelism' involved inviting friends to church, as with the twenty-year-old typist mentioned above, it could also involve 'door-bell evangelism'. In one early visitation project, the door of every home in Slough was knocked on over a seven-year period by a group of thirty church members, mostly young people.[61] The normally ebullient Richards conceded that its impact in 'getting people to church' might have been limited, as 'not everyone is interested, but everyone knows we are here'. Later, the only other churches that seemed able to marshal the resources for such work were the so-called sects (Jehovah's Witnesses, Latter-Day Saints and Seventh-Day Adventists), whose enthusiasm relative to his own congregation had so concerned the Methodist Francis Burns.[62] It is noticeable from Tables 1 and 2 that alongside from the Tabernacle it was these groups that saw absolute and relative growth in the post-war period.

The Gospel Tabernacle demonstrated that strong leadership, a contemporary message, a focus on families and the young and an activist gospel directly relevant to everyday life could stimulate a high level of commitment. But this was based on a traditional theological understanding of the Christian message. As some ministerial colleagues sought to 'modernize' the content of the Christian message to make it more appealing to modern sensibilities, for Richards the 'old fashioned messages' were as valid as ever, it was simply that they had not been delivered effectively. In his *Slough Observer* 'sermonettes', he expounded an unapologetically evangelical message, defending traditional Christian positions on theology, behaviour and morals.[63] During the 1960s, through the letters pages of the *Slough Observer*, Richards debated regularly with the liberal vicar of Colnbrook, on the east side of Slough, issues such as miracles, divorce and remarriage, evangelism, contraception and the virgin birth.[64]

---

[60] *Dedication*, May 1969, 7.

[61] 'The Church in Slough', *SO*, 1 June 1956.

[62] 'Jehovah's Witnesses get Land for Church', *SE*, 23 July 1965; 'Bibles in Hand – The Mormons are in Town', *SO*, 19 May 1961; 'They aim to Collect from every House in four Towns', *SO*, 24 March 1972.

[63] For example, 'One Minute Sermon'; 'Monthly Message'.

[64] 'Around and About: Controversial Priest', *SO*, 3 February 1956; 'Vicar challenges Ban on Divorcees', *SO*, 8 November 1957; 'Colnbrook: Vicar criticises Crusade', *SO*, 6 May

Richards's methods were not to everyone's taste, and he did not always defend them in language that endeared him to clerical colleagues, as seen in his condemnation of the mainstream churches quoted above.[65] The debates with the vicar of Colnbrook revealed deep-seated differences, and when another Anglican priest described some clergymen as 'theatre-managers', one of his targets was clear: 'with an anxious eye on the empty seats, may God forgive us [if] we have often found ourselves ordering not public worship but public entertainment'.[66] In 1963, Richards conceded: 'some people may find our methods unorthodox but I think they are justified because we get the message over', and in 1969 he pointed to the results:

> I have been preaching the same message in Slough for 25 years as the preachers of the early Church, and have found that it works. There has been constant growth for a quarter of a century and still hundreds of folk from various walks of life pack the Gospel Tabernacle each week to listen to the Gospel of the New Testament. It is obvious that it has lost none of its attractiveness. I see no reason to abandon it now for empty speculations or a sophisticated religion that is devoid of spiritual life.[67]

Locally, then, within thirty years Richards had established through his inspirational leadership a substantial institution, the largest Nonconformist church in the town, with premises to match a committed congregation of all ages, and a high local profile. But the institution had influence well beyond Slough.

From early on in his Slough ministry, Richards had looked beyond the UK for his own inspiration, while at the same time his own ministry provided inspiration for others. In 1953, he spent three months in the United States, combining a preaching tour with studying the methods of Christian youth movements.[68] Later, he set up 'Christian Witness', a training and publishing venture based in Slough, with the declared purpose 'to help build the Church of Christ by endeavouring

---

1966; 'Letters Extra: The Pill for Teenagers', *SO*, 24 January 1969; 'Letters: Vicar offers Pastor a Debate on Virgin Birth', *SO*, 5 September 1969.
[65] 'Blame Churches'.
[66] 'The Church in Slough', *SO*, 7 May 1954.
[67] 'The Church in Slough', *SO*, 1 February 1963; 'Letters: Pastor won't debate with Vicar', *SO*, 12 September 1969.
[68] 'Off to USA – With a Bible in his Pocket', *SO*, 27 March 1953; 'Travelling Pastor converts 100 Americans', *SO*, 24 July 1953.

to promote evangelism in the local church by seeking to train Christians in personal work at home and abroad'.[69] *Dedication* was a monthly (later bi-monthly) magazine for church leaders and ministers, with a circulation of up to six thousand.[70] Other materials included a correspondence course in evangelism, and a regular flow of written publications and cassette tapes of instructional material. One issue of *Dedication* listed around one hundred individual items that could be ordered.[71] From the early 1960s, an annual week-long Christian Witness convention was arranged, usually at a holiday camp. The 1970 convention in Paignton attracted over seven hundred residential delegates, including over one hundred ministers and their wives.[72] The twelfth convention took place shortly after Richards's death and attracted 'the largest company ever to attend'.[73] Early camps included young people, but as the work grew separate youth camps were organized. For example, in 1974, whilst the main convention took place in late September, a separate youth camp was held in North Wales with 'several hundred' attending.[74] It was claimed that over ten thousand students had been enrolled in the ten-lesson correspondence course, which was supported through ten international centres across Europe, Africa, Australia and North America.[75]

There had been inspirational preachers in Slough before; for example, a young Methodist minister had drawn large congregations to the Central Hall in the years before the Second World War.[76] However, that inspiration did not translate into widespread institutional renewal. Central Hall congregations fell following this minister's departure and, as noted above, the following years saw the church's leaders struggling with decline and perceived apathy. The Tabernacle's '12 reasons' perhaps read like a 'to do' list for many a church but were hardly revelatory. The question is: why did Richards succeed locally where other able and experienced ministers struggled, and why did ministers both nationally and internationally look to his organization for support, guidance and inspiration?

---

[69] *Dedication*, November–December 1974, 39.
[70] Kay, 'Assemblies of God', 199–200.
[71] *Dedication*, November–December 1974, 22.
[72] *Dedication*, October 1970, 8–10.
[73] *Dedication*, November–December 1974, 27–34.
[74] Ibid. 34.
[75] Ibid. 39.
[76] 'Slough Central Hall: Departure of the Rev. R. Brighton', *SO*, 13 August 1937.

INSPIRATION AND INSTITUTION

During his lifetime, the Gospel Tabernacle and Christian Witness ministries had been driven by the force of Richards's personality and, he would have claimed, the inspiration of the Holy Spirit.[77] However, growing and scaling the work required many people to be inspired to support the work practically and financially. The first step in institutionalization was therefore to mobilize a growing team of volunteer workers. Significantly, the principal of London Bible College, Gilbert Kirby, described Richards as 'a man with a vision who inspired others to follow where the Lord was leading him' with 'a wonderful capacity for enthusing others'.[78] David Powell, principal of the Assemblies of God Bible College, said:

> Brother Richards was wise in allocating responsibility. This was one of the main reasons for his God-given success ... He believed God would raise up people to help him and He certainly did so. Those who are fully acquainted with the Gospel Tabernacle system and its outreach will know what wonderful people God has raised up ... so that the work of the Gospel Tabernacle and its outreach ministries could go on without let or hindrance.[79]

Children and young people's work, as well as door-to-door visitation, required armies of volunteers, which many churches and secular youth groups struggled to attract during this period. The periodic expansion of the church building cost at least £26,000; in addition, funds were raised for the regular work of the church. All these are marks of a committed church congregation. Moreover, this army of workers was not just in support of a programme; they were key agents of the work itself, as the Methodist Burns had realized. Richards sought to inspire others to be in themselves inspirational. In 1970, he wrote of the greatest need of the local church being 'Attractive Members':

> The masses are on the search for a people possessing a steadfast serenity, a glowing faith, a transcendent joy, who can speak with conviction 'this is the way, walk ye in it' ... but oftentimes are only seeing the leaves of a cold, lifeless religion. The result is they turn a deaf ear to our message.

---

[77] *Dedication*, January 1971, 10–12.
[78] 'A Man of Vision and Inspiration'; 'The Pentecostal Fire inspiring human Leadership', *Dedication*, November–December 1974, 12.
[79] *Dedication*, November–December 1974, 11.

… In other words, live attractive lives for Christ, so that the unbelievers will be compelled to listen and consider the Gospel.[80]

Those thereby recruited would add to the base of support and growth of the local institution. But inspiring others in this way went beyond Slough. *Dedication* magazine regularly included contributions from other ministers, many from Richards's own denomination, but also including Lloyd-Jones, Kirby and the chairman of the Keswick Convention.[81] The Christian Witness camps were similarly addressed by speakers from the wider church. The 1974 conference advertised six main speakers, of whom Richards was one, the other five being from churches other than the Gospel Tabernacle.[82]

Further steps in securing the growing institution were in building a facility for Sunday worship and the addition of various meeting rooms, offices for the full-time staff and, later, the Christian Witness ministry, which represented at least four phases of expansion in thirty years.[83] Leadership began to be shared, with the establishment of a team of elders and deacons and another team of leaders for the children and young people's work. In January 1974, Richards took a further significant step in strengthening the core of the ministry by appointing three new assistant ministers.[84]

As noted above, Richards was a member of the Assemblies of God denomination, and was playing an active part in denominational matters at the time of his death.[85] More widely, he sought to set the Tabernacle and its ministries within the institutional context of the evangelical movement. Kirby described him as 'a convinced Pentecostal and a thoroughgoing evangelical [who] opened his pulpit to men who shared his basic beliefs and yet were not necessarily of his own denomination'.[86] Contemporary influences included Westminster Chapel, London Bible College, the Keswick Convention and Billy Graham, of whose various 'crusades' Richards was the most committed local supporter from as early as

---

[80] *Dedication*, April 1970, 18–19.
[81] For example, *Dedication*, March–April 1973.
[82] *Dedication*, July–August 1974, 12–13.
[83] 'Built their own Church', *SO*, 15 November 1946; 'Tabernacle Rebuilt', *SO*, 6 May 1955; 'After only 16 Years Gospel Tabernacle is a £25000 Building', *SO*, 13 May 1960; 'Tabernacle's Boom Plans', *SE*, 11 January 1974.
[84] 'Boom Plans'.
[85] *Dedication*, September–October 1974, 16.
[86] *Dedication*, November–December 1974, 12.

1954.[87] Issues of *Dedication* regularly reprinted works by evangelical 'greats' such as Spurgeon, Moody, A. W. Tozer and Bishop J. C. Ryle.[88]

Perhaps one of the most significant tests of whether this work had taken an institutional form greater than the personality of one man, however inspirational, would come after his death, especially since that death came so suddenly. That the 1974 Christian Witness conference could be a success, only two weeks after Richards's death, was a first sign that his work was underpinned by a wider institutional base. Another was the way his local church responded to his loss. Under the leadership that Richards had appointed early in 1974, within three years the Gospel Tabernacle had outgrown its premises and began meeting in a local theatre with an expanded congregation.[89] In following years, the church spawned new congregations in Langley and Windsor, and through partnerships created a network of churches along the Thames Valley. Over forty years on, the church, now known as Kings Church International, continues. The church's website proclaims its historical roots and provides six podcasts of sermons preached by Richards in 1973.[90]

In conclusion, without the story of the Gospel Tabernacle, the experience of organized religion in Slough after the Second World War, or at least that of mainstream Protestantism, could be characterized within Morris's framework of institutional marginalization and attenuation.[91] However, the ministry of Billy Richards offers both a case study in how inspiration and institution can work together and a formula for successful urban mission in the third quarter of the twentieth century. Again using Morris's words, as one example of 'the adaptive strategies of churches' employed to counteract apathy, marginalization and secularization, it may contribute to 'a different reading of British religious history'.[92] Inspirational leadership was needed, focusing on the relevance of Christianity to everyday life and concerns and building a community of mutually supportive

---

[87] 'The Church in Slough', *SO*, 5 March 1954.

[88] For example, *Dedication*, October 1970, 4–6.

[89] 'Church in Fulcrum attracts New Faces', *SE*, 21 October 1977.

[90] See: <https://kcionline.org/about>, accessed 30 July 2019. Wesley Richards, Billy Richards's son, is now the church's leader, although he was not one of the assistant ministers at the time of his father's death.

[91] Morris, 'Strange Death', 975.

[92] Morris, 'Secularization and Religious Experience', 197, 219.

like-minded people. This became both the institutional core and an inspiration to others to investigate, and perhaps join, that community. Appealing to the young and families was crucial, both in building a congregation for all ages and in securing the future. While the Tabernacle's focus on 'miraculous' divine intervention might have appealed to a minority, the '12 reasons why you should attend the Gospel Tabernacle' could have been a manifesto for any church. The Tabernacle presented an unapologetically traditional understanding of Christian doctrine and morals, but sought to adapt the presentation to modern expectations and means of communication while retaining its core values.[93] Through this, Billy Richards demonstrated to evangelical ministers one example of (as Martyn Lloyd-Jones put it) 'what we all should be doing' in the changing urban landscape of late twentieth century Britain.[94]

---

[93] 'Old Fashioned Religion'.
[94] *Dedication*, November–December 1974, 21.

The Church of America and the Heresy of Peace

Dominic Erdozain[*]
Emory University

America, said G. K. Chesterton, is a nation with the soul of a church. It is a sacred community commanding sacrificial loyalty. It is also a violent and weapon-loving civilization, in which force is tethered to patriotism and national identity. American culture is at once militarist and theological, Christian and violent. How can this paradox be explained? This article discusses the role of New England puritanism in establishing a providentialist nationalism that would define war as a theological prerogative and non-violence as heresy. It shows how theologians such as Cotton Mather identified the emerging nation of America with the sacred vessel of the Christian church to the point that 'chosenness' or divine election represented a blank cheque for military adventure. It also shows how theologies of peace and restraint were anathematized as not merely heretical but a form of spiritual violence against the American project. In this sense, American nationhood functions as a controlling consideration akin to an institution, and Christian pacifism serves as a charismatic critique – or inspiration. To what extent were attitudes to violence framed by models of salvation? How did identity or chosenness trump ethics or the duty of love in the puritan imagination? The article concludes with more recent observations about the relationship of the 'institution' of nationhood to the troublesome, fissiparous energies of peace.

The Russian novelist Leo Tolstoy called patriotism 'the savage superstition', a dissembling preoccupation that can turn black into white, and white into black. It was, he argued, a force at war with the universalizing principles of the Christian faith. Indeed, it was the foundation of war. Patriotism, Tolstoy argued, allowed Christian nations to fall back into what he called 'the pagan conception of life', centring on 'the family, the tribe, and the nation'. Patriotism effected a dechristianization of Christianity by subordinating the love of neighbour to the love of self. It was, he said, egoism dressed up as duty and loyalty to the state or the sovereign. Ultimately, he warned, everyone has to make a choice between a flag-waving orthodoxy or the Sermon

* E-mail: dominic@erdozain.net.

Studies in Church History 57 (2021), 364–385 © The Author(s), 2021. Published by Cambridge University Press on behalf of Ecclesiastical History Society.
doi: 10.1017/stc.2021.18

on the Mount. He quoted a pacifist Christian minister who had said at a recent conference: 'If I understand the Scriptures, I say that men are only playing with Christianity so long as they ignore the question of war.'[1]

Polemical as it is, Tolstoy's perspective resonates with the history of the United States, where attitudes to education, health care and economics, not to mention war itself, have been coloured by notions of exceptionalism and divine favour. During the Cold War, economic individualism was sacralized as a godly antidote to the atheistic collectivism of the Soviet Union. Jill Lepore's magnificent recent history of the United States, *These Truths* (2018), shows how resistance to the ostensibly neutral project of providing national health insurance mobilized around fears of the 'Prussianization of America'. When California passed a constitutional amendment providing for universal health insurance in 1917, it was opposed as something that would spell ruin for the United States. Every voter in the state received a pamphlet in the mail with a picture of Kaiser Wilhelm II and the words: 'Born in Germany. Do you want it in California?' The amendment was defeated. California's attempt to provide a European-style health system was defeated, washed away on a flood of patriotic sentiment.[2]

If progressive reform on healthcare represents 'inspiration' in this particular conflict, nationhood was the 'institution', the higher meaning that moderated and ultimately crushed the energies of dissent. Nationhood, in other words, frames what is permissible in the body politic: an invisible yet controlling consideration that transcends even the hallowed terms of the United States Constitution. This may be seen in many areas of public life and policy, but in none more strikingly than in attitudes to firearms and violence. Speaking at the annual meeting of the National Rifle Association in Phoenix, Arizona, in 1983, Ronald Reagan swatted away anxieties about what guns actually *do* with a political sermon about what they *mean* within the larger history of America. 'We're a free people, a democratic people,' said Reagan, 'we believe in God and we love peace. But let us remember what George Washington warned in 1790 – that to be prepared for war is one of the best means of

---

[1] Leo Tolstoy, *'The Kingdom of God is within you': Christianity not as a Mystic Religion but as a New Theory of Life* (London, 1894).
[2] Jill Lepore, *These Truths: A History of the United States* (New York, 2018), 379–80.

preserving the peace.' 'The United States remains the last, best hope for a mankind plagued by tyranny and deprivation', he continued, borrowing a phrase from Abraham Lincoln, which was itself a modification of a phrase of Thomas Jefferson. The effect was to trounce disagreement as a failure to grasp America's inner meaning. The goodness of guns rested on the goodness of America: a nation of innocence and force, goodness and power. 'Standing up for America', Reagan concluded,

> ... also means standing up for the God who has so blessed this land. If we could just keep remembering that Moses brought down from the mountain 10 Commandments, not 10 suggestions – and if those of us who live for the Lord could remember that He wants us to love our Lord and our neighbor, then there's no limit to the problems we could solve or the mountains we could climb together as a mighty force for good.[3]

Reagan's speech, like his better-known animadversions on 'the evil empire' of the Soviet Union, is an example of what the psychologist Rollo May has termed 'pseudoinnocence', a device which processes power through imagined virtue. This can be personal or national. For '[i]n America,' May writes, 'pseudoinnocence has a history as long as the country's. A "Chosen People" set sail from England, turning its back on a Europe that ... stood for sin, injustice, aristocratic exploitation, and religious persecution' to establish 'righteousness, justice, democracy, and freedom of conscience'. This doctrine of chosenness turned ego into piety, 'and the genocide of the Indians – an enterprise the guilt for which we have not yet confronted – is the will of God. This is the hallmark of pseudoinnocence: always identify your self-interest with the design of Providence.' May speculates that America's exceptionally high homicide rates – three to ten times higher than those of European nations – are connected to this exalted pedigree. 'This violence', he observes, 'exists side by side with a remarkable tenderness and warmth in the American character. We cannot escape the conclusion that some special conflicts must be present in the consciousness of

---

[3] Ronald Reagan, 'Remarks at the Annual Members Banquet of the National Rifle Association in Phoenix, Arizona', 6 May 1983, online at: <http://www.presidency. ucsb.edu/ws/?pid=41289>, accessed 17 November 2016.

Americans to account for the simultaneous existence of violence and tenderness.'[4]

This article will discuss the role of puritan theology in creating the 'institution' of nationhood and the resulting force field of innocence, before exploring the 'inspiration' of charismatic sects, and what was seen as the heresy of peace. Anthony Berens has written of the 'New Englandization' of America in the eighteenth and nineteenth centuries,[5] and others have identified the salience of puritan ideas in the Civil War, not least in the mystical providentialism of Abraham Lincoln.[6] In 1901, Albert Beveridge could describe the American conquest of the Philippines as an event 'divinely logical' and a continuation of the New England idea. America was 'a land set like a sentinel between the two imperial oceans of the globe, a *greater England with a nobler destiny*'.[7] From John Winthrop's famous sermon on the *Arbella* in 1630 to the great histories of the Indian Wars written by Increase and Cotton Mather towards the end of the seventeenth century, the concepts of land as entitlement and war as divine activity have been powerful considerations in decisions to go to war.

Charity is central to Christian discipleship, argued Winthrop and the Mathers, but it focuses on the family. God's love is uneven. As Increase Mather put it with ominous equanimity: 'the dealings of God with our Nation ... and with the Nations of the World is [*sic*] very different'. The sins of 'other Nations', he explained, God ignores up to a point, 'and then he utterly destroyeth' them. In contrast, 'our Nation', God watches, protects and reproves, 'so he may prevent our destruction'.[8] Puritan theology created an aristocracy, and grace became a principle of war.

'Consider', boasted Increase in 1675, '[t]hat there are no persons in all the world unto whom God speaketh by Providence as he doth to us. ... Mention, if you can, a People in the world so priviledged as we

[4] Rollo May, *Power and Innocence: A Search for the Sources of Violence* (New York, 1998), 50–2.
[5] John F. Berens, *Providence and Patriotism in Early America, 1640–1815* (Charlottesville, VA, 1978).
[6] Harry S. Stout, *Upon the Altar of the Nation: A Moral History of the American Civil War* (New York, 2006).
[7] Albert J. Beveridge, 'The March of the Flag', 1898, online at: <https://sourcebooks. fordham.edu/mod/1898beveridge.asp>, last accessed 26 January 2021 (italics mine).
[8] Cited by Sacvan Bercovitch, *The Puritan Origins of the American Self* (New Haven, CT, 1975), 55.

are!' We of 'this New-English Israel ... are more involved than any men Living' in a new 'Age of Miracles'. We are, said Cotton Mather, 'the Apple of God's eye, ... prospered ... beyond ordinary ways of providence'. We have been 'dandled in the lap of his providence'.[9] A humourist expressed the logic of a Puritan town meeting thus: 'Voted, that the earth is the Lord's and the fullness thereof; voted, that the earth is given to the Saints; voted, that we are the Saints.'[10] Under the doctrine of election, violence was destiny. Killing was divine.

Histories of the Pequot War (1638) and King Philip's War (1675–8) reveal the stabilizing power of puritan mythology, to the point of crediting God with the accuracy of their weapons. This was perfect innocence. In Captain Underhill's narrative of the Pequot War, one can sense the power of theology to settle nerves and ease consciences. Underhill described the 'dolefull cry' of the Pequots as English fire rained down on them 'at the breake of day'. He recalled the hesitation of his men, adding that 'if God had not fitted the hearts of men for the service, it would have bred in them a commiseration towards' the Indians; 'but', he noted, with a chilling turn of phrase, 'every man being bereaved of pitty fell upon the worke without compassion'.[11]

The slaughter was no different, he said, from scenes in the Old Testament in which David 'harrowes' and 'sawes' whole peoples, under God's instruction, putting them 'to the most terriblest death that may bee'. Indeed, 'sometimes the Scripture declareth women and children must perish with their parents; some-time the case alters: but we will not dispute it now. We had sufficient light from the word of God for our proceedings.'[12] Emboldened by Scripture, Underhill could marvel at the efficiency of the English weapons against the ineffectual arrows of the Indians. Mocking the indecision of the natives, 'changing a few arrowes together after such a manner', Underhill said 'they might fight seven yeares and not kill seven men'.[13] But 'finding our bullets to outreach their arrowes', the Pequots were overwhelmed.

---

[9] Ibid. 51, 53.

[10] Francis Jennings, *The Invasion of America: Indians, Colonialism, and the Cant of Conquest* (Chapel Hill, NC, 2010), 83.

[11] John Underhill, *Newes from America; Or, A New and Experimentall Discoverie of New England; Containing, A Trve Relation of Their War-like Proceedings These Two Yeares Last Past, with a Figure of the Indian Fort, or Palizado*, ed. Paul Royster (London, 1638), 32–3.

[12] Ibid. 35–6.

[13] Ibid. 36.

And, he added, 'wee could not but admire at the providence of God in it, that souldiers so unexpert in the use of their armes, should give so compleat a volley'. It was 'as though the finger of God had touched both match and flint'.[14] Some friendly (Narragansett) Indians 'rejoyced' at the manner of the victory, amazed to see a man turned 'over with his heeles upward' by a single shot. But even admirers came to think that the English mode of war was 'too furious, and slaies too many men'.[15] Underhill was acknowledging the other side of the affair. It did not stop him reporting coldly on the war's greatest atrocity, in which hundreds of Pequots were burnt alive at Fort Mystic. Underhill's men were shocked 'to see so many soules lie gasping on the ground so thicke in some places, that you could hardly passe along', but he ascribed the slaughter to a stern and nerveless deity who 'hath no respect to persons'.[16]

In his account of the slaughter, William Bradford, governor of the New Plymouth colony, revelled in the terror that befell the Pequots. He found providence in every detail, including the assistance of the wind:

> It was a fearful sight to see them thus frying in the fire, and the streams of blood quenching the same, and horrible was the stink and scent thereof; but the victory seemed a sweet sacrifice, and they gave the praise thereof to God, who had wrought so wonderfully for them, thus to enclose their enemies in their hands, and give them so speedy a victory over so proud and insulting an enemy.[17]

The importance of theology was not simply to establish the righteousness of the conquest, but the efficiency. The two concepts were linked. 'Sermon histories', as Richard Slotkin has written, distorted chronology and censored the details. Time and again, one reads of battles in which enemies fall like flies and, in Cotton Mather's words, 'not one of ours was wounded'.[18] War is clean, decisive and godly. For Cotton, holy warfare was an 'antidote' to the 'poison' of unbelief, a living sermon. 'The power of God', he argued with

---

[14] Ibid. 36, 32.
[15] Ibid. 38–9.
[16] Ibid. 35.
[17] William Bradford, *Of Plymouth Plantation: Sixteen Twenty to Sixteen Forty-Seven* (New York, 1952), 296.
[18] Cotton Mather, *Magnalia Christi Americana*, 2 vols (Hartford, CT, 1820), 1: 50.

Augustinian relish, 'is the glory of God'.[19] Following his account of God's 'revenging flames' at Mystic Fort, when 'five or six hundred of these barbarians were dismissed from a world that was *burdened* with them', Cotton reports that one of the Indian allies was converted to Christianity: 'Know, reader, that after this battel *Wequash* had his mind wonderfully struck with great apprehensions about the glory of *the Englishman's God*'.[20] He introduced a sequence of slaughters in the same book: 'Let us adore the justice of that God, who thereby many times has cut off his adversaries; and let us adore the goodness of that God who therein preserves us from imminent and impending desolations'.[21]

In Cotton Mather, faith is strongly identified with national honour. Unbelief is insult and insolence. His account of a battle with the 'nation of the *Narragansetts*, ... one of the most populous and powerful among all the *Indians* ... [in] this mighty wilderness', shows how gospel and honour were fused.

> It was not long before this nation ... engaged in acts of hostility against our people. Whereupon, ours, with a force much inferiour unto theirs, but with a marvellous valour and success, in the depth of winter, made a descent upon 'em. The glorious Lord Jesus Christ, whom they had slighted, was with our *army*, and the day was wonderfully carried against the tawny Infidels. Their city was laid in ashes. Above twenty of their chief captains were killed: a proportionable desolation cut off the inferiour savages: mortal sickness, and horrid famine pursu'd the remainders of 'em, so that we can hardly tell where any of 'em are left alive upon the face of the earth. Such was thy speedy vengeance, O *blessed* JESUS, on the heathen that would not know thee, nor call upon thy name.[22]

When Metacom is finally 'shot ... thro' the heart', Mather describes the event as justice for a 'monster' who had pulled a button off the coat of '[t]hat renowned evangelist of our *Indians*, the reverend [John] ELIOT. ... So do the rejecters of thy grace, perish, O Lord!'[23]

---

[19] Ibid. 2: 317.
[20] Ibid. 482.
[21] Ibid. 318.
[22] Ibid. 336.
[23] Ibid.

Gospel, war and English honour are one. And Mather promises more, adding:

> ... the *Indian* savages are not the only instances of the divine revenges, which have ensued on mens undervaluing the gospel of the Lord Jesus Christ, among us. Travel with me, sirs, to the eastern parts of this province; *O come and behold the works of the Lord, the desolations he has made in those parts of the earth!*[24]

One part of the country where 'the *ordinances* of the gospel of our Lord Jesus Christ' have been rejected, has 'now been made an *Aceldama*' ('field of blood'). 'The jealousie of the neglected Lord Jesus Christ, has *broke forth* like an unquenchable fire against those plantations; the fiery *wrath of heaven* has brought a *swift destruction* upon them.' Their punishment for 'prodigious ... enmity against the *gospel of* the Lord Jesus Christ' was to be 'horribly roasted alive'.[25]

Time and again, Providence tidies up the ethics and mechanics of war. Increase described a scene in which some soldiers crept up on a large number of Indians camping near one of the English garrison houses. The darkness was such that 'an English man could not be discerned from an Indian, yet ours being forty in number, discharged several times upon the enemy, and (as Indians taken since that time do confess) *God so disposed of the bullets* that were shot at that time, that no less then [*sic*] thirty Indians were wounded, of whom there were fourteen that dyed'.[26]

Where Indian violence is bloody, messy and perfidious, English gunfire is clean, decisive and effective. In a sermon for soldiers, delivered during King William's War (1688–97), Cotton Mather addressed the difficult question of how to combine courage with trust in God. How could soldiers be aggressive without compromising the passive dependency of faith? The answer was to understand war as an expression of faith, love by another name. When you fight, it is not you who fight, Mather preached: 'Tho' you carry your *Lives* in your *Hands*, yet they are not in your own *Hands*; no

---

[24] Ibid.
[25] Ibid. 336–7.
[26] Richard Slotkin and James K. Folsom, *So Dreadfull a Judgment: Puritan Responses to King Philip's War, 1676–1677* (Middletown, CT, 1978), 114.

they are in the Hands of that God, without whom not a *Sparrow* falls, and by whom every *Bullet* is directed.'[27]

In the same sermon, Mather advised soldiers to think of 'the Glory of God' as they discharged their weapons, arguing that if God may be worshipped in ordinary toil, how 'much more' may he be honoured in war.

A Godly Man, among our first Planters here, while he was cutting of Wood, being asked, 'Who it was for?' answered, 'I am Cutting of Wood for God.' If in Cutting of Wood, much more in *Killing* of Men, you should be able to say, *I am at work for God.* Be not the Souldiers of Fortune, as they are called; but be the Souldiers of Jesus; and let the Account that you may give of your Concerns be this, I would do all I can, that the Churches of God may have Rest, and that therefore those may be cut off, who Trouble them.[28]

The act of killing is a sacred event. He quotes a Spanish soldier who said '[t]*hat if we have a Good Cause, the smell of Gunpowder in the Field is as sweet as the incense at the Altar*', to which he adds: 'Let the Reader judge after these things, what scent there was in the *Gunpowder* spent for Nine or Ten years together in our *War* with the *Indian Salvages* [*sic*].'[29]

Mather was no crank. He was a vastly learned and intelligent man, a pioneer of smallpox vaccination, a future Fellow of the Royal Society, a man of extensive charities. He thought of himself as a serious historian. 'We have', he writes, 'by a true and plain history secured the story of our successes against all the *Ogs* in this *woody* country from falling under the disguises of *mythology*'.[30] But his history *is* mythology, and one that blends Christian theology with the martial imagery of pagan antiquity:

And we will not conceal the *name* of the God our Saviour, as an heathen country sometimes would … No, 'tis our Lord Jesus Christ

[27] Cotton Mather, *Souldiers Counselled and Comforted. A Discourse Delivered unto Some Part of the Forces Engaged in the Just War of New-England against the Northern & Eastern Indians. Sept. 1. 1689* (Boston, 1689), 34.
[28] Ibid. 26.
[29] Cotton Mather, *Decennium Luctuosum. An History of Remarkable Occurrences, in the Long War, Which New-England Hath Had with the Indian Savages, from the Year 1688 to the Year 1698* (Boston, 1699), 24.
[30] Mather, *Magnalia Christi Americana*, 2: 501.

worshipped according to the rules of his blessed gospel, who is the great Phoebus, that *SUN of righteousness*, who hath so saved his churches from the designs of the *generations* of the dragon. 'Tis to our Lord Jesus Christ that we offer up our *hallelujahs!*[31]

Mather's glee is unending, his delight centring on the conviction that the *'armies of the Aliens'* are comprised of those who 'are *not a People'*.[32]

In one especially disturbing image, Mather invites soldiers to think of God as 'the *Star* to Guide us' in battle, and then suggests that this light may twinkle in the eyes of the enemy, disclosing their location: 'Let every *Bullet* be shot with an Eye taking aim at this *White*, when you are Firing upon the *Blacks* in the *Swamps* of the *Howling Wilderness*.'[33]

> Yea, when once you have but got the Track of those Ravenous howling *Wolves* then pursue them vigorously; *Turn not back* till they are *consumed*: *Wound* them that they shall not be *able to Arise*; Tho' they Cry; Let there be none to *Save them*; But *Beat* them small as the *Dust before the Wind*, and *Cast them out*, as the *Dirt in the Streets*. Let not the Expression seem Harsh, if I say unto you, *Sacrifice them to the Ghosts of the Christians whom they have Murdered*. ... *Vengeance, Dear Country-men! Vengeance upon our Murderers*. Let your *Courage*, in the Name of God be daring enough to Execute that *Vengeance* on them.[34]

The Quaker, Edward Wharton, wrote to a friend in London during King Philip's War: 'Our Rulers, Officers, and Councellors are like as men in a maze, not knowing what to do: but the Priests spur them on, telling them the *Indians* are ordained for destruction; bidding them go forth to Warr, and they will Fast and Pray at home in the mean time: yet', he said, in a poignant corrective, 'their General, with some other Officers, complain and say, with tears, They see not God go along with them.'[35]

---

[31] Ibid.
[32] Ibid. 462; Mather, *Decennium Luctuosum*, 29.
[33] Mather, *Souldiers Counselled and Comforted*, 26, 27.
[34] Ibid. 28.
[35] Edward Wharton, *New-England's Present Sufferings under Their Cruel Neighbouring Indians Represented in Two Letters Lately Written from Boston to London* (London, 1675), 4, online at: <http://name.umdl.umich.edu/A65574.0001.001>, accessed 7 January 2021.

Theologians found God where soldiers did not. And they were managing the narrative to ensure that the mythology outlived military realism. When the Quaker, Thomas Maul, disputed the morality of conquest, Mather accused him of 'goring the sides of New-England', as if he, the critic, were the aggressor. Maul had complained that the puritans had dealt cruelly with the native Indians from the start, a charge Mather refused to take seriously: 'And those *Unrighteous Dealings*, he Explains, to be the Killing of the *Indians*, (or Murdering of them) by the Old Planters of these *Colonies*, in their *First Settlement.* ... Thus are the Ashes of our *Fathers* vilely *staled* upon'.[36] In the mirrored chamber of puritan ethics, a complaint against the 'murdering' of natives is sacrilege, whilst the act of killing is holiness.

In her excellent history of violence in the puritan imagination, Susan Juster describes warfare as a Protestant substitute for sacrament. It binds the community in holy awe.[37] It also involves a ruthlessly selective approach to Scripture that has been weakly acknowledged by historians. Were the Calvinists people of the book? Or did they, as Spinoza accused, *raid* it rather than read it, ransacking its pages for the febrile rationality of war? Speaking of Mather's Dutch Reformed contemporaries, Spinoza alleged: 'There is nothing they interpret with less hesitation and greater boldness than the Scriptures.'[38] Three Quaker missionaries who suffered the removal of their ears in Boston in 1659 made the same point. Had Jesus left 'any Precept' for cutting off ears?[39]

But the future was with Mather, or rather an Americanized version of the New England creed. Theological nationalism was blown across the colonies in the first Great Awakening and it provided one of the motors of the War of Independence. The Great Awakening made a sectarian idiom the common sense of the colonies. As John Berens writes, when 'a New England Calvinist and a non-New England Anglican' could speak in 1763 with the same 'intensity' on the theme of national election, the political salience of a revival becomes apparent. New England became America.[40]

---

[36] Mather, *Decennium Luctuosum*, 163.

[37] Susan Juster, *Sacred Violence in Early America* (Philadelphia, PA, 2016).

[38] Benedict de Spinoza, *Theological-Political Treatise*, ed. Jonathan I. Israel (Cambridge, 2007), 97–8.

[39] Meredith Baldwin Weddle, *Walking in the Way of Peace: Quaker Pacifism in the Seventeenth Century* (Oxford and New York, 2001), 90.

[40] Berens, *Providence & Patriotism*, 50. Bercovitch likewise writes that '[t]he myth of America is the creation of the New England Way': *Puritan Origins of the American Self,* 143.

Jonathan Edwards was no less inclined to nationalized readings of divine activity. His vision was more expansive than classical puritanism but ultimately no less divisive. Christians can kill because God has killed first. His famous sermon, 'Sinners in the Hands of an Angry God', is a frenzy of loathing and anthropomorphic petulance, picturing the deity as an enraged schoolmaster who has finally cracked and has now decided to torture the children. God hates you, Edwards tells his congregation after what must have been a very bad week, and it is only by his sovereign 'pleasure' – 'the mere arbitrary will, and uncovenanted unobliged forbearance of an incensed God' – that they are not already in hell:

> The God that holds you over the pit of hell, much as one holds a spider, or some loathsome insect, over the fire, abhors you, and is dreadfully provoked; his wrath towards you burns like fire; he looks upon you as worthy of nothing else, but to be cast into the fire; he is of purer eyes than to bear to have you in his sight; you are ten thousand times so abominable in his eyes as the most hateful venomous serpent is in ours.

'You are', he says, 'a burden' to creation. And 'the sun don't willingly shine upon you'.[41] Edwards describes a God toying with his progeny, and delighting in their destruction. If you call out to God after you die, Edwards warns, 'he will only laugh and mock'. He 'will inflict wrath without any pity'. Indeed, Edwards continues with truly disturbing imagery:

> If you cry to God to pity you, he will be so far from pitying you in your doleful case, or showing you the least regard or favor, that instead of that he'll only tread you under foot: and though he will know that you can't bear the weight of omnipotence treading upon you, yet he won't regard that, but he will crush you under his feet without mercy; he'll crush out your blood, and make it fly, and it shall be sprinkled on his garments, so as to stain all his raiment. He will not only hate you, but he will have you in the utmost contempt; no place shall be thought fit for you, but under his feet, to be trodden down as the mire of the streets.[42]

---

[41] Jonathan Edwards, 'Sinners in the Hands of an Angry God', in *The Works of Jonathan Edwards Online*, 22: *Sermons and Discourses, 1739–1742*, ed. Harry S. Stout (New Haven, CT, 2003), 410–11, online at: <http://edwards.yale.edu/archive?path=aHR0cDovL2Vkd2FyZHMueWFsZS5lZHUvY2dpLWJpbi9uZXdkaaGlsby9nZXRvYmplY3QucGw/Yy4yMTo0Ny53amVVv>, accessed 10 May 2018.
[42] Ibid. 414.

Edwards peppers his sermon with martial imagery:

> The glittering sword is whet, and held over [you]. ... The bow of God's wrath is bent, and the arrow made ready on the string, and Justice bends the arrow at your heart, and strains the bow, and it is nothing but the mere pleasure of God, and that of an angry God, without any promise or obligation at all, that keeps the arrow one moment from being made drunk with your blood.[43]

It should be no surprise that, with this foundation of theological wrath, Edwards should have fallen back on standard puritan positions on war and divine providence. Edwards writes with formulaic enthusiasm of British prerogative and British success, describing for a friend in Scotland how God was governing their fortunes during King George's War (1744–8). With 'the air ... full of bombs', during the siege of Louisbourg, Edwards said it was a 'miracle' that so few Englishmen had died. The bombardment had continued day and night:

> But yet the whole number that were killed by the enemy's fire, from the town and forts, during the whole siege ... did not amount to twenty. Our men at length were so used to their bombs and cannonballs, and found them harmless for so long a time, that they learned at length but little to regard them; so wonderfully did God cover their heads ...[44]

In fact, Edwards noted, God even used enemy fire to clear obstacles out of their way:

> Once in digging a trench, our men came upon a rock, which they fatigued themselves in vain, in endeavoring to remove, and labored till they were quite discouraged; and just as they had left it, there came a bomb from the enemy, and fell under that very rock, in the most suitable spot, so as at once to do their work for them, and cast the rock quite out of the way; so that then their work lay fair before them, and they went on with digging their trench.[45]

---

[43] Ibid. 406, 411.

[44] Jonathan Edwards, 'To a Correspondent in Scotland', in *The Works of Jonathan Edwards Online*, 16: *Letters and Personal Writings*, ed. George S. Claghorn (New Haven, CT, 1998), 179–97, at 193–4 (no. 63), online at: <http://edwards.yale.edu/archive?path=aHR0cDovL2Vkd2FyZHMueWFsZS5lZHUvY2dpLWJpbi9uZXdwaGlsby9nZXRRvYmplY3QucGw/Yy4xNTo1OjYyLndqZW8=>, accessed 10 May 2018.

[45] Ibid. 194.

The English God was guiding the French bombs, turning destruction into deliverance.

Edwards joined a long line of clerical cheerleaders, making war attractive by parsing the details. Historians have noted errors in Edwards's account of the battle,[46] and the notion that soldiers actually bask in the impotence of the enemy stretches a theory. So does the Mather-like claim that by the end, 'it was apparent to the French ... that God fought for the English, and some of them said, "that their God was turned an Englishman"'.[47] Noting the decisive role of the weather in the taking of the French stronghold, Edwards again pointed to the mind of a partial and protective deity: 'Thus the clouds and winds, and sun, moon and stars in their courses, from the beginning, fought for us.' 'This place,' he added, 'since it has fallen into our hands, has proved a snare to our enemies abroad'.[48] This is theology in the first person. Jehovah was English. 'Edwards was a patriot, a loyal British subject', writes James Byrd. His participation in 'one of the great moments of colonial American patriotism' was as an Englishman.[49] His theology of violence, complete with its images of a God crouching with bow and arrow, was unavoidably anthropomorphic. He was swimming in the same water as Mather, ennobling violence by moulding Christianity around national concerns.

Of Christ's celebrated response to Pontius Pilate, 'If my kingdom were of this world, then would my servants fight', Edwards offered imperious evasion. Jesus, Edwards reasoned, did not mean anything theological or existential. What he meant was that, since his followers were not in secular authority *at that particular time*, they would not fight. Were they in charge of an earthly kingdom, as modern Christians are, then of course they would. So when Christ said, 'If my kingdom were of this world, then would my servants fight', what he actually meant was 'that it is lawful and necessary to fight for the maintenance and support of temporal kingdoms'.[50] Voltaire

---

[46] James P. Byrd, 'Jonathan Edwards, War, and the Bible', in David P. Barshinger and Douglas A. Sweeney, eds, *Jonathan Edwards and Scripture: Biblical Exegesis in British North America* (Oxford, 2018), 192–211, online at: <http://www.oxfordscholarship.com/view/10.1093/oso/9780190249496.001.0001/oso-9780190249496-chapter-12>, accessed 28 June 2018.

[47] Edwards 'To a Correspondent in Scotland', 196.

[48] Ibid.

[49] Byrd, 'Edwards, War, and the Bible', 194.

[50] Quoted ibid. 198.

would have had a field-day. The Bible was a fountain of innocence, a treasury for the warrior. As Byrd remarks drily, the palpable drift of the New Testament passages on 'the kingdom of God' was that 'Jesus and his disciples advocated peace, not violence – an otherworldly kingdom instead of a worldly one. If Edwards saw this difficulty, he ignored it.'[51] As Spinoza contended, theologians such as Mather and Edwards were not servants of Scripture: they were masters.

In the French and Indian War (1756–63), Edwards galvanized Mohawk and Mohican co-operation by situating the Catholic enemy outside the will of God. He rallied the English troops with David's challenge to Goliath: 'Thou comest to me with a sword, and with a spear, and with a shield: but I come unto thee in the name of the LORD. ... I will smite thee, and take thine head; ... for the battle is the LORD's, and he will give you into our hands'[52] The fair-skinned youth standing before the grizzled warrior is a picture of innocence for a naval superpower fighting what Winston Churchill called 'the first world war'.[53] Edwards concluded with a warning against the sin of pride.[54] The idea was to master the weapon but to trust in the weapon-giver to direct its power.

Like Mather, Edwards holds a cosmic struggle between God and Satan as the basic reality of international affairs. As such, he recasts ethics and strategy as secondary concerns. Enemies were 'Edomites' and minions of 'Antichrist'. When the choice is between Light and Darkness, it is difficult to see grey. When the enemy is a concept, not a person, it is easier to kill. With their 'miracles' and 'remarkable judgments of God', men such as Mather and Edwards were sanctifying war as Providence. They were also trivializing it as a game of easy wins and guaranteed outcomes. And with ominous deference to the will of the state, Edwards denied that ordinary subjects had a right to oppose war, saying, 'God has not made them judges.'[55] Christianity's

---

[51] Ibid. 197.

[52] Ibid. 203.

[53] Charles Royster, 'The War to begin all Wars', *New York Times*, 13 February 2000, Books section, online at: <https://www.nytimes.com/2000/02/13/books/the-war-to-begin-all-wars.html>, accessed 11 January 2021.

[54] Jonathan Edwards, 'In the Name of the Lord of Hosts', in *The Works of Jonathan Edwards Online*, 25: *Sermons and Discourses, 1743–1758*, ed. Wilson H. Kimnach (New Haven, CT, 2006), 680–4, at 682, online at: <http://edwards.yale.edu/archive?path=aHR0cDovL2Vkd2FyZHMueWFsZS5lZHUvY2dpLWJpbi9uZXdwaGlsby9nZXRXmplY3QucGw/Yy4yNDozNS53amVv>, accessed 10 May 2018.

[55] Byrd, 'Edwards, War, and the Bible', 198.

inversion was complete. What Christianity once condemned outright was not only acceptable but spiritual and sacramental. As Samuel Davies preached to the militia of Hanover County, Virginia, when the cause is right, 'the *Sword* is, as it were, *consecrated* to God; and the Art of WAR becomes a Part of our Religion. Then happy is he that shall reward our Enemies as they have served us. Blessed is the brave Soldier; blessed is the Defender of his Country, and the Destroyer of its Enemies.' In such circumstances, the curse of God was not on the soldier but on him '*that keepeth back his sword from blood*'.[56] The rules had changed, as Davies was honest enough to admit: 'we have no Method left, but to repel Force with Force, and to give them Blood to drink in their Turn, who have drunk ours'.[57]

The force of this gospel of violence was evident in the capacity of war to build patriotic unity from sectarian division. 'Old Lights' and 'New Lights' (as opponents and exponents of the revival were known) settled their differences under the banner of nationhood. Preaching in July 1745 in celebration of the victory that had thrilled Edwards, Charles Chauncy, the 'Old Brick' of Boston and original scourge of the revivalists, drew the same lessons about military success. 'I scarce know of a Conquest, since the Days of *Joshua* and the *Judges*, wherein the Finger of God is more visible', he told his congregation.[58] Meanwhile in Philadelphia, Chauncy's theological opponent, Gilbert Tennent, proclaimed: 'How admirable ... is the mercy of God in giving into our Hands this strong Hold of the Enemy of our Religion and Liberties!' Evangelicals could do theology in the first person as well as any puritan. There was universal rejoicing that 'British colours once more adorn the walls of Louisbourg ... Thus the kind Hand of Providence, has been pleased to assist us in our undertaking, to crown our Endeavours with Success, and make all our Enterprizes terminate to our wishes.' 'A gracious God', marvelled Tennent, had 'sent undeserved and almost

---

[56] Samuel Davies, *The Curse of Cowardice: A Sermon preached to the Militia of Hanover County, in Virginia at a General Muster, May 8, 1758* (London, 1759), 2, online at: <https://quod.lib.umich.edu/e/evans/N06566.0001.001?rgn=main;view=fulltext>, accessed 11 January 2021.
[57] Ibid. 5.
[58] Charles Chauncy, *Marvellous Things done by the right Hand and holy Arm of God in getting him the Victory* (Boston, 1745), 12.

unexpected Salvations to us.'[59] George Whitefield, the flamboyant revivalist, had coined a Latin dictum for the assault on Louisbourg: *Nil Desperandum, Christo Duce* ('Never despair, Christ leads!'). All of this suggested that patriotism, the god of us, trumped Christian universalism in a time of war.[60]

Within a decade, the very arguments used by theologians such as Jonathan Edwards in the French and Indian War of 1754–63 were turned back on the colonial parent, as Britain attempted to pay for its adventures with a series of ill-conceived taxes. Indeed, one of the ironies of the Revolution was that it was motivated in part by a Whig- and Enlightenment-inspired anti-militarism: a seething resentment of gun-toting Redcoats, military chieftains and martial law. In consequence there was a kind of Lockean and Jeffersonian Revolution, on the one hand, and a theocratic or Calvinist Revolution, on the other. These tensions are still with us.

Representing the theocratic tradition was John Witherspoon's sermon, 'The Dominion of Providence over the Passions of Men' (1776), in which the Princeton president implored soldiers to perceive 'a spirit of revenge' as a 'necessary and laudable' aspect of war.[61] War 'praiseth God' and 'promotes the good of his chosen', he argued. 'There is no part of divine providence in which a greater beauty and majesty appears, than when the Almighty Ruler turns the counsels of wicked men into confusion'.[62] In early Christianity, Witherspoon observed, it was noted 'that the blood of the martyrs was the seed of christianity'.[63] God was working the same miracle now, but with the blood of the proud British. 'Has not the boasted discipline of regular and veteran soldiers been turned into confusion and dismay, before the new and maiden courage of freemen … ?'[64]

---

[59] Berens, *Providence and Patriotism*, 43.

[60] James P. Byrd, *Sacred Scripture, Sacred War: The Bible and the American Revolution* (Oxford, 2013), 22.

[61] John Witherspoon, 'Dominion of Providence over the Passions of Men', in *Political Sermons of the American Founding Era: 1730–1805*, vol. 1, 2nd edn (Indianapolis, IN, 1998), 529–58, at 537, online at: <http://oll.libertyfund.org/pages/1776-witherspoon-dominion-of-providence-over-the-passions-of-men-sermon>, accessed 4 May 2017.

[62] Ibid. 538, 541.

[63] Ibid. 542.

[64] Ibid. 547.

In 'God Arising and Pleading His People's Cause' (1777), Abraham Keteltas declared more plainly that 'God loves his people, infinitely more than all the rest of the world.' 'God so loved the church, that he redeemed it by his own blood, he spared not his own Son, but gave him for his chosen people.'[65] So the dominion was not of Providence over the passions of men but of passion over theology. Not that Britain could complain. The tug of Providence was felt on all sides, except perhaps amongst those who deconstructed it on theological grounds.

When a group of Quakers were brought before a court at Plymouth in 1678 for 'declineing to preserve his majesties intrest' during King Philip's War, both the accusers and the accused cited the same biblical passage about love. By refusing to fight, said the petitioners, the Quakers violated Jesus's command to love one's neighbour as oneself. The defendants agreed that the command to love neighbours was sacred. But they defined 'neighbour' to include the 'enemy'.[66] The Quaker peace testimony developed unevenly, but it found a rock and a foundation in the concept of universal love. The new covenant was open to all. Puritan gunfire smelled not of God but of man. It suggested a narrow and anthropomorphic deity. As Samuel Fisher challenged the defenders of the eternal decrees around 1660: 'Are ye not ashamed thus to engross the grace of God ... among yourselves and a few like your sinning selves? ... For the elect are very few with you.'[67]

Explaining his alienation from Reformed orthodoxy, the Quaker apologist, Robert Barclay, made the same point about salvation and charity: 'such as confined *God's Love*, did consequentially confine their own'.

> [T]hey think not Men worthy to live as Men, or breath the common air. ... Surely this is far from the *Nature of God's Love*, that causes his Sun to rise both upon the Just and Unjust. ... Now none of these Men, without manifestly contradicting their own Principles, can pretend to have Love to any of those that are thus predestinated to Death ...[68]

---

[65] Abraham Keteltas, 'God arising and pleading his People's Cause' (1777), in *Political Sermons*, 1: 579–606, at 586, online at: <http://oll.libertyfund.org/titles/sandoz-political-sermons-of-the-american-founding-era-vol-1-1730-1788–5>, accessed 4 May 2017.

[66] Weddle, *Walking in the Way of Peace*, 202.

[67] Christopher Hill, *The World Turned Upside Down: Radical Ideas during the English Revolution* (Harmondsworth, 1978), 260.

[68] Robert Barclay, *Universal Love Considered and Established upon Its Right Foundation, Being a Serious Enquiry How Far Charity May and Ought to Be Extended towards Persons of Different Judgments in Matters of Religion and Whose Principles among the Several Sects of*

Predestination was unchristian. It was to toy with 'heathen' notions of 'blind' fate. And it was an idea that 'so leaveneth and defileth with an unlovely humour, such as strictly and precisely hold it, that for most part they are observed to be Men of peevish and persecuting spirits', Barclay ventured. This principle of 'absolute Reprobation among Protestants [was] the very root and spring, from whence flows that Bloody and Antichristian tenet of Persecution'. 'And this', he maintained, 'goes directly against, and destroys the nature of *Universal Love*'.[69] 'God never loved the world, according to this doctrine, but rather hated it greatly', Barclay indignantly inferred. So, he concluded, '[t]his doctrine is highly injurious to mankind.'[70]

Barclay's judgement was echoed by Jean-Jacques Rousseau, in his vastly influential treatise *The Social Contract:* 'It is impossible to live in peace with people you think are damned. To love them would mean you hate God who punishes them. You have either to convert them or torment them. Wherever theological intolerance is allowed, it necessarily has civil consequences.'[71] Quakers, on the other hand, preaching 'love to enemies' and 'suffering Injuries without Revenge,' held 'it Unlawful for Christians to fight or use carnal Weapons'.[72]

For another influential Quaker, Anthony Benezet, war was not a Christian affair but 'a sad consequence of the apostacy, and fall of man'. It grieved him to see the American colonies sliding into European sin: 'look at all European Christendom sailing round the globe, with fire and sword, and every murdering art of war, to seize the possessions and steal or kill the inhabitants of Africa and the Indies'.[73]

Christians Do Most Naturally Lead to That Due Moderation Required (n.pl., 1677), 23, 28, online at: <http://quod.lib.umich.edu/cgi/t/text/text-idx?c=eebo;idno=A30906.0001. 001>, accessed 18 December 2015.

[69] Ibid. 29, 24.

[70] Robert Barclay, *Apology for the True Christian Divinity* (1676), Propositions 5 and 6, online at: <http://www.qhpress.org/texts/barclay/apology/props5-6.html>, accessed 17 December 2015.

[71] Jean-Jacques Rousseau, *The Social Contract and other later Political Writings* (Cambridge, 1997), 151.

[72] Barclay, *Universal Love Considered.*

[73] Anthony Benezet, *Serious Considerations on Several Important Subjects: Viz. on War and Its Inconsistency with the Gospel; Observations on Slavery. And Remarks on the Nature and Bad Effects of Spirituous Liquors* (London, 1778), 7, 15; online at: <https://quod.lib. umich.edu/e/evans/N12457.0001.001?rgn=main;view=fulltext>, last accessed 4 February 2021.

Again, he came back to the doctrine of salvation, that Christ's love
extended to all:

> 'Christ hath tasted death for *every* man,' not only *for all kinds of men*, as
> some vainly talk, but *for every one of all kinds*; ... The Quakers abso-
> lutely declare against being concerned in the destruction of their fellow
> men, who equally with themselves are the object of saving grace; hence
> they can take no part in war ... 'He came not to destroy men's lives, but
> to save them,'(Luke ix. 56.) ...[74]

The peace testimony, writes Meredith Weddle, was 'the
foolishness ... and the magnificence of a people whose time has
not yet come'.[75] This is true, but it perhaps understates the degree
to which such thinking succeeded in the political and legal realms,
when it failed in the church as such. The democratic tradition
retained some of this theological generosity, what one scholar has
termed 'the loving heresy of universal salvation'.[76] Benjamin Rush,
physician and social reformer and a signatory of the Declaration of
Independence, couched his republicanism on 'the original and natural equality of all mankind'. It was a Christian conviction that defined
his politics: 'A Christian, I say again, cannot fail of being a republican,
for every precept of the Gospel inculcates those degrees of humility,
self-denial, and brotherly kindness, which are directly opposed to the
pride of monarchy and the pageantry of a court.'[77] War and capital
punishment were the echoes of European despotism. But Christianity
taught otherwise:

> When two of his disciples, actuated by the spirit of vindictive legisla-
> tors, requested permission of him to call down fire from Heaven to
> consume the inhospitable Samaritans, he answered them 'The Son of
> Man is not come to destroy men's lives but to save them.' I wish these
> words composed the motto ... of every nation upon the face of the
> earth. They inculcate every duty that is calculated to preserve, restore,
> or prolong human life. They militate alike against war – and capital
> punishments – the objects of which, are the unprofitable destruction

---

[74] Robert Barclay and Anthony Benezet, *A Concise View of the Chief Principles of the
Christian Religion: As Professed by the People Called Quakers* (Baltimore, 1840), 6, 15, 17.
[75] Weddle, *Walking in the Way of Peace*, 200.
[76] Donald J. D'Elia, 'The Republican Theology of Benjamin Rush', *Pennsylvania History*
33 (1966), 187–203, at 188.
[77] Benjamin Rush, *Essays, Literary, Moral & Philosophical* (Philadelphia, 1798), 9.

of the lives of men. How precious does a human life appear from these words, in the sight of heaven![78]

Or take 'Brutus', one of the most eloquent of the anti-federalist writers to whom we owe the measured grandeur of the Bill of Rights: 'The European governments are almost all of them framed, and administered with a view to arms, and war, as that in which their chief glory consists; they mistake the end of government – it was designed to save men[']s lives, not to destroy them.' 'Let the monarchs, in Europe, share among them the glory of depopulating countries, and butchering thousands of their innocent citizens, to revenge private quarrels, or to punish an insult offered to a wife, a mistress, or a favorite: I envy them not the honor, and I pray heaven this country may never be ambitious of it.'[79]

Finally, Thomas Jefferson, on assuming the presidency in 1801, said that America's part would be 'introduce between nations another umpire than arms',[80] and in 1814 disdained the wisdom of the war 'hawks' with the opinion that 'it is better to suffer much from the scalpings, the conflagrations, the rapes and rapine of savages, than to countenance and strengthen such barbarisms by retortion.' '[M]y hope,' he said, 'is in peace. ... One war, such as that of our revolution, is enough for one life'.[81]

Alexis de Tocqueville had a slightly rosy appreciation of American liberty, but it is remarkable that as late as 1835 he could marvel at America's immunity to European sins of militarism and national honour:

The Americans have no neighbors and thus no great wars, financial crises, devastations, or conquests to dread. They need neither heavy taxes, nor a large army, nor great generals; they have almost nothing to fear

---

[78] Ibid. 176.

[79] 'Brutus VII' (1788), online at Teaching American History: <http://teachingamerican-history.org/library/document/brutus-vii/>, accessed 28 March 2019.

[80] Thomas Jefferson to James Madison, 24 March 1793, in *The Letters of Thomas Jefferson 1743–1826* [online collection], at: <http://www.let.rug.nl/usa/presidents/thomas-jefferson/letters-of-thomas-jefferson/jefl103.php>, accessed 11 May 2019.

[81] Thomas Jefferson to José Corrêa da Serra, 27 December 1814, in *The Papers of Thomas Jefferson, Retirement Series*, 8: *1 October 1814 to 31 August 1815*, ed. J. Jefferson Looney (Princeton, NJ, 2011), 166–9, online at 'Founders Online': <http://founders.archives.gov/documents/Jefferson/03-08-02-0143>, accessed 11 May 2019.

from that scourge which is more terrible for democratic republics than all these put together, namely, military glory.[82]

This was a generous appraisal, and Jefferson's stance was, by the time the Frenchman was penning his eulogies on the new nation, a minority report. By the time that Theodore Roosevelt and William Jennings Bryan sparred over America's place in the world in 1899, a position that had been normative for Jefferson and Rush had assumed a texture of idealism. And if the First World War prompted an unprecedented effusion of American pacifism, as coalitions of Christians, socialists and anti-imperialists opposed a war that seemed to be destroying what it attempted to save – democracy – the rise of Hitler and Italian fascism settled the argument in the other direction.[83] The justice of America's involvement in the Second World War was clear to most Christians outside the radical firmament of Dorothy Day and the *Catholic Worker*,[84] a position articulated by the most influential public theologian of the day, Reinhold Niebuhr.[85]

Yet history can resuscitate this tradition of peaceable scepticism simply by showing that it was there and it never died. De Tocqueville was appalled and embarrassed by the election to the presidency of Andrew Jackson, a brutal killer known to the Native Americans as 'Sharp Knife'. De Tocqueville tried to explain it away as an exception to the rule of American wisdom and liberty. But his idea that American exceptionalism could exist as a reluctance to fight is surely a valuable one, and a concept that occasionally resonates in liberal and conservative commentary.[86] In a nation that continues to think like a church, such a re-centring of the heretics and peacemakers at the heart of the American story seems an urgent task. As Boris Pasternak wrote in *Doctor Zhivago*: 'Happy are the downtrodden. They have something to tell about themselves.'[87]

---

[82] Alexis de Tocqueville, *Democracy in America and Two Essays on America*, ed. Isaac Kramnick, trans. Gerald Bevan (London, 2003), 324.

[83] Michael Kazin, *War against War: The American Fight for Peace, 1914–1918* (New York, 2017).

[84] John Loughery and Blythe Randolph, *Dorothy Day: Dissenting Voice of the American Century* (New York, 2020).

[85] Thanks to Tim Grass for making this important point.

[86] David Brooks, 'The Brutalism of Ted Cruz', *New York Times*, 12 January 2016, online at: <http://www.nytimes.com/2016/01/12/opinion/the-brutalism-of-ted-cruz.html>, last accessed 26 January 2021.

[87] Boris L. Pasternak, *Doctor Zhivago* (New York, 1991), 50.